Answering the Call

RELIGION AND GLOBAL POLITICS

SERIES EDITOR
John L. Esposito
University Professor and Director
Prince Alwaleed Bin Talal Center for Muslim-Christian Understanding
Georgetown University

ISLAMIC LEVIATHAN
Islam and the Making of State Power
Seyyed Vali Reza Nasr

RACHID GHANNOUCHI
A Democrat Within Islamism
Azzam S. Tamimi

BALKAN IDOLS
Religion and Nationalism in Yugoslav States
Vjekoslav Perica

ISLAMIC POLITICAL IDENTITY IN TURKEY
M. Hakan Yavuz

RELIGION AND POLITICS IN POST-COMMUNIST ROMANIA
Lavinia Stan and Lucian Turcescu

PIETY AND POLITICS
Islamism in Contemporary Malaysia
Joseph Chinyong Liow

TERROR IN THE LAND OF THE HOLY SPIRIT
Guatemala under General Efrain Rios Montt, 1982–1983
Virginia Garrard-Burnett

IN THE HOUSE OF WAR
Dutch Islam Observed
Sam Cherribi

BEING YOUNG AND MUSLIM
New Cultural Politics in the Global South and North
Asef Bayat and Linda Herrera

CHURCH, STATE, AND DEMOCRACY IN EXPANDING EUROPE
Lavinia Stan and Lucian Turcescu

THE HEADSCARF CONTROVERSY
Secularism and Freedom of Religion
Hilal Elver

THE HOUSE OF SERVICE
The Gülen Movement and Islam's Third Way
David Tittensor

Answering the Call

Popular Islamic Activism
in Sadat's Egypt

by

ABDULLAH AL-ARIAN

OXFORD
UNIVERSITY PRESS

OXFORD
UNIVERSITY PRESS

Oxford University Press is a department of the University of Oxford.
It furthers the University's objective of excellence in research, scholarship,
and education by publishing worldwide.

Oxford New York
Auckland Cape Town Dar es Salaam Hong Kong Karachi
Kuala Lumpur Madrid Melbourne Mexico City Nairobi
New Delhi Shanghai Taipei Toronto

With offices in
Argentina Austria Brazil Chile Czech Republic France Greece
Guatemala Hungary Italy Japan Poland Portugal Singapore
South Korea Switzerland Thailand Turkey Ukraine Vietnam

Oxford is a registered trade mark of Oxford University Press
in the UK and certain other countries.

Published in the United States of America by
Oxford University Press
198 Madison Avenue, New York, NY 10,016

Library of Congress Cataloging-in-Publication Data
Al-Arian, Abdullah
Answering the call : popular Islamic activism in Sadat's Egypt / By Abdullah Al-Arian.
p. cm. — (Religion and global politics)
Includes bibliographical references and index.
ISBN 978-0-19-993127-9 (hardcover : alk. paper) —
ISBN 978-0-19-993128-6 (ebook) — ISBN 978-0-19-937378-9 (online content)
1. Jam'iyat al-Ikhwan al-Muslimin (Egypt)—History. 2. Islamic fundamentalism—
Egypt—History—20th century. 3. Islam and politics—Egypt. I. Title.
BP10.J383A427 2014
322.4'2096209047—dc23
2013043924

In loving memory of Adel

Contents

Foreword

THE MUSLIM BROTHERHOOD (*al-Ikhwan al-Muslimun*) began as a small religious study group in the Suez Canal Zone in Egypt in 1928. By the twenty-first century, the Brotherhood had become one of the most well-known and influential Muslim organizations in the world. The candidate of its political party won the first democratic presidential elections in Egypt following the overthrow of Egypt's military dictator in the Arab Spring of 2011, and following the military coup of 2013, the Brotherhood became the largest organized opposition force in the country.

This long and dramatic history of the Brotherhood has many periods of crisis and change. The organization maintains a strong sense of continuity from the days of its founder, Hasan al-Banna, but each period in its history has a distinctive character, reflecting the challenges of that particular time. Its development reflects the broader themes of modern Egyptian history.

In the late 1960s, many observers argued that the Brotherhood was basically no longer an important force in Egyptian society. It had lost its charismatic founder-leader and was brutally suppressed by the authoritarian military regime that had been established by Gamal Abdel Nasser following the revolution of 1952. Many believed that its fundamentalist message was out of step with the times. Writing in 1968, Richard Mitchell, the author of an influential study of the history of the Brotherhood, concluded that "the essentially secular reform nationalism now in vogue in the Arab world will continue to operate to end the earlier appeal of this organization."[1]

By the early 1980s, however, the situation was very different. Analysts and political activists spoke of an Islamic resurgence throughout the Muslim world. An influential study of Egyptian militants of the late 1970s argued that Nasserism "seemed to have run out of steam," providing an opening in which "Islamic militancy began its present surge."[2] Observers spoke of "Egypt's militant Islamic movement" as "more vocal, active, and committed on political issues than any other in Egypt today [1980]."[3] The old "secular reform nationalism" was no longer important in the thinking of the Islamic resurgence (or even among the more secularist educated elite). "In terms of the religious dimension of ideology, their reading of history and their overall vision for the future, the militants expressed no differences with the Muslim Brotherhood."[4]

This transformation—from being the core of a movement with fading popular appeal into being central to an Islamic resurgence in Egypt—was dramatic. Between the 1967 Arab-Israeli war and the assassination of Egyptian President Anwar al-Sadat in 1981, the Brotherhood reorganized its structures and rearticulated its message in ways that established the organization as a major force in politics and society. In the early 1980s, many people even suggested the possibility of an Islamic revolution in Egypt, led by the Brotherhood, similar to the revolution that established the Islamic Republic in Iran in 1979.

The visibility of small extremist Muslim groups in Egypt during the 1970s led many to fear that the larger Brotherhood would be in the vanguard of violent militancy during the 1980s. Instead, the Brotherhood emerged as a mainstream Islamist organization, minimizing the influence of hard-line extremists in the movement who criticized the Brotherhood for "its commitment to gradualism and its willingness to participate in a political system not based on the laws of Islam."[5] It was as a gradualist advocate of social transformation, not a militant inciter of violence, that the Brotherhood emerged from the period when Anwar al-Sadat ruled Egypt.

Abdullah Al-Arian presents a comprehensive, in-depth account of the main Brotherhood organization during this time of dramatic growth and development in the 1970s. Other studies of Muslim groups at that time have concentrated on the more militant and violent groups, which gained more headlines but represented small extremist minorities in the developing Islamic resurgence. Al-Arian provides a broader picture of the emerging Islamist movement that recognizes the diversity of organizations and tendencies within the movement during the 1970s and 1980s. This diversity received less attention in the earlier and still influential studies of the period. In those studies, the Islamist movement is defined primarily in terms of the ideology of Sayyid Qutb, the Egyptian radical who was executed in 1966. Qutb provided the rationale for the militant jihadism that developed in the 1970s and even in the twenty-first century has some continuing influence among Muslim militant extremists. He argued that Muslim societies had fallen so far from the true message of Islam that they should be regarded as unbelieving and in the state of belligerent ignorance, or *jahiliyya*. Qutb argued that *jihad* against this *jahiliyya* was the obligation of those who continued to be actual believers.

The jihadist ideology provided the foundations for the small militant groups of the 1970s, but it was not the foundation for the thinking and programs of the Muslim Brotherhood. Recent studies by scholars like Barbara Zollner have shown that Hasan al-Hudaybi, who led the Brotherhood from the time of al-Banna's death until 1973, presented "the first substantial refutation of Sayyid Qutb's ideas."[6] Al-Arian shows how the mainstream Brotherhood leadership developed this non-jihadist perspective in the era of its transformation. Qutb remained a revered martyr, but his ideology was not central to Brotherhood perspectives.

Al-Arian argues that the central message of the mainstream Brotherhood was not Qutb's *jihad* but rather, it was *da'wa*, the "mission" or "call," urging Muslims to live their lives more in accord with Islamic teachings. This distinction was emphasized in the title of the book by Hudaybi that argued against Qutb's views: *Preachers, Not Judges (Du'at la qudat)*. Al-Arian shows how the concept of *da'wa* was developed by the Brotherhood during the 1970s, distinguishing it from other groups within the Muslim movement who called for militant and revolutionary *jihad*. Scholars who emphasized the Qutb tradition argued at the time that "by deliberately opting for moderation, the neo-Muslim Brethren failed to capture the spirit of the Society of Muslim Brethren of Hasan al-Banna's time. . . . In the ramshackle dwellings of the suburbs ringing the large Egyptian cities, people bypassed by progress and development turned toward other, more radical tendencies of the Islamicist movement."[7] This prediction was incorrect, as the jihadists lost influence even among the poorer Egyptians, who turned to the welfare services of the Brotherhood for support in their misery. In the long run, the *da'wa* approach gained more support than the jihadist. Al-Arian's study examines how opting for moderation was, in fact, in the tradition of al-Banna, and how the jihadist approach became marginal within the Islamist movement in Egypt in the final decades of the twentieth century.

The reorganized Brotherhood that developed during the 1970s was, according to Al-Arian, the product of the cooperation of older Muslim Brothers with new and dynamic Islamist student groups. In the early 1970s, the Islamic student movement created a new culture of activism that replaced the old, previously dominant leftist student groupings. As

Al-Arian shows, the leadership of the major group, al-Gama'a al-Islamiyya, joined with the Brotherhood and provided an important support base for the reestablished Brotherhood. The student jihadists, in contrast, became a marginalized minority and tended to create or work within groups outside the Brotherhood. Al-Arian's analysis of this process is a major addition to the scholarship dealing with the evolution of Islamism in the era of the "Islamic resurgence."

Al-Arian's study provides an important corrective to the common view that all Islamists are militant and extremist advocates of violent *jihad*. The Islamist mainstream in Egypt, as it developed in the 1970s, was gradualist and reformist, and it is this majority mode that set the tone for what came to be called Political Islam in the 1980s. Despite the repressive policies of Sadat's successor, Hosni Mubarak, the Brotherhood remained committed to the *da'wa* approach rather than calling for revolutionary *jihad*. As Al-Arian shows, the foundations for this commitment were set by the ideas and actions of the Islamist students and the Brotherhood leadership during the 1970s.

In many ways, the Brotherhood of the 1970s set important patterns for the Political Islam of the 1980s and later in many parts of the Muslim world. The Islamic youth movement in Malaysia (Angkatan Belia Islam Malaysia, ABIM) was established in the early 1970s and became a major force in Malaysian politics and society. In many ways, it explicitly modeled itself on the Muslim Brotherhood, especially as a *da'wa* organization. The translation of Hudaybi's *Preachers Not Judges* provided an important guide for ABIM members.[8] A similar student movement emerged in Tunisia (Mouvement de la Tendance Islamique; MTI) by the early 1980s under the leadership of Rachid Ghannoushi. Although he was "strongly influenced by the thought of the Egyptian Muslim Brotherhood and particularly Sayyid Qutb in his early development and Islamic activism, Ghannoushi came to realize that though Qutb was a great man, he is 'not the spokesman for Islam.'"[9] The MTI and al-Nahdah, the political party that it established in the late 1980s, were not jihadist but rather followed the *da'wa* approach, even under the repressive military regime of Ben Ali. Other major manifestations of Political Islam in the 1970s and 1980s show these same tendencies.

The marginalization of radical jihadism in favor of policies of *da'wa* is an important feature of the development of Islamism from being the approach of fringe extremists to an important expression of the vision and hopes of mainstream Muslims. Al-Arian shows how the Muslim

Brotherhood was able to make the transition from marginal to mainstream in Egyptian politics and society. The jihadist approach would not have been able to mobilize populist support for participation in movements of democratization. In many ways, it was the transformation of the Brotherhood in the 1970s that made the electoral victories of the Brotherhood in 2012 possible.

John O. Voll

Preface

ON THE MORNING of January 25, 2014, Cairo's Tahrir Square was eerily quiet. The epicenter of a popular uprising that brought down the authoritarian rule of Hosni Mubarak only three years earlier now stood devoid of life, with only a hastily built monument serving as a haunting reminder of the fleeting nature of the country's revolutionary moment. As though to cement the emerging order even further, later in the day crowds rallied in the square in support of yet another military man's bid to become Egypt's uncontested ruler. Elsewhere around the country that day, clashes continued between the security forces of General 'Abd al-Fattah al-Sisi and supporters of the ousted Mohamed Morsi, a Muslim Brotherhood leader and the nation's first democratically elected president until his removal by the military exactly one year into his term.

In the span of just three years, Egypt's oldest social movement organization experienced the most dramatic oscillation in fortunes, with both highs and lows unprecedented in its storied history. Seemingly overnight, the Muslim Brotherhood was transformed from officially outlawed—but tolerated—opposition to ruling party in the post-revolutionary transition. But its moment in the sun was to be short-lived, as the Muslim Brotherhood's domination of the political transition and its failure to fulfill the demands of the revolution, coupled with the resurgence of deeply entrenched state institutions combined to overturn its narrow short-term gains and thwart the possibility of real systemic changes to Egypt's authoritarian political order. By the time of the third anniversary of the launch of the January 25 movement, the promise embodied in the remarkable uprising had become all but a distant memory. The renewed repression of the Muslim Brotherhood (and indeed, all of Egypt's independent political forces) and the subsequent struggle against the military's attempts to reassert its will has ensured that the final chapter in the confrontation between the regime and the society it seeks to control is far from written.

When I set out to conduct the research for this book, I did not antici-
pate that the experiences of Egypt's activists during the 1970s would take
center stage in an impending revolutionary moment. As I attempted to
chart the displacement of Nasser era political activism by a young and vibrant Islamic student movement that eventually linked with veterans of
the society founded by Hassan al-Banna, the stakes did not appear to be
particularly high. The legacy of this era was rarely discussed in the open,
even as the apparent contemporary divisions within the Muslim Brotherhood, following its reconstitution in the mid-1970s, were a direct consequence of major experiences and critical decisions that can be dated back
to this period. A new generation of youth took to the streets to challenge
Mubarak's rule in 2011, just as past leaders of the Egyptian student movement, such as 'Abd al-Mon'eim Abul Futuh, 'Esam al-'Erian, and Helmi
al-Gazzar, had taken on the excesses of the regime of Anwar al-Sadat several decades earlier.

In the aftermath of Mubarak's overthrow, however, it would be those
veteran activists, having been fully enmeshed within the rigid hierarchical structure of the Muslim Brotherhood, who would attempt to exert their
influence over the emerging political order. Along with outsiders from the
same generation who eventually became insiders, including Morsi and
Khairat al-Shater, Egypt's future would be shaped in large part by contending visions of Islamic activism that have been playing out since the Sadat
era. In the pages that follow, I attempt to recreate a historical moment that
has been neglected for far too long. Years before the legacy of this era
became a contentious topic in the political campaigns of the post-Mubarak
transition, the 1970s were one of the most dynamic and captivating eras of
the last half-century of Egyptian history. In retelling the story of this
period, it is my hope that the free-spirited and uninhibited nature of these
experiences comes across with minimal attempts to provide a guiding
structure where one was rarely exhibited at the time. To that end, I rely on
the voices of that period as much as possible, for it is their story to share.

I am deeply appreciative for all those who agreed to speak with me regarding experiences that in some instances spanned over half a century.
This book could not have been possible without the wealth of information, written and recollected, that was provided by all of the subjects who
appear here. I would also like to thank my relatives in Cairo for their
warmth and hospitality throughout the course of my field research.
Indeed, the comfort and support they provided ensured that this project
would remain a labor of love, even on the most trying of research days.

I am incredibly grateful for the many teachers and mentors I have had the privilege of encountering throughout my intellectual formation. I would like to thank Robert Keohane, David Paletz, miriam cooke, and Sarah Shields for the unbelievable patience they demonstrated while sharing their wisdom and guidance with a mystified undergraduate and for their mentorship in the years since. I am also incredibly indebted to Judith Tucker and Emad Shahin, both of whom helped plant the seeds that were eventually to become this research project through their transformative courses and their diligent supervision of my work from its earliest stages. Nathan Brown was kind enough to have suffered through an earlier version of my manuscript and has served as an invaluable resource throughout the formative years of my academic career. To John Voll and John Esposito, I owe my deepest debt of gratitude. It is the passion and precision they have demonstrated in their scholarship for decades that inspired me to pursue this path. Their generosity of spirit and unwavering commitment to illuminate the path before their students has made this work possible. I could not have asked for better mentorship. Any insight offered by this study is due to the commitment, patience, and wisdom of all of my mentors. Whatever shortcomings it contains are purely my own.

I am also grateful to the many friends, classmates, and colleagues I have had over the years, for the long talks about subjects ranging from the trivial to the hyperintellectual, the sharing of our mutual frustrations, and the opportunity for critical engagement of each other's work. Adel Ait-Ghezala was a constant source of inspiration to all those he encountered, and with his untimely passing, I have lost a kindred spirit.

Finally, I would like to recognize what we have always said is the most important thing: family. Without their unconditional love, guidance, and support I could not have faced any of life's challenges, or endeavored on the path of scholarly pursuits. My parents, Sami and Nahla, instilled in me a thirst for knowledge and a desire to share it with others. My siblings, Laila, Leena, Ali, and Lama have shown me the importance of listening to and appreciating the individual experiences of others. Together, they have all taught me more than I can ever hope to repay.

Abdullah Al-Arian
Washington D.C.
February 2014

A Note on Sources

SOCIAL MOVEMENT HISTORY, by its very nature as a phenomenon arising in opposition to the state, does not lend itself to the production of systematized and organized materials to be discovered years later in a central state archive. In the case of the Muslim Brotherhood of Egypt, the sensitivity surrounding the persistence of an organization that has been officially outlawed since 1954 ensured that the process of collecting primary source documents of an official nature would be even more daunting, if not outright impossible. Whatever official records exist about the Islamic movement reside strictly in the domain of Egypt's state security agency and are unavailable to the public.

Nonetheless, the story of the 1970s Islamic movement, especially the segments of it that have pursued their mission in public and have engaged with the larger society, provides for a number of ripe sources for the investigation of popular religious activism. Newspaper archives, even as they frequently reflect the cynicism of an authoritarian regime, provide meticulous daily accounts of events as they were experienced by many Egyptians. This includes those responsible for creating headlines, whether as student activists marching through the gates of Cairo University or movement elders who recently won their release from prison. Other publications, including those of the Islamic movement itself, from monthly magazines like *al-Da'wa* to occasional booklets, pamphlets, student wall magazines, and even conference programs, offer particular insight into the vision and functions of groups like Shabab al-Islam and al-Gama'a al-Islamiyya.

The period also generated a considerable number of personal accounts, recorded in the form of memoirs, from central leaders making crucial decisions to peripheral figures observing events from the margins of the Islamic movement. Other figures have either published shorter pieces recounting their experiences from the era, or have been interviewed for various publications in the past. Additionally, for the purposes of this study, interviews were conducted with a number of individuals who played an important role in shaping events surrounding the Islamic movement of the 1970s. These oral histories enhance the understanding of events for which published accounts provide little context or explanation, while also granting insight into the internal dynamics and relationships at work in any social movement.

Another body of literature that delves into the experiences of Islamic activism in the 1970s emerged out of internal studies conducted by members of the group, who often meld their own personal experiences with those of comrades and even opponents, and incorporate public documents, such as university records, whenever possible. Taken together, these sources provide a narrative rich in detail, weaving together the events and experiences that precipitated the rise of popular Islamic activism in Egypt during this era.

A Note on Transliteration

THIS STUDY EMPLOYS a simplified form of transliteration of Arabic words. Diacritical marks are not included for the sake of readability. The ' symbol represents the letter *'ayn* and the ' symbol represents the *hamza*. A number of words are transliterated into the colloquial Egyptian dialect, which features a hard "g" sound (as in *gama'a*) in place of the "j" of modern standard Arabic (as in *jama'a*). Popularized English spellings of prominent names, such as Gamal Abdel Nasser, are utilized in this text. The *ta marbuta* word ending is translated only as "a" and not "ah," as in the aforementioned *gama'a*.

Answering the Call

Introduction

CAIRO'S OPPRESSIVE SUMMER weather had yet to subside as the third general guide of Gama'at al-Ikhwan al-Muslimin (the Society of the Muslim Brotherhood) languished in the damp heat of an Egyptian prison. It was the fall of 1981, and he had not expected to be back inside so soon. By now an old man, 'Umar al-Tilmisani was a lawyer by training but had spent nearly twenty years of his life as a political prisoner. In the decade since his release, however, he had attained the top leadership position in the Muslim Brotherhood and helped restore it to its former status as the chief opposition movement in the country, largely through the successful recruitment of a vibrant student movement. Along with several colleagues from his inner circle, Tilmisani had traveled across the nation speaking at conferences, attending summer youth camps, and meeting with students on their campuses, preaching the *da'wa*, or call, of the Muslim Brotherhood to tens of thousands of young Egyptians in the process.

In contrast to the relative openness that had characterized much of his time in office, on September 5 President Anwar al-Sadat ordered state security agents to conduct a massive sweep of the country, arresting hundreds of members of the political opposition in all of its ideological stripes, from Nasserists and Marxists to the Islamic movement, represented chiefly by the Muslim Brotherhood. Feeling threatened by the rising tide of fervent political opposition, Sadat abandoned his rhetoric on democracy, opting for a return to the repression that had characterized the era of his predecessor, Gamal Abdel Nasser, by quashing all political dissent. A month later he would be assassinated.

From the confinement of his cell, Tilmisani could do no more than pen his prison memoir, recounting his experiences under the Sadat regime, and commenting on the daily news items that trickled into the prison through smuggled newspapers. In one entry, he lamented a news story about Sadat's meeting with the Higher Council of the Press. According to the article, on his way out of the meeting, Sadat stopped to greet one of the council's members, 'Ihsan 'Abd al-Quddus, a notable newspaper editor, literary writer, and liberal commentator. Sadat smiled at his old friend, shook his hand warmly, and spent a moment catching up with him. Though he tried to muster a smile in return, 'Abd al-Quddus could not help but be reminded of the loss of his son Muhammad, who at that very moment was in an undisclosed location, along with the hundreds of other activists arrested by Sadat.[1]

Muhammad 'Abd al-Quddus was a leader in al-Gama'a al-Islamiyya (the Islamic Society), the powerful organization that represented religious student activists in universities throughout the country. He had also recently joined the Muslim Brotherhood and, carrying on the family tradition, had taken up journalism as a career and a personal passion. But Muhammad did not report for one of the liberal, secular newspapers. He was a writer for *al-Da'wa*, the Muslim Brotherhood's monthly magazine. When security agents raided the offices of *al-Da'wa* and arrested the editors and staff members, Muhammad 'Abd al-Quddus was the youngest person apprehended.[2]

In commenting on this chance encounter between Egypt's authoritarian ruler and a grieving father, Tilmisani wavered between unrestrained condemnation of Sadat's behavior and sadness at the pain that 'Ihsan 'Abd al-Quddus must have felt by coming face to face with the person responsible for his son's dismal fate. Sadat "was flexing his muscles, demonstrating his power . . . and reproaching ['Abd al-Quddus] for allowing his son to go along the path of the call to God." Or, he pondered, was it possible that Sadat was genuinely attempting to flatter his old friend? "His tenderness did not end with a smile to the father he had deprived of his son . . . no, not only did he smile at him, but he went out of his way to greet him. Have you ever seen humility more charming than this?" Tilmisani concluded sarcastically.[3]

This story serves as a symbolic representation of a number of transformative developments of the Sadat era in modern Egyptian history. The anguished father unable to confront the president in defense of his son is a testament to the decline of liberalism in Egypt's political culture, which witnessed the replacement of the traditional political forces, the "centers of power" as Sadat termed them, with a new political base made up of ideologies antagonistic toward the liberal, nationalist, and radical socialist forces of old. The assumption of leadership by Tilmisani, who expressed his deep outrage at Sadat in no uncertain terms, signaled the arrival of the Muslim Brotherhood as the chief opposition movement leading the popular contention against the state. In fact, Tilmisani's role extended to that of paternal caretaker to Muhammad 'Abd al-Quddus, who along with thousands of young Egyptians, joined in this movement at the expense of the ideology of their parents. Finally, Sadat replicated the dualism for which his regime had become known, warmly greeting his friend while knowing that his policies had caused 'Abd al-Quddus and his family so much harm.

As a leader who in the span of a decade pursued war and peace, populism and free enterprise, democracy and despotism, Sadat was said to have met his untimely demise at the hands of a movement he helped create. Following a turbulent history of social activism, political contention, and militant resistance, the Muslim Brotherhood had experienced such a crushing blow early in the Nasser era that few in Egypt would have expected it to reappear. Yet after two decades of absence from society, the Muslim Brotherhood re-emerged as a social movement organization spreading a religious and political message and expressing its opposition to the state. This study explores the underlying social developments, political conditions, and historical events that permitted the return of the Muslim Brotherhood to the fore of Egyptian society and politics in the 1970s. Additionally, it investigates the internal factors within the organization's disparate parts: its leaders, members, ideological mission, and social program—to explain its stunning resilience in the face of severe repression and its ability to reclaim its position at the head of an increasingly diversified Islamic movement.

Beginning after Egypt's defeat in the June War of 1967 and gathering momentum with Sadat's assumption of the presidency following Nasser's death in September 1970, religiously inspired social movements took on a renewed urgency in their activist missions. By the middle of the 1970s, the trajectory of Islamic activism reached its height, as a vibrant and dynamic student movement became dominated by religious youth who put forward a multifaceted program of social advocacy and anti-state contention, built on an intellectual project that incorporated a wide array of sources and influences. Finding strength in its youth and diversity, the religious student movement, led by al-Gama'a al-Islamiyya, swept the Student Union elections at nearly every Egyptian university, adding legitimacy to its cause and raising its ambitions. Meanwhile, following their gradual release from prison, the Muslim Brotherhood's former leaders cemented their determination to continue their mission by reorganizing their movement into something akin to the former organization.

By the end of the decade, the Muslim Brotherhood had been successfully reconstituted, due in large part to the ability of the senior leadership to assimilate the Islamic student movement into the ranks of a new hierarchical structure. Although the end of the Sadat period in 1981 occurred at a time of renewed political repression and the mass imprisonment of the leadership of the Islamic movement, young and old alike, the era itself would be remembered for ushering in the return of Islamic activism in the public sphere, a phenomenon that many have termed the "Islamic resurgence."[4] Even Sadat's assassination at the hands of a group of Islamic militants was not enough to subdue a movement that established a permanent presence in Egyptian society beginning in the critical decade of the 1970s.

Islamic Movements: Toward an Approach

This study engages and critiques the traditional method for the study of Islamic movements, adopting a methodological approach designed to most effectively capture the phenomenon under examination. In attempting to explain the rise of Islamic movements in the twentieth century, traditional Orientalist studies often fell prey to an essentialist paradigm, problematizing Islamic activism due to the fact that it purportedly stood in opposition to long-standing modernization theory, which viewed the path to progress in traditional societies as one of increased secularization, coinciding with economic, political, and social development. For much of the 1950s, as most Muslim-majority countries were run by conservative secular rulers or radical socialist and nationalist leaders, this view remained dominant.[5] The fact that most early expressions of Islamic activism had largely retreated to the margins of society by the mid-1960s appeared to give more weight to this perspective.

By the mid-1980s, however, following a number of events—the revolution in Iran, the Sadat assassination, and the launch of religious resistance movements in Afghanistan, Lebanon, and the Palestinian territories—analysts and scholars were at a loss to explain the rise of religious activism in large parts of the Muslim world. They termed the new phenomenon the "Islamic resurgence" and set out to depict it as a temporary expression of frustration and disillusionment with nationalist projects, a product of the stagnation and underdevelopment afflicting many Muslim societies and an outgrowth of the uneasy tension between tradition and modernity. Ultimately, it was decided, there was some essential quality about Islam that prevented its societies from breaking free from the past and embracing the present.[6] Considerable ink was spilled in attempting to uncover the aspects of Islamic history, culture, and thought that would contribute to the rise of an Islamic response to modernity. In any case, this phenomenon was still largely viewed as an aberration, a detour from the unrelenting march of modernization and progress.

But then something strange happened. By the early 1990s, a new trend had emerged that saw Islamic movements transformed from voices of opposition on the margins to permanent fixtures of society. They became mainstream political trends, competing for elections and gaining power in legitimate fashion. They utilized modern political institutions and tactics. This could be seen in places like Algeria, Pakistan, Malaysia, Turkey, Lebanon, Jordan, Sudan and Egypt. No longer were scholars talking about an "Islamic resurgence," but rather "political Islam," a phrase that became the buzzword of this period. Writers attempted to temper their earlier assessments by exploring whether this unlikely union of Islam and democracy was simply a temporary marriage of convenience, or whether there could be a future in the Muslim world that embraced both modernity, with all that accompanies it, and traditional Islamic values and political principles.[7]

By the beginning of the century, it appeared that many of these experiments had failed. As Islamist gains were turned back in a number of Muslim countries, scholars began to speak of an age of "post-Islamism."[8] Additionally, Islamic activism had increasingly taken on a shape completely on the fringes of society, and through a hybrid with advanced technological means and an outlook that transcended the state, had begun to express itself on a global scale, and with increasing militancy. To some, it seemed that events had come full circle. With slight adjustments to the earlier thesis and a few methodological advancements, such as the study of "human development" as a quantitative analytical category, the original assessment of Islamic movements as a rejection of modernity and the established state system seemed appropriate in the wake of Al-Qaeda's rise to prominence.[9]

This paradigm was problematic for a number of reasons. First, it failed to assess these movements on their own terms, and to utilize the historical and political contexts to explain their origins, their aspirations, and their methods. It could not separate particular political grievances from this notion of a larger rejection of modernity. Furthermore, it did not take into account the world as seen through the eyes of those involved in these movements. Rather than looking at these phenomena as isolated aberrations, or interruptions within the broad march of modernity, it is more useful to observe them within the context of a larger process at work in much of the Muslim world since the late nineteenth century. This intellectual current sought to explain the decline of Islamic civilization, to reconcile Islam and modernity, to respond to European imperialism and Western hegemony, and ultimately, to tend to the crisis of leadership in the Muslim world resulting from the collapse of the caliphate, the symbol of political and religious authority for thirteen centuries of Islamic history.

Thinkers, scholars, and intellectuals, like Jamal al-Din al-Afghani, Muhammad Abduh, and Rashid Rida, contemplated these questions at the turn of the century and through the early period of independence. Activists like Hasan al-Banna and Mawlana Mawdudi founded popular organizations to promote a social and political agenda within their respective contexts. In Banna's case, the Muslim Brotherhood was an expression of the loss of the Islamic state, the advent of foreign encroachment, and the desire for an Islamic character for the developing Egyptian state.

In response to these problematic approaches, in the early 2000s, a number of scholars began to apply social movement theory (SMT), a theoretical subfield employed in the study of Western movements, to the study of Islamic movements for the first time.[10] Three subsets of SMT guide the analysis that follows, allowing the study to consider the major factors involved in the development of the 1970s Islamic social movement.

The examination of political opportunity structures seeks to explain "the emergence of a particular social movement on the basis of changes in the institutional structure or informal power relations of a given national political system."[11] By focusing on external factors, as opposed to isolating grievances, this approach helps to explain why in some instances movements formed around a given issue, while in others they did not.[12]

Defined as "those collective vehicles, informal as well as formal, through which people mobilize and engage in collective action," the study of mobilizing structures draws heavily from two theoretical schools, resource mobilization theory and the political process model.[13] It is observed through what Charles Tilly and Sidney Tarrow referred to as repertoires of contention, "existing performances from an array chosen by the actors" in an attempt to explain and perhaps even predict collective behavior.[14] The means by which mobilization is acted upon is dependent upon a "toolkit" that contains familiar modes of collective action.

Resource mobilization frequently occurs through formal structures, such as religious institutions, nongovernmental organizations, professional or student associations, and political parties.[15] But it can also occur through the course of informal networks and social relationships. In fact, Quintan Wiktorowicz made the case that Islamic movements are best studied as informal networks, since they are rarely constituted as formal organizations recognized by their governments.[16] This presents a challenge for researchers of Islamic movements, since the official record rarely offers a complete picture of the group in question. Even the Muslim Brotherhood, which maintains a formal organizational structure, relies heavily on informal networks to mobilize its followers.

The third subset of SMT is cultural framing processes, defined as "the conscious strategic efforts by groups of people to fashion shared understandings of the world and of themselves that legitimate and motivate collective action."[17] By infusing the preexisting theory with a discussion of culture and its central role, the literature on framing provides the logical bridge between political opportunities and mobilizing structures. It is also an essential tool for defining the role of religion within a social movement in a field that has not traditionally shown religious movements the same treatment as their secular counterparts.

In SMT, the use of cultural symbols, historical narratives, and shared experiences is understood as intended to appeal to individuals outside the movement, motivating them to join its mission. Collective action frames are identified within three categories: diagnostic, prognostic, and motivational frames.[18] Diagnostic frames identify grievances, usually directed toward the state or social elites. Prognostic frames articulate the solution in an accessible manner, aiming to attract a large following. Finally, motivational frames provide the "call to arms," the rationale for taking corrective action.[19]

Within the context of this burgeoning field of methodological research, the Islamic movement in Egypt during the 1970s emerges as a ripe subject for investigation. The political climate of the period does not simply offer the backdrop against which the developments in society were occurring. Rather, the Sadat regime was a key actor in the rise of the Islamic movement, whether by consciously creating the political space to allow the growth of a religious trend, or by constricting its movements, thereby pushing many of its members to the margins of society, where they would wreak havoc in the form of violent contention against the regime.

Similarly, the rise of a distinct religious movement characterized by its youth and dynamism facilitated the development of innovative mobilization structures. Reflecting a new protest culture and an unprecedented ability to operate within important institutions such as the student unions, this movement also proved able to adapt to pressures from a "mother" movement in the form of the Muslim Brotherhood's return and its subsequent efforts to co-opt the student movement. Finally, with the exceptional openness of the Sadat era, in comparison to that of his predecessor, the cultural framing activities that the Islamic movement engaged in were unlike anything the country had witnessed since before the revolution of 1952. During the course of Sadat's presidency, the Muslim Brotherhood and religious student groups published books, periodicals, and wall magazines, and produced pamphlets, cassette tapes, and banners, all of which reflected the group's mission and ideological outlook. Taken together, this era presents a particularly fascinating period of study, given the ways in which the movement's decisions and actions interact with all of the theoretical subsets.

An Old Call, A New Call

Though he wrote his seminal work, *The Society of the Muslim Brothers*, in the late 1960s, Richard Mitchell nevertheless considered the Muslim Brotherhood a bygone movement, with no realistic chance for regaining its prior position in society. Mitchell's groundbreaking historical study concluded with Nasser's repression of the organization in 1954. In addition to the prevailing winds of secular Arab nationalism, his study cited the lack of a central charismatic leader and increased internal divisions for the final decline of the movement. The ideology itself could not gain any permanence because of the failure of the organization to fulfill its stated goal of reconciling acceptable portions of modern political thought and traditional Islamic principles. In this belief, Mitchell was not alone. Most commentators believed the age of the Muslim Brotherhood had long passed.[20] In his 1972 review of Mitchell's book, L. Carl Brown argued that not only was there no possibility for the return of the Muslim Brotherhood as an active force in Egyptian society, but that religious activism of any kind had no future role to play in the politics of Muslim societies.[21]

Indeed, Mitchell's assessment was to fall flat in the face of the events of the 1970s, and Brown's critique of Mitchell was to provide an accurate prediction of later studies of the Muslim Brotherhood. Arguing that Mitchell "tends to minimize the terrorist wing of the Ikhwan," Brown foreshadowed the increased emphasis on militancy as the basis upon which to study Islamic activism in successive years.[22] By the early 1980s, the notion of an Islamic revival typified in the Iranian Revolution would remove from contention the narrative of Islamic activism giving way to secular nationalism in the linear march of history. While much scholarship emerged that focused on the rise of Islamic militancy, others were more critical of the prevailing view of an "Islamist threat" that rejected the West, offering a more nuanced view of the revival.[23]

The Sadat era in the history of the Muslim Brotherhood has received the least amount of attention by Western scholars, though it proved to be a period of bustling activity. Briefly, various works mention that the organization reconstituted itself following the release of its members from the prisons of Nasser; that it benefited from Sadat's attempts to weaken the political Left, remnants of Nasser's failed socialist experiment; that, under Tilmisani's leadership, the organization operated openly, publishing books and periodicals, engaging the government in public debate; and that it ultimately reclaimed its place as the most potent opposition to the secular regime. Yet beyond this basic skeleton, little study was done on the mainstream Muslim Brotherhood organization of the 1970s. Instead, the bulk of the research focused on the other major development on the Islamic activist scene during this period: the rise of underground militant groups.

Whereas Mitchell put forth the idea that the Muslim Brotherhood had sought to bridge the supposed gap between Islam and modernity, another view emerged arguing that not only did this endeavor fail, but subsequent leaders of the movement, most notably the commentator Sayyid Qutb, had rejected such a project as contrary to the core values of their faith. Some of Qutb's supporters, survivors of Nasser's concentration camps, as Gilles Kepel termed them, saw such an effort as not only futile, but blasphemous as well. Emmanuel Sivan focused on the intellectual and ideological development of what he termed the "New Radicalism."[24] The concepts developed by Qutb in the mid-1960s laid the groundwork for the rise of extremist groups, such as al-Takfir wal-Higra, a decade later. Sivan's study lacked a wider discussion of Qutb's concepts within the framework of mainstream Muslim Brotherhood thought, as articulated by Banna and promoted by his successors.

Other writers were similarly inclined.[25] By diminishing some of the major differences between the mainstream and the fringe, it becomes easier to understand how the bulk of the scholarship would focus on the group of only a few thousand radicals, as opposed to the hundreds of thousands of self-declared Muslim Brothers.[26] This was also accomplished by scholars altering the external character of the organization itself. Though the Muslim Brotherhood of the 1970s remained intact as an organization, maintaining its name, organizational structure, and hierarchy, Western scholars chose to refer to it by other titles.[27]

Kepel's historical study, published in 1984, was indicative of this tendency to offer a different narrative of the Islamic movement in Egypt.[28] While freely acknowledging that a major split occurred between the traditional Muslim Brotherhood and the followers of Qutb's teachings, primarily embodied in the tome *Milestones*, Kepel made the case that it was this radical fringe that was the direct heir to the Muslim Brotherhood of previous generations. His work focused almost exclusively on groups emerging out of Qutb's intellectual movement, such as al-Takfir wal-Higra and al-Gamaʻa al-Islamiyya, while relegating Tilmisani's Muslim Brotherhood to only one chapter that focused on its (largely failed) attempts to compete in what was becoming a crowded marketplace of Islamic trends.

Kepel summed up the prevailing view of the Muslim Brotherhood by scholars of this period, juxtaposing the organization's strong rhetoric with its lack of an actionable program, in contrast to the fringe movement, which supposedly offered a more accessible platform. He argued that "by deliberately opting for moderation" the Muslim Brotherhood under Tilmisani failed to capture the essence of Banna's mission, and with that, could never recapture its place in Egyptian society.[29]

This dominant narrative did not go unchallenged. A number of scholars issued their response to the resurgent Islam paradigm.[30] John Voll argued for the need to expand the scope of scholarship on Islamic movements beyond narrow political considerations to their historical causes. He wrote that the Islamic movement of this era "is a response to the particular conditions of the late twentieth century and must be seen in the context of the conflicts and challenges of the modern world. At the same time, it is also part of the historical experience of renewal within Muslim societies over the centuries."[31]

Even Mitchell contributed to the growing critique, challenging the periodization of the Islamic resurgence prevalent in the literature. These studies, which placed the origins of the Islamic resurgence in the aftermath of the Six Day War, were once again too narrowly defined. "Thus the events of 1967 and 1973 should be seen as moments intensifying a long-term ongoing historical process. It does not make analytical sense to regard the events in the Middle East commonly referred to as the Islamic resurgence as a response to crises so narrowly defined as the 1967 defeat or, paradoxically, the 'victory' of 1973."[32]

Nonetheless, no major studies emerged during the successive period that examined the recent history of the Muslim Brotherhood following the events of 1954. Some scholars made mention of the development of the movement, citing the intellectual and organizational continuity following Banna's assassination and the rise of new leaders. The successor to Banna, Hasan al-Hudaybi, confronted the challenges from within the organization and safeguarded its mission as a primarily *da'wa*-oriented movement. "For Hudaybi and the other old-guard Brotherhood leaders, the problem was that Egyptians needed to be educated and called to the faith, not that Egyptians had ceased to be Muslims. Hudaybi rejected the practice of *takfir,* thereby rejecting the rationale for active revolution."[33] Voll emphasized the continuity from Banna's original vision to the reformist, nonviolent goals pursued by the reconstituted movement that even saw fit to incorporate elements of Qutb's thought into its mission.[34]

As proponents of this narrative became increasingly vocal, a number of recent studies on the Muslim Brotherhood have ushered in a new period of scholarship over the last two decades. These works have shifted from the paradigm of resurgent Islam to examining the Islamic movement on its own terms, free of the ideological underpinnings that marked prior efforts.[35] Moreover, an increasing number of studies in recent years have utilized the theoretical tools offered by SMT in the study of the Islamic movement in Egypt. Collectively, these works have advanced a different view of the Muslim Brotherhood as an organization that addresses the needs of a modern, middle-class polity in Egyptian society.[36]

Two important developments will inform the emerging literature on this movement. First, the abundance of newly available source material will allow for more thorough historical accounts of the Muslim Brotherhood, with a potential for revising the current narrative. Second, the increasing interaction between scholars of Islamic movements and proponents of SMT will provide valuable tools for analysis of this and other groups in the Islamic world.

Tracing a Movement

This historical study examines the rise of a religious social movement in Egypt during the period 1968–1981. While it utilizes the methodological tools provided by social movement theory, it is ultimately rooted in the desire to uncover and explain the past. Historical studies of social movements can fall short without the theoretical construct to contextualize and explain events and developments. By that same token, as Tilly explained, the study of social movements is rendered deficient without identifying the historical underpinnings of these social phenomena. He wrote:

> History helps because it explains why social movements incorporated some crucial features (for example, the disciplined street march) that separated the social movement from other sorts of politics. History also helps because it identifies significant *change* in the operation of social movements (for example, the emergence of well-financed professional staffs and organizations specializing in the pursuit of social movement programs) and thus alerts us to the possibility of new changes in the future. History helps, finally, because it calls attention to the shifting political conditions that made social movements possible.[37]

As a social history, this study takes social movements as its basic unit of analysis.[38] In the Egyptian context, two main social movements at work during the 1970s are examined in detail: the student movement and the Islamic movement. The student movement comprised the generation of Egyptian youth who entered the universities from the late 1960s to the early 1980s and pursued social and political activism. The student movement had no distinct ideological orientation, though at various moments it was populated heavily by, and featured the leadership of, leftists as well as Islamists. The Islamic movement, on the other hand, was not made up of a particular social segment, but was distinct in its all-encompassing ideological orientation.

Although they were by no means identical, for a brief historical moment, the student movement and the Islamic movement converged. With the absence of a significant presence of Islamic activists due to the period of repression instituted by the Nasser regime, and with the rise to power of the religiously motivated contingent within the student movement, the Islamic movement was, for all purposes, based in the student movement, and for its part, the student movement experienced a homogenization under self-assured Islamic leadership.

During the course of this study, several social movement organizations are considered for analysis, not the least of which is the Muslim Brotherhood, the dominant organization within the Islamic movement which, during this period, found itself in the rare situation of having to contend with new groups that staked their claim for authority. Similarly, the student movement featured numerous groups, including some with a decidedly religious orientation, such as Shabab al-Islam and al-Gama'a al-Islamiyya. Historically, it was a rare occurrence when an organization could successfully take command over an entire movement, a lesson that the youth leaders of al-Gama'a al-Islamiyya would learn during the course of their activism.

By exploring the recent historical experiences of the Islamic movement and the student movement, Chapter 1 sets the stage for the ensuing discussion of these movements during the late 1960s and early 1970s. Picking up where Mitchell's study leaves off, the role of the Muslim Brotherhood in the 1952 Free Officers Revolution is examined from the perspective of key actors from the Muslim Brotherhood and the nascent revolutionary regime. Following the total breakdown in relations and the subsequent era of political repression, the Muslim Brotherhood was outlawed and disbanded as an organization, but through informal networks that existed within the prison system, its intellectual program continued to evolve and progress.

It is noteworthy that Sayyid Qutb, one of the most prolific figures in the Islamic movement, wrote the bulk of his commentaries at a time when the Muslim Brotherhood did not exist in its traditional form. The collapse of its organizational structure and the effects of regime repression brought about a crisis in thought, during which a minority faction asserted a new interpretation of the Muslim Brotherhood mission, founded upon the language of resistance that Qutb employed. The internal debate that followed featured the reassertion of the original Muslim Brotherhood *da'wa*, redefined in opposition to the emerging militant discourse.

Translated as "mission" or "call," an examination of the concept of *da'wa* is critical for a proper understanding of the Muslim Brotherhood's ideological and organizational development. While it traditionally referred to the process of calling others to the Islamic faith, the term was redefined in the early period of the modern Islamic movement to denote calling others from within the faith, who were thought to have been negligent with regard to fulfilling basic religious obligations. With the spread of the Muslim Brotherhood's organization under Banna's leadership, the *da'wa* came to be regarded as the process of spreading the Muslim Brotherhood's program and recruiting outsiders to join in its mission. Finally, following the intellectual schism brought about by Qutb's supporters, who sought to legitimize violent contention against the state, Hudaybi attempted to put the matter to rest by reemphasizing the role of the Islamic activist as one of caller, not judge. The concept of *da'wa* continued to evolve throughout the 1970s, when it was employed to raise awareness of the Muslim Brotherhood's mission among a new generation, while also distinguishing the organization from other factions within the Islamic movement that had abandoned the call in favor of isolation and militancy.

Parallel to the developments within the Islamic movement, this chapter also addresses the rich legacy of student activism in the pre-revolutionary era, when Egyptian youth made up an important base of all political parties and factions and helped to shape the outcome of political crises through direct action campaigns. Although the student movement was subject to the same political repression that afflicted all independent social forces after the revolution, it ultimately proved to be the most resilient. Led primarily by leftist students, it was the first opposition force to emerge after the 1967 war, awakening the nation by leading the massive popular protests of 1968, and paving the way for its permanent return as a social movement actor.

Finally, Chapter 1 charts the political landscape in Egypt on the eve of Sadat's accession to the presidency. The failure of Nasser's project, culminated by the 1967 defeat, ushered in a new era of politics in Egypt, a development with major implications for the resumption of Islamic activism on a large scale.

The impact of the state's shift in policy could be observed very early in the Sadat period, through an examination of an oft-forgotten organization that signaled the return of Islamic activism in Egypt. Shabab al-Islam, the subject of Chapter 2, emerged from the open space actively cultivated and promoted by the Sadat regime. It advanced a broadly Islamized social and political program, articulated generally in the Islamic modernist tradition. Based on the excitement and widespread support generated by this organization, it proved to be a breath of fresh air for the public expression of an Islamic political program and a frame of reference after two decades in which such talk was taboo.

Through its debates, conferences, and publications, Shabab al-Islam infused the public discourse with discussions on the place of religion in the state and society. The group's leaders were also determined to engage in contentious politics, joining in the student protests of 1972–1973, and agitating for democratic reforms and a war to liberate occupied lands. While the organization was also notable for its strong opposition to the leftist trend dominant within the student movement, a position that won it favor with some regime officials, the manner in which it conducted its activism embodied the spirit of the radical politics associated with the Nasser era. The organization ultimately succumbed to internal structural weaknesses and external pressures, but it proved to be a sign of things to come, as the rise of a potent Islamic movement, led by the return of the Muslim Brotherhood, was not far behind.

When Sadat decided in 1971 to free the Muslim Brotherhood leaders and members from Nasser's prisons, he could not have envisioned the vigor with which the organization would return by the end of the decade. But based on the internal discussions of the group at the time, neither could its leaders. Chapter 3 details the early attempts at reconstituting the Muslim Brotherhood following a change in regime and with it, a change in policy toward the political opposition. Indeed, external factors played a critical role in shaping the debate around the organization's return. An increasingly crowded field of Islamic activism featured groups that offered alternative programs to the traditional Muslim Brotherhood mission, while Sadat attempted to throw his hat into the ring as well, by appropriating religious rhetoric and pledging to build a state based on "science and faith."

Internally, the Muslim Brotherhood had just consolidated its intellectual position vis-à-vis the rising militant fringe. Senior figures in the group then reached a compromise decision to stake their claim for leadership of the Islamic movement, but also to disavow any aspirations for a clandestine unit within the organization. Before the Muslim Brotherhood could spread its traditional *da'wa*, however, the group's leaders had to contend with more practical challenges of readapting to a changed society. Following Hudaybi's death in 1973, Tilmisani emerged as his successor, pledging himself to transmit the message of the Muslim Brotherhood to a new generation that would make up the energetic base of the organization and the future of the *da'wa*.

Completely independent of the Muslim Brotherhood's attempts to re-constitute its organization, a process that would only gain momentum after 1975, a vibrant Islamic student movement was already making waves within Egypt's colleges and universities. Building on the failed attempts by Shabab al-Islam to establish a lasting presence of religiously based activism on campuses, a new class of students, representing the fruits of Sadat's push to expand education to the urban poor and rural areas in greater numbers, developed a fresh Islamic student organization. Chapter 4 chronicles the rise of al-Gama'a al-Islamiyya through the students who built it. It traces the process of their intellectual discovery and the development of the group's religious mission.

Featuring a confluence of ideological trends from within the Islamic movement and an organic process of building the organization, al-Gama'a al-Islamiyya experienced considerable success, taking hold of student unions across the country, thereby institutionalizing its gains and securing access to resources essential for the perpetuation of the group's beliefs and programs. The leaders of the youth movement became notable not only for the effective promotion of the *da'wa* as they understood it, but also for the development of a distinct culture of activism representative of the new Islamic student movement. Internally, what had long been the movement's greatest strength—its ideological diversity and lack of a rigid dogma—became a liability as factionalism and radicalism took hold of some segments of al-Gama'a al-Islamiyya.

Chapter 5 details the process by which the internal divisions within al-Gama'a al-Islamiyya were resolved. Coinciding with the Muslim Brotherhood's reconstitution, or perhaps because of it, the dividing ideological lines within the student movement were more clearly drawn, with a majority of its leadership, especially at the senior level, making the decision to join the Muslim Brotherhood as members. Espousing support for the Salafi and *jihadi* trends, the minorities within al-Gama'a al-Islamiyya were gradually marginalized, with some even branching off into independent organizations, or managing to wrest control of local chapters of the student organization from the hands of the Muslim Brotherhood's supporters, especially in upper Egypt.

For its part, the Muslim Brotherhood's leadership proved extremely adept at recruiting the next generation of Islamic activists to join its ranks. In promoting the concept of *tawrith al-da'wa*, or bequeathing the call, Tilmisani and other senior figures relied on the Muslim Brotherhood's rich history on the front lines of the struggle for the promotion of Islam, as well as its ability to convey a complete program, respond to competing trends, and demonstrate flexibility in its views. Once the intellectual congruity was reached, during the course of countless meetings, lectures, camps, and conferences, the parties moved closer to organizational coordination, and ultimately, the organizational structure of the Muslim Brotherhood was rebuilt. The student leaders made up the base of the newly reestablished Muslim Brotherhood, which by the close of the decade, had proved to be a major thorn in the side of the Sadat regime. Based in its safe haven within the universities, the Muslim Brotherhood's student members and their elders from the organization pursued an active agenda of opposition to Sadat's policies, from the peace treaty with Israel to the government's refusal to institute provisions of Islamic law.

Examining the critical issues around which the Muslim Brotherhood organized its activism in the second half of the 1970s, Chapter 6 isolates the organization's chief publication, *al-Da'wa* magazine, for a discussion on cultural framing. The monthly periodical was a focal point of the group's activities, bridging the generational divide by publishing commentaries by senior group leaders and articles by student reporters. It featured the active construction of the Muslim Brotherhood's *da'wa* for the next generation, detailing not only the group's grand vision for an Egypt that fulfilled the tenets of Islam, but also its reaction to current events and a thorough appraisal of government policies. The magazine proved doubly effective, generating a mass audience of readers, as well as earning the ire of Sadat, who railed on the magazine's content in a speech before parliament, then resolved to shut down its operations permanently. Tensions were heightened during a series of confrontations, ultimately leading to Sadat taking authoritarian measures against the rising voices of dissent. But by the time Sadat decided to clamp down on all opposition in 1981, arresting figures from the Muslim Brotherhood, young and old alike, the successful reconstitution of the organization ensured that the *da'wa* would be preserved into the next era of Egyptian history.

I

The Islamic Movement on the Eve of Sadat

THERE ARE FEW events in contemporary Middle East history that can be said to have single-handedly transformed the course of the region's future as did the Six Day War of June 1967. The *naksa,* or setback, as it came to be known, reinforced the initial defeat at the hands of Israel two decades earlier, and destroyed the mighty pillar of Nasserism that had captivated Arab audiences since 1952. The ideologies of Arab nationalism and socialism, upon which an entire regional project had been built, were thoroughly discredited once their prime objective of liberating Arab lands and defeating Zionism proved too tall an order. As for the man himself, Egyptian president Gamal Abdel Nasser's rhetorical power and mythic persona were no match for the glaring reality on the ground: Israel had occupied Arab lands in every direction, more than doubling in size, and had delivered a fatal blow to the militaries of its most powerful adversaries. Millions of Egyptians would take to the streets in support of their president's continued leadership, but as one Egyptian would later write of Nasser, "he may have been buried on September 28, 1970, but he died on June 5, 1967."[1]

Nasser's demise exposed the deep-seated weaknesses of Egypt's revolutionary regime. It lacked independent social movements and was devoid of free intellectual development. It possessed no civil society institutions offering competing political ideologies to fill the void left by the collapse of the Nasserist project. The vacuum that emerged in the wake of 1967 was to be filled by a number of underdeveloped political trends representing mostly recycled platforms, several of which predated the revolution. As a result, Nasser's final years and the early period of Anwar al-Sadat's presidency, already notable for the absence of a distinct ideological orientation, featured no sufficient substitute for the failed policies of old.

Although it has been argued that regional and international pressures dominated Nasser's decision-making process after the war, domestic considerations also played a significant role.[2] However, it was not the liberal, Marxist, or Islamic political movements that exerted their influence over the suddenly weakened regime, for they had all been systematically repressed by Nasser early in his presidency. Rather, it was a revitalized student movement, having no particular political affiliation, which presented the most immediate challenge to the state. Throughout the course of the late 1960s and into the early 1970s, student activism represented the principal force of political opposition, paving the way for the emergence of distinct ideological trends, most notably in a revitalized Islamic movement.

This chapter begins with a brief discussion of the political trends that existed in the early period of the revolution, illustrating the ways in which the Free Officers dealt with them, with a particular emphasis on the fate of the Islamic movement as represented by the Muslim Brotherhood. With the ban on all independent political activity under Nasser, these forces disappeared from the scene. Different aspects of the young regime's relationship with the Muslim Brotherhood are highlighted to demonstrate that the two powerful political forces were at once intimately familiar with one another through their early partnership, and yet deeply distrustful as a result of divergent visions and the mutual desire for political supremacy. The thread of regime involvement continues as we explore the internal evolution of the Muslim Brotherhood's program, as Nasser became both an unwitting accessory (through his repressive policies) to the shift away from ideological moderation and a willing collaborator (through his promotion of religious officials) in the Muslim Brotherhood's effort to reassert its missionary roots.

After describing the state of the Islamic movement during the twilight of the Nasser era, the next section examines the legacy of student activism, which dates back to the days before independence, when Egypt was still fighting for an end to British rule. In order to better understand the rise of student activism, it is essential to expound on the profile of the educational system, along with the goals and modes of mass mobilization. Despite its rich tradition, the student movement was also subjected to severe repression during the Nasser regime, but it possessed a quality that no other movements could claim: the ability to operate from within an existing state institution, the Egyptian system of education.

The final section explores how the movement re-emerged onto the landscape of political activity after the Six Day War, witnessed in the 1968 student revolt, the first action of its kind in decades. Contrary to the prevailing notion that the national response to the war exposed ideological cleavages within Egypt, the student movement was notable for the unity that it demonstrated, along with the lack of a distinct ideological orientation—at least in its earliest stages. It would not be until several years later that the student movement would witness the rise of an Islamically oriented trend within the student movement, symbolized in the organization Shabab al-Islam (The Youth of Islam). What all of the discussions in this chapter aim to do is provide the historical context for the Sadat era in modern Egyptian political history, drawing attention to some of its most salient features. By elucidating the motivations and actions of the newly politicized population in the late 1960s, the stage is then set to explore the rise of a reenergized Islamic movement that came to define Egyptian oppositional politics throughout the decade that followed.

Free Officers and Repressive Politics

On July 23, 1952, a group whom Baker refers to as "fundamentally non-ideological, elitist military conspirators" swept to power by overthrowing the Egyptian monarchy in a largely nonviolent coup d'état.[3] While the Free Officers Revolution is known for its vehement rejection of a status quo characterized by a failing liberal political system, a discredited monarchy, and an unpopular foreign occupation, it is also notable for its opposition to the existing alternatives, whether from the Left or the Right. Inasmuch as the Free Officers aspired to overthrow a corrupt ruler backed by an oppressive colonial enterprise, they also sensed the revolutionary winds blowing from within the depths of society, representing political factions that had gradually become more radicalized with the near collapse of the liberal regime. So not only did the coup claim to be saving Egypt from foreign domination, but in essence, it was also saving Egyptians from themselves.

In spite of the fact that the clandestine military group maintained strong contacts with leaders of all political factions representing the spectrum of ideologies, including Young Egypt, the Wafd Party, the Marxists, and the Muslim Brotherhood, the core of the Free Officers were enormously distrustful of the political trends. It came as no surprise then, that less than six months after the revolution, the Revolutionary Command

Council (RCC), the makeshift body that had assumed control of the government, ordered the dissolution of all political parties. It was Anwar al-Sadat who oversaw the tribunal that attempted to rid the country of the pre-revolutionary political forces permanently. In addition to dismantling all independent political parties, this move had the added effect of debilitating intellectual life in Egypt, a change that would have profound effects two decades later, as Sadat attempted to build his legitimacy as president. The only exemption to this political clampdown was given to a small group that surrounded Nasser and helped cultivate his ideas and affirm his legitimacy. Muhammad Hassanein Heikal, a prominent journalist and intellectual, is most emblematic of this group.

Although he maintained a leftist and revolutionary character, Nasser demonstrated little tolerance for communists in Egypt, and his relationship with the Soviet Union was a complicated one, full of suspicions of its intentions toward Egypt and dissatisfaction with its inadequate aid when compared to that of US support for Israel. Upon the exclusion of communists as well as liberals, who embodied the failures of the parliamentary regime and faced charges of elitism and cooperating with Egypt's enemies, the state's sights were set on the Muslim Brotherhood, the remaining freestanding social movement with the ability to pose significant opposition to the revolution.

From Potential Partners to Outlawed Opposition

The story of the Muslim Brotherhood's brief honeymoon with and subsequent persecution at the hands of the RCC has been recounted in many places. In spite of the incomplete facts and at times contradictory accounts, there are several aspects of these events that are of direct relevance to the discussion of the Islamic movement's resurgence in the 1970s. For one, the first three presidents of Egypt, Muhammad Naguib, Gamal Abdel Nasser, and Anwar al-Sadat, all had personal relationships and experiences with the Muslim Brotherhood, which directly impacted the decisions they made in dealing with the group. For its part, the Muslim Brotherhood's leadership in the early 1950s exposed its inability to address basic questions such as its desired relationship with the state and the nature of its internal structure. The events of the critical years of 1952–1954 turned what was initially a *fursa*, or opportunity, into a *mihna*, or ordeal, with consequences that reverberated long after Nasser's death.

Upon ridding the new regime of the secular opposition, Nasser turned his attention to the Islamic movement and its chief representative, the Muslim Brotherhood. There is widespread disagreement among scholars as to whether Nasser deliberately devised a "divide and conquer" strategy to neutralize his political rivals, or whether circumstances eventually necessitated the clampdown on the Muslim Brotherhood. What is known is that the RCC was in need of the Muslim Brotherhood's support in order to survive the uncertainty of the first two years, while the Muslim Brotherhood was eager to take advantage of the new political space to advance its own program.

In gauging the Muslim Brotherhood's support for revolutionary action prior to the coup by the Free Officers, Mitchell emphasized that the picture was rather mixed.[4] As with many social movements that encompass an array of classes, the views of the Muslim Brotherhood's members on this issue generally reflected their social standing. Hasan al-Hudaybi, for instance, came from a respected lineage and enjoyed a successful career as a judge under the liberal regime, and as such was not receptive to the idea of overthrowing the existing system. Other figures, however, such as Salih al-'Ashmawi and 'Abd al-Rahman al-Sanadi, already leading members of the Muslim Brotherhood's Secret Apparatus, were far more open to working with the military conspirators. Actual contacts between the Free Officers and the Muslim Brotherhood date back to over a decade prior to the revolution. In 1940, prior to joining the group that was to become the Free Officers, Sadat met Hasan al-Banna. Soon thereafter, he became acquainted with 'Abd al-Mon'eim 'Abd al-Ra'uf, a Muslim Brotherhood member and military officer who participated in subversive activities. 'Abd al-Ra'uf continued to work with both groups, eventually joining the Free Officers and becoming the strongest advocate for the Muslim Brotherhood within its ranks.[5] Another disaffected military officer and Muslim Brotherhood member, Mahmoud Labib, met with Nasser in 1944 and addressed him passionately about the need for dramatic changes in Egypt. Mitchell contended that this meeting was responsible for orienting Nasser toward planning the coup.

In fact, Mitchell rightly pointed out that reports of such high-level contacts were later buried in order to create a historical record that minimized the Muslim Brotherhood's role in the coup. Early records of the meetings between Nasser and the Muslim Brotherhood, such as the one detailing the critical 1944 encounter, were created prior to the falling out between Hudaybi and the Nasser regime.[6] By contrast, Sadat's memoirs, published several years after the purge of the Muslim Brotherhood, diminished the role played by its leadership in the revolution. Sadat was appointed by the revolutionary committee as the liaison with the Muslim Brotherhood and met regularly with Banna, whom he lauded as "a theologian with a sense of reality, a man of religion who recognized the existence of facts."[7] In spite of his personal admiration for the Muslim Brotherhood's charismatic leader, Sadat stressed the group's failure to live up to its promise of joining the military collaborators in their plot to overthrow the corrupt and subservient Wafdist government during a critical juncture at the height of World War II. Moreover, he characterized the Muslim Brotherhood in the aftermath of the revolution as "an organization of unbounded fanaticism, and a menace to public order."[8]

Regardless of whether these historical interactions were framed with political considerations in mind, their significance lies in demonstrating the extent of the relationship between two important forces in Egypt in the critical time before and after the revolution. Sadat wrote that the Free Officers believed that "the Brotherhood was a powerful group, and the only one with which we could safely cooperate in the difficult years which lay ahead. It was vital that we should strengthen our position by such alliances."[9] In laying out the events that preceded the coup, Sadat emphasized that the military officers were cautious in their relationship with the Muslim Brotherhood, describing the cooperation between the two as "at best a makeshift affair; soon there were frequent clashes and misunderstandings."[10] He continued in this vein, laying down the gauntlet with his description of the events that resulted in the final break between the two groups in the aftermath of the revolution:

> The Revolutionary Council's first action after the coup d'etat was to pardon the Brotherhood, believing that its members had sufficiently expiated their crimes. This generosity was ill-rewarded, for the Brothers whom we had rehabilitated and given a fresh chance in life, turned against us savagely.[11]

Before moving on, it is necessary to investigate the drastic transformation of the relationship between the Free Officers and the Muslim Brotherhood. In spite of Sadat's simplistic characterization of the tenuous partnership as one of benevolence repaid with betrayal, the relationship was far more complex. It involved common causes, from the nationalist struggle against foreign hegemony and political corruption to the regional war for Palestine. It included powerful personalities, from Naguib and Nasser, to Banna and Hudaybi. Ultimately, however, it succumbed to conflicting interests between the two parties, whether it was over the targets for recruitment, which frequently overlapped due to the Muslim Brotherhood's interest in spreading within the military, the negotiations with the British for their withdrawal from Egypt (which both sides pursued separately), or the right to determine the nation's future, which exposed deeply diverging visions for Egypt.

Hasan al-Banna's sudden death in early 1949 was a watershed event in the relationship between the Muslim Brotherhood and the emerging opposition within the military. In addition to the previously recounted high-level meetings between leaders in both camps, the two fought side by side in the Palestine war in 1948, where the Muslim Brotherhood's volunteer corps performed admirably to such an extent that its heroics were recounted by members of the Free Officers. As late as 1949, Nasser himself spoke openly in defense of the Muslim Brotherhood during an interrogation by the prime minister regarding Nasser's political affiliations.[12] Earlier that same year, however, Banna was killed in a wave of political violence that swept Egypt. His organization was held responsible for several of those attacks, and an era of mistrust of the Muslim Brotherhood by the Free Officers, the presumptive keepers of order, began. While the organization's fallen leader was largely exempted from the accusations of supporting violence, his successor was viewed with suspicion by Nasser and his comrades.

As a long-standing member of the Egyptian elite, Hudaybi was already unpopular among the revolutionary officers and their sympathizers within the Muslim Brotherhood. However, several incidents accelerated the demise in the relationship. The first involved the Muslim Brotherhood's role in the revolution of July 23, 1952. Mitchell recounted that, with the exception of a few members, the Muslim Brotherhood was largely in the dark about the specifics of the coup. Even 'Abd al-Ra'uf, to this point a central figure in both movements, was excluded from the Executive Committee of the Free Officers in the months prior to the coup. In fact, the Free Officers kept the entire Muslim Brotherhood organization at bay, reserving its role primarily for contingency plans in the event of the coup's failure or the breakdown of civil order.[13] Hudaybi was not known to have had any personal knowledge of the coup in the days leading up to it. Whereas the overwhelming majority of Egyptians immediately welcomed the revolution, Hudaybi's offense was in waiting a full three days to officially recognize the new regime. Conveniently for many of his critics, Hudaybi's July 26 statement followed the king's abdication of his throne, signaling the official end of the old regime and the beginning of revolutionary politics in Egypt.

The Muslim Brotherhood's perceived lukewarm reception of the revolution was an early sign of the mistrust that would continue to build over the next few years, culminating in the dramatic events of the Manchiyya incident in 1954. Despite the Muslim Brotherhood's characterization of the new regime as "our revolution," the contending visions for the future of Egypt would become apparent just days after the RCC dismissed the parliament and attempted to form its own cabinet. The Muslim Brotherhood's desire for a government based on Islamic principles was quietly sidelined by the RCC, whose sole gesture toward the group was to offer three cabinet posts, upon Nasser's approval of the candidates. This story (with its many versions) has been recounted in several scholarly sources.[14] Resulting from this tense encounter was the expulsion of Ahmed Hasan al-Baquri from the Muslim Brotherhood following his acceptance of a cabinet post with the RCC. The power struggle between the two groups played out in this episode, as the Free Officers, achieving firm control over the new government, blocked Hudaybi's cabinet choices and effectively limited the role of the Muslim Brotherhood, which claimed to be the sole remaining voice representing the Egyptian people.

These events also exposed the internal challenges to Hudaybi from within the Muslim Brotherhood, as he was accused of frequently acting without the approval of the Guidance Council and alienating his organization from the new government at the expense of those elements within the group's leadership that desired a more meaningful partnership with the RCC. Although the damage done by this incident was not irreparable, Mitchell argued that it nonetheless changed the nature of the relationship, as the two forces grew further apart. He wrote that, "the feelings of the regime towards the Society remained positive but their basis shifted from friendship to need."[15]

The next major incident that affected the standing of the Muslim Brotherhood with the new regime concerned the question of the continuing British occupation. Hudaybi's meetings with the British Embassy in early 1953, ostensibly to negotiate the terms of a treaty ending Britain's presence in Egypt, roused the anger of the RCC, which felt betrayed by the Muslim Brotherhood's leader and undermined in its efforts to negotiate a treaty on its own terms. Hudaybi claimed that he had entered the discussions with Nasser's blessing and only to bolster the impression of a united front among Egypt's various political forces. However, his voice was drowned out by the strident agitation against the Muslim Brotherhood taking place in the Egyptian press, along with Nasser's exploitation of this sensitive situation to begin the process of ridding his government of the Muslim Brotherhood once and for all.

This process was completed the following year in dramatic fashion. On October 26, 1954, an assassination attempt against Nasser while he was delivering a speech in Alexandria served as the final blow to the Muslim Brotherhood's relationship with the regime. The perpetrator was a member of the organization and was accused of having received his orders from the highest levels. Following a reluctant attempt earlier in the year to ban the Muslim Brotherhood, this time the action was decisive and the retribution swift. Hundreds of Muslim Brotherhood members, especially those in the organization's leadership hierarchy, were arrested and charged with various crimes, ranging from specific knowledge of the plot against Nasser, to more broadly supporting sedition and counter-revolutionary activities. The attempted assassin and five others, including the most recent head of the Secret Apparatus, were executed shortly after their trial. Hudaybi's death sentence was reduced to life imprisonment. The Muslim Brotherhood's headquarters was ransacked and burned by angry mobs, who only days earlier had exhibited serious misgivings about the RCC.

The Ordeal and Its Consequences

By early 1955, the Muslim Brotherhood had entered a new phase in its existence. With its organization outlawed, its institutions dismantled, its rank and file members imprisoned, and its leader under house arrest, the group founded by Hasan al-Banna less than three decades earlier ceased to exist. It is no wonder that in the decade that followed, scholars wrote of the Muslim Brotherhood in the past tense. Even in his seminal study of the organization, Mitchell structured his chronology with a defined beginning and end to the group.[16] This was not without good reason. An independent social organization with a broad political platform was part of a bygone era of liberal parliamentary politics in Egypt and was largely out of step with the development of authoritarian rule in the tightly held political program of the revolutionary regime. Few would have predicted a future for the Muslim Brotherhood in this context, and whatever remained of the organization itself had to come to terms with the radically altered picture.

Even at the height of Nasser's repression, however, the remaining leadership of the Muslim Brotherhood attempted to forge a new body out of the ashes of the old organization. More recent scholarship has explored the evolution (or regression, as the case may be) of the Islamic movement during the revolutionary period, highlighting its enduring quality even as it faced the rising tide of secular nationalist ideologies that swept Egypt and the Arab world at large. The Muslim Brotherhood's experience culminated with the development of Organization 1965 and the state's response the following year, which once again sought to extinguish the flames of Islamic activism that threatened the Nasser regime. In addition to its continuing feud with the state, however, this period was also marked by the gradual materialization of distinct ideological fault lines within the Islamic movement. As the self-proclaimed mother organization of the movement, the Muslim Brotherhood was forced to bear the burden of this growing divide and to oversee the transition to a phase of competitive trends that fought eagerly for followers and the right to determine the future course of Islamic activism in Egypt.

By the late 1950s, the Nasser regime was at its zenith and the ideology of Arab nationalism had galvanized populations throughout the region to lend their support to Egypt's project for the Arab world. This period also marked the first wave of the state's relaxation of security measures and resulted in the release of some Muslim Brotherhood members from prison. Almost immediately, former high-ranking members of the organization's leadership hierarchy set about to revive the Muslim Brotherhood, albeit in a modest, simplified form. Members met in small groups to chart the future of the organization, eventually seeking (and by most accounts, receiving) the blessing of General Guide Hasan al-Hudaybi, who remained their leader, at least nominally. Zollner pointed out that the reorganization efforts conducted by these groups, which included such figures as 'Abd al-Fattah Isma'il, Shaykh Muhammad Fathi Rifa'i, Ahmed 'Abd al-Majid and 'Ali al-'Ashmawi, run counter to the prevailing narrative that the Muslim Brotherhood revival occurred within Nasser's prisons.[17] Although there was a significant amount of communication and coordination between those inside and outside prison, especially through the family support network led by Zainab al-Ghazali and the Muslim Sisterhood, the bulk of the activities took place outside prison and was concentrated in the urban centers of Cairo and Alexandria. There, small groups met in secret to conduct study sessions that continued to propagate Banna's message, while also discussing political matters and their experiences under the Nasser regime.

In its renewed existence, the Muslim Brotherhood was only a shadow of its former self. While it traditionally relied on its public character to spread its message and generate goodwill within the society at large, the new organization maintained secrecy as its most valued quality and limited its engagement to those with a preexisting relationship with the group. Furthermore, it no longer sustained itself financially, but rather relied increasingly on outside support, especially from the Gulf countries. Finally, the traditional structural hierarchy was replaced by an ad hoc leadership that maintained far less transparency than it had previously, and even bypassed the general guide on many important matters. In fact, it is during this period that Sayyid Qutb became the Muslim Brotherhood's most influential figure, not only on matters of ideology, but in directing the organization's movements as well. Although he remained in prison until 1964, Qutb's continued presence in the hospital wing of Liman al-Turra ensured that he would interact with the many Muslim Brotherhood members who passed through the hospital for treatment.[18]

There can be no doubt that the extreme conditions brought about by Nasser's pervasive security apparatus and the oppressive nature of the prison camps stunted the growth of the Islamic movement, engendering competing claims for authenticity based on conflicting responses to the challenges posed by the state's policies. When Qutb was released from prison in 1964, he found himself the spiritual head of a burgeoning movement for confrontation with the Nasser regime. The following year, before the group could act, state security agents once again pounced on what they perceived to be a revolt in the making, and conducted a new wave of arrests across the country. Hundreds of Muslim Brotherhood members, even with the most tangential connection to the alleged coup conspirators, were imprisoned after a series of military trials that produced little or no evidence. For his part in providing ideological guidance through his written works, Qutb was sentenced to execution. The order was carried out in August 1966.

Once again, the Muslim Brotherhood found itself in a state of complete disarray. Its leaders had either been killed or imprisoned and its members scattered within society, hoping to suppress any ties that would identify them with the outlawed organization. For the moment, the Nasser regime had thwarted every attempt to rebuild the Islamic opposition. It would take an entire year and a cataclysmic defeat on the level of the Six Day War to once again open the door for the Islamic movement.

Internal Debates and the Evolution of Ideas

Nasser's policy of total repression unwittingly contributed to the continuing development of Islamic political thought, as it became an extension of the revolutionary zeal with which he imbued Egyptian society, as well as the severity of the measures inflicted upon the Islamic movement. The trajectory of Sayyid Qutb's career is perhaps most emblematic of this point. Trained as an educator and writer, he specialized in literary criticism, writing a number of commentaries on pre-revolutionary Egyptian literature and culture early in his career. Published in 1947, his *al-'Adala al-Ijtima'iyya fil Islam* (*Social Justice in Islam*) was in its time the fullest expression of Qutb's attempt to reconcile traditional Islamic values with the challenges of modern society. Though it appeared prior to the coup by the Free Officers, the work in many ways embodied the promise of the revolution and helped to chart a course in which the Islamic movement could lend its credibility to the socialist policies of the Nasser regime. In fact, it was during this period that Qutb became editor of the Muslim Brotherhood's official magazine, propagating a message that departed from some of the traditional rhetoric associated with the liberal era in Egyptian politics and evoking the views of some of Qutb's associates from among the coup conspirators in the military.[19]

By late 1954, however, Qutb had suffered the same fate as other senior leaders of the Muslim Brotherhood. For the next decade, he was to make his home in the notorious Liman al-Turra. It was within this prison's walls that Qutb completed his magnum opus, the multivolume *Fi Dhilal al-Qur'an* (*In the Shade of the Qur'an*). Through its sobering portrait of modern society, it offered a reinterpretation of scripture for a different age in which believers suffered from alienation in the expanding gulf between their faith and the world around them. Departing from the traditional methodology for Qur'anic exegesis, Qutb's approach attempted to historicize the Qur'an's chapters, looking at the Causes of Revelation (*Asbab al-Nuzul*) as a means of distinguishing the earliest community of Muslims from later generations, while at the same time drawing upon that model to provide a "clear legal framework" to govern the lives of Muslims in contemporary society.[20] It was his holistic approach to Qur'anic interpretation that allowed Qutb to adapt traditional concepts such as *jihad* and *jahiliyya* for the modern age.

In the trajectory of Qutb's intellectual development, the final phase was marked by the short-lived publication of his most heavily referenced work, *Ma'alim fil Tariq* (*Milestones Along the Path*). Appearing for the first time in 1964, this work earned the ire of the Nasser regime and ultimately cost Qutb his life, as the only connection between him and the accused conspirators of Organization 1965 was that illegal copies of *Milestones* were discovered in their homes. Qutb was soon after arrested and later executed as the alleged inspirational leader behind the coup attempt. The book has been compared with Lenin's *What Is to Be Done*, as a tract that went beyond Qutb's previous works, which had identified the problems plaguing Muslim society or had outlined the solutions, by putting forth an outright call to action.[21] In examining the motivational message of *Milestones*, Kepel considers it as "both an instrument for the analysis of contemporary society and a guide for a vanguard whose task is to inaugurate the resurrection of the *Ummah*. In short, it is a manifesto."[22]

Qutb's final book was at once the culmination of his previous works and a dramatic departure from them. It built on many of the concepts developed in *Social Justice in Islam* and *In the Shade of the Qur'an* while also signaling the final break, not only with Egypt's revolution, but with society as a whole. Though written several years prior to the 1967 defeat, *Milestones* foreshadowed the utter failures of Nasser's program and, had he been alive to witness it, Qutb would probably have expressed no surprise at the *naksa*. There has been some debate over whether *Milestones* was the direct product of the harsh conditions in Nasser's prisons or whether it reflected the natural progression of thought during the so-called Islamic resurgence of the 1960s and 1970s. Kepel wrote that "Islamicist thought was reconstructed after 1954 primarily in the concentration camps, which were felt by Qutb and his disciples to symbolize the relationship of the state to society. The camp experience must therefore be assessed, before considering Qutb's major writings."[23] On the other hand, Zollner argued that:

> [T]his rather psychological explanation for the radicalization somehow hides the fact that key ideas of his arguments, as given in his later work, were already present in earlier stages. Additionally, by singling out Qutb's experiences and giving them a psychological

explanation, one can easily overlook that his radical interpretation was also embedded in a debate among Muslim Brothers, a network of relations to other detainees and to supporters outside the prison.[24]

Scholars have also pointed to the influence on Qutb by Abul 'Ala al-Mawdudi and Abul Hasan 'Ali al-Nadawi, two thinkers from the Indian subcontinent who developed key concepts that became central to the call to believers in *Milestones*.[25] Another argument that further undermines the notion of prison radicalization involves the fate of other Muslim Brotherhood prisoners. Leading figures such as Mahmoud 'Abd al-Halim, Mustafa Mashhur, 'Umar al-Tilmisani, and of course Hudaybi were undoubtedly subjected to many of the same conditions as Qutb but, as discussed below, continued to espouse the original Muslim Brotherhood message, with only slight modifications.

Qutb's departure from the traditional thought of the Muslim Brotherhood centered on the fundamental belief in a bottom-up versus top-down strategy for reform. That is, the Muslim Brotherhood of Banna and Hudaybi dedicated the bulk of its efforts to grassroots social activism, even as it engaged the centers of power. Qutb, on the other hand, shifted the emphasis from *da'wa*, the most essential part of the Muslim Brotherhood's program, to the pursuit of political empowerment and the implementation of the Shari'a. This was both a strategic and ideological change, informed in large part by a transformed worldview. By Qutb's account, the purity that marked the early generation of Islam was shortly thereafter consumed by a re-emergence of the various aspects of *jahiliyya* society, to such an extent that it persisted throughout the march of history. According to Qutb's analysis of the contemporary situation:

> Today too we are surrounded by *jahiliyya*. Its nature is the same as in the first period of Islam, and it is perhaps a little more deeply entrenched. Our whole environment, people's beliefs and ideas, habit and art, rules and laws—is *jahiliyya*, even to the extent that what we consider to be Islamic culture, Islamic sources, Islamic philosophy, and Islamic thought are also constructs of *jahiliyya*! This is why the true Islamic values never enter our hearts, why our minds are never illuminated by Islamic concepts, and why no group of people arises among us equal to the caliber of the first generation of Islam.[26]

By this reasoning, existing structures, whether it was the nation-state system as a whole, a recent introduction to the Muslim societies, or the Nasser regime ruling Egypt in particular, were beyond the pale of Islam and therefore were subject to being overturned through an intellectual project as well as through active struggle. Haddad described the revolutionary nature of Qutb's Islamic activist agenda thus:

> The task of Muslims today . . . is to reappropriate the understanding of true Islam so as to be able to apply it to the contemporary circumstances, for which task a rewriting of Islamic history is crucial, *and* to reappropriate the political power which was historically theirs so that the true *din al-wasat* can be actualized as God's divinely ordained and guided community on earth.[27]

It is in the final section of *Milestones*, in Qutb's call to arms, that he displayed most vividly his split from the Muslim Brotherhood's traditional intellectual framework. In defining the mission as being the replacement of "this *jahiliyya* with Islamic ideals and traditions," Qutb proceeded to note that "this cannot be brought about by agreeing with *jahiliyya* and going along a few steps with it, as some of us think we ought to do, for this would simply mean that from the beginning we have accepted defeat."[28] The critique of *du'a*, or callers—a central facet of the Muslim Brotherhood's program—signaled Qutb's final break with his intellectual tradition. In one of the final sections of *Milestones*, he noted that "the history of the Call to Allah has witnessed various endings in this world in its struggle with other movements."[29] These various endings, however, were merely different methods of "annihilation," violent ends that beset past civilizations. In other words, according to Qutb, *da'wa* is largely a failed endeavor. However, as is discussed below, it would be left to others to reach the conclusion that the label of *kafir* could be justifiably employed in reference to self-professed Muslims.[30]

While Qutb did not make any specific calls for the violent overthrow of the state, and even as he did not explicitly disavow the *da'wa* paradigm, it occurred to Muslim Brotherhood leaders to refute the arguments offered in *Milestones*, especially as it became apparent that some contingents within the rank-and-file membership and the rising generation of youth activists were adopting Qutb's words as the basis for their anti-state actions. Even after its official ban, *Milestones* spread across the country, as students huddled together to make copies by hand for distribution.

The state's policy of banishing Qutb and his memory from public life had seemingly backfired:

> [B]anning Qutb's works drew attention to the importance of his appeal. Forcing intellectuals to keep silent and not to discuss Qutb's works left the field completely open for the younger individuals and groups to interpret Qutb's thought as they wished. Consequently, waves of violence in the decades after Qutb's death, were inescapably the result of ignorance and stupidity.[31]

A generation had found in *Milestones* a call for action against the state. The practice of *takfir*, or declaring Muslims to be unbelieving, was utilized by a number of groups that sought isolation from society in the form of *hijra*, or migration, as the Prophet had done fourteen centuries earlier in leaving Mecca for Medina. This movement embarked on a new path, transforming modern Islamic political thought into a revolutionary force, willing to confront the regime head-on and to halt the march of secular nationalism in the pursuit of power.[32]

The most prominent response to the emerging oppositional front from within the Islamic movement came from none less than the general guide himself, in the form of Hudaybi's famous book, *Du'a la Quda* (*Preachers Not Judges*).[33] In her study of this period, Zollner offered important insights into the composition of this work. For one, she made a strong case that called Hudaybi's sole authorship of the book into doubt.[34] This is important for a number of reasons. The considerable number of contributors to the refutation demonstrates that the issues raised in Qutb's work were widely read and discussed within the Islamic movement. Moreover, the possibility that senior figures from al-Azhar were involved in the authorship of *Preachers* suggests that these issues were taken seriously by the regime, which undertook a proactive policy to combat the spread of subversive ideas among Qutb's followers. The latter point also exposes the fact that state officials closely monitored the internal debate within the Islamic movement, and possibly even contributed to it, undermining the notion of the debate being "internal" at all. As Zollner further elucidated, this process was facilitated by the limited modes of communication among Muslim Brotherhood leaders, who relied heavily on prison networks and the support of family members to remain in touch with one another.[35]

The work was notable for both its simplicity and its reliance on established Islamic legal and theological norms. In his opening chapter,

Hudaybi listed a set of guiding principles that set the tone of his rebuttal. First, judgment of individual faith was for God alone, and not intended to be in the realm of human beings. Second, it was incumbent upon those who make claims to particular religious decrees to bring proof from the main sources of Islam, the Qur'an and the Sunna. It was not up to those who deny the authenticity of religious claims to provide the evidence. Finally, the human intellect was not permitted to devise matters of legal prohibition or permissibility without corroboration from the divine source of Shari'a.[36] By laying out these criteria, Hudaybi calibrated the terms of the debate, placing the onus on the opposing side to respond with proof of its claims.

The first section defined the true believer, an indirect response to Qutb's assertion that society was in a state of total ignorance. Hudaybi quickly dispatched such an absolutist judgment in favor of the traditional Islamic definition of a Muslim as one who declared belief in the basic tenets of the faith. Even those who erred in their deeds were not to be cast out from the tent of the faithful, as sin was a natural part of every believing society. Moreover, he argued that the concept of passing judgment on an entire population without any distinction reflected poor acumen and was profoundly un-Islamic. In the event that individuals in society demonstrated "ignorance" (jahl, as opposed to the loaded term jahiliyya), it was not the place of the preacher to pass judgment against them.

The issue of divine sovereignty was another central theme in Preachers, prompted by the need to respond to Qutb's excoriation of man-made governments and his argument that rule was for God alone. Hudaybi countered that an Islamic state cannot exist without some degree of agency given to the people themselves who, rightly guided by divine decree, were apt to rule over the temporal world. This analysis also alluded to the visible contradiction in Milestones that granted Qutb's followers the right to condemn society as unbelieving while reserving sovereignty to God alone.

In many ways, Hudaybi's text hinged on the Muslim Brotherhood's claim to authority. It frequently faulted the group's rivals for failing to properly interpret Islamic sources, and even offered a miniature guide to evaluating religious texts. One chapter, titled "Obedience and Assent," stressed the need to conform to established norms, accepted interpretations, and recognized authority. To some extent, and in the face of an extraneous threat, the movement led by Hudaybi supported a declared orthodoxy and warned against any deviation from it. The recurring theme of Preachers defined the role of the movement's rank-and-file membership as simply callers to the faith. The figure of the *da'i*, a humble community servant, appeared in sharp contrast to the scathing judgment passed on society by Qutb.[37]

The period surrounding Hudaybi's publication of *Preachers* marked an important turning point in the history of the Muslim Brotherhood. Whereas in the previous era of the group's existence, it was possible to talk about the Muslim Brotherhood and the Islamic movement in Egypt as nearly interchangeable entities, the ideological (and the ensuing strategic) split within the movement's ranks were such that the Muslim Brotherhood would now have to contend with an emerging fringe opposition within the movement that vied for the hearts and minds of the nation's youth.

As the next section demonstrates, this was a young man's game. The discourse initiated by Qutb and elaborated upon by Hudaybi would only pick up steam after both figures had left the scene. It would be left to the new generation of Islamic activists, coming primarily from the ranks of Egypt's growing population of students, to determine the future of the movement. As its leaders continued to languish in prison, even as Nasser took his last breath in late September 1970, the Muslim Brotherhood's existence depended on its ability to overcome its logistical and organizational limitations and to spread its message to the youth. This was the key to maintaining its supremacy in the field of Islamic activism. Before proceeding to the next phase in the Islamic movement's history, however, it is essential to provide a historical overview of student political activism in Egypt, highlighting its relationship (both harmonious and contentious) with the Islamic movement along the way.

Student Activism in the Liberal Period

The modern system of education in Egypt is the product of developments stemming from several periods of recent history, beginning with the Napoleonic invasion of the late eighteenth century. The abrupt exposure to European imperialism, followed by a half century of rapid modernization at the hands of Muhammad 'Ali Pasha, signaled a break from traditional modes of learning and ushered in an era of modern, standardized education in Egypt. This process continued into the late nineteenth century, until it was hindered by the advancement of the British colonial regime in Egypt in 1882. Lord Cromer set British educational policy in Egypt in an attempt to preserve a status quo favorable to British interests. Educational reform was perceived to enable political instability by expanding upward social mobility and resulting in the rise of a widespread nationalist movement.[38] As a result of Cromer's policy, 73 percent of Egyptian students were paying for their education in 1892, a rise from 30 percent only a decade earlier.[39] The cultivation of an elite educated class separate from the rest of society was an integral part of maintaining British supremacy in colonial Egypt.

Following the Egyptian nationalist movement's achievement of nominal independence in 1922, efforts were made to standardize the system of education, with particular emphasis placed on primary education, provided to all Egyptians for free.[40] Despite numerous efforts throughout the liberal period, Egypt was still unable to shake off the dualism in its system of education, one that maintained two types of institutions, one for the dominant, landowning elite and future government leaders, and another for the rest of the population, a minimalist system targeting basic literacy for the rural majority.[41] In the area of higher education, Egypt's first modern university was established in 1925 by combining previously existing colleges and attempting to standardize the curriculum. As a remnant of British colonial rule, however, Egypt's university system was largely used to feed employees into government ranks, a phenomenon that became unsustainable as the number of university graduates exceeded the demand for government bureaucrats. These developments increased the strain on the Wafdist government, resulting in political instability in Egypt during the 1930s and 1940s:

> As the university students' perceptions of the future that awaited them became increasingly dismal, they turned to political activism. . . . Strengthening such feelings were the many physical, psychological, social, and economic problems which students, particularly those from more traditional backgrounds, encountered in attempting to adjust to the demands of university life.[42]

The achievements of these politically conscientious students can best be measured by examining periodic moments of crisis that beset Egypt during the era of liberal parliamentary politics. The first major political crisis surfaced in the aftermath of the 1930 revisions to the constitution that granted Britain increased rights in Egypt and marginalized the parliament, Egypt's only representative body. After Isma'il Sidqi Pasha's government collapsed in 1933, the Wafd-led government of Tawfiq Nasim

Pasha was tasked with the responsibility of reforming the constitution, following widespread outrage at the changes. The student movement was instrumental in this effort. When, in November 1935, Wafd Party leaders officially called for non-cooperation with the British, the students at Fuad University (later Cairo University) responded by taking to the streets. Nearly two thousand students marched from Giza to Cairo on the first day of the strike, and that number doubled on the second day, when students were met with a violent response by state security officers.[43] Although workers and professional unions sympathized with the protests and frequently joined them, it was the university students who took the lead in this unprecedented action.

On the political front, the students pressed for unity from their party leaders, an effort that yielded the United Front, the political coalition that forced the palace to restore the 1923 Constitution and set the stage for the signing of the Anglo-Egyptian Treaty of 1936. Made up of independents as well as representatives from all major political factions, from the Wafd to Young Egypt, and the communists to the Muslim Brotherhood, the student movement was free of domination by one political faction, and actually asserted its own power on the elders within these groups. So significant was the rise of the student movement as a force in its own right on the political stage that this period became known as the "years of youth."[44]

The political situation in Egypt remained relatively pacified during World War II, but as the war drew to a close, the country's popular factions began to agitate for full independence, and once again the student movement played a pivotal role in these events. Student protests in late 1945 in solidarity with Palestine as it battled increased Jewish migration and British rule gave way to the establishment of the Mixed Committee of Students (MCS) in early 1946. As one of its first acts, the MCS issued a National Charter, calling for the evacuation of the British from all of Egypt, the inclusion of the United Nations in determining the country's future, and the pursuit of just economic policies.[45] These lofty demands came on the heels of a significant event that provided the momentum for the student movement to strengthen its resolve and widen its appeal in the months to come. On February 9, thousands of students assembled within the university's walls to listen to passionate speeches calling for Egypt's full independence. When many of them set off on a march through Cairo, they were once again met with the brute force of Egypt's police, which proceeded to raise the Abbas Bridge as hundreds of students were crossing over it. Scores were injured as a result of this incident, and confrontations continued to escalate in the ensuing weeks, resulting in the deaths of more than twenty students in clashes with police on February 21 alone.

The instability caused by these student protests and the subsequent workers' strikes generated some important results, as the palace offered to dismiss the current government in favor of more popular political leadership, while the British authorities made the decision on March 8 to withdraw from all parts of Egypt with the exception of the Suez Canal Zone. In an effort to restore order, however, the government began preemptive raids on the student leadership, arresting two hundred of them in July, banning their publications, and later that year temporarily closing the universities in Cairo and Alexandria. In fact, the closure of universities was a frequent occurrence throughout the late 1940s, as the government attempted to assert its control over the students as they, in turn, demonstrated their power as a force for political change in the face of a liberal regime in rapid decline. In late December 1947, the military surrounded the gates of Cairo University, but following a week-long student sit-in, the soldiers were withdrawn.[46]

As the situation in Egypt deteriorated further in 1951, the Wafdist government of Nahhas Pasha abrogated the unpopular Anglo-Egyptian Treaty of 1936. But rather than appease the protestors, this move emboldened the student movement, which escalated the number of general strikes, and issued a new National Charter through the student government that called for armed struggle against the continuing British occupation. University grounds became a center for military training for ten thousand students, and the first student battalion was deployed to the Suez Canal Zone in November. Under pressure from solidarity protests across the country, the government was forced to quickly reverse its ban on military training on university grounds in support of the guerrilla movement. The student movement's dominance in the nation's political affairs continued into the turbulent year of 1952 and well after the Free Officers Revolution, until it was repressed along with all other independent political forces, as described below.

Even as it remained fiercely independent and loosely affiliated with every political faction in Egypt during this two-decade period, the student movement was nonetheless strongly tied to the fate of the Islamic movement, especially as the Muslim Brotherhood gained in power and prominence. Since its inception, the Muslim Brotherhood preserved a special place for students within its program. Hasan al-Banna had only recently graduated from Dar al-'Ulum when he founded the organization in 1928.

When he established the first chapter in Ismailia, Banna was spending his days as a government-appointed teacher at a secondary school. Many of the first individuals to join the organization were his former colleagues and students. During his many travels throughout Egypt in the 1930s, Banna made a point of meeting with groups of students, and many of them were organized into families within the hierarchy of the Muslim Brotherhood. Soon after the headquarters was set up in Cairo, a special office devoted to student affairs was put in place.

The Rover Scouts, frequently the subject of controversy but also the means by which the Muslim Brotherhood defended its interests within an increasingly crowded and confrontational field of political activism, relied heavily on student recruits. Estimates of the Rover Scouts in the mid-1940s placed their number from 20,000 to 45,000, with most coming from the ranks of students, and once the Muslim Brotherhood was banned by government decree in 1948, one thousand of its members were dismissed from universities and secondary schools.[47] As stated previously, a feature of the independent student movement was the fierce competition between the political factions, as no single party effectively dominated the scene. Consequently, the university grounds were often the site of violent confrontations between student militias representing the various factions. Previously popular among only a minority of students, the Muslim Brotherhood made great gains in the mid-1940s, especially as it exploited the deterioration of the Wafd Party and the increasing disillusionment with it from within the student population. In 1946, a British embassy official observed that "[t]he rise of the Moslem Brethren has weakened the Wafd, particularly in the University and Schools, where they have recently become stronger than the Wafd as an element of disorder."[48]

The Muslim Brotherhood's influence within the student movement reached its apex on the eve of the revolution. In 1951, students affiliated with the Muslim Brotherhood swept the Student Union elections throughout Cairo University, winning all the available seats in the colleges of agriculture and science, and a majority of seats in the colleges of engineering, arts, law, and commerce.[49] Though frequent, the clashes between the Muslim Brotherhood and the other factions, especially the Wafdists and the communists, were occasionally interrupted by moments of coordination and cooperation, especially during times of national political crisis. The Muslim Brotherhood's growing power and influence also made it an appealing partner for these groups, and eventually it became a focal point for the coup conspirators in the military as well. The nexus between the student movement, the Muslim Brotherhood, and the Free Officers was a natural extension of the military action in Palestine and the Suez Canal Zone. The Muslim Brotherhood relied on student recruits to fill the ranks of its battalions, provided them with arms, and coordinated the volunteers' participation with officers in the Egyptian military. This relationship was to inform the future dealings between these groups in the aftermath of the Free Officers Revolution.

Student Activism after the Revolution

Despite the numerous advancements made to Egypt's system of education during the liberal era, including the increased availability of primary education and the standardization of the curriculum, the fundamental problem of elitism in the system remained:

> Thus by 1952 Egypt was rift by numerous social, political and cultural cleavages, a state of affairs to which the educational system had contributed greatly. Its elitist, fragmented structure ensured that divisions between elite and mass, town and country, graduates of the religious system and of the secular schools, would become ever deeper; its ethos ensured that even the graduates of the modern schools would be ignorant automatons possessing . . . negative attributes.[50]

As such, one of the top priorities of the Revolutionary Command Council was to pursue reforms in the system of education, just as it advanced new programs in other areas of Egypt's political, economic, and social infrastructure. Szyliowicz categorized the development of Egyptian education under the revolutionary regime according to three phases, which largely coincided with the major political transformations that marked the Nasser regime.[51]

The first phase lasted until 1956, falling under the period of Nasser's consolidation of power. During these years the state aggressively pushed a national plan toward universal primary education and the diversification of post-primary education, seen through its emphasis on technical and vocational training. The second phase lasted until 1961 and was marked by the central role that the state's emerging political ideology played in determining the course of the educational system. School and university instruction was heavily politicized as students were expected to internalize the Nasser regime's nationalist rhetoric and to lead the way in meeting its ambitious development goals. The third phase lasted through most of the 1960s and reflected Egypt's growing dependence on foreign support, as it advanced radical socialist policies at all levels of domestic policy, including education. The regime also attempted to address some of the failures of the previous period, including the inability to meet development targets and the strains placed on its educational system due to overcrowding and aging facilities.

The government's reforms brought about some welcome changes to Egypt's system of education. Though it did not attain its goal of universal education, the Nasser regime abolished school fees and saw the number of students in higher education increase by more than 50 percent in the first six years after the revolution.[52] Additionally, public expenditure on education rose from 2.5 million Egyptian pounds under the last Wafd government to 33.3 million Egyptian pounds under the RCC. Nasser also attempted to do away with the dualism in education by providing a standardized curriculum and opening the doors of Egypt's universities to greater numbers of students from the middle and underprivileged classes. These changes saw a dramatic qualitative shift in the profile of students who attended Egypt's colleges and universities. Nasser later set his sights on the historically independent al-Azhar University, revamping its curriculum and diminishing its capacity to influence matters of policy and law in Egypt, another major change that was to have a profound impact on the future relationship between the student movement and the state.

In the immediate aftermath of the revolution, secondary and university students supported the RCC in large numbers. Students welcomed the promise of greater reforms to a system that had only catered to the elites in society. They continued to lend their support, even when "the new regime offered to do away with the parliamentary system in return for providing a number of social achievements which that system had notably failed to produce."[53] Nasser proceeded to dismiss hundreds of teachers, seen as representatives of the old regime, replacing them with those loyal to the revolution.

The breakdown in relations between the students and the government did not occur, however, until the RCC itself faced an internal split. Much like the Muslim Brotherhood's leadership, a large number of students supported Naguib, who ultimately lost out to Nasser in the ensuing power struggle. Sensing an immediate threat from within the ranks of the students, many of whom shared loyalties with the recently banned Muslim Brotherhood, Nasser established a student wing of the Liberation Rally, the first official political party after the revolution. On Egyptian campuses, this group's sole purpose was to undermine the efforts of preexisting student groups, eventually hoping to overwhelm them and to establish its presence as the sole representative of students. Following a turbulent period of violent confrontation between a state-supported organization and the remaining independent factions, the student movement was effectively suppressed by the end of 1954.

The absence of student activism, which lasted until 1967, "was engineered through the combination of coercion and socialization."[54] Nasser's clampdown on political freedom and his development of a robust security apparatus extended to the university campuses, where surveillance of students and professors was standard and armed guards patrolled the grounds and its surroundings. Moreover, administrators developed policies to keep students busy with day-to-day distractions, both welcome and unwelcome, such as the addition of intensive midterm examinations and various athletic clubs. It was also understood that students who affiliated themselves with the regime's various student organizations, from the Liberation Rally in the early years after the revolution to the Arab Socialist Union's Socialist Youth Organization (SYO) in the mid-1960s, stood a far better chance of attaining employment opportunities after graduation.

The degree to which student activities were closely monitored and controlled can be observed most closely through the experience of the Student Union at Cairo University. After 1953, school officials suspended elections and began appointing the leadership. Even after elections were restored in 1959, they were closely controlled and resulted in much the same type of pliant leadership.[55] For the first time in the organization's history, students did not enjoy full autonomy within their union, but instead deferred to faculty advisors, whose approval was required on all major issues. Furthermore, the mandate of the Student Union did not extend beyond academic, social, and cultural functions. Political activism was strictly off limits to students, except insofar as it served to echo the message of the regime. Faculty control over union membership dues ensured that resources were not allocated to independent student activities.

By the early 1960s, a combination of widespread student disinterest and frustration, along with Nasser's perception that he had solidified his regime's control over civil society, led to a slight relaxation of the state's grip on the Student Union, with reforms to its constitution passed in 1963 to allow greater student control. As the events of 1968 would demonstrate, however, students had long ago given up on the Student Union as a vehicle for their activism, and instead sought new alternatives. The June War of 1967 was a watershed event that drastically changed the nature of the Egyptian regime's relationship with its citizens. This was especially true of the students. An entire generation that was raised knowing no other form of government but that which came out of the revolution, and no other leader but Gamal Abdel Nasser, was suddenly left to question everything it had ever been taught. As one student leader later recalled, "only after the massive defeat of 1967, and the slowing down of the regime's social program due to the burden of military expenditure, did an eventual split between the regime and its student body become a real possibility."[56]

The Student Movement Returns

The last three years of Nasser's rule were notable for the shifts in the political order brought about by two incidents of civil unrest, both of which featured a prominent role by a student movement determined to reclaim its role in Egyptian political life. Both protests brought to a head larger concerns about the future direction of the nation in light of the unsuccessful war, along with localized grievances about the nature of the university environment. The defeat acted as a catalyst that:

> shattered the remaining sense of dynamism and momentum among the youth and created a climate wherein their frustrations concerning the university environment, the kinds of positions to which they could aspire, and the repressive political context became as explosive as in the past.[57]

The verdicts by the military courts in February 1968 sparked the first wave of protests. Although it was factory workers in Helwan who initiated the street demonstrations, students quickly joined in the efforts, infusing the growing opposition movement with momentum that would see the uprising last for one week. Following a flurry of discussions and debates in campuses in Cairo and Alexandria on February 21, students would take to the streets of those cities the following day, resulting in clashes with police followed by mass arrests. According to the recollections of one student leader at the Engineering College at Cairo University, it was the Law College students who initiated the protests, but their colleagues in engineering quickly took the lead and played a central role in the events that followed, as indicated by the selection of several students from the college to represent their peers in a meeting with the Speaker of Parliament, Anwar al-Sadat, on February 24.[58]

When the march reached the gates of parliament, a student delegation was admitted to the chamber and delivered a passionate address to the body. Addressing student concerns, Sadat assured them that state security agents would not retaliate against the students for their public display. In fact, he even provided them with his personal telephone numbers in case they were harassed following the meeting.[59] Sure enough, that night security agents conducted raids that netted all the student leaders. The following morning, a student assembly to discuss the next course of action turned into a second street demonstration once news of the arrests spread. This time, however, the police forces were ready to confront the students. The demonstration was violently repressed through the use of clubs and tear gas, and the students eventually retreated to their campus, where hundreds of them staged a sit-in. It took three days for faculty members and parents to convince the students to end their protest, and only after government officials agreed to another meeting to hear student demands.[60]

The meeting and its outcome were a major point of contention as student leaders recalled that their key grievances were obfuscated by the media and government officials. For his part, Sadat attempted to narrow student demands to the issues of the perceived leniency of the military sentences and the abuses committed by the university guard. Complicit in the effort to trivialize student concerns and discredit their leaders, the press portrayed the students as spoiled children of the old elite who called for the execution of Egyptian military generals following the national defeat. So careful was the regime in attempting to isolate the students and their message from reaching the wider public that Cairo police rerouted city traffic from passing the university gates in order to prevent Egyptians from reading the signs and banners hanging from the walls.

In separate accounts of this period, Ahmed Abdalla Ruzza, president of the Higher National Committee of Cairo University Students, and Wa'il 'Uthman, an Islamic activist and co-founder of Shabab al-Islam, stressed that the student movement united around a comprehensive program that called for liberalization of the political system and the restoration of rights and freedoms. A statement released by student leaders on the eve of their meeting with Sadat called on all students to come together for the sake of demanding their freedom which, according to them, had to be taken, and would never be given. The statement concluded with a list of eight demands:

1. The release of the detained students;
2. Freedom of opinion and of the press;
3. A free assembly practicing normal parliamentary life;
4. Removing the intelligence and security agents from the universities;
5. Issuing and enforcing laws to restore rights and freedoms;
6. A serious investigation into the incident of the Helwan workers;
7. Clarification of the truth of the air force trial matter;
8. An investigation into the conduct of the university guard.[61]

Of these demands, only half dealt with immediate problems arising out of the protests. The rest drew attention to larger political issues and called for fundamental changes to the system. The issue of the air force trial, with which the parliament and the media had been obsessed, was listed as the seventh demand and was not greatly emphasized by the students. Despite concerted efforts to minimize the scope of the student movement's demands, the protests did have a lasting impact on Egypt's political scene, signaling a point of no return for the Nasser regime. In the aftermath of the February protest:

> [n]ationally, it forced Nasser to order the retrial of the officers charged with negligence and to form a new cabinet with a civilian majority, mostly of university professors, for the first time in his rule. More significantly, it made him seek a renewed legitimacy for his regime through the promulgation of the Program of 30 March, with its promised liberal reforms of the political system.[62]

Within the university, students were satisfied to see that some of their demands were met, such as the lifting of censorship restrictions and the limitations on the University Guard's ability to intervene in political activities. A new constitution for the Student Union brought an end to faculty control and offered new welfare benefits for students. As Abdalla recalled, "the most important legacy of the uprising, however, was the spirit of self-confidence which spread through the student body in its aftermath."[63]

That spirit carried over into another protest later in the year. In November 1968, students united in their opposition to a new education law that raised testing and graduation standards in order to ease pressures on Egyptian schools. The protests began with secondary school students marching through the streets of Mansoura but spread to other cities in Egypt, beginning with al-Azhar students in Cairo and moving on to Alexandria, where students held the city's governor on their campus until he agreed to release their arrested colleagues. The situation escalated as the street protests in Alexandria and the subsequent response by police resulted in the deaths of sixteen people, scores of injuries, and widespread destruction of property. Meanwhile in Cairo, students attempting to organize a response were preempted by an aggressive effort by government and university officials to prevent the spread of the protest. Class meeting times were changed and ultimately canceled as officials closed the university's gates to prevent students from convening.

For the time being, the regime's aggressive response had proved effective in quelling the spread of another protest. In what Abdalla referred to in hindsight as a "step backwards for the student movement," some of the credibility it had built up in February was lost in November.[64] Without much popular outrage, students were arrested but never tried, and ultimately released after some months. The government went on an all-out offensive, with Nasser giving several speeches condemning the rash behavior of the youth and its effect on Egypt's image abroad. The media did its part to trumpet this position, while some regime officials hoped that the failure of the movement to achieve popular support could be used as a pretext to roll back some of the liberalization measures of the March 30 Program. For their part, the students recognized that the immediate cause around which they rallied during this protest was not likely to resonate with their compatriots. Regardless of how unfair they may seem to some students, the tougher educational measures were meant to improve standards, a goal with which many Egyptians would agree, at least in theory.

Movements Converge on the Eve of Sadat

In the long term, however, the November 1968 protest did much to continue to awaken the spirit of political activism within the nation's student body. By the end of the year, it became clear to the regime's highest officials that the status quo of the pre-1967 period was no more, and Nasser would have to rethink the means of maintaining his authority. His sudden death in 1970 would mean that this task would fall to someone else. With a new ruler in Sadat, whose Nasserist credentials were frequently questioned, and a reinvigorated student movement, the stage was set for some historic developments in Egyptian political life.

When examining these critical years of transition in Egypt's modern history, a degree of nuance is essential. Understanding the behavior of social movement actors can often become obfuscated by relying too heavily on rigid dates and landmark events. Though only a few years apart, the student protests of 1968 and those of 1972 fall on either side of the divide in Egypt's political timeline, and are accordingly treated as having occurred under vastly different state systems. In reality, however, the latter protests were an extension of the earlier ones and part of the same movement, evolving within a political climate that had been undergoing gradual change for a number of years.

Thus, the Sadat period can actually be said to have begun prior to his assumption of the presidency in late 1970. In contrast to his essentially marginal role during the early years after the revolution, Sadat enjoyed a sudden rise in the ranks of the Egyptian regime throughout the late 1960s, serving as prime minister and then becoming Nasser's vice president during the transitional final years of the Nasser presidency.

Additionally, many of the political transformations that would mark Sadat's term as president were actually set in motion prior to his assumption of power, in the immediate aftermath of the 1967 War. Egypt's gradual detachment from the Soviet Union, its warming up to the West, efforts toward greater political and economic openness, and even the possibility of a peace settlement with Israel were all pursued by Nasser during his final days in office. Finally, and perhaps most directly related to the subject at hand, the student movement's interaction with the regime during its post-1967 activism usually entailed filing grievances with Sadat in the dramatic scenes that unfolded in parliament. The buck stopped with him as far as many of the students were concerned. They met with him repeatedly and depended on his promises as representative of the regime's commitment to their demands. This is not to diminish the importance of Sadat's corrective revolution and consolidation of power that took place in May 1971 (and was further cemented in the October 1973 War) but rather to emphasize that many of these developments were set in motion prior to his assumption of the presidency.

It is in this context of political uncertainty and ideological fluidity that the student movement took form. In the late 1960s, the strength of the student activist movement lay in its unity. Scholars who have examined the responses to the June War list at least three ideological factions to

emerge from the defeat: secular liberal, radical socialist, and Islamic fundamentalist.[65] But if one examines the response at the level of the student
body, the most vocal and active segment of society during these critical
years, a different picture emerges. This was a period of dynamism and
fluidity of thought and action. Though representing different intellectual
trends, the student movement united in many of its activities and shared
largely the same feelings with regard to the issue of the defeat. It was
not until several years later, in the early 1970s, that one begins to witness the student movement divided according to rigid ideological lines.
This feeling was shared by a number of student leaders who later wrote
on their experiences during the protests of 1968. Abdalla and 'Uthman,
who represented the leftist and Islamist trends, respectively, would later
assert that the consolidation of ideological trends and inter-student competition did not develop until the protests of 1972–1973.[66] Until then, students united around the universal issue common to all them: the call for
freedom.

But it is to that process of diffusion of political activist trends that we
now turn. In the early 1970s, the Islamic movement developed a voice
of its own, independent of any preexisting organization and purely as
a force within the student movement. It became dedicated primarily to
ending nearly two decades of leftist dominance and reinserting Islam into
the field of student political activism. Though it is frequently excluded
from the standard history of the Muslim Brotherhood and its presence
within Egyptian society in general and universities in particular, Shabab
al-Islam, the short-lived organization founded by students at Cairo University's College of Engineering, emerged as the first true heir to the Muslim
Brotherhood's student chapters. Its experience during the critical years of
political transition served as an important stepping stone in the resumption of organized Islamic activism in Egypt. The students who founded
and led Shabab al-Islam signified the evolving nature of the Islamic movement, at once demonstrating that the moderate Islamic movement had
evolved beyond the monopoly established by the Muslim Brotherhood,
while also displaying the durability of Banna's mission in a debilitating
political climate.

2

The Youth of Islam

IN THE HISTORY of Islamic activism in the 1970s, the sheer volume of organizations—whether public advocacy groups or secret underground movements, mainstream or militant—has ensured that some actors will inevitably be lost in the chaotic shuffle of history. Such has been the case with Shabab al-Islam, a movement that emerged from the shadow of the unified student movement in the late 1960s to become a key actor in the protests of 1972–1973. Despite its initial success and its enduring status as the first public expression of religious activism in Egypt in the late Nasser era, Shabab al-Islam's term was short-lived, and its legacy often forgotten.

Upon providing the political and social context that gave rise to this group, this chapter traces the history of Shabab al-Islam, detailing its intellectual and organizational roots, along with its experiences confronting internal and external challenges. The successes and failures of the organization are closely examined through the experience of its leaders. Finally, this chapter concludes with a brief analysis that attempts to explain why Shabab al-Islam did not survive its first generation of leaders or develop into a sustainable movement. Though the two groups never encountered one another, Shabab al-Islam's infusion of Islamic politics into Cairo University paved the way for the Muslim Brotherhood to resume its status as the leading Islamic movement organization, built in large part on the success of the student movement. While Shabab al-Islam ultimately proved to be a mere forerunner of the widespread Islamization of Egyptian youth that took hold in the mid-1970s, it was notable for being years ahead of its time, melding Islam and politics at a moment in modern history when the risks were prohibitive for most other groups.

Student Activism: Sustained or Contained?

Along with its rich legacy of political activism, a primary reason that the student movement was the first independent force to resume its place on the national stage was its presence within an existing state institution, but one whose members could not be as tightly controlled. While Gamal Abdel Nasser could easily clamp down on the communists and the Muslim Brotherhood, he could not simply shut down the universities. And while he could placate the endless ranks of bureaucrats and soldiers by controlling their livelihoods, students were less dependent on the state for their survival, and thus had less to lose. Finally, there is something to be said about the idealism, zeal, and vitality that are often associated with youth, and those should not be discounted as factors in mobilizing the student movement after years of its effective dormancy.

In the aftermath of the 1967 defeat, students were at the forefront of the political discussions and debates taking place in Egypt. Many of them explored the spectrum of ideological and intellectual trends available within a closed and controlled political system. Because Nasser had built his regime around an Arab nationalist and radical socialist program, the majority of students had moved toward leftist political ideologies ranging from outright communism (though it was technically banned by the state) to moderate socialism. The state promoted groups that it hoped could channel the activist tendencies of the student movement within acceptable boundaries. The Socialist Youth Organization (SYO) fulfilled this purpose for several years, until it was withdrawn following the events of 1968.

The protests demonstrated that students naturally gravitated toward forces of opposition, rather than the "mindless exhibitionism" of pro-regime groups.[1] The government took a different approach with the Socialist Vanguard (SV), an underground organization meant to take on the appearance of an independent student voice for political activism, though it continued to reflect the will of the regime. The group's leaders recruited many student activists into its ranks and politicized the student unions of several colleges, after years in which the regime had kept politics out of the university. This reflected Nasser's new understanding, in the aftermath of the 1967 defeat, that the politicization of students was inevitable, and as such it was best for the regime to offer a formidable alternative to the independent voices sprouting out of the postwar climate. The Socialist Vanguard, along with the reforms to the Student Union's constitution that included provisions for political action, ensured that the state would preserve at least some degree of control over this process.

An Islamic "Idea" Takes Shape

Along with the leftist forces that dominated campus politics during the late 1960s by virtue of their being the only acceptable outlet, Islam-based activism was posed to make yet another comeback. Much as Nasser tried to erase its presence, the specter of his old foe, the Muslim Brotherhood, continued to maintain a presence in the intellectual life of Egypt. Following the events of 1965 and the subsequent execution of Sayyid Qutb, the organization was once again relegated to Nasser's concentration camps and had no official presence in Egyptian society in the late 1960s. Yet the intellectual tradition that inspired the organization could not be eradicated from the scene. The Muslim Brotherhood "idea" continued to live on, even when it appeared to most observers that the organization would not. This was accomplished in a number of ways.

First, the legacy of Hasan al-Banna was such that even a leader as charismatic and domineering as Nasser could not erase him from the Egyptian collective memory. Though difficult to find in bookshops, his writings continued to be a source of inspiration for many Egyptians who exchanged them quietly. The amount of goodwill generated by the Muslim Brotherhood during its early period was too deeply rooted to do away with, even after the events of 1954 and the group's supposed betrayal of the revolution.[2]

Second, there existed in Egypt a number of prominent individuals—former Muslim Brotherhood officials or at least sympathetic to its mission—who continued to thrive even during the period of repression. At a time when the organization's name could not even be spoken in public, these men ensured that the spirit of its Islamic modernist mission would persist. Individuals such as Salih al-'Ashmawi and Sheikh Muhammad al-Ghazali, both of whom left the Muslim Brotherhood after their disagreements with Hudaybi, were spared Nasser's prisons. While they could not openly propagate for the organization, they kept its tradition alive. Sheikh Yousuf al-Qaradawi, who had since relocated to the Gulf, also ensured that the Islamic trend made popular during the 1930s and 1940s would continue to spread well into the 1960s, and would achieve the status of most prominent Islamic intellectual school in the Arab region. This was a significant departure from the early years of the Muslim Brotherhood, when its ideology and its organization were virtually inseparable. Consequently, a generation emerged that was exposed to the ideas of the Muslim Brotherhood, even if it had never heard the name.

Third, the Qutb experience, along with that of Organization 1965, sent shockwaves throughout Egyptian society, which had not witnessed such ruthlessness by the Nasser regime toward its political opponents in over a decade. Even those who may have strongly opposed Qutb's message were sympathetic to his plight and were horrified at the possibility that someone who was at one time Nasser's personal colleague could be sent to the gallows. Less than a year after Qutb's execution, the *naksa* sent many youth in search of answers, and some of them found solace in his writings, which had presciently condemned the nation to misery and defeat until it turned toward God. The 1967 defeat, which shattered Nasser's image, had the opposite effect on his opponents. Within some circles, Qutb's message seemed more in tune with the experience of the 1960s, and thus superseded the traditional Muslim Brotherhood ideology. Stories of young people huddling together to read handwritten copies of *Milestones* were as widespread as the government's efforts to crack down on them.

Rise of the Religious Youth

This revived interest in religious texts appeared despite the government's success in limiting any institutional avenue for Islam-based activism. At the universities, the only club available for religious expression was al-Gam'iyya al-Diniyya, the Religious Group, whose functions were severely restricted to those of basic rituals such as prayers and fasting. Its members were few in number, and most expressed no interest in engaging in the protests of 1968. Instead, they preferred to engage in religious learning on matters of belief and practice, all of which was free of any political content.[3]

It is thus remarkable that, in a climate so devoid of opportunities for religiously based political expression, a group such as Shabab al-Islam could emerge. The organization, which dated its official launch to the fall of 1972, was the product of several unique circumstances. It was founded in Cairo University's College of Engineering, an institution that featured the best and brightest that Egyptian schools had to offer during a period of increased mechanization and industrialization. Colleges of law, religion, and the humanities had suffered as a result of the push that the Nasser regime had made in the fields of science, medicine, and engineering. In the case of engineering in particular, many of the top students spent their summers in Europe for professional training, and were therefore exposed to a more open environment that allowed them to contemplate and explore issues facing their countrymen at home.

Additionally, the activists of the 1970s increasingly reflected yet another demographic shift within Egyptian society. Whereas historically, educational opportunities were far greater for members of the old elite, the Nasser regime paved the way for the inclusion of the urban poor in greater numbers. However, the late 1960s saw the rise of a new middle class in Egyptian society that had greater resources at its disposal. In the case of Wa'il 'Uthman, one of the founders of Shabab al-Islam, his family had temporarily relocated to Kuwait, where he spent his high school years; as a result, he was influenced by the intellectual currents there, which were more openly Islamic in nature.[4] Perhaps the most important development during this critical period, however, was the transition of power at the highest levels of Egyptian politics, with Sadat's accession to the presidency. Although Islamic activists from this era generally refuted the assertion that Sadat actively aided the rise of Islamic movements, many of them readily acknowledged that his desire for a corrective revolution to combat leftist forces and Nasserist remnants provided them with the space to operate.[5] This was especially true of Shabab al-Islam, the first such expression of popular religious advocacy.

'Uthman, in his memoir recounting his college experience, recalled that the 1968 protests, even as they were led by leftist students, had a profound impact on the students of his generation who would pursue the resumption of Islamic activism.[6] For the few students such as 'Uthman who were not part of the leftist wave, they remained uncomfortable with many of the inconsistencies in the burgeoning student movement. Some student leaders were quietly members of the Socialist Vanguard, even as they purported to reject the state's intrusion into the universities. Still others would later come to the defense of Sha'rawi Gom'a, Nasser's interior minister who directed the crackdown against the protests of 1968, but was later removed from his post and arrested during Sadat's corrective revolution of May 1971.

What made students such as 'Uthman wary of the dominant student leadership was its propensity to change stripes depending on the political winds, while hiding its true nature. They would operate "with two faces:

unabashed communism, as they were not shy to declare their atheism in our personal discussions, and a revolutionary nationalist façade that appealed to the students to join the struggle of world socialism against American imperialism."[7] They moved frequently from one organization to another, taking on such names as Ansar al-Thawra al-Falastiniyya (Supporters of the Palestinian Revolution) and Gama'at Gawwad Hosni (Gawwad Hosni Group). By invoking causes with widespread appeal, these groups succeeded in broadening their base of support, albeit from students who may not have otherwise supported an overtly communist organization.

For students who claimed to see through the veneer of leftist activists (in fact, 'Uthman and others routinely referred to them only as "communists"), the period that followed the 1968 protests was a critical juncture in which each side rallied its troops for the ensuing battle. While the leftist students had the luxury of nearly two decades of dominance, along with some important friends and considerable resources, the Islamist students could not even count on the support of the sole religious organization on campus, and were forced to commence their mission at a severe disadvantage.

At the beginning of the 1968–1969 academic year, 'Uthman appealed to leaders of al-Gam'iyya al-Diniyya to publish a political wall magazine. These bulletins, which covered the walls of the university, were the most unambiguous measure of student activism, which 'Uthman boasted were "the freest press in Egypt."[8] Leftist students had honed their skills by publishing dozens of regular wall magazines around which hundreds of students had crowded every morning and then continued to discuss throughout the day. Independent wall magazines were few in number and ran infrequently. Al-Gam'iyya al-Diniyya declined 'Uthman's offer and continued its habitual reposting of a Qur'anic verse or a Hadith, which attracted few readers.[9] 'Uthman then took it upon himself to found a new bulletin, entitled *Ara' Hurra* (*Free Opinions*), which he proceeded to edit until 1975. Initial articles focused on the general issues of corruption in Egypt and the reaction to the defeat. While most leftist students asserted the need for a renewed alliance with the Eastern Bloc, 'Uthman argued for a "return to God and the rebuilding of the Egyptian citizen on the basis of Islamic values and principles."[10]

The dominant discourse within the university was challenged for the first time in years, and the leftist student groups were alarmed at this sudden arrival of a new opponent. Nonetheless, the subsequent months would witness the rise of a spirited discussion among students that would be unique to Cairo University's College of Engineering. Students debated the merits of the political trends available to them, while the leftists hoped to solidify their place in the leadership of the student movement. The two academic years from late 1969 through the spring of 1971 featured no major outbreaks from the student movement. It was notably quiet for at least two major reasons. For one, there were no significant events or incidents to provoke the students into action.[11] Moreover, these years witnessed the final decline of the Nasser regime, culminating with his death in September 1970. Many students preferred to approach the rise of his successor with cautious observation before determining their next course of action. Not long thereafter, however, this period proved to be, as 'Uthman later recalled, the calm before the storm.

The Diverging Path of Student Protests

The process of lifting Egypt out of the Soviet camp became an early priority for Nasser's successor. Sadat's consolidation of power depended highly on his ability to remove long-standing figures from the so-called centers of power and to cultivate a new ideological program that centered on his own claims to power. It was thus no surprise that leftist student activists felt threatened after the events of May 1971, while students such as 'Uthman and his colleagues discerned a real sea change that would pave the way for the resumption of Islamic activism for the first time in a generation. These young men believed the first step in that direction was to exploit the developing rift between Sadat and the Soviet Union, revealing that it was not in Egypt's interest to forge ahead with that relationship, and thereby discrediting the leftists who had staked their reputations on the ascendency of the communist East in the face of the imperialist West.

'Uthman spent the summer of 1972 working in an engineering training program in Holland, an opportunity provided to a select number of Egyptian students each year. While there, he came upon an article in *Newsweek* that detailed Sadat's growing differences with the Soviets, especially on the issue of whether Egypt could go to war to reclaim the territories occupied by Israel in 1967. Such a topic was considered a taboo subject for discussion in Egypt, and as such, no one had reported on these developments. Few Egyptians were aware of the seriousness of the differences in the Egyptian-Soviet relationship, especially the fact that Moscow was obstructing Egyptian preparations for war. When the academic year began that fall, the newest issue of *Free Opinions* carried a full translation of the *Newsweek* piece, along with a commentary by 'Uthman. The article was so explosive that angry leftist students and security agents repeatedly tore down the bulletin, only for more copies to pop up on walls around the university grounds. The article was the first in a series of events that was to dent the credibility of the leftist student leadership, which had reached its zenith earlier in the year.

In January, the first phase of protests threatened to undo Sadat's gradual consolidation of power. Although 1971 was to be "the year of decision" vis-à-vis Israel's continued occupation of Egypt, months passed without any resolution to the untenable situation of "no war, no peace." Students began to pressure the government into action by publicizing the issue of Israel's military presence and highlighting the plight of Palestinians during a "Palestine Week" held in December at the College of Engineering.[12] Sadat responded with a speech on January 13, 1972, in which he cited the instability caused by the war fought between India and Pakistan, along with an analogy of "the fog" in previous attempts to take on Israel, as the reasons for the lack of action. The infamous "fog speech," which was intended to justify the regime's inaction and allay growing restiveness, had the opposite effect of riling the anger of many Egyptians, especially among the student population. Under the banner of the Supporters of the Palestinian Revolution, leftist university students led a series of protests and sit-ins in mid-January.

In order to bypass the weak and ineffective Student Union, student leaders combined the movements across multiple colleges to establish the Higher National Committee of Cairo University Students (HNCCUS). After a heated assembly dominated by leftist students, the committee issued a list of demands for the government and staged a sit-in to demonstrate their commitment to the issues. Although the Islamist students joined in the effort, 'Uthman noted that he became critical of the leadership when they continued their protest even after most of their demands had been met.[13]

In fact, 'Uthman was selected as part of a student delegation that met with Arab Socialist Union (ASU) officials, including Sayyid Mar'i, the minister of agriculture and a regime insider. The following day, the national press announced the government's plans to take serious steps to prepare for the war, including suspending classes to allow students to commence military training. Rather than end the protests, however, the Supporters of the Palestinian Revolution staged a new round of sit-ins and agitated a large number of students to resume their anti-government positions. 'Uthman recalled:

> I asked myself, what do they want? What is the point of another protest? ... I replayed the events of the previous three days in my mind and concluded that the matter was a communist attempt to sow chaos and seize control of the student community. Their reneging on the training agreement confirmed it.[14]

As the sit-ins spread beyond Cairo University's campus to other parts of the city, the regime took more decisive action against the students and their supporters. Following a series of police raids on January 24–25, the protests were broken up and hundreds of people were arrested. The government also withdrew its support for the statement in which it had pledged to include the students in war preparations.[15] Though it had failed to achieve its primary objectives, the January 1972 protest allowed the student movement to consolidate its power under a mostly leftist leadership and saw the convergence of a burgeoning anti-communist bloc and the decline of the Student Union, which became one of the weakest official student organizations in Egyptian history. The long-term effects would also be felt by the regime, as "this was the first occasion on which President Sadat had had to face street riots, and it set a precedent which he never forgave or forgot."[16]

It is in this context that the student movement entered the fall 1972 semester, full of hope, energy, and dynamism. Though the momentum was clearly in favor of the leftist students, who had helped establish the Higher Committee only to take full control of it, 'Uthman and his colleagues believed the supremacy of the leftist movement was ripe for confrontation. Both sides acknowledged that the weeks that followed featured fierce attacks against the views of the other, both in print, as 'Uthman had done with his wall magazine's opening issue of the term, and in person, as supporters of both camps exchanged strong words and, on occasion, blows over their political ideology of choice.[17]

For its part, the regime attempted to use this situation to its advantage. On the one hand, the fact that neither side supported the government was of concern to Sadat, who considered the wall magazines and their highly critical viewpoints "obscene" expressions on the part of the students.[18] Both the leftists and the Islamists opposed the delays in the war of liberation and pushed an agenda of expanded freedoms and the restoration of democracy in Egypt. On the other hand, Sadat stood to benefit from the exploitation of the fundamental differences between the emerging factions. He took specific measures that created the political space to allow for the resumption of Islamic activism. Among these was the appointment of Ahmed Kamal Abul Magd as general secretary of the ASU Youth Organization in August 1971. Abul Magd was a prominent attorney with close ties to the Muslim Brotherhood, though he himself was not a member. As Beattie noted, "His directorship augured well for some degree of Islamization of that organization's curriculum and activities. This heightened the likelihood of Egyptian youth receiving a new type of political socialization—one with a much heavier religious coloration."[19] During the student protests nearly six months later, it was Abul Magd on whom the regime relied to quell the protesters, sending him to Cairo University's auditorium to hear their concerns and provide reassurances, only for him to be taunted and ridiculed by the students.[20] When Sadat met with students only days before Abul Magd's appointment, he "told them that the state would no longer interfere in student activities."[21] However, these signals were precisely the impetus needed to encourage the rise of new groups within the student movement.

The New Face of Islamic Activism

On November 16, 1972, 'Uthman and several of his friends in the College of Engineering, including 'Esam al-Ghazali, an older student who had become well-known for his political poetry, and 'Adli Mustafa, a popular student who had served as vice president of the Student Union and captain of the national volleyball team, came together at the college's auditorium to announce the establishment of Gama'at Shabab al-Islam (the Society of the Youth of Islam). They were joined by Sheikh Muhammad al-Ghazali, the prominent scholar and thinker. As 'Uthman reminisced, the event was a smashing success. "In the history of student meetings held at the college, never was the auditorium so full. My eyes welled with tears as I witnessed the widespread popular affirmation of our Islamic movement."[22] That evening, the British Broadcasting Corporation (BBC) radio news service reported on the event, announcing it as a takeover of Cairo University's Engineering College by the Muslim Brotherhood, although the organization had not been mentioned at all during the event.[23] Perhaps this was a sign of the magnitude of the establishment of Shabab al-Islam, as it was difficult to envision an active Islamic movement organization in Egypt that was not affiliated with the Muslim Brotherhood.

In the weeks leading up to the announcement, several developments paved the way for the establishment of the first political Islamic organization in nearly two decades. Mustafa, who had spent his summer working in Germany, returned to Egypt with the determination to launch a student group with an Islamic orientation to face off against an increasingly polarizing leftist movement. 'Esam al-Ghazali had been at the university for many years and was on the verge of graduating, but believed in the importance of this project and became a figure around whom many students rallied. Known for his incisive poetry, Ghazali was viewed by many of his peers as the visionary behind the movement and the heart and soul of Shabab al-Islam. Together, Mustafa, Ghazali, and another student, 'Abd al-Hamid Bahgat, traveled to the three-day conference of Cairo University's Student Union that was held in Mansoura beginning on October 9, 1972. The delegation proposed the formation of a new group, and despite fierce opposition from leftist student leaders, the Student Union's Committee on Religion and Society decreed the establishment of Shabab al-Islam at the different faculties within Cairo University, with a mission "to create an Islamic environment at the university and to inform students of Islamic principles."[24]

Shabab al-Islam's account of this meeting, reported by 'Uthman and confirmed by Mustafa and Ghazali, differs from the Student Union's official conference report, which makes no mention of the organization's establishment. 'Uthman maintained that this report was later amended to remove any mention of Shabab al-Islam, a likely explanation considering that the organization could not have been announced and functioned as openly as it did without some degree of official sanction. According to the group's recollection, Shabab al-Islam was a designated organization within the Student Union, but was to operate with its own independent budget. Its president was to have a seat on the council of the Student Union, while the group itself could select a faculty advisor and maintain its own membership list. The Cairo University Student Union officially established Shabab al-Islam at the Engineering College on October 21. In early November, the organization held a closed camp to determine its internal structure. Mustafa was elected president. Additionally, five committees were created: (1) Thought and Callers; (2) Publication and Outreach; (3) Communication; (4) Preparation; and (5) Follow-up. Finally, a larger coordination committee combined the heads of the five committees

with the group's president, faculty advisor, and the college dean to determine the organization's agenda.[25]

Almost immediately, the group began to hold events, inviting guest
speakers, hosting student-led political discussions, and posting articles in
'Uthman's wall magazine. It also used a series of press releases to set the
stage for Shabab al-Islam's arrival on the scene of student activism. One
of the first statements called attention to the threat of external forces to
Egypt's Islamic identity. While the obvious fear was the military danger
brought about by Israel's occupation, a far greater danger lay in the ideological campaign waged to discredit Islam and replace it with foreign systems of social organization. Once the threat was sufficiently described,
Shabab al-Islam issued its call to action:

> Patience has run out, for there is no path but that of serious, hard
> work. We need to be sprung out of this false world that has brought
> us nothing but backwardness and defeat. We need to spring forth
> this faith through honor and victory, to use its glimmering light to
> launch us toward redemption. Our brothers, this is the path of re-
> demption. Get out of the path of the weak slaves to the path of God,
> the almighty and powerful.[26]

The group's leaders identified weakness, fear, and disunity as the major
obstacles to its success and called on students to face these three dangers
head-on through embracing their faith.[27] However, another impediment
to the young organization's progress came in the form of state efforts to
undermine its success. Shabab al-Islam's first brush with authorities occurred on November 14, when ASU officials sabotaged a scheduled lecture by al-Bahi al-Khouli, a well-known Islamic thinker. According to
Ghazali, security agents visited Khouli at 3 AM the previous night and told
him that they feared retaliation by leftist students at the event. Concern
over Khouli's personal safety was a pretext, Shabab al-Islam would contend, since the method and manner in which the message was delivered
was meant to intimidate the guest speaker, as well as to send a message to
the new organization that it would not survive for long without the active
support of the regime. At the scheduled event, Ghazali revealed the entire
incident to the audience and vowed that Shabab al-Islam would not be
deterred from its mission.

Two days later, its official launch event was held to great fanfare. Six
hundred people joined Shabab al-Islam that night alone, with hundreds

more joining in the days that followed. Its membership numbers swelled to become far and away the largest student organization. Students from other faculties came to sign up for membership, as did young professionals and workers from outside the university. 'Uthman recalls that it made his group "resemble a political party at a time when such a venture was unheard of."[28]

Organizational Challenges

The group's activities continued with great success in the weeks that followed, but a set of new challenges was not far behind, whether from the government or fellow students. Shortly after the initial announcement, Shabab al-Islam's leadership was contacted by Muhammad 'Uthman Isma'il, an ASU official and future governor of Assiut who had joined Sadat's inner circle and was intent on restraining leftist elements. At a meeting in his office, Isma'il offered Mustafa and 'Uthman the regime's full support for their activities. He hoped to expand the organization's efforts within the university and pledged a sum of 10,000 Egyptian pounds (a hefty amount in that period) to that end. He promised the two students freedom to hold an annual summer camp for activists from all Egyptian universities: in effect, the regime was determined to orchestrate Shabab al-Islam's control over the entire student movement. 'Uthman recalled that they were not being asked to spy on other students or take orders from any higher power, but simply "to continue doing what we were doing."[29]

Tempting though the offer was, both Mustafa and 'Uthman politely declined and promptly returned to their normal course of action, trying to reach out to the student body.[30] On December 21, Shabab al-Islam hosted a meeting of student leaders from other faculties at the student cafeteria in the College of Engineering. What brought all the groups together was their common interest in combating the leftist forces dominating student activism. With the regime now supporting the repression of communists, Marxists, and Nasserists within the student movement, the Student Unions were tasked with carrying out this mission, but had little credibility or legitimate following within the student population. Thus, they hoped to ride the coattails of the newly established Islamic organization and sought to utilize its growth to the regime's advantage.

'Uthman later wrote that the discussion reflected a fundamental misunderstanding among the students. Shabab al-Islam members had to continuously repel suggestions of violent confrontation with the leftist students, for which the Student Union leaders were agitating. They insisted that violence was not to be used, even in the face of violence on the part of the leftists and regardless of how abhorrent they found their views.[31] Mustafa also consistently had to push back suggestions to form an anti-leftist student militia, and was ready to call off the summit when Ghazali intervened. He thought the groups could still find some common ground and suggested that they release a joint statement announcing their platform. It began by requesting the Egyptian president to fulfill his motto of "science and faith" by allowing Islamic thought to flourish alongside capitalist and socialist ideologies.

Shabab al-Islam's leaders were stunned when one student stepped forward, offering to print ten thousand copies of the release, not an easy sum of paper to come by for most student groups, suggesting that he enjoyed the support of far more powerful forces. The following day, the release was issued in the name of the various student groups, but with a number of notable omissions, such as the call for the republication of works by Hasan al-Banna and Sayyid Qutb. According to 'Uthman, "the overall statement was nothing more than an attack on communism phrased in Islamic terms."[32] Shabab al-Islam immediately issued a statement denouncing the press release and producing the unedited version.

This was not the first incident in which the organization was mischaracterized by outside forces affiliated with the regime, who wished to exploit its credibility with the student body. Shortly after the November announcement, a group within the College of Law calling itself Shabab al-Islam disrupted a meeting of leftist students, using knives to attack the other students.[33] As 'Uthman wrote, "we immediately disavowed and exposed them . . . and later discovered that the orders to this group came from the office of the Arab Socialist Union's general secretary."[34]

Indeed, by early 1973, and especially under the cover of the new round of student protests, Shabab al-Islam's leaders struggled to control the name of their organization. It was consistently cited in violent confrontations between leftist students and security forces. Mustafa repeatedly heard of new chapters of the group sprouting up in various colleges, without the approval, or even knowledge, of Shabab al-Islam's founders at the College of Engineering. The leaders took measures to limit the damage that foreign elements could inflict on the organization. Mustafa issued a statement announcing that the only official chapter of Shabab al-Islam was the one at Cairo University's College of Engineering and even announced a list of just five students who were authorized to speak on behalf of the organization. As Ghazali had already graduated, the list included Mustafa, 'Uthman, Bahgat, Sayyid 'Azzazi, and Mustafa al-Simari.[35]

Additionally, Mustafa proceeded to expunge the membership list of students who previously had acted as provocateurs or who were known to have ties with leftist groups or the regime. "All were still welcome to attend our events," he said, "but only we could speak on behalf of the organization."[36] These efforts did not stop others from attempting to represent or associate themselves with Shabab al-Islam. 'Uthman reported that, "[s]tate security tried to spread the rumor that we were their creation. Known informants would try and defend us publicly knowing it would ruin our reputation."[37] So severe was the problem that the sides occasionally came to blows over the attempts by some to usurp the voice of Shabab al-Islam. Mustafa acted as the enforcer in these instances, at one point beating a student who continued to claim to speak for the organization, and in another instance, even calling on the assistance of his volleyball teammates in a showdown with other students.[38]

Direct efforts by the government to co-opt Shabab al-Islam continued through a variety of tactics that included inducements as well as threats. Following the rejection of Isma'il's offer and then the renunciation of the united student press release (which ostensibly had the backing of the regime), state security agents conducted overnight raids of the student movement on December 30, 1972. Approximately seventy students were arrested; the overwhelming majority of them were leaders of the various leftist groups. One of those arrested, however, was 'Esam al-Ghazali, the unifying force within Shabab al-Islam. The arrest delivered a devastating blow to Shabab al-Islam. Without its charismatic elder, internal divisions became more acute. The group's leaders were divided as to whether or not to combine their efforts with those of the leftist students to free their abducted comrades.

The government raids were conducted in the shadow of renewed efforts by the student movement to lobby for more freedoms and political space. Only days earlier, a summit by a student organization called the National Democratic Group issued demands for new Student Union elections, or in the event that they did not take place, the establishment of an independent union that genuinely represented student interests. While some students saw this move as the legitimate expression of student aspirations for freedom and democracy, Shabab al-Islam was highly critical of the proposal, believing it to be a new tactic to legitimize leftist leadership of the student movement.[39] Mere hours before the mass arrests, Sadat gave an angry speech calling for "'the practice of democracy without fear' and stated that 'as of this night' he would not allow the country's youth to be misled by 'the fanatical right or the adventurist left.'"[40] These events were the spark that officially brought about the student protests of 1973. As 'Abdalla described it:

> A wave of protest broke out in five Egyptian universities and in a number of higher institutes. This took the form of mass meetings, sit-ins in various faculties, leaflets and wall-magazines and confrontations with security forces around the university campuses, which resulted in serious disruption of studies.[41]

Efforts by Shabab al-Islam to unite with other groups were often ineffective and disjointed. Mustafa and 'Uthman refused to adopt a broad platform of political demands because of the major differences they had with the leftists, agreeing only to call for the release of the arrested students. On issues of tactics, the groups also voiced major disagreements. Leftist students proposed to lead a march outside the university walls, in which Shabab al-Islam's leaders refused to participate, because they believed it would serve as a pretext for the government to shut down the university and lock its gates, as they had done a year earlier, forcing the students to disperse and effectively ending the protests. 'Uthman worried that, as a new group, the university's closure would be the worst possible outcome for Shabab al-Islam because it would slow the movement's momentum and possibly destroy the organization.

Instead, his colleagues determined to take a different course of action: on January 2, 1973, they staged a sit-in at the office of Dr. Fu'ad 'Asal, the dean of the College of Engineering. With only a handful of students joining Shabab al-Islam's chosen method of protest, the sit-in quickly turned into a hunger strike, the first of its kind in several decades. Although the hunger strike made waves within the university, prompting professors and administrators to plead with students to end their demonstration, the move failed to gain traction with the public at large, and went unnoticed by the media. It ended a day later, as 'Asal successfully convinced the students to leave his office, and they eventually dropped their protest altogether. 'Uthman later expressed his regret that Shabab al-Islam had not taken a stronger stand from the outset and had not capitalized on the large number of students willing to participate in a protest within the university walls rather than joining the leftists in their march through the streets of Cairo.[42]

Not wanting to take any more chances, the government shut down the university. Protests continued for weeks across the country, with Assiut University students engaging in historic marches never before seen in upper Egypt. On occasion, Shabab al-Islam came together with the leftist groups to issue joint statements demanding the release of the detained students, the withdrawal of university police, and the lifting of restrictions on student activism. In several speeches, Sadat responded with a hard-line position that was highly critical of the student movement and implied that a larger conspiracy was at work. A parliamentary investigation concluded that outside forces—from the Left and the Right—were responsible for corrupting the students and using them in their bid to destabilize the government. Despite accusations that the student movement stood against democracy, it was actually the regime that continued to restrict the activities of Egyptian students, banning wall magazines and placing universities under the control of security agents, in addition to expelling hundreds of ASU members, as Muhammad 'Uthman Isma'il had done.

While participating in the protests, Shabab al-Islam also began to engage members of the regime to pursue the release of their arrested leader. An attempt to visit Ghazali in prison failed after a verbal altercation with a prison guard who insulted the female president of the Student Union. Subsequently, however, 'Uthman recalled that in meetings with ASU officials, some of them at the senior levels of leadership, he and Mustafa were consistently surprised at how friendly and gracious the officials were, with many of them hoping to impress their Islamic credentials upon their young visitors, visibly praying as they came in to the office, or placing Qur'ans prominently on their desks. Most of them stressed how supportive they were of Shabab al-Islam's mission, and some even offered to lend their support, including Isma'il, who continuously offered financial incentives and the full backing of the ASU. 'Uthman noted the irony in that, while regime figures constantly lavished his organization with praise, one of its leaders continued to languish in prison without any officials working toward his release.[43]

In fact, it was only after Shabab al-Islam retained the pro bono services of a prominent attorney, Muhammad Shawkat al-Tuni, that Ghazali was eventually released from prison without charges, on March 24, nearly three months after his arrest. The 1973 protests ended with the release

of most students, though some still had to face trials on charges related
to their political activities. On the eve of the October War, however, the
regime dropped the charges and ended the trials in an effort to galvanize
the nation in support of the war effort.

Multidimensional Activism

Shabab al-Islam resumed its activities that fall, taking on a number of
important issues, not the least of which was the impending war to reclaim
the occupied territories. Sadat successfully galvanized the nation in support of the war effort, including the leaders of the student movement, who
established defense committees in the various universities across Egypt.
In its activities, Shabab al-Islam also led the way in educating students
about the plight of Muslims in other parts of the world. Speakers, from
Eritrea to the Philippines, were invited to give presentations on the oppressive conditions facing Muslims in these countries. As Mustafa later
recalled, for most Egyptians, it was the first time they were even made
aware that these places were home to Muslims.[44] An occasional lecture
on the situation of Muslim communities in the various Soviet republics
was sure to raise the ire of leftist students, already under attack for their
support of the Soviet Union at a time when the political winds in Egypt
were steadily shifting from East to West.

In regular study circles, Shabab al-Islam members read and discussed
works by many of the most influential modern Islamic thinkers, from
Banna to Qutb, and Mawdudi to ʿAli ʿAbd al-ʿAzim. The students were also
frequently joined by prominent figures such as Muhammad al-Ghazali,
ʿIsa ʿAbduh, and Sayyid Sabiq.

Although dominated entirely by male students, Shabab al-Islam also
sponsored occasional activities for female students. Segregated meetings
and conferences were organized and led by women, focusing on many
of the same issues as the events organized by their male counterparts.
These events also tackled the larger political questions facing the country, as well as matters of ritual and practice, some of which were tailored
specifically to their female audience. In contrast to the year he began
university, when virtually no women wore the headscarf, Mustafa observed that the practice had spread considerably by the time he graduated in 1975. Indeed, though Islamic student activism was largely a male
domain, its success was partially measured by the visibility of female religious observance.

In addition to the wall magazines, by 1974, Shabab al-Islam had also launched an official publication, *Wa Islamah*. The sixty-page magazine produced six issues over the course of a year and covered topics ranging from religious instruction and student mobilization to national politics and international causes. In a typical issue, for example, Mustafa's opening editorial lamented the aggressive posturing on the part of some students as they attempted to coerce their colleagues into joining the Islamic movement. This was followed with a critical book review by 'Uthman of a recent work on *da'wa* by a popular Islamic writer. Another article made an impassioned plea to unify the Islamic movement in the university, asking the rhetorical question, "If we as students cannot realistically impact the state of despair and disunity afflicting Muslims throughout the world, then can we not at least change our own state of affairs?"[45] The remaining pieces included an article challenging the minister of information over censorship policies, reports about the plight of Muslims in Eritrea and Somalia, and a political poem entitled, "A Window onto Hell." The magazine demonstrated the evolution of Shabab al-Islam, as it was a more sophisticated vehicle for transmitting its message and providing more depth to the issues it advocated. But it was to be short-lived, as the organization itself was nearing its end.

An End and a Beginning

In spite of its successful infusion of an Islamic component to the student movement, Shabab al-Islam ultimately succumbed to both external as well as internal pressures and ceased to function after 1975. Efforts to co-opt the organization for the regime's purposes continued to take their toll on student leaders. 'Uthman and Mustafa had yet another meeting with a top government official in 1973. This time it was Ahmed Kamal Abul Magd who offered the young men incentives to coordinate their group with the regime. Additionally, Abul Magd hoped to instill some degree of fear into the student leaders should they proceed independently. He told them that they had earned Sadat's anger and that it was only through his own intervention that they were spared a fate worse than 'Esam al-Ghazali's brief imprisonment. Mustafa became angered at the suggestion that Abul Magd had saved Shabab al-Islam from the wrath of Sadat, and abruptly left the meeting. He later recalled that he "could not sit down with someone who did not treat us as equals, someone who believed they had us by the neck and held something over us."[46]

Shabab al-Islam's relationship with al-Gam'iyya al-Diniyya also played an important part in the decline of the former, as the latter reached its ascendancy in the mid-1970s. As early as November 1972, Shabab al-Islam hoped to include the religiously observant contingent of students at Cairo University in charting out its organization. While links were forged between the leaderships of both groups, al-Gam'iyya al-Diniyya repeatedly withdrew its support for the overtly political activist organization. On the eve of Shabab al-Islam's announcement, a meeting between the core members of both groups at al-Gam'iyya al-Diniyya's modest prayer hall, led by Mustafa of Shabab al-Islam and 'Esam al-Sheikh of al-Gam'iyya al-Diniyya, ended in agreement to jointly announce the launch of the new group, only for Sheikh to withdraw his organization's support at the eleventh hour. Another attempt to unify the groups a month later ended in failure when, according to Mustafa, al-Gam'iyya al-Diniyya insisted that 'Uthman and al-Ghazali be removed from Shabab al-Islam as a condition for its members joining. Elections scheduled for that day were hampered by al-Gam'iyya al-Diniyya's change of heart, as it moved its meeting to a different location from the agreed-upon site of the elections.[47]

The disagreements between the two groups stemmed from their different visions of Islamic activism. Shabab al-Islam's model grew out of the student movement of the 1960s. Though it staunchly disagreed with its leftist counterpart, in many ways it captured the essence of its activist trend. As is detailed in Chapter 4, al-Gam'iyya al-Diniyya (subsequently, al-Gama'a al-Islamiyya) relied on a different model, one that emphasized strong hierarchical leadership and an Islamic basis for the organizational structure, complete with a position of "amir." Their camps and activities also maintained a far more rigid religious tone, one that was influenced by the steady infusion of Salafi thought—a mark of the 1970s shift in Egyptian religious culture. One of Shabab al-Islam's main critiques of al-Gam'iyya al-Diniyya was its unwillingness to allow its rank-and-file members the freedom to think and decide for themselves. Without Sheikh's approval, no member of al-Gam'iyya al-Diniyya was allowed to join Shabab al-Islam, forcing Mustafa to rely on the general student population, whose religious credentials were less assured, to make up the bulk of Shabab al-Islam's base.[48]

Indeed, the tension between the two groups was palpable, as one organization's downfall meant the ascendancy of the other. Opinions varied within Shabab al-Islam as to whether al-Gam'iyya al-Diniyya actively aided the government's tactics against it, or if it simply offered an alternative for the regime to co-opt once Shabab al-Islam refused overtures by state officials. Mustafa believed that not only did its leaders help to propagate rumors that Shabab al-Islam was secretly an organ of the state, but that it was in fact al-Gam'iyya al-Diniyya that actually accepted the government's offer of support for its activities, evidenced by the lavish camps organized in the years following Shabab al-Islam's departure.[49] While 'Uthman did not go so far as to suggest collusion on the part of Sheikh, he believed that al-Gam'iyya al-Diniyya stood to gain the most from the organizational failure of Shabab al-Islam; its overly cautious political strategy allowed it to survive efforts to subdue the most vocal wing of the student movement, while Shabab al-Islam was on the front lines of that struggle.

On the other side, depictions of Shabab al-Islam by members of al-Gam'iyya al-Diniyya (and later, the Muslim Brotherhood) were often quite derogatory. It was frequently portrayed as a creation of the state, not only to combat the leftist student movement, but also to undermine the legitimate Islamic movement as led by al-Gam'iyya al-Diniyya. Its failure in that effort, according to some accounts, was because the students of Shabab al-Islam failed to embody Islamic ideals in their daily lives, by openly smoking and engaging female students. They also could not build their credibility because at the events they held, their guest speakers were regime officials.[50] According to this narrative, Shabab al-Islam was a government tool that failed in its mission to bring all Islamic activism under its control. A more recent academic study on the Islamic movement during this period relates the same picture: that Shabab al-Islam was the brainchild of Muhammad 'Uthman Isma'il, which failed to attract "genuinely Islamic" activist students to it.[51]

In any case, 1974 was the pivotal year during which Shabab al-Islam was succeeded by al-Gama'a al-Islamiyya, whose leaders held their first major camp that summer. The principal figures of Shabab al-Islam had either already graduated, or were on the verge of completing their studies. When its founder graduated a year later, he told the remaining members to join al-Gama'a al-Islamiyya to avoid any divisions in the Islamic movement. According to Mustafa, most did not mind, as the younger members had only recently joined Shabab al-Islam and were not party to the divisions that defined the 1972–1973 period. Those who did not join generally quit activism altogether, but no one tried to form a competing group out of the ashes of Shabab al-Islam.[52]

Islamic Activism for a New Age: The Legacy
of Shabab al-Islam

In the broad narrative of Islamic activism since the late 1960s, Shabab al-Islam is almost universally excluded from the standard timeline. Whatever brief mention it receives is usually dismissive and accusatory in tone. This is partly a product of the reality that contemporary Islamic activism in Egypt is dominated by the Muslim Brotherhood, to which Shabab al-Islam had no direct connection. In contrast, al-Gam'iyya al-Diniyya is frequently portrayed as the predecessor to the resumption of Islamic activism on a large scale, due primarily to the fact that most of its members eventually joined the Muslim Brotherhood. It is therefore instructive to reflect on the legacy of Shabab al-Islam and its contribution to Egyptian society. In a critical period of transition, Shabab al-Islam acted as the bridge between the radical politics that defined the student movement of the late 1960s and the emergence of a rejuvenated Islamic movement in the mid-1970s.

The founders of Shabab al-Islam, young men like 'Adli Mustafa, Wa'il 'Uthman, and 'Esam al-Ghazali, traced their intellectual upbringing to the Islamic trends that dominated that era: the ritualism of Ansar al-Sunna, the legalism of al-Gam'iyya al-Shar'iyya, and the social consciousness of al-Ikhwan al-Muslimun. Despite these influences, this generation of youth did not join any of these groups and lacked the organizational structure to guide its activities. 'Uthman recalled that they "did not have elders to look up to, there was no generation of mentors in our group. We were on our own."[53] The message that was distilled from the many intellectual currents was a simplified version of Islamically conscious politics, as Mustafa summed up in his statement, "We are an organization to announce the word of God. We believe that no one should determine the fate of Muslims but Muslims, and that the student leadership should be Islamic, not communist, socialist, Nasserist, Western, or secularist."[54] Following years of frustration due to individual efforts, the Islamically conscious students came together to form an organization that united their beliefs and their mission under one banner.

Although it was religious in character and, as its leaders maintained, the first political Islamic organization of that period, Shabab al-Islam did not hark back to a bygone era of Islamic politics or adopt the model established by organizations such as the Muslim Brotherhood in the 1940s. Rather, it operated within the same vein as its ideological foes and appropriated their system of organization. Thus, while it blanketed its message in an Islamic hue, Shabab al-Islam relied on much the same modes of pursuing its mission as its leftist adversaries. For one, Shabab al-Islam adopted the vanguardist model that saw the newly urbanized and privileged middle class youth as part of a unique generation destined to become the future leaders of society. 'Uthman stated that much of Shabab al-Islam's activities were only possible because of the commitment of its leaders, who spent their own allowances to fund them.[55] These students also believed it was their role to lead the laborers and bureaucrats who were energized by the group's mission but were too afraid to become involved in its daily activities.

In the course of its activism, Shabab al-Islam's repertoire consisted of many of the same traits that defined the broader student movement: wall magazines, banners and slogans, sit-ins and marches, heated wars of words and the occasional violent brawl. It also released formal statements, ratified resolutions, and joined in larger institutional efforts, whether by endorsing ad hoc unity organizations or imploring the Student Union to take official action. In short, the students of this period were the children of the revolution and embodied its spirit in their actions, even when the focus of their advocacy was contrary to the prevailing political ideology of the time. Their model was the protest movement of 1968, not only in Egypt's universities, but also in the educational halls of France, where student fervor was at its height and the collective action of the youth reverberated among Egyptian students, some of whom were directly exposed to European political culture during their summers abroad.

In addition to its own methods and motivations, Shabab al-Islam succeeded in galvanizing support for religious activism in part due to the timing of its emergence and the external factors that paved the way for its arrival.[56] By all accounts, the period that witnessed the decline of the Nasser regime and Sadat's consolidation of power was strategically significant, if not imperative, for the rise of new opposition movements in Egypt. Nasser's decade and a half of repression successfully excluded opposing political forces and silenced all dissent, but the shock of the 1967 defeat provided just the opportunity for the opposition to coalesce. As Nasser attempted to correct the course of his regime, de Tocqueville's words from two centuries earlier rang true: "the most perilous moment for a bad government is when it seeks to mend its ways."[57]

Egyptians, led by the students, guessed correctly that the regime was in no position to repress the new opposition with the same ferocity that it had previously enforced internal security measures. Consequently, the slightly opened political space provided just the opportunity for students to express their frustrations. In the university environment, this manifested in the relaxation of censorship laws, resulting in the highly politicized wall magazines and the gradual withdrawal of the university guard, creating the space for mass demonstrations and marches. Moreover, students found a moderate degree of success when their pleas to the state were heard at the highest levels. The dramatic scenes of student delegations confronting the prime minister in a public forum established a new precedent for social movement interactions with the state, one that was to be repeated throughout the 1970s. Students were given more room to operate because their protests were not viewed as a threat in the same light as movements with fuller political objectives, such as the Muslim Brotherhood. As the frustrations of Sadat, Isma'il, and Abul Magd demonstrate, at its worst, the student movement was still only perceived as the product of youthful indiscretions or the plotting of some foreign political forces. As Mustafa recalled, the burning question that he and his colleagues faced constantly during interrogations was "Who is behind you?"[58]

While Shabab al-Islam generally experienced the same opening as the broader student movement, its position as an Islamic movement gave it an occasional slight edge over its leftist counterparts. During his consolidation of power, Sadat repeatedly threatened political agitators from "the fanatical Right" to "the adventurist Left" and even made good on those threats with the 1972 wave of arrests that afflicted students from both camps. However, in its recalibration of the country's political identity, the regime also specifically reached out to leaders of the Islamic movement, thus providing Shabab al-Islam with opportunities to pursue its agenda in a variety of other ways. The multiple meetings between regime officials and leaders of Shabab al-Islam added another dimension to the group's activities and granted the students a greater understanding of the inner workings of the political machine. However, this too came with a cost. Whatever Shabab al-Islam gained from its ability to hold direct talks with the state, it lost in credibility with the student population, at times giving the appearance that the organization was yet another government arm. In fact, the organization suffered a double blow, as its dealings with the state often served only to prove the organization's limitations. Shabab al-Islam's members continued to suffer intimidation, repression, and arrests, and ultimately found it impossible to free their imprisoned comrade through these back channels. Mustafa later conceded that "[w]hen they arrested 'Esam, they almost killed the movement because he was our elder. . . . We looked up to him and rallied around him."[59] Thus, while Shabab al-Islam enjoyed a wider array of political opportunities than its adversaries, it also experienced firsthand the constraints imposed by a closed system.

As a smaller movement that did not have the benefit of years of wide-spread political indoctrination, the burgeoning Islamic movement was frequently working against the odds established by Nasser's ideological project and promoted by leftist students. Shabab al-Islam had the benefit of the rich legacy of Islamic activism, symbolized in the Muslim Broth-erhood, but the organization could not rely solely on past successes. It needed to present a vision of Islam in sync with contemporary times and in the language of its generation. The framing processes of Shabab al-Islam signaled the first active construction of an Islamic paradigm in the post-1967 era. Just as Qutb's *Milestones* epitomized the state of Islam during the darkest years of the Nasser period, Shabab al-Islam attempted to find a glimmer of hope in the receding of Nasser's regime. The concept of the Islamic system was developed and articulated in direct opposition to the prevailing ideological trends of the time: communism and capitalism.

From 'Uthman's first wall magazine and Shabab al-Islam's earliest press releases to its later publications, a concerted effort was undertaken to establish the threat of external political ideologies and to position Islam as the natural alternative to these foreign systems by contrasting their failures with Islam's rich legacy of success. In the face of immense chal-lenges ranging from Israeli occupation to economic stagnation and un-derdevelopment, Islamic concepts were utilized to provide a solution, a source of empowerment, and a means to achieve what had eluded the nation for far too long. Additionally, Shabab al-Islam engaged in a process of internationalization of the Islamic movement, aiming to impress upon Egyptian youth that their struggle was a universal one, part of a broader movement to overcome adversity throughout the Islamic world. It used its platform to raise awareness of the plight of Muslims the world over, with the hopes that deeper bonds of religious solidarity would overcome the nationalist sentiments on which Nasser had built his entire enterprise.

Along the timeline of Islamic activism in Egypt, Shabab al-Islam stands alone as the unique expression of a generation that came of age during a critical period of transition in Egypt's modern political history. It marked the return of the Islamic movement and paved the way for the re-emergence of some of its most significant actors, such as the Muslim Brotherhood. Through its interactions with the state, Shabab al-Islam also revealed the intentions of the nascent Sadat regime to cultivate its religious credentials, possibly sooner than it otherwise would have done. On the popular level, it contributed to the reassertion of Islamic identity within Egyptian society, demonstrated by the massive reception to its programs and activities. This process gathered more steam and continued long after Shabab al-Islam had left the scene. It also helped to usher in a new era of a globalized Islamic consciousness that would come to epitomize the Islamic movement during the latter decades of the twentieth century.

Despite its many contributions, however, Shabab al-Islam also suffered from a number of shortcomings that spelled its failure to persist beyond the generation of its founders. As occurs with many social movements, especially those that are defined by the age group of its members, the ability to sustain the movement beyond the initial phase is highly dependent on a strong organizational structure. In the case of Shabab al-Islam, the idea for which it stood was far stronger than the organization's ability to control its direction. Internally, the group's founders acknowledged that they lacked the knowledge and experience to maintain a rigid organizational structure, and were too often concerned mainly with Shabab al-Islam's message, rather than its structure. External forces, in the form of rival student groups and meddling state officials, contributed to Shabab al-Islam's inability to maintain control over its public image as the actions of others were often attributed to the organization. As Mustafa lamented, "we allowed too many people to enter, which gave us less control. . . . We were hit organizationally."[60]

This was to have direct implications for the future of the Islamic movement. A primary reason that al-Gam'iyya al-Diniyya eventually succeeded where Shabab al-Islam failed is that it focused an immense amount of its energies on building a strong centralized organizational structure. Not only did it adopt the Muslim Brotherhood "idea," as Shabab al-Islam had done, but it also embraced the Muslim Brotherhood's organizational model. In its failure to endure, Shabab al-Islam would unwittingly demonstrate that, although the Muslim Brotherhood was more than an organization, the organization was vital to sustain the movement's efforts in the long term. 'Uthman recalled that during the interrogation of Shabab al-Islam leaders by state security officials they were told, "you were the spark that became the flame. If we had let you continue, your flame would have engulfed the entire country."[61] While Shabab al-Islam's flame may have been extinguished prematurely, these officials could not comprehend that the dying embers would give life to a new fire, one that saw the Islamic movement established as a permanent fixture in Egyptian political life through a familiar name that was destined to return.

3

Return of the Brothers

IN FEBRUARY 1971, as Anwar al-Sadat released the first wave of Muslim Brotherhood leaders from the prisons of Gamal Abdel Nasser, an elder in the group, a lawyer named 'Umar al-Tilmisani, immediately set out for the 'Abdin Presidential Palace. Upon entering the lobby of one of Egypt's most impressive modern structures, a relic of the monarchy that was seamlessly transitioned into a symbol of the revolution, Tilmisani walked to the guest registry and wrote down a message of gratitude to Sadat for the compassion he showed in freeing him and his long-imprisoned colleagues.[1] With that gesture, the Muslim Brotherhood appeared ready to turn the page—quite literally—on its relationship with the regime that had been in power since the Free Officers revolted in 1952. Less than three years later, as Egyptians celebrated their nation's impressive showing in the October 1973 war with Israel, Tilmisani was in the process of becoming the newest general guide of the organization, a development that was to foreshadow the Muslim Brotherhood's re-emergence as Egypt's chief Islamic movement organization and the leading force of political opposition in the decade that followed.

The Muslim Brotherhood's path to reclaiming its place in Egyptian society was by no means decorated with flowers. Rather, it was long, arduous, and fraught with new challenges, the likes of which the organization had not experienced in its four-decade history. Following an intricate yet at times inexact process of reappraisal and adaptation, this period resulted in a Muslim Brotherhood that was well suited to operate within a new set of constraints and tackle the pressing issues of the day. This chapter chronicles the experiences of the Muslim Brotherhood's leaders in the critical years after attaining their newfound freedom. Because the organization was in such a state of disarray following a nearly twenty-year absence, it is no surprise that most historical studies of the organization during the 1970s do not begin until the middle part of the decade, with some even dating the Muslim Brotherhood's re-emergence to the 1976 inaugural publication of its monthly magazine, al-Da'wa.[2] In order to grasp the progression in the group's makeup, however, it is vital to examine the tenuous period that preceded it, taking into account both the internal and external forces that would shape the future course of the Muslim Brotherhood.

In contrast to earlier periods, the intellectual project around which the Muslim Brotherhood was established no longer held sway as the only activist-oriented ideology within the Islamic movement. To the surprise of many of the organization's leaders, other Islamic intellectual trends had begun to compete for followers in the Muslim Brotherhood's absence. Du'a la Quda, the tract penned by Hasan al-Hudaybi, turned out to be just the opening salvo in a drawn-out battle between the Muslim Brotherhood's leadership and its ideological competitors, a rivalry that would come to define the entire decade. In addition to Sayyid Qutb's eager followers, however, a number of other intellectual currents began to permeate Egypt from across the Islamic world. The first section of this chapter addresses the increasing diversity within the field of Islamic activism, with the aim of disambiguating the various trends and identifying what relationship, if any, they had to the Muslim Brotherhood and its intellectual school.

Dovetailing with the exploration of competing ideological trends is a section on the consequences these had in the form of new organizations to house them. If the traditional strength of the Muslim Brotherhood lay in its ability to bring people within its organizational fold, the rise of competing groups who claimed to represent more fully the needs and aspirations of everyday Egyptians could (and often did) pose an unwanted challenge to its authority. In fact, as demonstrated in greater detail below, the existence of a range of Islamic organizations played an important role in the Muslim Brotherhood's determination to reconstitute its structure at a time when such a decision was by no means inevitable. Moreover, the diversity of groups, some of which operated completely in secret, provided the Muslim Brotherhood with an opportunity to distinguish itself from the rise of fringe elements pursuing a militant path and possibly to attain for itself a better standing with the state.

However, the posture of the regime was not a constant in this equation. The next section addresses the role that Sadat played in bringing Islamic politics in Egypt once again to the fore and the benefits as well as barriers that this placed before the Muslim Brotherhood. Despite the outwardly welcoming attitude to the space created for the discussion of Islam in the public sphere, the Muslim Brotherhood's leaders would find themselves facing yet another challenge in the form of the regime's appropriation of religion for its own purposes. Reaching its zenith with the October War, which featured "Allahu Akbar!" as the Egyptian military's battle cry, this process forced the field of Islamic activists to rethink their strategy and tailor their mission to the changing political and social environs.

Upon identifying the range of external pressures that guided the trajectory of the Muslim Brotherhood following the prison exodus, it is essential also to take stock of the internal factors that would determine the future of the organization. All indicators point to the fact that, even in the aftermath of Nasser's second wave of repression in 1965, the Muslim Brotherhood still aspired to return to the scene. This effort was stepped up following the 1967 defeat and picked up even more steam with Sadat's accession to power. It was not a question of "if" the Muslim Brotherhood would return, but "how" it would reappear and in what capacity it would pursue its mission. Divisions appeared within the ranks of the senior leadership, and the debate over the nature of the organization's renewed structure ultimately yielded a solution built on compromise.

But efforts to implement the agreed-upon strategy to restore the Muslim Brotherhood were interrupted by the more practical need for many of the leaders and members to reclaim their place, as individuals, in a society that had witnessed tremendous change in the two decades when many of them were away. In most cases, this meant reconnecting with one's family, finding steady employment, and adjusting to the cultural changes in Egyptian society. As this process wore on, it became clear that the prison years took a terrible personal toll on the Muslim Brotherhood members and this, in turn, complicated the process of regrouping the members under an organizational umbrella.

It is no surprise then, that in attempting to reach out to the group, Sadat set his sights on the exiled former members of the Muslim Brotherhood living abroad in other Arab countries. With those initial contacts, the stage was set for the resumption of *da'wa* activities on a limited basis, as the leadership of Hudaybi proceeded with his trademark policy of extreme caution. The events of late 1973 were of particular consequence for the Islamic movement, which had to contend with Sadat's strong showing in the war, followed by Hudaybi's death. The immediate decisions that followed, whether on the structure of the organization or the essence of its message, would shape the future of the Muslim Brotherhood.

A *Marketplace of Ideas*

In his investigation into the reappearance of medieval texts in 1970s Egypt, Emmanuel Sivan noted that as he came upon fresh editions of works by Ibn Taymiyya and Ibn Kathir in many a Cairo bookshop, he "was struck by the degree to which the basic message of these writings had been driven home."[3] Describing the motivations of their audience, he continued, "it is a response to contemporary problems they sought in these exegeses of five-to-seven-hundred-year-old texts, trying to weave them into the texture of their own, quite modern, life."[4] Chronicling the phenomenon that he termed "the New Radicalism," Sivan proceeded to declare it a "reaction to Nasserism and Ba'thism," tracing its origins to Qutb's *Milestones* and viewing its core idea as "the total rejection of modernity . . . since modernity represents the negation of God's sovereignty (*hakimiyya*) in all fields of life and relegation of religion to the dustbin of history."[5]

Taken in isolation from the larger context, Sivan's argument certainly holds considerable merit. Indeed, the examples he provided, from the militant activism of Shukri Mustafa and 'Abd al-Salam Faraj, lend credence to the notion that, aided by the restoration of medieval texts (complete with new commentaries), a radical intellectual current took hold of a small segment of Islamic activists, resulting in a rejection of mainstream society and violent contention against the state. However, Sivan's analysis did little to explain how texts representing such a seemingly isolated trend could have made such waves across Egypt that they "were quickly snatched off the bookstalls by people in all walks of life, but especially by youngsters in modern garb."[6] A wider look at the burgeoning marketplace of religious ideas in Egypt during the late 1960s and early 1970s reveals a more vibrant and diverse field, one in which young and old alike could easily wade into intellectual waters of varying consistencies and depths.

In the mid-1930s, Hasan al-Banna described the Muslim Brotherhood, his blossoming new organization, as "a Salafiyya message, a Sunni way, a Sufi truth, a political organization, an athletic group, a cultural-educational union, an economic company, and a social idea." The first of those qualities refers to the intellectual school from which Banna's idea for the organization originated. The movement of Islamic modernism was given life by such figures as Sayyid Jamal al-Din al-Afghani and his Egyptian disciple, Muhammad 'Abduh, who went on to become the rector of al-Azhar at the dawn of the twentieth century. But just as these early thinkers contemplated the challenge of bringing Islam into accord with a rapidly changing modern world, later thinkers, such as 'Abduh's disciple, Muhammad Rashid Rida, had to contend with the reality of Western encroachment on Islamic societies, and saw the challenge as one of bringing the external influences of modernity in line with basic Islamic precepts.

The abolishment of the caliphate in 1924 heightened the crisis facing the Islamic nation in the minds of many Muslim thinkers, some of whom began to refocus their energies on more innovative methods to rejuvenate the Ummah (the global body of Muslims). The modernist Salafi school advanced a program centered on the return to the classical age of Islamic history, following in the footsteps of the Prophet Muhammad and the first generation of believers, or al-Salaf al-Salih. This movement also featured a renewed emphasis on the textual authenticity offered by the Qur'an and the Hadith as the primary sources governing society. It is in the spirit of this intellectual movement that Banna founded his organization in 1928, with the blessing of Rida, from whom he inherited the seminal reformist periodical, *al-Manar*.

However, the turn-of-the-century modernists were not the only thinkers to invoke the memory of the golden age of Islamic history. In fact, the medieval scholar Taqi ad-Din Ahmad Ibn Taymiyya, also writing at a time of crisis in the Muslim world, called for a return to the original sources of Islam, seeking to purify the existing body of religious knowledge from centuries of innovation and foreign influences. This conservative Salafiyya, as it were, resonated with a later movement, that of Muhammad ibn 'Abd al-Wahhab, an eighteenth-century reformer in the Arabian peninsula. 'Abd al-Wahhab's efforts to purge his society of all un-Islamic elements entailed a literalist interpretation of classical texts and eventually took on a state-building function to enforce a rigid application of the law. This vision was realized with the establishment of the Saudi kingdom, which adopted the Wahhabi school of thought as the state's official ideology.

Thus, by the mid-twentieth century, two varying strands of Salafi thought had come to dominate different parts of the Muslim world. But the combination of Nasser's policy of repression in Egypt and the rise of Saudi wealth and regional influence saw the trajectories of modernist and traditionalist Salafi trends heading in vastly different directions. As the Muslim Brotherhood's leaders, the self-proclaimed heirs to modernist Salafi thought, disappeared into Nasser's prisons, the intellectual vacuum they left behind was filled by the rise of popular preachers spreading a conservative interpretation of Islamic texts. Through the sermons of 'Abd al-Hamid Kishk and the writings of Muhammad Nasiruldin al-Albani, Egyptians were exposed to a more rigid, if decidedly apolitical, Islamic current that influenced their understanding and practice of Islam. Men were seen growing their beards and wearing traditional Islamic dress, while women donned the headscarf in greater numbers than at any time in the previous half-century.

In the absence of modernist lay thinkers without formal religious training, such as Banna, Qutb, and their intellectual heirs, these scholars set out to reaffirm the historic authority of traditional Islamic institutions, led by al-Azhar. This was a two-step process: the first involved dissociating the leading institution of Islamic learning from the secular state by disavowing Nasser's modernization efforts in al-Azhar; the second was to push for populist reforms that would distance al-Azhar from the instruments of the state and bring its scholars closer to their constituency. In the battle for the hearts, minds, and souls of ordinary Egyptians, scholars such as Kishk, Sayyid Sabiq, and Muhammad Mitwalli al-Sha'rawi hoped that their classical training in the Islamic sciences and popular modes of communication to a wider audience would see them surpass the popularity of Qutb's cadre of youth followers, the "pubescent thinkers" and their shallow education, limited to "three pages of Ibn Taymiyya."[7]

In addition to mosques teeming with congregants, these preachers relied on a new technological advancement to spread their message, the growing use of the cassette tape. Recordings of Kishk's sermons were as pervasive as they were fiery, and Egyptians were affected by his message in far greater numbers than ever before.[8] By the mid-1970s, he had also emerged as a leading critic of the Sadat regime, further signaling the break between the religious establishment and the state. In response, the state attempted to promote Sha'rawi as a more acceptable alternative, since his message was limited to issues of beliefs and ritual practice.

Further east, 'Abd al-'Aziz ibn Baaz was promoted to president of the Islamic University of Medina in 1970. The future grand mufti of Saudi Arabia took a great interest in the up-and-coming generation of Muslims. Boxes of Saudi religious texts appeared in Egyptian universities with greater regularity in the last years of the decade and were distributed among students for free. Moreover, Egyptians who had migrated to the Gulf for work in the 1950s and 1960s returned to their country in the 1970s having been influenced by the religious climate of their host nations. Many student leaders who later joined the Muslim Brotherhood readily admit that they were strongly affected by the intellectual current characterized by conservative Salafi scholarship that permeated Egypt during this period.[9]

As the domestic religious activists continued to be absent from the scene, another external influence that appeared at around the same time was the missionary movement represented by the Jama'at al-Tabligh. Based in the Indian subcontinent, this revivalist group spread through much of the Muslim world seeking to bring non-practicing believers back into the fold of Islam. Stressing individual piety and teaching orthodox ritual practice, the Tabligh leaders were known for their unyielding commitment to their mission and their aggressive outreach. The movement did not gain the same footing in Egypt as it did in other Muslim countries, but its followers were highly visible contributors to the landscape of religious activism. Ibrahim 'Ezzat, a popular Islamic preacher associated with the Tabligh, ensured that even those who did not join the organization were keenly aware of its presence and mission, especially among the youth. Also led by Sheikh Farid al-'Iraqi, a former Muslim Brotherhood member, the Tabligh became a safe alternative for Muslim Brothers who wished to continue their activism but without the risk of state repression.[10]

In the realm of popular religion, figures emerged who capitalized on the growing pervasiveness of Islamic thought in mainstream culture. Though they often did not pertain to a particular ideological current, or perhaps because of it, these individuals were successful in amassing a large following and became celebrities in their own right. Mustafa Mahmoud serves as an illustrative example. Trained as a doctor and closely allied with leftist politics in his youth, Mahmoud underwent a personal journey of spiritual renewal in the early 1960s, eventually coming to disavow Marxism in a number of written works. Moreover, he quit his medical practice to devote his life to writing and speaking on matters of Islam, spirituality, and philosophy, along with developing a number of charitable institutions.

In addition to his dozens of books, Mahmoud gained his fame through the popular television program *Faith and Science*, in which he sought to demonstrate the divine presence through nature and scientific discovery. Contrasting his earlier alienation by Nasser, coupled with lawsuits against his teachings by the religious establishment of al-Azhar,

Mahmoud became a proponent of Sadat's religious policies. In turn, he was offered a ministerial position, which he declined in order to focus on his many projects. His charitable association provided free medical care to poor Egyptians and built a mosque that was named after him in the Mohandesin neighborhood of Cairo. Through his writings, television programs, and social services, Mahmoud offered Egyptians an accessible and positive spiritual path, balancing against the more austere and rigid trends in the broader field of Islamic thought.

Similarly, Sufi orders gained prominence during the 1970s. Though it was nowhere near the role they played in the early modern period more than a century earlier, *tariqas* such as the Burhaniyya Disuqiyya Shadhiliyya found new life in Sadat's Egypt. Under the visionary leadership of the Sudanese Sheikh Muhammad 'Uthman 'Abduh al-Burhani, the thirteenth-century order was renewed throughout the Middle East in the mid-twentieth century, amassing a following of three million people in Egypt alone, during the 1970s.[11] The re-emergence of Sufi *tariqas* such as the Burhaniyya represented a spiritual revival that succeeded the Nasser era and its relegation of faith to the realm of private affairs. Just as the Islamic resurgence led by political and militant groups is often explained as the product of countervailing forces in Nasser's Egypt, so, too, must the rise of Sufi orders seeking spiritual revival be viewed in that light.

The trend that would have the most direct impact on political events in the 1970s, especially the ways in which the decade has been portrayed since, was the jihadist current. The development of militancy within the Islamic movement was the result of a number of factors: the legacy of religiously inspired resistance in the earlier period of the Islamic movement; the political, cultural, and socioeconomic changes that came with the revolution; the evolution of religious thought; and the breakdown of leadership hierarchy within the Islamic movement. This current had considerable impact within the Islamic movement, though it was not as momentous or dominant as some commentators have suggested.

The development of jihadist discourse was in part an unintended consequence of Nasser's policy toward the Islamic movement in the late 1960s. Not only did his repressive measures in the concentration camps result in the radicalization of a segment of young prisoners, as Kepel and Ibrahim have demonstrated, but the clamping down on the public debate of Qutb's ideas also had the negative byproduct of relegating the discussion to the fringes of Egyptian society. In the aftermath of Qutb's execution, the Nasser regime burned his books, ordered writers not to mention him by name, and even removed references to his writings in later editions of works by prominent authors.[12]

Without the necessary space to combat the spread of militant views, the Muslim Brotherhood found itself on the defensive. In the aftermath of the events of 1965, Hudaybi demanded that young followers clarify their interpretation of the *takfir* concept. In response, he issued seven prison letters with the goal of reorienting the youth cadres back toward the mainstream Muslim Brotherhood school of thought.[13] These modest efforts appeared to have had little effect, however. By 1967, on the eve of the June War, the Islamic activist prisoners were divided into three ideological camps, whose views on the impending struggle against Israel varied widely. The self-proclaimed Qutbists viewed the Egyptian regime as illegitimate and refused to support Nasser, even as the threat of a foreign enemy loomed large. Hudaybi's camp, meanwhile, believed in uniting all Egyptians, regardless of political allegiances, in the face of an external threat. Even those critical of Hudaybi's leadership, and referring to themselves as supporters of Banna's original mission, agreed that supporting the state's war efforts took precedence over internal political differences.[14]

The prevalent historiography has shown that Nasser's defeat at the hands of Israel emboldened the Qutbists, who continued to develop their ideology, adopting the concept of *hijra*, in addition to *takfir*. Their belief in separation from the larger community for the sake of spiritual purity led to their segregation from fellow prisoners in Liman al-Turra and Abu Za'bal camps, years before they would continue the practice outside the prison walls.[15] In fact, though they had yet to take a concrete position on the use of violence to accomplish their goals, the major ideological differences they had with the mainstream Islamic movement ensured that not only would these groups engage in a heated war of words, but that they would occasionally resort to force to defend their views. Prison gang fights were not uncommon, and served as a warning sign for the patterns of violence that marked many of the important events of the decade.

Because these budding fringe groups could not openly preach their calls of excommunication of fellow Muslims and publicly assert their belief that society was in a state of *jahiliyya*, they relied heavily on the establishment of a strong underground network. They eschewed the traditional Muslim Brotherhood model of a popular grassroots organization that operated from a prominent position in society, instead forming secret groups whose sole purpose was to evade the state security forces while pursuing their strategic goals, often militant in nature. The Islamic

Liberation Organization, known popularly as al-Fanniyya al-'Askariyya because it launched its coup attempt from the Technical Military Academy, was the first of these groups to emerge on the scene. Led by a Palestinian named Salih Sirriya, this organization believed in the Islamization of society from above, with its chief goal to displace the nation's ruler and seize political power. Sirriya recruited dozens of Egyptians, mostly young military academy students and, in April 1974, set out to stage a coup from behind the walls of the Technical Military Academy. Following a violent confrontation with the Egyptian military, the plan quickly fell apart. After a swift trial, Sirriya was executed and most of his supporters were imprisoned.

Similarly, a group that called itself Gama'at al-Muslimin, or the Society of Muslims, was at the center of events in mid-1977, culminating in the assassination of Azhari Sheikh and former Awqaf Minister Husayn ad-Dhahabi. A subsequent police raid led to the apprehension of the group's leader, Shukri Mustafa, and his cadre of followers. Known in the Egyptian press as al-Takfir wal-Higra (Excommunication and Flight), this underground organization became notable for the erratic behavior of its followers, who shunned mainstream society as corrupt and relocated to communal homes, whether in out-of-the-way suburban furnished flats or the caves of the upper Egyptian countryside. Among other things, the group believed it was not permissible to hold government jobs or pray in public mosques. Al-Takfir wal-Higra more fully realized the reformulated theory of *jahiliyya* than any prior group.

Its gestation occurred in Nasser's prisons a decade earlier. Mustafa, having been recruited into the latest attempt at the reorganization of the Muslim Brotherhood, was imprisoned along with Qutb's other followers in 1965. Holding tightly to his *takfiri* views, Mustafa found himself alone after Hudaybi's followers succeeded in dissuading the emerging Qutbist fringe, including one of its leaders, Sheikh 'Ali 'Abduh Isma'il, from following a path of isolation and militancy. Starting from a position of weakness, Mustafa recruited several close friends to begin the effort anew, with an eye toward establishing a separate organization upon their release from prison, which occurred in mid-1971.[16]

While al-Takfir wal-Higra represented the most forceful and abrupt break from the Muslim Brotherhood's traditional school of thought, it was by no means the only expression of the growing ideological divisions within the Islamic movement. By the late 1970s, the Muslim Brotherhood was successfully rejuvenated, due in large part to its effective co-optation of the student movement. In some corners of the youth activist community, however, especially that based in upper Egypt's universities, the Muslim Brotherhood was met with staunch resistance by the local campus chapters of al-Gama'a al-Islamiyya. The dispute was as much ideological—with the minority advocating a militant outlook—as it was about appearances. Competing factions fought over the use of the name al-Gama'a al-Islamiyya, with the only thing distinguishing them from one another being the logo: one group adopted the classic Muslim Brotherhood logo, featuring two swords crossed over the Qur'an, while the opposing side's logo featured only one sword raised in the air. Eventually, as the Muslim Brotherhood's sympathizers formally merged with it, the latter group monopolized the name al-Gama'a al-Islamiyya, by the early 1980s becoming an independent organization unaffiliated with the universities. At its prime, al-Gama'a al-Islamiyya proved to be the most formidable opponent to the Muslim Brotherhood from within the Islamic movement, and was responsible for a number of violent incidents across Egypt.

In addition to the jihadist organizations that grabbed the most headlines, several smaller underground groups espousing similar views sprang up in the mid-1970s. Groups such as Tahrir Islami, Jund Allah, and Jama'at al-Amr bi-l-Ma'ruf wa-l-Nahy 'an al-Munkar became a thorn in the side of the Sadat regime at a time when it was attempting to develop its own Islamic credentials. Meanwhile, by October 1981, Jama'at al-Jihad went from being an obscure militant organization with fewer followers than any other group, to gaining international notoriety for its role in the assassination of the Egyptian president.

Taken together, the various intellectual currents within the Islamic movement presented a formidable challenge, as well as an opportunity for the Muslim Brotherhood. As it faced little external competition throughout its early history, the organization could not refer to the Banna years for guidance on how to assert itself as the veritable head of the Islamic movement. Instead, its leaders emerged from prison to discover a dynamic and multifarious scene of Islamic intellectualism and activism. Though many of these figures would express genuine delight at finding Islamic identity so firmly established across the country, they faced an uphill struggle to impress upon the up-and-coming generation the need to restore the Muslim Brotherhood to its rightful place as the leader of the Islamic movement. This process entailed responding to all of the prevalent ideologies, from conservative Salafism to popular Sufism and especially the dangers posed by groups promoting jihad against the state. Adding to the complexity of the Muslim Brotherhood's enormous task was the appearance of the state as a puissant actor within the realm of Islamic politics.

The Believer President

In the process of reorienting his regime away from the failed policies of Nasser and toward a new vision for Egypt, Sadat attempted to infuse his government with an Islamic persona. All indicators point to the fact that Sadat perceived this to be a crucial element in his mission to shift the country away from a socialist system in the Soviet camp to a liberal economic system allied with the West. Mining Islam's rich legacy as a defining facet of Egyptian culture, the new regime utilized religion as a legitimating force for its policy realignment.

This transformation began with Sadat himself. Taking on the title of the "believer president," he embodied the characteristics of piety and devotion in his daily life. In sharp contrast to his predecessor, who had relied exclusively on secular nationalist rhetoric, Sadat frequently intoned Islamic expressions and Qur'anic verses in the course of his public speeches. Moreover, he restored his given name of Muhammad and used it exclusively in official settings. The state media was enlisted to transmit this persona to the Egyptian public. Scenes of Sadat listening intently to the Friday sermon and praying in many of Egypt's mosques became commonplace on television screens across the country. Close associates of Sadat had no reason to doubt the genuine nature of his spiritual awakening, but the political utility of a state-sanctioned Islamic platform to combat leftist members of the old guard could not be denied.

Soon thereafter, Sadat's policies began to reflect this increased religiosity. A new constitution passed in September 1971 established the Shari'a as a source of legislation, while later that month, Sadat announced that his state was to be built on the principles of "science and faith."[17] Continuing to rely on this slogan several years later, Sadat expounded upon his vision for the interplay between the two, careful to distinguish the official vision of faith from those of competing forces in society:

> The faith we defend and abide to is a faith devoid of hatred and fanaticism which encourages work, research, and knowledge. . . .
> It is also the faith expounded by Islam and which fixed the human spiritual values and established the Islamic state on the basis of political and social legislations based on justice, amity and equity.[18]

Sadat then proceeded to illustrate how together with faith, science played a vital role in pursuing national goals and meeting development targets:

> Faced with an increasing population and the increasing demands of modern life upon natural resources, we have no alternative but to push towards the desert, reclaim its land, to look for its riches and to encourage settlement therein, so that our society might be secure, prosperous, generous with its resources and invincible by its people. . . . Science is our ideal mean to achieve these targets and Faith is the decisive weapon to face the challenges of the march.[19]

This outlook was pursued through a number of new initiatives to place Islam at the center of public life in Egypt. In Cairo, "the city of a thousand minarets," Sadat ordered the construction of one thousand new mosques, in addition to the forty thousand already in place.[20] By 1973, he had returned to the Ministry of Awqaf the lands confiscated by Nasser and invested the ministry with greater autonomy in regulating Islamic endowments. Institutions such as al-Azhar and recognized Sufi orders were permitted to operate with greater freedom than at any point since the revolution. Religious programming on television increased substantially, and the call to prayer interrupted even live presidential speeches, an unthinkable act under the prior regime. Sadat succeeded in creating the impression that Egypt had become one nation under God, deriving his legitimacy from his image as a righteous leader serving the interests of his people as determined by Islam.

There is perhaps no better scenario to illustrate the sharp contrast between Nasser and Sadat than the October War of 1973:

> Whereas Nasser had employed the secular motto "Earth, Sea, and Sky" in the 1967 war, Sadat used "Allahu Akbar!" the opening words of the call to prayer and the traditional Islamic battle cry. *Allahu Akbar!* was on the lips of Egyptian troops as they stormed across the Suez Canal. . . . The war itself was in every sense portrayed as a *jihad*; religious language and symbolism were freely employed. As a result, Egypt's success in penetrating Israeli positions was seen as an Islamic victory. Sadat emerged as a Muslim hero.[21]

The war itself occurred during the holy month of Ramadan and in his secret preparations, Sadat gave it the code name Operation Badr, in reference to the Prophet Muhammad's famous inaugural victory over the Meccan army. In the aftermath of the war, Sadat appeared to have reached the height of his popularity, successfully combining his strong Islamic credentials with his resolute command of the Egyptian forces in its most successful campaign against Israel to date. In an ironic twist, the reversal of fortunes under Sadat's divinely inspired war effort served to affirm the common Islamist critique that Egypt's continued defeat at the hands of the Israeli military was due to the state's failure to uphold Islamic values.

Indeed, even as Sadat emerged triumphant from his early challenges, be it the Corrective Revolution of May 1971 or the October War in 1973, not all segments of Egyptian society were convinced of the country's new direction. The student protests of 1972 reflected the backlash from a generation raised in Nasserist rhetoric that saw their world rapidly collapsing around them. For the staunchly secularist leftists, a return to religion was perceived as a cheap tactic to shore up a new political base upon which Sadat could forge his revised policy agenda, and this was sure to fail because of Islam's incompatibility with the challenges of the modern world. Furthermore, in the hands of "rightist" forces, Islam could only amount to capitalist economic policies and exploitation of the nation's workers and resources.

On the other side, Islamic activists responded to the state's newfound religiosity with a combination of bemusement and skepticism. Whereas Tilmisani was grateful for Sadat's apparent change of heart regarding the Muslim Brotherhood, other groups were weary of the state's legacy of repression of independent political voices, especially those inspired by Islam. The fact that the violent confrontation at the Technical Military Academy occurred only a few months after the October War, at a time when Sadat was seemingly at the height of his popularity, was a telling sign that not all Egyptians believed in the "believer president."[22]

Stemming the Opposition

Early on, Sadat's Islamization policy appeared to be aimed at shifting the country's political capital away from traditional "centers of power"—institutions and individuals with strong leftist leanings—to an as yet undefined alternative that relied on Islamic principles for its legitimacy. Therefore, in Sadat's estimation, the formidable opposition from the prior regime was the only factor worth consideration, at least in the initial stages of this policy. Long repressed and much defeated, the Islamic movement's response did not enter into the state's calculations, and there-fore no reasoned strategy was ever devised to address it. Instead, Sadat's policy toward Islamic forces in society was an incoherent patchwork that faced much opposition and displayed frequent contradictions.

On the one hand, Sadat offered some gestures to the Islamic movement through the appointments of Kamal Abul Magd and 'Abd al-'Aziz Kamel, the latter a former Muslim Brotherhood member, to strategic posts within his government. A respected scholar who had credibility in the eyes of many Muslim Brotherhood leaders, 'Abd al-Halim Mahmoud was appointed Sheikh of al-Azhar and was given considerable independence to resurrect the institution's place in society following its marginalization by Nasser.

In addition to these public moves to appoint figures with perceived Islamist sympathies to influential positions in the new government, the regime also utilized covert measures to spread its influence within an Islamic movement undergoing a pronounced resurrection. The previous chapter detailed the ways in which Shabab al-Islam, one of the earliest public expressions of Islamic activism in the Sadat era, was subjected to co-optation efforts by government officials. The group was frequently forced to push back against external elements utilizing its name, mission, and momentum in pursuit of their own agendas. Muhammad 'Uthman Isma'il and 'Uthman Ahmed 'Uthman, two figures close to Sadat who promoted the policy of creating an Islamic youth movement to combat leftist activists, utilized their considerable influence with the president and access to the sizable resources of the Arab Socialist Union to sponsor student groups to advance the regime's interests. Just as Nasser had cre-ated the Socialist Vanguard for this purpose, Sadat had lent his support to the unaffiliated Shabab al-Islam chapters and later the Gama'at Islamiyya.

Through these wide-ranging policies targeting the rise of an Islamic alternative, the Egyptian state itself became an important actor in the emergence of a reconstituted Islamic movement. Even in later years, as the danger of fringe elements within the movement made itself apparent, the security apparatus took special care to monitor these groups closely, infiltrating them when it felt it necessary. The ideological and organiza-tional diversity of the Islamic movement ultimately served to bolster the regime's position in confronting the growth of a new threat to its political agenda. As Kepel contended, "It was this climate of fragmentation of the movement into rival sects and of incidents between them that gave the police the opportunity to intervene in the internal affairs of the Islamicist movement."[23]

By late 1972 then, at the same time that Shabab al-Islam held its initial launch event, Sadat had formally severed his special relationship with the Soviet Union, leaving Egypt to pursue a course independent of communist influence for the first time in nearly two decades. Meanwhile, the Muslim Brotherhood's leadership emerged from prison to discover a vibrant field of religious activism made up of veteran former members, an independent student movement, and an unproven president seeking to bolster his Islamic credentials in society. Echoing the scene on the eve of the revolution in 1952, both the Muslim Brotherhood and the new regime quickly came to realize that they were in need of one another, even if their political visions did not often converge. The real question would be what lessons each side had learned from previous encounters that had ended in violent confrontation and years of repression.

Old Wounds and New Beginnings

Only four months into his presidency, Sadat launched the first wave of prison releases that freed several high-ranking Muslim Brotherhood leaders, including Hudaybi and Tilmisani, in February 1971.[24] By August, Sadat's new interior minister, Mamduh Salem, announced the release of an additional 134 political prisoners and proclaimed an end to the "political isolation" of 13,000 Egyptians by the following year.[25] Though it fell short of full legalization of the group for the first time since its ban in the early years of the revolution, the policy revision that coincided with Sadat's accession to power ushered in a new era for the Muslim Brotherhood in Egypt. Three main issues occupied the leadership during this early phase of the group's reappearance.

The first and most immediate area of concern involved the adaptation of Muslim Brotherhood leaders and members to the changes in Egyptian society. For many of them, the prison experience had come to define the majority of their adult lives. The psychological effects of years of torture and isolation took their toll on the rank-and-file members to such an extent that the thought of resuming political activism could not be further from their minds. Instead, they faced the complex task of reconnecting with their families and resuming normal life within their communities.

Second, any attempt to reconstitute the organization had to take into account Sadat's policy toward Islam in general and the Muslim Brotherhood in particular, taking great care to avoid another wave of repression. The regime's new posture toward the Muslim Brotherhood was reflected in Sadat's efforts to reach out to exiled members and to form an under-standing on the future of their activities within the limited political space created for them by the state.

For those who wanted to reignite the mission of the Muslim Brother-hood, especially among the senior leadership, a third challenge emerged in the form of internal conflicts regarding the future course of the orga-nization. Upon taking stock of the current political situation in the early 1970s, several competing viewpoints developed, each representing a dif-ferent outlook for the future of the Muslim Brotherhood. Before confront-ing the obstacles from the society at large or the challenges posed by the regime's stance toward Islamic activism, these leaders had to face an inter-nal struggle to determine the course of the Muslim Brotherhood and its revised mission. Ultimately, this was a period marked by widespread con-fusion and a high degree of uncertainty, even by the standards of a social movement that was historically subject to the whims of the ruling power.

Picking Up the Pieces

In his memoir recounting the devastating conditions in Egypt's prison camps, Ahmed Ra'if described in vivid detail the scenes of physical and psychological abuse. In one instance, he and four other Muslim Broth-erhood members were tortured for three continuous days, resulting in the death of two of them, while the others sustained permanent impair-ments.[26] The punishment meted out by Nasser's security forces built such a wall around each of the prisoners that Ra'if concluded by wonder-ing: "[W]hat would an individual subjected to all of this do once they leave this place, if they ever could leave this place?"[27]

Indeed, the transition from an outlawed movement subjected to unspeakable atrocities to individual activists seeking a return to main-stream society was the foremost obstacle to the Muslim Brotherhood's re-emergence. Describing this process, 'Esam al-'Erian, a young student activist later commented that the group's elders "faced enormous difficul-ties in preparing for the reentry into society. This was the most difficult challenge."[28] This process was laden with sociocultural, psychological, and economic implications.

The cultural landscape of Egypt in the early 1970s was markedly differ-ent from that of the mid-1950s. The decline of the old landed elite in favor of a developing middle class, more educated and technically able than any previous generation, meant that a small segment of the population isolated from these developments had to determine how it fit into the new social categories. Moreover, they had to come to terms with the fact that, while they had seen the ugly side of the Nasser regime over the course of two decades, other Egyptians had only recently come to understand the failures of the prior government. Regardless of how openly critical Sadat and other state officials were of Nasser, the former Muslim Brotherhood prisoners were too far ahead in their denunciation for most people to catch up, leading to continued feelings of alienation among them.

The prison camp experience took an enormous psychological toll on the Muslim Brotherhood members. Many of them had to endure years of isolation and hard labor. Reports of torture were common and became immortalized in the Muslim Brotherhood's historiography throughout the memoirs and publications that appeared in the years that followed.[29] Even outside observers noted the severity of Nasser's treatment of his political foes, citing the constant fear of outright extermination, actual massacres within the prison walls, and show trials followed by public executions, as in the case of Organization 1965.[30]

In his methodological note regarding research conducted on prisoners in the late 1970s, Saad Eddin Ibrahim noted that the activists he approached expressed hostility and suspicion toward independent researchers. Their initial refusal to cooperate stemmed from a determination by some to avoid contact with members of a "corrupt society," while the majority simply believed that the researchers were government agents.[31] The culture of fear and paranoia was a lingering effect of the Nasser era that extended throughout the Sadat period. It perpetuated a siege mentality that existed within the community of Islamic activists long after their release from the prison camps, and helps to explain why the Muslim Brotherhood experienced such a dearth of numbers compared with its membership of over a million two decades earlier.

As a younger activist recalled, the prison environment continued for some time after the release of the Muslim Brotherhood leaders.[32] Feelings of isolation continued, as some members found it difficult to reconnect with family members and struggled to find employment. Others found support from preexisting Muslim Brotherhood networks, as those from the organization who had found economic security working in the Gulf countries provided employment opportunities to their newly freed comrades, often after having assisted their families in previous years. Most former prisoners dreamed of starting a new life in the Gulf, while some even learned German in prison for a new life in Europe, which they claimed was even more tolerant of Islam than most Arab states.[33] For those who were determined to remain in Egypt or who had no alternative, their struggle for reintegration required them to track down old community ties or establish new ones. These early encounters with Egyptian society in the pursuit of employment required the former prisoners to adapt to the changes around them and to temper their expectations for reintegration.

However, as another student leader recalled, many Muslim Brotherhood leaders were stunned to discover a new religiosity in society that had not been a product of the Muslim Brotherhood *da'wa*.[34] While this was a welcome surprise to many Islamic movement elders, it ran contrary to their belief, developed over the course of the prison experience, that society had abandoned all claims to its Islamic identity through its embrace of Nasserism, complete with its hostility to the Muslim Brotherhood. Within an emergent cultural context that was both alien and strangely familiar, discussions among the movement's leaders centered on what role, if any, the Muslim Brotherhood stood to play in a society eager to fashion a new national project out of the ashes of the failed policies of old.

Sadat Extends a Hand

While the former prisoners were still adjusting to a life of new challenges, Sadat marched on with his policy of de-Nasserization and its concomitant attempts to infuse his regime with Islamic values. Some of his early appointments, including Abul Magd and Isma'il, were instrumental in this process. Not only were they the public face of this campaign, but they also provided the necessary links between the state and prominent Islamic figures in society. Others have pointed to additional influences, such as Sadat's first vice president, Hussein al-Shafi'i, and his budding relationship with Saudi Arabia's leaders, who had looked favorably on the Muslim Brotherhood in their regional rivalry against Nasser.[35]

In the course of these contacts, Sadat shifted his attention to the Muslim Brotherhood figures abroad. Given that those living in exile fared far better than their comrades who had endured Nasser's prison camps, this seemed like a more prudent step on the part of the Egyptian president. It would be far easier to turn the page on that dark moment in history with individuals who were more likely to reciprocate the conciliatory gestures. Moreover, the social standing of the local Muslim Brotherhood leaders as recently released prisoners complicated the ability of the regime's top authority from granting them any formal recognition. In February 1971, an exiled Muslim Brotherhood member living in Qatar was allowed to make a trip to Egypt. During the course of his short visit, Kamal Nagi delivered a letter to Sadat on behalf of other exiled figures that signaled their desire for a fresh start. Their grievances were with Nasser's enforcers, they argued, not with Sadat.[36]

Repaying this visit with a gesture of his own, Sadat enlisted the help of one of his confidants, a doctor affiliated with the Islamic movement. In his memoirs, Mahmoud Gami' recalled that Sadat pondered asking the Muslim Brotherhood to join in his efforts against the Nasserist remnants in Egypt, but preferred to call upon those who had fled, since they would be more likely to cooperate with him. To that end, Gami' traveled to a number of Gulf countries on behalf of Sadat, meeting with the likes of Yousuf al-Qaradawi, Ahmed al-'Asal, 'Abd al-Ra'uf Mashhur, and Salim Nigm.[37]

With these meetings, Sadat meant to accomplish a number of things. First, he hoped to enlist the help of individuals who had long been responsible for making considerable financial and moral contributions to Egyptian society. Rather than as a force of subversion, their efforts would now be treated as an asset to the regime. Second, Sadat also believed that the exiled Muslim Brotherhood figures were instrumental to enhancing Egypt's relationship with the host countries. As he attempted to rectify the mistakes of the past, Sadat believed in cultivating strong ties with the Gulf states, and he was determined to take advantage of the community of Egyptian exiles who had already made significant inroads with the rulers of several Arab countries.

Third, by circumventing the recognized leadership of the Muslim Brotherhood in favor of fringe figures of questionable influence in the command structure, Sadat was also employing a strategy of divide-and-conquer. Sadat made no secret of his distaste for Hudaybi, whom he once described as "a singularly dull-witted and colorless ex-magistrate."[38] For his part, Hudaybi and others within his inner circle had refused to pledge their allegiance to Sadat following their release from prison, further complicating the early encounters between the Muslim Brotherhood and the state.[39] Internally, the group's leaders were faced with a new challenge, that of coordinating between factions that were separated by both geography and historical experience. As al-'Erian later acknowledged, reorganization efforts in Egypt were actually hindered by the challenge of dealing with al-Aqtar al-'Arabiyya, or those exiled figures who would command some authority by virtue of their reputable social standing and access to the Egyptian regime.[40]

Charting a New Course

While the majority of Muslim Brotherhood members spent the initial months following their release from prison focusing on personal matters, the surviving core group within the leadership contemplated the future of their organization. The years of repression had decimated the organizational structure of the Muslim Brotherhood, which had been carefully developed by Hasan al-Banna and inherited by his successor, Hasan al-Hudaybi. The Consultative Assembly, which elected the leadership, was no more. The Field Apparatus, which oversaw individual localized cells known as "families," had ceased to exist, as the families themselves had disbanded. Even the Guidance Bureau was a shell of its former self, with many of its original members having died or fled in the intervening years, leaving a handful of figures, such as 'Umar al-Tilmisani, Ahmed al-Malt, and Farid 'Abd al-Khaliq, as the only contemporaries of Banna, along with Hudaybi.

It had been nearly two decades since the last round of internal elections, and with no membership or institutional structure to speak of, the Muslim Brotherhood could not be reconstituted through a simple resumption of its internal mechanisms for the selection of leadership and secretarial positions. In fact, a decision to resume activism under the banner of the Muslim Brotherhood had yet to even be taken. What followed was a spirited internal debate among leading members of the Muslim Brotherhood, continuing the discussions that marked the prison years, but with the added insight that came with assessing the political and social situation that was developing in a post-Nasser Egypt.

Several factors helped drive the discussion on the future of the Muslim Brotherhood's mission. For one, the Islamic movement had appeared to outgrow the need for a centralized organizational structure such as that offered by the Muslim Brotherhood in its early years. Reputable thinkers from the Muslim Brotherhood's school of thought, such as Muhammad al-Ghazali, Yousuf al-Qaradawi, and Sayyid Sabiq, had enjoyed a high degree of success despite the lack of organizational backing for their activities.

Moreover, a new generation of youth activists had clung to Islam as their primary frame of reference and motivational force, without having come up in the traditional Muslim Brotherhood *da'wa*. Some wondered if it could be that the future of Islamic activism was in safe hands due to the unexpected rise of this vibrant movement. On the other hand, the ideological divisions that marked the prison years had already begun to permeate among ordinary Egyptians. Though the existence of underground militant groups such as that which stormed the Technical Military Academy in 1974 was not known to the recently released Muslim Brotherhood leaders, they were certainly aware of the subculture that would cultivate such expressions among zealous youth and disaffected veteran activists. Combating militant views would require strong organizational backing and a reassertion of the Muslim Brotherhood's core message.

In addition to the existing social conditions, consideration also had to be given to the political situation. The Muslim Brotherhood had become an outlawed organization by official decree in 1954. Though Sadat had seemingly extended an olive branch to its leaders, he had not sanctioned the organization's return. The ban would remain in effect throughout the Sadat presidency. Any decision on the part of the group to resume its activism under the Muslim Brotherhood banner was sure to set off a new round of confrontation with the state. The dreadful memories of Nasser's prisons were ever present, casting a dark shadow over these deliberations.

Additionally, Sadat's expressions of personal piety, along with the appointment of reputable Islamic leaders to key posts in the new regime, raised the question of whether the Islamic movement should abandon its traditional mode of operating through a nonstate organization. Instead, it would join in national efforts to instill society with Islamic values and govern on the basis of the Shari'a. After all, if Banna founded the Muslim Brotherhood in part as a response to the fall of the caliphate, then Sadat's apparent willingness to revive the Islamic basis of the state was cause enough to alter the nature of the group's mission, if not abandon it altogether.

These and other questions weighed heavily on the minds of the leading Muslim Brotherhood figures. By 1973, three camps emerged, reflecting the multiple viewpoints expressed in the course of these discussions.[41] The first camp believed that the Muslim Brotherhood's moment in the sun had passed. They argued that the body of the organization should not be revived, but rather its spirit should live on in the form of public advocacy on the part of its veteran leaders. Acknowledging that this was "a completely new idea," its main proponent, Mahmoud 'Abd al-Halim, argued that the Islamic movement should set aside its traditional proclivity for working under a particular banner. He suggested instead that "its activism should take on a cultural and intellectual character."[42]

A former close associate of Banna, 'Abd al-Halim believed that there was much in the Muslim Brotherhood's past experiences that would dissuade its members from wanting to build the organization anew. Most obviously, the years of repression at the hands of the Nasser regime, which he witnessed firsthand in the torture chambers of Liman al-Turra prison, were cause enough to force a recalculation on the part of the Muslim Brotherhood. It would be tragic, 'Abd al-Halim argued, if the lessons of this painful experience were lost on old and young alike, only for it to be repeated with a new regime and a revived Muslim Brotherhood. Additionally, he was critical of the exclusivity and secrecy with which closed organizations by their very nature operate. It is this type of partisanship that would preclude the group from working closely with some of the period's intellectual luminaries who may not have joined the Muslim Brotherhood, or in the case of Sheikh al-Ghazali, were dismissed from its ranks under specious circumstances many years earlier.

As an alternative, proponents of this view advocated for the continuation of an open and fluid Islamic movement, one that would continue to spread the message articulated by Banna, but that also would possess the flexibility to adapt to its changing surroundings and incorporate the positive contributions of leading thinkers and popular social forces. It would focus its efforts on indoctrinating the youth, especially the rising generation of student activists, without interfering in their organizational structures or imposing on them membership in a new group. Instead, the veteran leaders would channel their energies through public initiatives, such as the convening of lectures and dissemination of literature. In essence, the traditionally rigid organizational structure of the Muslim Brotherhood would transform into something akin to a publishing house with its own speakers' bureau.

Indeed, proponents of 'Abd al-Halim's vision, who included 'Abbas al-Sisi and 'Abd al-Halim Khafaga, would pursue this strategy independently of the outcome of the Muslim Brotherhood's internal debate. Based in Alexandria, al-Sisi founded Dar al-Sawtiyyat wal-Mar'iyyat, a media company that produced Islamic audiovisual materials for distribution across Egypt. Following his emigration to Germany, Khafaga founded Bavaria Publications, an Islamic publishing house that served Muslim communities in Europe. 'Abd al-Halim himself would take his vision to heart, writing a three-volume history of the early Muslim Brotherhood—the first such work of its kind by an insider—and committed himself to other intellectual endeavors.[43]

On the opposing side of this discussion was another group, led primarily by Mustafa Mashhur, along with Ahmed Hassanain and Kamal al-Sananiri, who argued for the return of the Muslim Brotherhood as the preeminent Islamic activist organization, complete with a strong internal structure and the rigid hierarchy that distinguished the group's Secret Apparatus. As former members of the Secret Apparatus themselves, Mashhur, Hassanain, and al-Sananiri strongly believed in the importance of a well-disciplined organization as the basis for spreading the *da'wa*. Rather than general social advocacy work, under this model the Muslim Brotherhood's main focus would be to recruit a strong membership base and devote its energies to religious training of members with the organization's official curriculum, a process known as *tarbiya*. This would ensure a disciplined and uniform organization capable of combating negative forces in society and, should the opportunity arise, it would be well positioned to exert political influence as well.

This vision could only be realized, Mashhur argued, by reconstituting the Secret Apparatus, an internal subunit within the Muslim Brotherhood's organizational structure that existed separately from the group's public face, thus avoiding the constraints placed upon it by the regime. The lesson of the Nasser period, according to this view, was that a strong internal organization was absolutely critical as an anchor for the endurance of Islamic activism. A mission that was purely outward and public could be easily washed away by the recurring tide of state repression. Thus, it was no surprise that, along with many of the surviving members of the original Secret Apparatus, proponents of this position also included most of the members of Organization 1965, the group that most recently witnessed the regime's obstruction of the Islamic movement to devastating effect.

In recounting the prison experience, Ahmed Ra'if described the reorganization efforts by imprisoned Muslim Brotherhood members in the late 1950s and early 1960s, which ultimately resulted in the 1965 crackdown and the execution of Qutb and two of the accused conspirators. But barely two years later, in the aftermath of the 1967 defeat, the prisons were again buzzing with discussions of reorganization in the event that Nasser released the political prisoners. Given the deepening divisions among the Muslim Brotherhood members, it is quite likely that the proponents of the Secret Apparatus had already launched preparations for the group's return, while leaving their opponents in the dark.

Another young activist recalled that Mashhur later discouraged students from interacting with a number of senior Muslim Brotherhood figures, including Farid 'Abd al-Khaliq, Salah Shadi, and Salih Abu Ruqayyiq.[44] In many instances, these divisions reflected ideological as well as personal differences. Mashhur's faction stressed the resolve they demonstrated in prison, highlighting their suffering in comparison with those who had either recanted their beliefs in the hopes of attenuating the authorities, or those who had avoided the prison camps altogether, like al-Ghazali and Salih al-'Ashmawi. The publication of graphic prison memoirs like Ra'if's were intended to reintroduce Muslim Brotherhood veterans to society, while also distinguishing between those who had paid the heaviest toll and sacrificed the most and those who wavered during the ordeal, or *mihna*.

Also unlike the members of the other faction, Mashhur and his supporters did not treat the recent surge in Islamic activism among Egyptians with cautious optimism. Rather, they were highly critical of the limited knowledge displayed by the student movement, and its penchant for focusing on narrow issues and outward matters of ritual practice.[45] This concern for the wayward youth further underscored the need for a centralized organization with a strong leadership that could instill its members with discipline and command their obedience.

In spite of the seemingly polarizing attitudes on the part of the veteran Muslim Brotherhood leaders, the anticipated impasse never materialized. This was partly a consequence of the fact that both factions independently pursued their own course, with 'Abd al-Halim's turn to publication and Mashhur's efforts to reorganize the internal structure quietly. The apparent lack of confrontation was also the product of the emergence of a third faction, proposing to combine elements of the two visions for the future of the Muslim Brotherhood. Coalescing around the figure of 'Umar al-Tilmisani, the centrist position saw the merits in both outlooks and attempted to incorporate them into a single project for the continuation of the Muslim Brotherhood's mission. Along with Tilmisani, who had begun to take on a more active role in leadership as Hudaybi retreated into the background, this group included Jaber Rizq, Muhammad Salim, Husni 'Abd al-Baqi, and later Farid 'Abd al-Khaliq.

They discerned a real need for a public presence for the Muslim Brotherhood, especially in the midst of a vibrant Islamic movement that lacked strong leadership. These figures took 'Abd al-Halim's proposal for an Islamic press to heart, vowing to introduce Egyptian society to the legacy of the Muslim Brotherhood and to lend its voice to the political and social issues of the day. Several years later, *al-Da'wa* magazine, and indeed, the associated publishing company with its vast library of Muslim Brotherhood literature, emerged from this commitment. Contrary to the beliefs of the Mashhur faction, the accommodationists perceived the Muslim Brotherhood's prominent presence in society as an asset, not a liability. The more deeply entrenched it was in social institutions, from schools and mosques, to factories and hospitals, the more difficult it would be for the regime to take action against it. The more visible it was in the hearts and minds of Egyptians, the more impossible it would be for Sadat to erase its presence.

Continuing to operate under the Muslim Brotherhood banner meant that some level of organization was essential. Witnessing the burgeoning field of Islamic activism, and perhaps even the state's foray into the religious student movement, the accommodationists tended to agree with Mashhur's supporters that a diffuse public *da'wa* campaign alone was not enough to sustain the Muslim Brotherhood's mission. Tilmisani envisioned the reconstitution of the Guidance Bureau and its affiliated branch sections simply as a mechanism to organize the existing Muslim Brotherhood members who wished to remain active in the group, but needed to be part of a coordinated effort. There was to be no active recruitment of new members, and more important, no establishment of any secret entities within the Muslim Brotherhood. The Secret Apparatus and its alleged plots against the state, whether real or imagined, had been the justification used by Nasser to dismantle and suppress the Muslim Brotherhood. The reconstituted group could not afford to provide Sadat with the same pretext upon which to act against it.

In this way, Tilmisani managed to combine elements of the conflicting perspectives to form a cohesive vision for the future of the Muslim Brotherhood. He envisioned a mission of public advocacy that focused its efforts on society at large, but utilized its organizational mechanisms to execute this mission. He reasoned that the organization's name was an asset that distinguished its followers from the competing Islamic trends, but that the next generation of activists should be encouraged to work within their existing institutions rather than being recruited to join the Muslim Brotherhood. The tension between the spirit of the message and the reality of the messengers was one that Tilmisani believed could be eased through such compromises and an ability to adapt to new surroundings. He was supported in this effort by most of the remaining Muslim

Brotherhood members, and he even succeeded in bringing figures from the opposing factions on board. Early on in the discussions, al-Sisi joined Tilmisani's middle position, and eventually even ʿAbd al-Halim reluctantly agreed to join in the reconstitution efforts, taking on a position in the new organization.

The Brothers Return

By early 1973, the decision to resume activism under the banner of the Muslim Brotherhood had been made by most of its surviving leadership. Due to the extraordinary circumstances surrounding its return, however, the group was in no condition to adhere to the organizational protocol, and this period became notable for signaling a true break from the past. As the Guidance Bureau was reestablished, only a handful of its original members had survived the prison years. In order to fill the open positions, the leadership relied on appointments rather than elections, which it lacked the ability to hold. For the first time in the Muslim Brotherhood's history, the Guidance Bureau became populated with figures who were not contemporaries of Hasan al-Banna and thus had not witnessed the first two decades of activism under his leadership. Moreover, the entire remaining membership comprised only about 100–200 individuals, a far cry from the days of Banna, when the Muslim Brotherhood boasted hundreds of thousands of members.[46]

Within the organization, the reshuffling saw the rise of a new leadership. Though in a position of seniority, ʿAbd al-Halim refused an appointment to the Guidance Bureau, instead agreeing to serve under one of his former pupils, al-Sisi, who was placed in charge of the Muslim Brotherhood's chapter in Alexandria.[47] Though he would have appreciated a greater degree of authority within the organization, ʿAbd al-Halim resolved himself to documenting the group's history so that its legacy would be preserved. Elsewhere, Mashhur, Hassanain, and al-Sananiri exerted greater influence within the organization than ever before, even showing early signs that they intended to institute part of their proposed vision for a clandestine unit.

Already in disarray following a tenuous organizational arrangement, the Muslim Brotherhood faced a number of challenges during the course of the year. Having largely taken a back seat during the student protests in the first months of 1973, the leadership struggled with its position vis-à-vis the broader Islamic movement, especially within the universities. It recognized the need to tread carefully, especially in light of Sadat's decision to bypass the domestic leadership in favor of exiled Muslim Brotherhood figures as the only recognized channel with whom he communicated. Adding insult to injury, Hudaybi's refusal to pledge his unconditional allegiance to Sadat ensured that the reconstituted group would remain under intense scrutiny by the regime.

When the October War broke out later that year, the Muslim Brotherhood's leadership knew that it would be expected to take a stand. In echoes of the heated prison debates that surrounded the 1967 war, the Islamic movement featured both conservatives, who refused to lend their support to the regime's war effort, and conciliatory gestures on the part of some activists who placed the national goal of liberation above domestic political considerations. Owing largely to the fact that it had yet to be sufficiently organized, the Muslim Brotherhood sidestepped this debate, though some figures took individual positions on the issue, lauding the gains made by Egyptian forces on the battlefield, but also criticizing the political leadership for its decision to cease hostilities prematurely.

Less than a month later, the Muslim Brotherhood was dealt another blow with the loss of its second general guide. Hasan al-Hudaybi died on November 11, at the age of 82, sparking another crisis of leadership in an organization that already was in a precarious position prior to the loss of its figurehead. As with the ad hoc reconstitution of the Guidance Bureau, the Muslim Brotherhood was not in any position to pursue its standard operating procedures with regard to selecting a new general guide. Moreover, given the organization's nebulous legal standing, what figure would willingly step forward and be declared its leader? As thousands of supporters, including former members and public officials, gathered to mourn Hudaybi's death, the Guidance Bureau quietly met to determine its course of action.

When no clear candidate or, for that matter, protocol for his selection, emerged from this discussion, the members turned to Sheikh Marzouk, a respected veteran of the Muslim Brotherhood who in the previous year had served as Hudaybi's stand-in at Bureau meetings when the general guide was unable to attend.[48] The Bureau asked Marzouk to fill in as general guide while they determined the future of the position, a process that was expected to take some time, given the organizational deficiencies faced by the Muslim Brotherhood. Marzouk initially refused, but after prodding by the other members, he reluctantly agreed to take on the responsibilities of the general guide.

While it was a short-term solution, this posed a problem for the Muslim Brotherhood. The Guidance Bureau refused to reveal the identity of the new general guide publicly, keeping its decision to install Marzouk a secret from its own members, as well as the society at large. Instead, members were requested to pledge their allegiance, the traditional *bay'a* given to all new leaders, to the position of general guide generically, without any knowledge of who had actually come to occupy the post. According to the recollection of 'Abd al-Mon'eim Abul Futuh, a student activist who later became one of the youngest members of the Guidance Bureau, the move sent shockwaves through the rank-and-file members, some of whom refused to give their *bay'a* to a "Secret Murshid." This was especially true among the community of exiled Muslim Brotherhood members, whose distance from the events made them all the more suspicious. But even within Egypt, figures like Mahdi 'Akef, a future general guide himself, reportedly spurned a delegation of Guidance Bureau members who attempted to obtain his *bay'a* to the general guide without disclosing his identity.[49]

The "Secret Murshid" period is an oft-forgotten episode in the modern history of the Muslim Brotherhood. It signaled one of the lowest points in the organization's existence, and became emblematic of the disarray characteristic of the group during its reconstitution phase. The idea that the organization founded by the visionary Hasan al-Banna, which had relied so heavily on his charismatic authority, would one day have a nameless general guide was unconscionable. This moment represented its internal divisions and its external apprehensions. With no strong leadership or unifying vision for the Muslim Brotherhood's future, members of the makeshift Guidance Bureau could not come to a concrete decision on the way forward for their organization, necessitating a temporary solution that all agreed was unworkable. Moreover, continuing concerns over the state's posture toward a reconstituted Muslim Brotherhood contributed to the need for confidentiality during this early stage. As with earlier periods in its history, the organization discerned a real need to protect its legacy and to conceal whatever internal divisions and structural weaknesses it possessed.

In that sense, the Muslim Brotherhood succeeded, even with the "Secret Murshid" debacle. Few outsiders were privy to the internal situation in the Guidance Bureau. Just over a year later, Tilmisani emerged as the agreed-upon choice for the position of general guide. As the most senior remaining Muslim Brotherhood figure and the only member of the

last Guidance Bureau prior to its dissolution in 1954, he was an obvious
choice and received the support of the majority of the organization's members. The only reservations were those of the Mashhur faction, which held
philosophical disagreements with Tilmisani's vision for the organization,
in spite of its declared support for the compromise position that emerged
from the internal debate.[50] These tensions would become a recurring
theme during the remainder of the decade, as the accommodationist outlook for the future of the organization was under constant pressure by
forces wishing to pursue their own vision. Nonetheless, with its legacy
largely intact, in that same period, the Muslim Brotherhood re-emerged
as the most prominent social movement organization in Egypt, resuming
its place at the head of the Islamic movement. This development, by no
means a certainty as Tilmisani assumed the reins of leadership from an
anonymous general guide in 1974, was due in large part to the infusion
of new lifeblood for the Muslim Brotherhood. Across the nation's colleges
and universities, Islamic youth groups had been busy developing a new
spirit of religious activism unlike anything that had been seen in Egypt
since the revolution.

4

Islam on Campus

IN FEBRUARY 1977, Anwar al-Sadat convened a meeting at his vacation home in al-Qanatir, the site of several defining moments of his presidency. In addition to his vice president, Hosni Mubarak, and several members of his cabinet, Sadat also invited ordinary Egyptians representing various segments of society: workers, professionals, and students. The town hall meeting format was a favorite of Sadat's, and one he tended to rely on in the face of an impending political crisis. Only weeks earlier, protests had erupted across Egypt in response to the regime's lifting of subsidies on basic staples such as flour and oil. These "Bread Riots" singlehandedly threatened to undo Sadat's liberalizing economic strategy, known as the *infitah* (opening) policy, and instantly became the most perilous moment of his presidency. The gathering, carried live on state television, was intended to mollify the seething populace and provide reassurances of Sadat's leadership at a time of political and social turmoil.

Following Sadat's opening remarks, the floor was opened for the audience to express their views and ask questions of their president. In the small crowd sat 'Abd al-Mon'eim Abul Futuh, a young medical student who was currently serving as the president of Cairo University's Student Union and the treasurer of the National Student Union's Media Committee. As a founding member of al-Gama'a al-Islamiyya, the most prominent religious organization within the university system, Abul Futuh's rise to the leadership of the Student Union was a sign of the times. Islamic-oriented student activists had finally reached a position of influence after a long and bitter struggle against their leftist rivals. And just as they had succeeded in silencing Sadat's most threatening political opponents, it appeared that the Islamic movement's usefulness to the regime was wearing thin. As Abul Futuh recalled, "I was the only bearded one in the entire meeting. . . . I rose my hand to speak several times but [Sadat] ignored me. When he did not permit me to speak, I rose to the microphone anyway, without permission, and my words were harsh."[1]

Abul Futuh spoke on the state's responsibility toward the youth and the apparent contradictions between Sadat's flowery rhetoric of a nation built on "science and faith" and the actual practices of his regime. As an example, he cited the case of Sheikh Muhammad al-Ghazali, one of the foremost Islamic figures in Egypt, who had been reassigned from his position as a teacher and scholar to an administrative post that did not afford students the opportunity to interact with him in a formal setting. Adding insult to injury, the state sent internal security forces to disperse students peacefully protesting this move.[2] Abul Futuh continued his point by asking, "Mr. President, why do you surround yourself with hypocrites who do not work for Egypt's interest? Why do you keep all the good people away, and where is this country going?"[3]

Before Abul Futuh could complete his remarks, Sadat interrupted him angrily. Seeing the entire purpose of the meeting undone by this brash student activist, the red-faced president yelled at him to "stop right there!" and proceeded to berate him with a lecture on respecting his elders. The meeting was abruptly adjourned and in the months that followed, Abul Futuh's family worried over his personal safety after this very public spat with the Egyptian president. Though no harm came to him personally, the incident signified a new period of confrontation between the Islamic movement and the state. Following the defeat of leftist elements in the universities and society at large, the only remaining potent force of political opposition was represented by al-Gama'a al-Islamiyya, the precursor for the return of the Muslim Brotherhood to Egyptian society.

Prior to Abul Futuh's brush with fame at the expense of Sadat, Islamic activism in Egypt had not made any significant waves. Only a few years earlier, in 1973, Shabab al-Islam had reached the limits of its influence, and al-Gam'iyya al-Diniyya, the predecessor of Abul Futuh's organization, restricted its efforts to modest activities such as providing a prayer space for students, conducting occasional Qur'an study circles, and hosting communal breakfasts during the month of Ramadan. In fact, with the exception of the underground organization behind the events at the Technical Military Academy in 1974, Islamic activism barely registered on the radar of most Egyptians in the early 1970s, while the state believed it would have a strong hand in nurturing the growth of an Islamic trend to combat remnants of the old regime. Following their release from Nasser's prisons, the Muslim Brotherhood leadership endured several years of external pressures and internal disarray, all of which made it unlikely that the organization would make an immediate impact on society. It was not until 1976, with the launch of its monthly magazine, *al-Da'wa*, that the Muslim Brotherhood announced its official re-emergence onto the national stage.

In the meantime, it would be left to young Egyptians at the university level, building upon the legacy of political activism by the student movement, to infuse society with a rejuvenated Islamic mission. The students who launched al-Gama'a al-Islamiyya into the orbit of political activism represented the next stage in an ongoing process that began in the twilight of the Nasser period. As regime sponsored platforms of Arab nationalism and socialism gave way to a potent wave of leftist opposition after 1967, the leftist movement was soon met with a nascent Islamic movement given tacit support by the new regime. By the mid-1970s, a burgeoning movement, more deeply rooted in the new social and cultural milieu, gradually positioned itself in deep opposition to Sadat, even as it continued to enjoy the opened political space provided by the regime.

This bloc of student activists expanded in several directions, its public mission culminating with its capture of the Student Unions of nearly every university, while tacitly its leaders forged links with the Muslim Brotherhood. These twin developments would come to characterize the rise of Islamic activism and the restoration of the Muslim Brotherhood's role at the head of Egypt's political opposition. This chapter begins with an examination of the characteristics that distinguish this generation of students. Separated only by a few years from their counterparts in Shabab al-Islam, the students who developed al-Gama'a al-Islamiyya into an outright political movement typified a number of new trends unique to the Sadat era. This transition is also of particular importance due to the fact that the thousands of rank-and-file activists in al-Gama'a al-Islamiyya would come to make up the base of the reconstituted Muslim Brotherhood, giving the organization a different character in the latter quarter of the twentieth century than it featured in the era of Hasan al-Banna or his successor, Hasan al-Hudaybi.

In addition to its social profile, the Islamic student movement was also distinguished by its intellectual roots. The influences of particular religious and political texts, along with frequent interactions with leading scholars and intellectuals, played an important role in forming the ideological basis upon which the student movement would pursue its activist mission. These foundational influences and early activities form the second key facet in the examination of al-Gama'a al-Islamiyya. Considering that this movement was led primarily by students in the colleges of medicine, engineering, and the hard sciences, external intellectual forces played a critical role in cultivating a generation of Islamic activists that did not otherwise produce its own scholars and thinkers.

Once the small and isolated religious groups on Egypt's campuses began to expand the scope of their mission and their ranks swelled with greater numbers of eager students, the organizational structure of the groups had to adapt accordingly, evolving to meet the growing needs of student activists and the lofty ambitions of the leadership. These institutional developments went hand in hand with the decision by many leaders to participate in Student Union elections. The newfound access to considerable resources and institutional support saw to it that not only would the Islamic movement leave its imprint upon the wider student movement, but the organizational mechanisms that it utilized would also help shape the future of Islamic activism. Participation in Student Union elections by leaders of al-Gama'a al-Islamiyya would eventually pave the way for young Muslim Brotherhood members to run for the leadership of professional syndicates and, beyond that, the Egyptian People's Assembly.

Though it was emblematic of the fragile relationship between the state and the Islamic movement, Abul Futuh's confrontation with Sadat was not the only occasion on which the two forces collided. The role of the Egyptian regime in forging the political and social space in which a revitalized Islamic movement could operate was an overarching theme of this period. Nevertheless, the state was also determined to place hurdles in the path of student activists to contain the growth of an Islamic current from overwhelming Sadat's political agenda. These external pressures ultimately helped to shape the development of Islamic groups, at times limiting their strategic choices, and in other instances offering them an outlet that would not have existed without the regime's consent, however indeterminate it may have been.

Finally, it is worth taking stock of the Islamic movement's achievements during the height of its public activism campaign. In universities across the country, students were exposed to similar campaigns of religious education and were given new avenues for public religious expression, most notably in the form of Islamic summer camps that attracted thousands of Egyptian youth. Additionally, the movement rallied around individual issues, ranging from social ills and public morality to the president's overtures to Israel and the deposed shah of Iran. On the level of organization building, the student leaders of al-Gamaʻa al-Islamiyya proved to be particularly adept, constructing a disciplined and structured group that was more resilient to external forces. In fact, it was only after the group's leadership made the conscious decision to subsume its mission under the larger umbrella of the Muslim Brotherhood that the student movement became subject to outside influences that successfully channeled its energies toward a larger purpose. But the dynamic and vibrant nature of the student movement was such that the influence was mutual, as the Muslim Brotherhood would find itself transformed by its new partnership with the youth of al-Gamaʻa al-Islamiyya.

"Religious from Birth"

Historically, Egypt's system of higher education was the exclusive domain of the privileged classes of society. Though students played a significant role in national politics throughout the liberal era, the student population was relatively homogenous, reflecting the socioeconomic imbalance that favored urbanized elites who could afford to continue their post-secondary education. Even after the revolution, as Gamal Abdel Nasser sought to expand social services to include free higher education, the process was slow and its effects on the majority of Egyptians remained limited. The student activists of the 1960s and early 1970s continued to reflect a common socioeconomic base, one that viewed itself as a vanguard for the leftist or Islamic transformation of society.

By the mid-1970s, however, Sadat's aggressive changes to state education policy had altered the landscape of higher education in Egypt. Upon rising to power, Sadat pursued a populist agenda designed to build a new base of support. He declared it a national goal that all secondary school graduates be admitted to university. Following the creation of an "admissions authority" in 1971, new standards were drafted, creating a hierarchy that would eventually allow all secondary graduates to pursue higher education, ranging from medicine, as the most selective, to vocational training institutes, whose requirements were not as stringent.[4]

Only four years later, the number of secondary graduates admitted to higher learning programs surpassed 400,000 students, more than doubling the 1971 figure of 199,074.[5] As would be expected, the sudden boom in the number of students put additional burdens on academic facilities, leading to a visible decline in the quality of education, and putting additional pressure on the state to respond. Hoping to ease the strain on Cairo and Alexandria, Sadat saw to the establishment of new universities in many provincial centers, including Tanta, Hilwan, Zaqaziq, and al-Minya.[6] For the first time in history, these institutions offered an outlet of higher education for rural Egyptians, thereby reversing the decades-old trend that saw urban middle class Egyptians make up over 85 percent of the university student population.[7]

In altering the social makeup of the student population, Sadat aspired to build a new political base, one that was not beholden to the elitist socialist politics advanced by Nasser. Instead, Sadat bet that by infusing the university environment with rural and working class students in greater numbers, the ensuing political movement within the universities would reflect more conservative and traditional cultural trends.[8] Various tactics also ensured that university faculty, suspected by Sadat of harboring Nasserist sympathies, would exercise minimal influence over the nascent student movement. A ballooning student to faculty ratio that would reach 666:1 by 1977 placed enormous teaching burdens on the faculty, leaving them with little time to connect with students outside the classroom.[9] Moreover, the state's 1971 decision to remove mandatory faculty advisors from student groups was indicative of Sadat's desire to cultivate a new student political culture free from the shackles of prior eras.

From the perspective of the regime, this development could be viewed as a cautious and calculated strategy to secure its legitimacy and consolidate its power. In reality, however, the rise of an Islamic movement within the new crop of students was due to forces largely outside Sadat's control, "partly rooted in an accumulation of rapid, unbalanced, social change."[10] In his analysis of socioeconomic developments during the early Sadat years, Hinnebusch described a society in flux, still reeling from the effects of Nasserization, and now being forced to contend with yet another transformation:

> Massive urbanization was uprooting a growing number of persons from the land and village community who could not be absorbed by the modern urban sector of the economy. Set adrift from the security of family and village, searching for a wider identity and solidarity, yet barely removed from traditional life and values, their heightened aspirations frustrated in a system dominated by a Westernized bourgeoisie, urban migrants were especially susceptible to recruitment by a nativist social protest movement.[11]

Though this assessment is limited by its consideration of socioeconomic factors as being at the root of the rise of a religious opposition, it nonetheless provides an added dimension to the explanation of why the Islamic movement took the form that it did by the late 1970s. In contrast to Shabab al-Islam, which was made up of cosmopolitan middle class youth who had come of age during the height of Nasser's popularity, only to see their hopes dashed by economic stagnation and the 1967 defeat, al-Gama'a al-Islamiyya harbored no illusions about the regimes of Nasser and his unproven successor.

Indeed, many of the youth of this period asserted that they emerged with a strong sense of religiosity. Islam played a formative role in their upbringing and the development of their identity. In describing his generation, which he defined as "those of us born in the 1950s," Abul Futuh argued that even during the staunchly secular and nationalist Nasser era, Islam was everywhere to be found in his community.[12] It is true, he said, "[t]he regime was against any Islamic movement, but it was not against Islam itself. The Islamic *da'wa* was present, represented by al-Azhar, and various associations and institutions."[13]

Ibrahim al-Za'farani attended the Medical College at Alexandria University, where he became active in the Islamic movement in the early 1970s. However, he maintained that his strong religious identity was not acquired during his college years. Rather, growing up in a village in the Kafr al-Sheikh region, Za'farani found Islam to be deeply rooted in the identity of Egyptian villagers.[14] Describing his family and other villagers as "religious from birth," Za'farani added that many villagers were also resentful of the state's land reform policies, which had dispossessed many families of their land plots.[15] In his study of Nasser and Sadat's domestic economic policies, Hamied Ansari confirmed not only the contention that land policies were utilized by both regimes as a means of empowering supporters and disempowering political opponents, but that opposition was also frequently expressed in religious terms.[16]

From the Ordinary to the Exceptional

While the changing socioeconomic landscape helped lay the groundwork for the transformation of political activism within Egyptian universities and society at large, it was only one of several developments critical for the rise of a renewed Islamic movement. Leaders within the Islamic student movement stressed that while their religious consciousness played an important part in developing their identities as youth, they experienced an "ordinary" or "general" Islam that was no different from that which was pervasive within Egyptian society as a whole.[17] This tended to include an emphasis on core Islamic beliefs and rituals, and the elementary study of Islamic history and Qur'anic exegesis. Abul Futuh recalled that the only religious societies allowed to operate during the Nasser era were ones that were avowedly nonpolitical, such as al-Gam'iyya al-Shar'iyya, Gama'at Ansar al-Sunna, and the Sufi tariqas.[18] For much of his childhood, there seemed to be no contradiction between supporting Nasser's decidedly secular agenda and adhering to a general religiosity in one's personal and family life.

As noted previously, it was only after the shock of the 1967 defeat that cracks appeared in this arrangement. The sentiment expressed by the youth of this era reflected a stark realization that they could no longer abide by the Nasserist program and continue to live as Muslims. At a time when the pillars that had stood strong for nearly two decades were crashing down around them, Egyptians turned to their religious roots for answers. Abul Futuh recalled that, after the 1967 war, his neighborhood mosque became full of congregants eager to dig beneath the surface of basic Islamic teachings for more fulfilling answers to the core problems facing their society.[19]

Likening the fall of the "Nasserist revolution" to an "earthquake" that befell Egypt, and the whole Arab world for that matter, Abul Futuh maintained that out of the rubble emerged a class of notable Islamic scholars who sought to push the boundaries of acceptable topics of exploration and discussion.[20] Led by Sheikh Muhammad al-Ghazali, who preached at the historic mosque of 'Amr ibn al-'As in Cairo, these scholars infused the public discourse with a critique of the old order within an Islamic framework. Sheikh Sayyid Sabiq also emerged from the margins to educate the public on the role that Islam had to play in the future of the nation.[21]

Moreover, the Muslim Brotherhood, the maligned group that had for so long played the role of enemy of the revolution (and accordingly, the nation) was for the first time publicly mentioned in sympathetic terms. For the many Egyptians who became completely disillusioned with Nasser's leadership, his longtime critics began to be seen in a new light. Abul Futuh credited his local imam, Sheikh al-Bihairi, with helping launch the process of reintegrating the Muslim Brotherhood into the public consciousness. "He would defend the Brothers and say that they were good men who only wanted to build Egypt and wanted the best for its people, but they collided with Gamal Abdel Nasser."[22] During this period, and especially following Nasser's death in September 1970, the image of the Muslim Brotherhood was radically altered in the minds of many Egyptians, becoming "models of sacrifice and redemption for the sake of the nation."[23]

By that same token, however, "the perception of the Muslim Brotherhood as the possessor of a program for revival" was still several years away.[24] This was simply the earliest form of a process that continued throughout the decade, gaining more steam with the release of the Muslim Brotherhood's leaders from prison; it was accelerated further by the air of tolerance toward religious expression promoted in the early part of Sadat's rule. Contacts between the student movement and the Muslim Brotherhood were extremely rare during this period. Instead, the youth relied on intermediary, public figures, such as al-Ghazali, or local imams like al-Bihairi, to learn about the banned organization.

The nascent forces of opposition were by no means limited to the religious sphere. Though they ultimately launched what would become a decidedly Islamic movement, young students such as Abul Futuh and 'Esam al-'Erian also found inspiration in the emergence of other cultural trends. The voice of the frustrated and disenfranchised masses of Egypt found expression in the songs and poems of folk performers like poet Ahmed Fu'ad Negm and singer/composer al-Sheikh Imam 'Isa. Both came from humble origins in the Egyptian countryside, and following a brief traditional education, began long careers representing the poor and working class of Egypt in their popular folk songs. They spoke out against the political order at a time when it was far from safe to do so. Negm was imprisoned by Nasser following his scathing critique of the regime in the aftermath of the 1967 defeat, which he mourned with the words:

> *The state of Egypt is submerged under lies*
> *And the people are confused*
> *But everything is O.K. as long as our damned masters are happy*
> *Because of the poets who fill their stomach with poems*
> *Poems that glorify and appease even traitors*
> *With God's will, they will destroy the country.*[25]

Indeed, Negm later echoed the sentiments of many Egyptians toward the political awakening brought about by the *naksa*. "The '67 defeat," he said, "made me into a poet."[26] Moreover, by virtue of their subversive art,

Negm and Imam led a wave of Egyptians who began to question their leaders. According to Negm, until the June War "we used to believe what the state media would tell us."[27] Up until this historical moment, "people were afraid to speak out, for fear of imprisonment. But this collective fear is what led to the defeat, so I promised myself not to be fearful after that day, regardless of the consequences."[28]

The process of self-empowerment and social consciousness proceeded out of this pivotal historical moment. As Negm and Imam sang folk songs about poverty, political corruption, and national pride in the face of Western imperialism, a rising generation of Egyptians developed self-awareness, a certain cynicism and disbelief toward political elites, and a strong desire to seek alternative sources of information and accultura-tion. The duo spared no one in their sardonic reflections on powerful figures, from Nasser and Sadat, to Sha'rawi Gom'a, the notorious interior minister, and Richard Nixon, the US president. Even Umm Kulthum, the iconic songstress revered across the Arab world, was disparaged for her perceived elitism and propensity to act on behalf of the regime. With each public performance to which hundreds of Egyptians flocked, it became increasingly clear that a new era of popular culture and political con-sciousness was at hand.

Recounting his early days of student activism, 'Esam al-'Erian credited the emergence of an oppositional culture, led by figures such as Negm and Imam, with creating the fertile ground necessary for the rise of a new movement.[29] Akin to Bob Dylan and Pablo Neruda in the West, these art-ists delivered their message in plain and accessible language, connecting directly with the people they represented, and giving voice to a population that for decades had been silenced. For their troubles, Negm and Imam were frequently imprisoned, late in the Nasser era, and several times by Sadat, who was doubtlessly irked that his attempts at populism were con-stantly undermined by those truly in tune with the hopes and aspirations of the Egyptian populace.

The emergence of this cultural trend played a pivotal role in the rise of student activism in the 1970s. It aided in the formation of a distinct identity to define the up and coming generation, featuring a unique and poignant message articulated by cultural icons in the buoyant vernacular of youth. The ability to challenge the status quo, a quality at the heart of any popular social movement, was developed as a result of the confi-dence imbued in the student population in the wake of one of the lowest moments in modern Egyptian history. This was no easy feat, one that required the coalescence of a variety of social forces and cultural symbols. Building upon this effort, the young men entering university in the early 1970s became determined to transform their surrounding environment and empower themselves through the use of existing institutions.

In the fall of 1970, Abul Futuh entered Cairo University's College of Medicine. Having received the highest marks in his secondary school's graduating class, he was admitted to the most prestigious college program in Egypt. During the one-year pre-medical preparatory education program at the College of Science, Abul Futuh recalled that there was no semblance of religious activity on campus. The modest prayer space was not put to use by students. Abul Futuh and only one other student, 'Abd al-Shafi Sawi, who had arrived at Cairo from al-Minya in upper Egypt, would convene regularly for prayers between their classes.[30] The few religious students on campus had even more reason to feel isolated. Coming out of sheltered, conservative backgrounds, the younger students were stunned to discover their older colleagues publicly denigrating Islamic teachings and promoting a cultural and national identity devoid of any religious attachments.[31] In Alexandria, Za'farani had witnessed a similar environment. His first day of class at the Medical College coincided with Nasser's death, and classes were promptly canceled to allow the long-standing leader to be mourned by the university community, an event that set the tone for the remainder of the year.[32]

In the summer of 1971, the first efforts to organize the activities of the religiously oriented students were under way. Though they had returned to their hometowns across the country for the summer holidays, the students were determined to return to Cairo and discuss the future of their campus-wide activities.[33] The meeting took place at the Medical Center for Cardiac and Rheumatoid Care, under the supervision of 'Abd al-Mon'eim Abul Fadl, an accomplished physician, scientist, and educator who served as a mentor to the religious students. At the gathering, the students resolved to take a more active role in the propagation of their faith, and expand the scope of their activities to take on a slightly more politicized bent. On one level, this last point was a reflection of the increasingly politically charged atmosphere in Egypt during the early months of the Sadat regime. More specifically, it was also a direct consequence of the difficulties the students had faced in their confrontations with leftist activists.

The following year, as the students began their medical studies at the Qasr al-'Aini Medical School, they were astonished to find that in the span of a year, the student population had changed substantially, with the campus mosque filling with congregants during prayer time. Encouraged by this sudden rise of religious consciousness, several students attempted to expand the offerings of religious services beyond prayers to include Qur'anic study circles and communal breakfasts during the month of Ramadan. Soon, a group of students also determined to initiate campus-wide outreach, reacting to the long-standing anti-Islamic sentiments expressed by the contingent of leftist student activists.

Responding to this general air of hostility to their faith, Abul Futuh and other students posted wall magazines providing basic religious lessons and exploring issues of *halal* and *haram* (lawful and impermissible) in Islam. They also proceeded to escalate their awareness campaign, printing and distributing pamphlets, leaving short religious messages on the chalkboards of classrooms, and ultimately engaging the leftist students in heated debates on questions such as the compatibility of Islam with modern systems of governance.[34] But the leftist students had honed their debating skills for years, while the younger and more inexperienced students wishing to defend their faith found it difficult to counter many of the complex arguments being tossed their way. Abul Futuh and his colleagues turned inward, embarking on a journey of self-reflection and more sophisticated religious education.

Joined by future student leaders such as Muhammad Yousuf, Hasan 'Abd al-Fattah, Sanaa' Abu Zayd, and 'Abd al-Rahman Hasan, Abul Futuh approached Sheikh al-Ghazali for answers to the complex questions that many of them had never contemplated. The elder scholar patiently offered his expertise in regular talks at the 'Amr ibn al-'As mosque, while also referring them to a number of texts that delved into such matters in greater detail. "During this period," Abul Futuh recalled, "we discovered the routes to all the major Islamic bookshops."[35] The youth eagerly read seminal religious texts such as al-Ghazali's *'Aqeedat al-Muslim* (*The Doctrine of the Muslim*) and *Khuluq al-Muslim* (*The Behavior of the Muslim*). They were taken by Sheikh Sayyid Sabiq's humorous and personable style, and found his *Fiqh al-Sunna* (*Jurisprudence of the Tradition*) to be a definitive work of Islamic jurisprudence. Bahi al-Khouli's series of articles left a strong impression on Abul Futuh and his classmates, while 'Isa 'Abduh's lectures on Islamic economics were the first that any of them had ever heard on the topic.[36]

On the whole, this exposure to an elder intellectual class was instrumental in cultivating the activist mindset of the student movement of the 1970s. In essence, this didactic enterprise marshaled the transformation from an "ordinary" religiosity to the "exceptional" vision of Islam put forth by scholars in the modernist tradition. This Islamic educational movement initiated the development of "the idea of a civilizational project for the Ummah" within a new generation. "Though I was religious from a young age," Abul Futuh stated, "I had never heard of this before."[37]

Structural Evolution: Rise of the Islamic Society

With the growing political awareness of the students and the steady development of a more comprehensive vision of Islam's role in public life came an evolution in the content produced in wall magazines, booklets, and pamphlets. Some of this early political content focused on general critiques of the country's political and cultural elites, while pointing to exemplary models of just leadership from classical Islamic figures such as 'Umar ibn al-Khattab, the second caliph. These elementary writings also took on a broad nationalist tone, expressing strong opposition to the Zionist project and calling for the liberation of Arab lands.

During the course of these events, student activists faced frequent obstruction by the leadership of the Student Union, "which rejected even this simple religious activity and wished to control all student activism."[38] Wishing to operate through legitimate and authorized channels, the students organized their activities through the Committee for Religious Awareness (al-Taw'iya al-Diniyya), an extension of the Student Union's Cultural Committee that was set up by Abul Fadl several years earlier. Even with this official recognition of the religious committee's work, the Student Union repeatedly refused to provide the resources required by the students to conduct their activities, such as a meeting space and printing supplies. For students like Abul Futuh, this served as an early lesson in the importance of achieving political clout for the pursuit of his group's activities.

Following a frustrating second year that saw their activities hampered by the authority of the Student Union, the Islamic activists at Qasr al-'Aini Medical School went about reorganizing their mission under the banner of al-Gam'iyya al-Diniyya (the Religious Association). This move effectively replaced the previous Committee for Religious Awareness with a new, independent organization that was not subject to the oversight of the hostile Student Union. Since the group had enjoyed few of the benefits associated with being affiliated with the Student Union, members viewed the break as a positive step forward.

Freed from administrative constraints following this internal restructuring, the movement's program underwent considerable expansion, especially in the printing and distribution of reading materials, and the frequency of religious lectures and study circles. The structure featured a simple hierarchy: at the top was the amir, or leader, chosen through informal consensus by a consultative council, *majlis al-shura*, made up of a core group of the most active members. Finally, there was the general membership, or those students whose level of activity was limited to engaging in occasional public forums and other open programs. As most leaders stressed, the Islamic student movement, in its various incarnations, never had an official process for membership, did not provide identification cards, and did not maintain records or rolls of all who joined in its activities. Nor were there any dues or other monetary requirements, though all students were encouraged to donate for the support of the group's programs.[39]

Looking outward, the student leadership of al-Gam'iyya al-Diniyya also resolved to take on the Student Union directly by standing in elections beginning in 1973. Even as its activities flourished within a hostile environment, the Islamic movement believed that its mission of spreading the *da'wa*, or calling on their fellow students to reassert the place of Islam in their lives, could not be accomplished without the institutional support provided by the Student Union.[40] As Abul Futuh noted, taking control of the Student Union was not an end in itself for al-Gam'iyya al-Diniyya. Rather, it was part of a strategy to marginalize the leftist forces that had dominated campus activities and to carve out a permanent place for the Islamic movement.[41]

Deciding to run candidates in all six Student Union committees in the Medical College, al-Gam'iyya al-Diniyya aspired to make its presence felt and to test its growing strength among the student population. By the leadership's own account, the group even ran a candidate for the Arts Committee who not only had no qualifications for the post, but actually expressed outright hostility toward the arts.[42] Though they had mobilized a wide network of supporters, the religious students were not considered to be a credible threat to the leftist hold on the Student Union. It was only after leaders from al-Gam'iyya al-Diniyya won four out of six committee chairs that the long-standing leftist leadership realized that the Islamic student movement was slowly taking the mantle of authority over student activism.

In the wake of al-Gam'iyya al-Diniyya's victory, the campus witnessed a sudden surge in Islamic activism. This was due in part to the emergence of strong leaders within the movement's ranks. Having just started at the university earlier that year, younger students, like 'Esam al-'Erian and Muhammad 'Abd al-Latif, energized the movement and began to focus their energies on organizing their peers. More directly, however, in his new-found position as president of the Student Union, Abul Futuh ensured that al-Gam'iyya al-Diniyya received the requisite funds and access to resources to see its activities flourish. Sanaa' Abu Zayd was chosen to serve as amir by an inner circle of active members of al-Gam'iyya al-Diniyya. Together, the two close friends saw to it that their respective positions allowed for a well-coordinated strategy for the student movement.

In the contest for influence over the student body, however, Abul Futuh leaves no doubt that it was not the Student Union president, but rather the amir of al-Gam'iyya al-Diniyya who held the most sway over the rank-and-file of the student movement. "The real power," he said, "was in the hands of the amir."[43] As a result of the close relationship between Abul Futuh and Abu Zayd, and the conscious process of dividing the functions of their positions, the two leaders saw their roles as complementary to one another rather than adversarial in nature. While the position of Student Union president was viewed as one of a necessary functionary capable of delivering the means for the Islamic movement to progress, the amir was the spiritual head of the movement and was entrusted with cultivating its overarching vision and managing its daily affairs.

The term itself was chosen because of its classical Islamic connotation, harkening back to an idealized historical era in which religious and political leadership were wedded in the position of the caliph, also known as *amir al-mu'minin* (commander of the faithful).[44] This choice also reflected the central role that classical Islamic texts played in the formative period of the student movement. In stark contrast to the recent failures of secular leadership in Egypt, the model of just rulers during the golden era of Islam left a strong impression on the youth. The students referred to a particular Prophetic tradition that states, "If you are three, make one of you an amir."[45] This Hadith provided the inspirational framework for a simple organizational structure with one figure at its head, whose legitimacy stemmed directly from the initial consent of the group.

The traditional concept of *al-sam' wal-ta'a* (to listen and obey) was adopted to strengthen the authority of the amir, and set the leader apart from the general membership. Though there was the potential for abuse of power by demanding blind loyalty to the leader, students repeatedly stressed that no amir was ever interested in power for the sake of power. Indeed, Sayyid 'Abd al-Sattar al-Meligi, a student leader at 'Ain Shams University, believed that observing this concept was critical to the success of the movement during this stage.[46] Moreover, the selection of leaders generally occurred organically, with some activists demonstrating their qualities and developing a large following. The internal dynamic was marked by strong feelings of camaraderie and brotherhood, especially in light of the multitude of external adversaries facing the nascent Islamic movement.

Hand in hand with this vision of leadership, al-Gam'iyya al-Diniyya developed its structural hierarchy. This process took off following the spontaneous reevaluation of the group's name. Abul Futuh recalled that one day in 1973, as he and 'Abd al-Rahman Hasan were leaving their customary short Islamic lesson on the chalkboard, Abul Futuh questioned whether they should sign it "al-Gam'iyya al-Diniyya" in their usual manner. "Why do we not sign it 'al-Gama'a al-Islamiyya'?" he wondered.[47] The description was more expressive of the group's true character. It also evoked the name of a popular social movement organization founded in Pakistan by Mawlana Mawdudi who, incidentally, also served as that group's amir. At a time when the Muslim Brotherhood of Egypt was still in disarray, the Jamaat-i-Islami provided an exemplary model of a modern Islamic movement that held to its religious tradition while also operating within a contemporary political context. From that moment, as Abul Futuh and Hasan decided to sign off their daily moral with "al-Gama'a al-Islamiyya" (the Islamic Society), the organization was officially renamed for the last time.

Unlike the transition from al-Taw'iyya al-Diniyya to al-Gam'iyya al-Diniyya, the move from the latter to al-Gama'a al-Islamiyya featured no change to the group whatsoever, whether in its ideology or organizational structure.[48] Rather, this simple alteration in name reflected the Islamic movement's growing confidence with its mission, a settling on a distinct identity, and increased comfort with the political and sociocultural space in which it operated.[49] It demonstrated maturity on the part of a vibrant youth movement that had entered its fourth year at Cairo University's Medical College, and had begun to spread widely to other colleges and subsequently to other universities throughout the country.[50] Although prior groups had defined themselves as explicitly Islamic (most notably, Shabab al-Islam), what distinguished al-Gama'a al-Islamiyya was the introspective nature of its decision to redefine its organization. It was not depicting itself in opposition to the dominant secular, leftist political youth culture. Nor was it distinguishing its religious identity from those of non-Muslim activists. Rather, it represented the culmination of the struggle to achieve organizational cohesion and the process of intellectual contemplation of the nature of Islamic activism itself. The "association" had become a "society." The "religious" had become "Islamic." The movement had become self-aware.

The Amir of Amirs

Within a year, al-Gama'a al-Islamiyya had spread to every other college at Cairo University and indeed, to nearly every university within Egypt. The growth experienced by the group after 1973 came as a result of a combination of factors: the appearance of a new class of energetic youth at other colleges and universities eager to extend the *da'wa* on their campuses; and the presence of a strong, centralized leadership at the Medical College willing to play the role of mentor to branch groups around the country. Following the initial stage of launching the movement and establishing its central organization, the period of 1974–1977 featured al-Gama'a al-Islamiyya's consolidation of the national Islamic student movement under its leadership.

The evolution of al-Gama'a al-Islamiyya's organizational structure granted the central leadership the institutional capacity with which to nurture the growth of corresponding groups. During the 1974–1975 academic year, the leaders at the Medical College created a council of amirs from every chapter of al-Gama'a al-Islamiyya at Cairo University. When the council convened for the first time, it elected 'Esam al-'Erian, the recently chosen amir of the Medical College chapter, as the head of this council.[51] In his capacity as the amir of Cairo University, al-'Erian effectively managed the mission and activities of the entire organization. During biweekly meetings, leaders at other colleges looked to his leadership on a number of fronts, from which texts and scholars to consult and how to confront challenges from leftist students, to how to attract a wide following, compete in union elections, and maximize the utility of resources available to them.[52] This disciplined and coordinated strategy was critical in establishing al-Gama'a al-Islamiyya as the preeminent student organization for the remainder of the decade.

In 1977, the organization decided to expand even further, calling for a meeting of all amirs from every university in Egypt. At the summit, student leaders selected Helmi al-Gazzar, the young activist from the Cairo University Medical College, as the amir of the council. This latest development saw the organization reach the fruition of its structural evolution. In the preceding years, it had succeeded in establishing a strong presence at every Egyptian university, and now it had seen to it that all of these chapters were linked directly through a communications and strategy network and were brought under the umbrella of a powerful, centralized leadership. In his capacity as amir of the body that oversaw every chapter of al-Gama'a al-Islamiyya, al-Gazzar became one of the most influential leaders in the history of Egyptian student activism. His command over a sizable contingent of the student body put him directly at odds with the president of the republic, who was becoming increasingly ineffective at reaching the restive youth. When al-Gazzar was among the many activists arrested in the expansive security sweeps in late 1981, Sadat mockingly referred to him as "amir-ul-umara" (amir of amirs).[53]

Al-Gazzar's selection as the head of a national council of amirs signaled the consolidation of al-Gama'a al-Islamiyya's authority over the national Islamic movement. Chapters at other colleges and universities looked to the movement that started it all, at the Cairo University Medical College, for wisdom and guidance on how to proceed in developing their own mission. This consultation required a high degree of coordination, and as such, leaders in Cairo engaged in frequent written correspondence and even took occasional trips to campuses throughout Egypt, "from Alexandria to Aswan."[54] The Cairo leadership would also take advantage of annual summer camps to spend time with leaders from other chapters.

A primary purpose of these meetings was to identify the most active figures at other universities and to designate an amir in the event that one was needed to fill an opening. Among the criteria Abul Futuh, al-'Erian, and al-Gazzar used to select a chapter head was their personal religious observance and general behavior, in addition to their record of student activism. In practice, however, this usually entailed simple affirmation of leaders already in place as the heads of their respective groups, rather than handpicking individuals who were otherwise unknown. The intra-organizational responsibilities added to the growing list of demands on the time and resources of the core group at the Cairo University Medical College, so much that the leaders would have to finance the long-distance trips out of their own pockets and in some instances delegate the task to their colleagues.[55]

In this fashion, al-Gama'a al-Islamiyya established a vast network that allowed for the growth of a vibrant movement with a strong structural hierarchy. Leaders in Cairo welcomed the opportunity to work with amirs across the country, such as veteran activist Za'farani in Alexandria, Anwar Shahata in Tanta, and Muh'iddin 'Isa in Assiut. Before long, the amir in Cairo became looked upon as a *murshid* (guide) to groups everywhere, according to Abul Futuh.[56] There was no conscious determination to emulate the model instituted by the Muslim Brotherhood and its role of *al-murshid al-'am* (general guide), but the fact remained that as it solidified its structural hierarchy, placing an authoritative head with symbolic as well as actual powers at the top, al-Gama'a al-Islamiyya was becoming increasingly akin to the banned organization. Due to his vast following and the respect he commanded, the student *murshid*'s authority trumped even that of the union president, though as long as the unions remained in the hands of the Islamic movement, the amir rarely had cause to exert his authority over a body that followed his lead on matters of activism.

Parallel with these developments was the continuing success of the Islamic movement within Student Union elections. Though it had enjoyed early victories at Cairo University, al-Gama'a al-Islamiyya's hold on the Student Unions remained tenuous for several years. When prominent leftist activist Ziyad 'Abd al-Qadir 'Awda ran against Abul Futuh in the 1976 union elections, Abul Futuh emerged victorious by only two votes, 86–84.[57]

Elsewhere, electoral advances were far more gradual. In Alexandria, the first elections contested by the Islamic movement came in 1973, when its leaders won 50 percent of the votes across the various positions. Za'farani recalled that, at the time, few students knew much about al-Gama'a al-Islamiyya, but the group benefited from the rampant corruption and nepotism for which the established union leadership had become known.[58] Framing themselves in contrast to their opponents, the Islamic movement's leaders became notable for their strong moral character, having worked for charitable causes and having denounced the corrupt practices and lack of transparency within the union. By 1975, their victory was far more sweeping, and only a year later, al-Gama'a al-Islamiyya had come to control virtually the whole Student Union at Alexandria University. Though he served as amir of the Medical College's chapter, Za'farani also served on political and cultural committees of the union, and later became its treasurer.[59]

Participation occurred even more slowly in upper Egypt. Abul 'Ela Madi, a student leader at al-Minya University, recalled that al-Gama'a al-Islamiyya was highly resistant to the idea of engaging the Student Union, because of the endemic corruption within it, and its connection to the regime.[60] On a fundamental level, though, there appeared to be an aversion among more traditional students in upper Egypt to participation in Western-inspired democratic models that did not preface their institutional structures with the supremacy of divine commandments. It was only after a series of intense discussions among student leaders on a national level that the last of al-Gama'a al-Islamiyya's leaders came around to the idea of institutional engagement.

Madi credited Abul Futuh in particular, whom he first encountered at the 1976 Islamic camp in Cairo, with convincing hesitant student leaders to participate in union elections. The following year, after Abul Futuh's confrontation with Sadat, Madi and several other student leaders visited him to demonstrate their solidarity in the aftermath of the affair. During the ensuing discussions, "he convinced us all to join the elections in November. Though many of us thought the Student Union was a corrupt institution, he told us it could be used for harm as well as good, and it contained many resources to help us expand our work."[61]

Sure enough, by late 1977, al-Gama'a al-Islamiyya had contested union elections at every major university in Egypt, sweeping leadership posts in all of them. Madi himself was elected to the national union, becoming vice president of the powerful body. For the student activists of upper Egypt, however, this experiment with institutional engagement would prove to be short-lived, as the regime clamped down on all participation in 1979, reversing all electoral gains made and handpicking future union leaders.[62] Nonetheless, the experience proved invaluable. According to its leading participants, success in Student Union elections proved that al-Gama'a al-Islamiyya represented a true vision of Islam with which many Egyptian youth identified, and that its leadership was capable of running state institutions and could be entrusted with the future of the nation more so than any of its rivals.[63]

The Freedom Factor

Early in the process of making significant gains in its program, the Islamic student movement became keenly aware that its behavior would be subject to the scrutiny of its peers and the regime. Long aided by the Nasser regime in its pursuit of a broad national consensus over major policies, leftist student groups found themselves in the unfamiliar position of being the most vocal opposition to the government beginning in 1968. Their conflict with the state escalated with the rise of Sadat, who had no socialist credentials to speak of, and was rapidly transforming the regime by expelling prominent leftist figures and initiating economic liberalization measures. With the rise of a new political force, diametrically opposed to the leftist political culture and vision that dominated the universities, the Islamic movement understood that it would face accusations of acting at the behest of the young regime.

Activists from the era acknowledged that they were frequently charged with being a tool of Sadat to quash the leftist movement. Abul Futuh responded simply that:

> as someone who lived this period, and was among those who founded the Islamic activism within it, I would have been in a position in which no details of an agreement between Sadat and the Islamic movement would have passed me by. In fact, I can say with certainty that any such agreement with Sadat would have been done with me personally, in my capacity as leader of the Islamic student movement, and God is our witness that we did not make an agreement with the regime, or with anyone.[64]

Badr Muhammad Badr, the amir at Cairo University's College of Communication in the late 1970s, echoed those sentiments, declaring that while Sadat was advised to capitalize on the rise of Islamic movements to suppress his leftist opponents, "these offers by the regime did not succeed in convincing the principled ones to work for its benefit."[65] Rather, most leaders from al-Gama'a al-Islamiyya maintained that the regime's efforts to co-opt Islamic activism came in the form of its support for (or according to some, creation of) Shabab al-Islam, the short-lived group that featured in the early 1970s. In support of this claim, they cite the observed behavior of this competing group's members, as well as the testimony of its leaders.[66]

Most leaders from al-Gama'a al-Islamiyya readily admitted that they judged the suitability and, indeed, the commitment of their fellow students to Islamic activism based on outward appearances: demonstrations of personal piety, observing regular prayers, maintaining beards and traditional dress, self-segregating from members of the opposite sex and non-religious students, and general avoidance of popular cultural practices like listening to music and going to the cinema. By these standards, some of the students who publicly proclaimed to be members of Shabab al-Islam fell fall short of expectations. Abul Futuh recalled hearing from 'Esam al-Sheikh, the amir of al-Gama'a al-Islamiyya at the Engineering College of Cairo University, that "'we did not know who these students were who made up Shabab al-Islam, for they did not join us in any prior activity, but now they speak openly to students about Islam, even standing with female students and talking to them about Islam. We came to the conclusion then that these students from Shabab al-Islam were not observant and therefore did not align with us."[67]

This was a widespread sentiment among Islamic activists, some of whom went further in condemning Shabab al-Islam's members for not adhering to "Islamic manners and behavior, for they would smoke cigarettes openly and engage female students in the colleges. This was unacceptable from the perspective of a Muslim youth fulfilling Islamic manners."[68] Moreover, critics added that Shabab al-Islam attempted to usurp the activism of al-Gama'a al-Islamiyya (and its forerunners) by holding its own lectures and seminars in which it would only invite state religious figures promoted by the regime.[69]

In support of their suspicions of Shabab al-Islam, these critics also noted that leaders such as Wa'il 'Uthman and 'Adli Mustafa readily admitted being approached by regime figures to promote the interests of Sadat.[70] Though this was in fact true, 'Uthman and Mustafa categorically denied making any agreement or accepting any offers of support, a point neglected by their detractors from al-Gama'a al-Islamiyya. As described in greater detail in Chapter 2, the distrust between the groups was mutual, and was owed in part to the cultural differences between them, but also to actual evidence of regime intervention in the form of copycat groups, unauthorized chapters of Shabab al-Islam that emerged in other colleges.

By characterizing the regime's attempts to incorporate the Islamic movement into its own program as having occurred solely through the efforts with Shabab al-Islam, al-Gama'a al-Islamiyya effectively removed any doubts about the genuine nature of its own mission. Abul Futuh repeatedly stated that his movement was "natural" and "spontaneous," without any guidance from the authorities. Though they frequently leveled charges of collaboration, even leftist critics of the Islamic movement have generally pointed only to indirect contacts, usually conducted through university officials, something al-Gama'a al-Islamiyya has also not denied.

An important figure whose name frequently appears in discussions on the rise of Islamic activism within Egyptian universities is Sufi Abu Talib. Trained as a lawyer, Abu Talib was an accomplished scholar who rose to become the vice president of Cairo University in 1973. His sympathies toward the Islamic movement were widely known, especially in the face of a leftist resurgence during the early Sadat years. Abu Talib was the architect of the effort to incorporate Shari'a statutes into Egypt's legal code; he became the speaker of the Egyptian parliament in 1978, remaining in that post through the end of the Sadat era.

During his tenure as a high-ranking university official, however, he was in frequent contact with student leaders, providing moral and logistical support for their activities. Abul Futuh recalled that in one instance during his time as Student Union president, he and Muhammad 'Abd al-Latif, vice president of the Medical College Student Union, were approached by Abu Talib, who was incensed about a demonstration scheduled by leftist activists. According to Abul Futuh, Abu Talib asked the two student leaders, "'How can you allow them to hold a protest?' so I said to him, 'they are free to do that.' He replied, provocatively, 'How? You are unable to stop them?' so 'Abd al-Latif responded to him, 'we are not batons to be used to club others.'"[71]

Though the student movement frequently challenged his authority to control its activities, youth leaders generally enjoyed a good relationship with Abu Talib. He helped the students organize the elaborate annual summer camps, and even felt comfortable enough with some of them to tell Abul Futuh, for instance, when he thought his beard had grown too long and needed to be trimmed.[72] Abu Talib's support for the Islamic movement could be (and often was) construed as official sanction of al-Gama'a al-Islamiyya by the regime.[73] Given the severe restrictions on independent student activism strictly enforced by the Nasser regime, the relative freedom provided by Sadat could easily be viewed through the lens of his narrow political objectives. But if that were the case, many student leaders argued, the regime would have placed barriers before other political movements and would have created a space in which only the

Islamic movement would be allowed to operate. In reality, Sadat granted equal freedom to all ideological trends. This was predicated upon an assumption by the president that, if left to their own devices, Egyptians would gravitate toward their Islamic identity and away from the leftist ideologies cultivated by Nasser.[74]

During the early years of the Sadat regime, this indeed appeared to be the case. Egyptians enjoyed political freedoms that had been unknown since the revolution two decades earlier. Abul Futuh emphasized that at no time during its rise did the student movement feel threatened by the regime. They met in the open, held meetings that brought thousands of students from across the country, marched through the streets of different cities in protest, distributed books of varying political viewpoints, and invited Islamic scholars of all ideological stripes.[75] According to student leaders, at no time did the regime attempt to block these activities. In fact, there was not even a sense among the students that the state security apparatus was monitoring these events with concern. The university guard was withdrawn early on, a move that sent a clear message to the student movement that it was free to organize and speak openly within the confines of its campuses.

In hindsight, this illustration may appear to have been exaggerated, given some of the periodic excesses of Sadat and the swift security clampdown that occurred after 1977, but in the promising early years, the students genuinely felt no fear of retribution and believed "the world was opened before us."[76] By 1975, as it appeared that even the Muslim Brotherhood, the banned organization regarded as the chief public enemy of the Nasser regime, was no longer subject to the same restrictions, the student movement believed strongly in the freedom to act without restraint. Viewed more critically, however, these policies were not part of a broad program of political liberalization, but rather a short-term effort to solidify Sadat's legitimacy that began with the Corrective Revolution of May 1971 and was extended after the October War of 1973 that saw Sadat's popularity reach unprecedented heights.

Additionally, the opened social space for political expression went hand in hand with the *infitah* policy for economic liberalization that sought to engage a greater segment of the Egyptian population—particularly young professionals and entrepreneurs—in the expanding national economy. The annual growth witnessed by the Egyptian economy, reaching 8 percent at its height, provided Sadat with a new political base of support that allowed him "to adapt the authoritarian state to the growing social and

ideological pluralization of the political arena."⁷⁷ In essence, the freedom experienced by the student movement was a transitory means to an
end: achieving full de-Nasserization and consolidating Sadat's authority.
However, this did not make it any less meaningful for the students of al-
Gama'a al-Islamiyya. And its effects were demonstrable.

Building the Complete Muslim

Rarely has a youth movement exhibited such ambition as the Islamic
student movement of the 1970s, and for it to have singlehandedly transformed the social and political scene in Egypt is even more extraordinary.
The accomplishments of al-Gama'a al-Islamiyya stem from its pursuit of a
simple objective: spreading its *da'wa*. In a typical early document entitled
"Our *Da'wa*," al-Gama'a al-Islamiyya declared to the student body that:

> [t]he *da'wa* of al-Gama'a al-Islamiyya is simple and clear. It is neither
> complicated nor ambiguous. Nonetheless, rarely do we find anyone
> in the university who understands it correctly. Our call is the call
> of Islam, the call to establish society on an Islamic foundation. Our
> thought is unwaveringly Islamic. And we understand Islam, good
> brother, within the bounds of these twenty principles.⁷⁸

The statement proceeded to list the famous Twenty Principles, first articulated by Hasan al-Banna, that detail the central beliefs of the pious
Muslim. They begin with a general statement on the comprehensive
nature of Islam as a system to govern all aspects of life, and move on
to describe particular ideals, such as following the exemplary model of
Prophetic leadership, emphasizing the centrality of holy scripture, implementing divine law, and remaining vigilant against forces that threaten
the faith.

This public pronouncement captures the first stage of the activist mission of the Islamic student movement, the practice known as *tarbiya*, or
religious instruction.⁷⁹ Programs for Islamic education accounted for the
vast majority of student activities, especially during the early period of
campus organizing. In fact, al-Gama'a al-Islamiyya developed a strict curriculum that it promoted among its members. In another document it
published, entitled "Why al-Gama'a al-Islamiyya?" the group declared,
"al-Gama'a al-Islamiyya fulfills its role in cultivating a generation of youth
able to face the plans of its enemies, the enemies of God, and calls on all of

you to join it in its educational program for the coming year."[80] In the long list of instructions, students were told to memorize the thirtieth part of the Qur'an, the first fifteen Hadiths out of a popular published collection of forty, and to study Qur'anic exegesis and the elementary procedures of Islamic jurisprudence, or fiqh. Alongside each instruction, specific book recommendations were listed, with Sabiq's *Fiqh al-Sunna* featuring prominently.

The program laid out by the *tarbiya* list was expected to be accomplished within an academic year. Additional lists supplemented the original program, suggesting more advanced texts to build upon one's knowledge and collectively expand the intellectual horizons of the student movement. Though these were individual targets that all committed members were expected to meet, the didactic process was in most instances a collective effort. Students shared books, many of which were loaned out from al-Gama'a al-Islamiyya's library collection. Weekly study circles were meant to enhance the knowledge achieved from texts and, at times, even afforded students the opportunity to meet the authors of some of the seminal works in contemporary Islamic thought.

But the activity most critical to the process of *tarbiya* was the annual summer camps organized by al-Gama'a al-Islamiyya in conjunction with the Student Union.[81] These camps featured intensive programs designed not only to instruct the students in matters of Islamic belief, but also to provide them with an avenue to practice an idealized interpretation of Islamic precepts during their daily interactions. Held at Cairo University in the summer of 1973, the first of these camps featured an appearance by Ahmed Kamal Abul Magd, Sadat's minister of youth.[82] Also in Cairo, 'Ain Shams University held a parallel camp that included forty students from al-Azhar University.[83] Shorter camps held at individual colleges during the winter holiday also became a regular occurrence. The following year, the Cairo University camp was greatly expanded, and welcomed the involvement of two Islamic luminaries, Sheikh Muhammad al-Ghazali and Sheikh Yousuf al-Qaradawi.[84] The camp format spread across Egypt in subsequent years until, by 1977, every major university in Egypt was holding its own Islamic summer camp. Though they were some of the latest to join in these programs, universities in al-Minya, Assiut, and Mansoura quickly became some of the most active in the country, while the impact of Alexandria University was second only to the developments in Cairo.

A look at a typical program from an Islamic summer camp is indicative of its rigorous nature, and illustrates how it was effective in accomplishing much in a relatively short time:[85]

3:00: Wakeup for overnight prayer
4:00: Call to prayer
4:20: Dawn prayer
4:50: Morning religious remembrance
5:20: Lessons in Qur'anic recitation
6:10: Prepare for morning exercise line
6:30: Morning exercise line
7:30: Prepare breakfast
8:00: Breakfast
9:00: Free reading period
10:00: Morning lecture
12:00: Noon prayer
12:45: Afternoon rest
15:00: Lunch
15:30: Afternoon prayer
16:30: Evening lecture
18:00: Evening religious remembrance
19:00: Sunset prayer
19:30: Dinner
20:00: Night prayer
20:30: Committee meetings
21:30: Sleep

In the midst of this intensive combination of spiritual observance and instruction, intellectual discussion, and physical activity, the youth developed and matured in all aspects of their lives and established strong bonds and feelings of camaraderie with one another. Moreover, the emphasis on discipline, which was at the heart of these activities, translated into a solid organizational foundation for the remainder of the year. In fact, one leader recalled that students living on the university campuses enforced a similar program in their dormitories year-round, observing regular communal prayers, sharing meals, and joining together in athletic events when they were not busy studying or pursuing their other intellectual activities.[86]

For many students, their first real exposure to the Islamic movement came in the form of attending these camps. Such was the case with Gamal 'Abd al-Salam, who would become active in al-Gama'a al-Islamiyya at the Medical College of Cairo University. Although he entered the university in 1975, it was not until he attended the summer camp of 1976 that he became dedicated to the Islamic movement.[87] There, he witnessed first-hand the *da'wa* of the elder generation of accomplished scholars tailored and delivered directly to the youth by figures like Qaradawi, Ghazali, 'Abd al-Mut'ali Gabr, and Mustafa Mashhur.

The process of indoctrination was reinforced throughout the year by similar events held within the university walls. Public lectures, closed seminars, and daylong conferences, all building on Islamic themes, became permanent fixtures on the academic calendar. Access to Student Union resources also provided al-Gama'a al-Islamiyya with the ability to publish Islamic booklets, many of which simply rehashed older texts, though they became available to a new generation for the first time. Abul Futuh edited a periodical entitled *Sawt al-Haqq* (*Voice of Truth*), one of the first to reintroduce the writings of Hasan al-Banna and Sayyid Qutb, which had been banned by Nasser, and was only permitted to resume publication in 1974. Mahmoud Ghozlan, an instructor at the Cairo University College of Agriculture, selected most of the excerpts, which included classical as well as modern scholars, and covered a wide array of issues.[88]

At al-Minya University, students even took liberties with these texts, refashioning them to suit the current political, social, and ideological climate. Madi, for instance, recalled that of the Twenty Principles of Hasan al-Banna, al-Gama'a al-Islamiyya only published eighteen, out of concern that two of Banna's points about the nature of spirituality and its practices would offend the sensibilities of the more conservative Salafi students who had adopted an outlook that was highly critical of Sufism.[89]

The Student Union also allocated a portion of its budget to subsidize student trips to the holy cities of Mecca and Medina, whether for smaller 'Umrah visits, or as part of the annual Hajj pilgrimage. Costing students a mere 35 Egyptian pounds, these trips were immensely successful, allowing up to 100,000 students, male and female, to visit Saudi Arabia during the mid-to-late 1970s, according to one estimate.[90] At a time when Saudi Arabia was expanding its regional influence, politically and economically, the effects of the cultural component that resulted from the interaction between impressionable Egyptian youth and established scholars trained in the Wahhabi tradition were rather considerable. Egyptian university students were attracted to the pure and uncompromised interpretation of their faith that they encountered in the holy cities, and attempted to incorporate some of these teachings in their own practices. This yielded the suspicious view of Sufism as a deviation from Islam, and the hostility toward music, film, and other cultural forms for which Egypt had been known.

Along with these brief but momentous trips, students were also influenced by the boom in book production coming from the Gulf. Upon returning home from the pilgrimage, students often discovered crates of books that had been shipped to them, free of charge, by their hosts in Saudi Arabia. Often focusing on matters of ritual practices and the interpretation of law, these texts, from groups like Ansar al-Sunna al-Muhammadiyya and al-Dar al-Salafiyya, made their way into the hands of many students, through the library of al-Gama'a al-Islamiyya, as well as the weekly book fairs.[91] These were typically held out in the open on the university grounds, and quickly became one of the most successful programs sponsored by the Islamic movement. Student leaders acquired Islamic books from publishers across Cairo and Alexandria, and offered them to their peers at discounted rates. This spurred an intellectualized campus culture that revolved around religious topics and provided a common frame of reference for the discourse of the student movement. As an added service to their fellow students, leaders also provided academic textbooks for a variety of courses at heavily subsidized prices. They even obtained permission from professors to photocopy their most important works to provide to the student body, a large percentage of whom could not otherwise afford to purchase textbooks.[92]

At a time when retail markets had not kept up with changing fashion trends among the youth, student vendors took pride in their ability to offer modest dress to female students. The Islamic headscarf and modern forms of traditional dress became widespread among the female student population. This initiative was consistent with the emphasis on outward appearances among the leadership of the Islamic movement. Female students also maintained regular study circles held in parallel with those of male students, and hosted female guest lecturers, like Zainab al-Ghazali. Another major project lauded by the Student Union was the establishment of segregated public transportation for female students. While this was occasionally billed as an issue of safety—providing female students with a secure means of traveling through the city without risk of harassment or attack—it was also part of the growing effort to enforce public morality by decreasing interaction between male and female students. Badr described the program as "highly successful," noting that it was particularly important at the Medical College at Cairo University, whose students often had to study long hours.[93]

In all, the religious and cultural activities made up the bulk of al-Gamaʻa al-Islamiyya's program. From its humble beginnings convening for obligatory prayers in the tiny college prayer room, it demonstrated great maturation as its lectures and camps witnessed thousands of eager youth clamoring to interact with their peers and learn from the established scholars of the day. Its activities soon spread beyond the university, epitomized in the biannual celebration of Islamic holiday by holding religious services out in the open, as per Islamic custom. By 1981, the last of these ʻeid prayers permitted by Sadat brought over half a million congregants, young and old alike, to the ʻAbidin Square in Cairo and to the Alexandria Stadium.[94] Additionally, al-Gamaʻa al-Islamiyya succeeded in generating goodwill among students and society at large by engaging in social services, such as providing volunteer medical care, handing out toys to children during the holidays, and organizing athletic clubs and tournaments. But while the expanding religious and cultural offerings of al-Gamaʻa al-Islamiyya reflected a group that had matured over the course of several years, its entry into political activism provides a more precise measure of its evolution.

Taking a Stand

During the formative years of the Islamic student movement, religiously oriented students rarely took an interest in politics. In this sense, the students who formed Shabab al-Islam were exceptional. They took an immediate interest in the political issues of the day and framed them from an Islamic perspective. On the whole, however, outright political activism remained the domain of the leftist movement. The relationship between the leftists and the nascent Islamic movement was tenuous at best. In the contentious political discourse between the students of al-Gamʻiyya al-Diniyya and their leftist peers who dominated the Student Union in the early 1970s, the religious students were quickly shown to have been out of their depth, even when the conversation touched upon the subject of Islam's role in public life.[95] In the face of complex political arguments that made use of modern historical experiences and recent intellectual trends, the young Islamic activists could do little more than recite simple religious morals.

In other instances, the Islamic groups followed the lead of the dominant political forces within the student movement, and even joined in their activities, such as the protest movement of 1972–1973, for instance, that were led by Ahmed Abdalla.[96] On broad issues with a national popular consensus, such as accountability for the 1967 defeat, readiness for a new confrontation with Israel, and the expansion of political freedoms, all students joined in solidarity with the leaders of the leftist opposition. In practical terms, however, the Islamic groups, according to Abul Futuh, "were still taking baby steps in the realm of student activism."[97] Instead, the formative period of the Islamic movement focused purely on the mission of *tarbiya*, and left political discussions aside.

In addition to the external pressures that came from the rivalry with leftist student activists, three factors can be singled out as drivers for the politicization of the Islamic student movement. They can be categorized, roughly, as intellectual, institutional, and social. As reading lists and symposiums became more varied and sophisticated, student leaders began to take on a more politicized outlook toward the issues of concern to them. Rather than engaging with the old guard on matters of belief and ritual practice, students probed them for their experiences in Islamic activism during the pre-revolutionary era, a time when all ideological trends were making competing claims for political authority. Moreover, the success in Student Union elections was an inherently politicized moment in the history of the young Islamic movement. As Za'farani recalled, this experience put the students in the unfamiliar position of having to take on immediate obligations within a state institution, compelling them "to learn responsibilities and attain leadership skills," and perhaps most important, to "know how the country works."[98]

Finally, the politicizing effect of the October War on a new generation of Egyptian youth was particularly significant within the budding Islamic trend. As a war that was framed in Islamic terms, the debate surrounding the role of religion in politics witnessed an immediate rejuvenation in the aftermath of the conflict. As Egypt emerged from the war in a stronger position and Sadat became known as the "Hero of the Crossing," political Islam's popular image was changed, virtually overnight, from a public menace that posed a threat to the regime, to offering a foundation for a new social contract. The only remaining question was who would impose their vision of Islam's role in the state: the regime to society, or vice versa.

Answering that call, many student leaders underscored the empower-ment they felt after 1973, which spurred a *sahwa diniyya* (religious awak-ening) across all segments of Egyptian society, but particularly within the student movement.[99]

As al-Gama'a al-Islamiyya settled into its political identity, the organi-zation displayed a strong ability to tackle issues that were local, regional, and global in scope. It responded to events as they occurred, even as it also set its own agenda. In the initial stages of political activism, the stu-dent movement focused on issues that were at the forefront of the public discourse in Egypt. Despite the strong showing by the military in 1973, the October War ended without the liberation of the occupied territories. The subsequent years would witness a tense national discussion on the strategy to capitalize on the gains of the war. By 1977, however, it had emerged that the regime's policy choices were diverging widely from the preferences of the Egyptian people, especially the increasingly vocal Is-lamic movement.

On the domestic front, zealous youth had taken to heart the message conveyed in the course of their religious education. They believed in the need to promote Islamic principles in public life, ranging from enforc-ing tenets of public morality, to rooting out corruption, promoting social justice, and enacting political reforms. According to this view, all of these goals could be accomplished through adherence to Islamic judicial codes. At a time when Sadat was pressing for reforms to the constitution, the Is-lamic movement advocated a revival of the Shari'a as the basis for govern-ing the Egyptian state. These two issues, the liberation of lands occupied by Israel and the implementation of the Shari'a, became the cornerstones of al-Gama'a al-Islamiyya's foreign and domestic policy agendas, as well as at the roots of the group's conflict with the state.

The activist strategy on political mobilization generally followed a common formula. As they became more politically aware, students closely monitored the issues of the day, reading newspapers and magazines, lis-tening to radio reports, and discussing the content with their peers and elders. Upon further deliberations among themselves, the student leader-ship would frequently articulate its position on a given issue in the form of a public statement or a wall magazine. These were intended to raise public awareness on the issue, as much as they aimed to advance a par-ticular position or response. In many instances, this initial consideration of the issue would be followed by an open lecture or conference featuring respected guest speakers or experts in a given area.

On matters that took on added significance within a broader political context, al-Gama'a al-Islamiyya would devote an entire week to events and activities covering a specific theme. These "awareness weeks" created a wide array of channels through which to communicate the critical nature of a given issue, including posters, photo displays, public statements, lectures, town hall meetings, and book fairs.[100] Student leaders chose the theme on the basis of its timeliness, such as the Soviet invasion of Afghanistan, but were also known to have impressed upon their classmates a number of issues that they thought were pertinent to the emerging public discourse, such as the status of women in Islam. Other topics included the Islamic position on Palestine, the status of Muslim minorities around the world, and secularism and Islam.

Finally, with regard to certain issues that took on a sense of urgency, the student movement would on occasion expand its mission beyond education and raising awareness to include anti-state contention. Leaders wrote letters and held meetings with regime officials and organized demonstrations and sit-ins within the university. In some cases, as in the 1977 Bread Riots, students even made a concerted decision to join in nationwide protests against the regime, taking to the streets of major cities and confronting security forces. On the whole, al-Gama'a al-Islamiyya shaped a unique political culture within Egyptian universities. Gone were the radical leftist politics of the 1960s and early 1970s. Catchy slogans, satirical articles, and political cartoons soon became obsolete.[101] They were replaced by long-winded and serious-minded explanations of religious principles and lofty calls for refashioning the Egyptian state on the basis of Islam.

Following Sadat's 1976 announcement of political liberalization measures, complete with the establishment of a multiparty system, the student movement expressed its opposition to what it perceived as an attempt by the regime to consolidate all independent political movements under its control. In a press release entitled "To God Is the Power, and to His Prophet and the Believers," al-Gama'a al-Islamiyya expressed its opposition to Sadat's policy and to the political system in general. "Islam cannot be established without politics, just as there cannot be politics without religion," it began.[102] "The parties established maintain that they cannot be built on an Islamic basis, based on the Law of the Parties, and even those that mention the Shari'a among their programs, it is listed as a low priority, and to shield the people from reality."

The emerging hard-line position against the state's political initiatives was due in part to Sadat's own hostile expressions toward the aspirations of the Islamic movement. Following his comment that "there is no politics in religion, or religion in politics," student leaders issued lengthy responses attempting to disprove the premise of Sadat's statement. By their own accord, the reaction among the student population was "full of anger, rejection, and denial."[103] Group leaders held a conference at Cairo University, attended by more than ten thousand students, and presided over by leading scholars, that engaged with the president's statement, paying particular attention to the legal justifications provided by high-ranking officials at al-Azhar. The conference issued a statement in the form of a letter addressed to the president, which was also sent to every major newspaper, though none chose to run it. The unpublished letter, dated February 28, 1979, stated in part:

> We begin with a specific question: is Egypt an Islamic state or a secular state? The answer must be based on the constitution, which states that Egypt is an Islamic state. So what does it mean for Egypt to be an Islamic state? Is Islam only worship and slogans, fulfilled solely in the mosques, without any relationship to organizing the affairs of life?
>
> The call to separate religion from politics has no basis in Islam. It is a concept that is imported from the West. As such, the accusation that the callers to Islam in its totality and perfection are hiding behind religion to achieve power is mistaken. It does not matter much to us who rules . . . what matters to us is what does he rule by, and how does he rule?[104]

The students carried the spirit of this message with them as they contested the regime's policies on a host of issues, such as the Personal Status Law passed in 1979. Known popularly as "Jehan's Law," because it was heavily promoted by Egypt's first lady, Jehan al-Sadat, the law challenged dominant social norms by granting increased marital rights to women, while restricting practices like polygamy. Chief among the opposition to the law was al-Gama'a al-Islamiyya, which characterized it as an affront to long-standing cultural practices that were sanctioned by Islam. They wondered, how Sadat (and his wife) could outlaw what God has ordained?[105] The vocal protest movement was ultimately successful in repealing several aspects of the law, especially those constricting the rights of men to marry only one wife.[106]

At a time when the Islamic world was experiencing considerable turmoil, international issues were also at the forefront of student activism in the late 1970s. Mobilization on the question of Palestine had been a permanent fixture of the student movement since before the revolution. However, by the time al-Gama'a al-Islamiyya became the dominant actor within the university, the discourse was altered to reflect the student movement's growing religious orientation. "The position on the Zionist entity," as it was called, in many ways represented the classical Muslim Brotherhood point of view, though it also took into account the changes in the regional situation that occurred in the late 1960s and 1970s.

For instance, in formulating their response to Sadat's peace overtures, student activists emphasized Israel's expansionist tendencies in the wake of its occupation of several neighboring countries during the June 1967 War. It was also Sadat's highly unpopular policy that spurred al-Gama'a al-Islamiyya from qualifying its traditional position on the issue, which viewed that "there is no means to reclaim Palestine . . . except by returning to God and establishing His rule in the land, and (then) declaring jihad as the only solution for recouping the country and reclaiming dignity."[107] However, by the time Sadat initiated his 1977 visit to Jerusalem and the subsequent Camp David negotiations, a sense of urgency replaced the traditional grand but abstract scheme for liberation for which the Islamic movement had become known. After providing the textual basis against normalization of relations with Israel, a statement by al-Gama'a al-Islamiyya condemned the president, stating in part:

> If our position was based on nothing more than his contravention of Qur'anic injunctions, that would be enough. But what of his endangering of our lands, our freedom, our lives, our wealth, and our future generations? He ignores the lessons of history and the truths of reality.[108]

The students relied heavily on a 1956 ruling by al-Azhar's Fatwa Committee which forbade making peace with Israel, calling on Sadat to recognize the decision of this state institution, and further calling on the people of Egypt to:

· Denounce the recognition of Israel, the peace agreement, and the normalization of relations;
· Boycott Israel completely: politically, economically, culturally, and in the media;
· Boycott any Egyptian who does not adhere to the previous decrees;

- Study the Qur'anic texts and the Prophetic traditions about the Jewish people;
- Uphold the rights of Muslims, not only in the West Bank, Gaza, the Golan Heights, and Sinai, but in all of Palestine.[109]

Student activists successfully mobilized a large segment of the university population on the basis of such calls to action, which were accompanied by large-scale activities that included campaigns in the independent media, educational events to raise awareness, and public protests. Similarly, as events in Iran led to a popular revolution that overthrew the dictatorial rule of Shah Muhammad Reza Pahlavi in February 1979, al-Gama'a al-Islamiyya felt compelled to comment on the situation. In a statement entitled "Lessons from Iran," student leaders highlighted a number of important observations from the revolution in Iran that were applicable to Islamic activists in Egypt. They lauded the impact of basic Islamic precepts on the mobilization of Iranian masses against one of the most powerful rulers in the region. These events proved, the document argued, that Islamic identity could not be suppressed by any force, and perhaps most important, that "the nature of this religion is that . . . it is comprehensive, for this world and the hereafter. It organizes all aspects of life, providing for just rule, just as it provides for the maintenance of prayers."[110] Moreover, the Iranian Revolution was described as "the first dent in the wall of secularism" and an unequivocal denunciation of "those rulers who would sell their countries and hasten in the service of the east and the west, and repress their people for the benefit of their patrons."[111]

Statements such as these were intended to send a message to governments around the region—particularly the regime in Egypt—that the Islamic movement represented a significant force in society that should be ignored only at the peril of the ruling regimes. Sadat's position toward the revolution in Iran was diametrically opposed to that of al-Gama'a al-Islamiyya, deepening the divisions between the state and the student movement. Tensions became particularly heightened over Sadat's decision to take in the exiled shah. Unlike the issue of the revolution generally, which was only used to educate students and inspire hope and confidence, the specific issue of the shah's arrival to Egypt was to mobilize thousands of students in opposition to Sadat.

On their university grounds, students held mass protests that numbered in the thousands. On March 26, 1980, noon prayers were followed by a student conference that condemned Sadat's admission of the shah into Egypt. The conference issued a statement under the heading, "The Bloodthirsty Shah is Unwelcome," in which it denounced a decision by Egypt that many other countries, including the United States, refused to make. Challenging Sadat's rationale, the students posed the rhetorical question, "Did the rest of the world forego humanitarianism and leave it for Egypt?" The statement continued:

> Or can we say that Egypt has become an outpost for the American intelligence agencies to plot their schemes while the Egyptians become a people without principles, or morals, or feelings, in the eyes of the Egyptian government? The government is mistaken if this is what it thinks. The whole world will know that Muslims reject injustice and oppression in Egypt too, and that they refuse to host the bloodthirsty Shah, the enemy of Islam, in their country.[112]

A third international issue of major importance to the student movement came in the form of the Soviet Union's invasion of Afghanistan in December 1979. As Abul Futuh later explained, the reaction to this event was a natural extension of the Islamic movement's feelings of "a strong allegiance to the Islamic Ummah."[113] He elucidated further, that "any Muslim country was, by necessity, our country, causing us to feel solidarity with all the peoples of the Muslim world, beyond our central issue of Palestine."[114] In fact, in articulating its position on Afghanistan, al-Gama'a al-Islamiyya drew parallels to the occupation of Palestinian lands, and advocated its unconditional belief in the liberation of Muslim lands from foreign occupation. Guided by the experience of the Muslim Brotherhood in Palestine in 1948, the youth believed that a similar effort would be required to liberate Afghanistan.

Although they advocated a united *jihad* across the Muslim world, student leaders stopped short of suggesting popular participation from the ranks of students. Instead, they continued to hold conferences and seminars on the issue, inviting the usual cadre of respected scholars, including 'Umar al-Tilmisani, Mustafa Mashhur, Hafez Salama, and Ahmed al-Mahallawi, and they issued a call to the governments of the Muslim world to take action in defense of a Muslim country that had fallen victim to a powerful and ruthless superpower. While it had reached the height of its power, the student movement only managed to offer "symbolic and moral support" on the issue of Afghanistan, but its awareness campaign in the early 1980s paved the way for the wave of volunteer fighters that were sanctioned to travel to Afghanistan by the Egyptian government beginning in 1984.[115]

Toward Confrontation

By 1977, the Islamic movement had solidified its control of the student movement and had succeeded in marginalizing leftist trends within the university. While this development probably met with Sadat's approval, he also appeared to understand that a popular movement united under one ideological banner was sure to pose a challenge to his attempt to chart a pro-Western path that included peace with Israel and economic liberalization. Moreover, the Islamic credentials that he meticulously had built for himself during the early years of his presidency were being swiftly eroded by his refusal to follow up symbolic gestures with meaningful policies that reflected his supposed desire to rule as "the believer president." Meanwhile, the Muslim Brotherhood had reorganized internally, re-emerged onto the scene, and began to exert its influence over the student movement, positioning itself as the alternative to a regime that was becoming increasingly unpopular.

All of these factors combined to create a situation in which the Islamic movement became the chief opposition force in Egypt in the late 1970s. Abul Futuh's confrontation of Sadat in early 1977 marked a major shift in the relations between the regime and the Islamic movement. Later in the year, as Sadat traveled to Jerusalem, the hostility between the two sides became more palatable. Public statements issued by al-Gama'a al-Islamiyya condemned Sadat in no uncertain terms, while within the university walls, student leaders discerned a changed demeanor on the part of administrators who had long supported and facilitated their activities. Sufi Abu Talib, in particular, had changed his tone. "He never refused me a request, as head of the Student Union," recalled Abul Futuh. "But his dealings with us changed thereafter, as he began to obstruct our work and place obstacles before our activities in the university."[116]

These obstructions took the form of new restrictions on student activism, from limiting al-Gama'a al-Islamiyya's ability to hold conferences and camps, to issuing new regulations and election lists for Student Union elections. Administrators withheld resources from Islamic camps, and even spread rumors that state security agents were going to raid the camps and arrest the student leadership. In 1978, student leaders at 'Ain Shams University became the first to experience disqualification from that year's Student Union elections.[117] The following year, the situation escalated, as ten students from al-Gama'a al-Islamiyya in al-Minya University, including Muhieddin 'Isa and Abul 'Ela Madi, were arrested by government agents and expelled from the university. Madi was serving as the vice president of the national Student Union, so his detention sent major shock waves across the country.

The government soon made its position toward al-Gama'a al-Islamiyya official. In late 1979, Sadat issued Law 265, which disqualified the existing Student Unions from reelection, froze the assets and locked the offices of all unions, and prohibited them from meeting.[118] In at least one instance, conditions escalated into violent confrontation between students and security agents.[119] At Alexandria, Za'farani recalled that he saw state security agents entering the university for the first time in a decade.[120] Once again, they became a permanent fixture on the university grounds, restricting student activity through coercion and intimidation. The same scene was repeated in Cairo, al-Minya, and across the country.[121] In 1980, the last Islamic camps were held in Assiut during the winter holiday and in Alexandria in the summer. Sadat ordered all student camps canceled thereafter. Student leaders tried in vain to soften the president's stance toward their movement. They wrote open letters and issued public statements to various state officials, responding to charges by security agents, and imploring officials to reconsider their cancelation of student elections.[122]

While the student movement, led by al-Gama'a al-Islamiyya, bore the brunt of the regime's repressive measures, these developments occurred within the larger context of confrontation between the state and an increasingly diverse Islamic movement. The violence that marked the activities of underground groups like Shukri Mustafa's Gama'at al-Muslimin (better known as al-Takfir wal-Higra) left a deep impression on Sadat. The group's 1977 abduction and murder of former Awqaf Minister Muhammad al-Dhahabi coincided with the beginning of Sadat's clampdown on student activism. Moreover, Tilmisani's famous 1979 confrontation of Sadat on national television had shone a light on the Muslim Brotherhood's deep frustrations with the regime, while also exposing Sadat as an unsettled and increasingly paranoid ruler. International considerations also played a role. Attempting to balance his alliance with the West, which had become rooted in the tenuous peace with Israel, Sadat became concerned with the growing tide of Islamic activism as a threat to established regimes, especially in light of the revolution in Iran. Students in

Egypt were accused of being "Khomeiniites" who wanted to overthrow the government.[123]

In an April 1979 speech, Sadat alleged that "[w]e are building Egypt with our own hands, and with our freedom. No one has power over us. . . . This is nonsense. For two years, they entered the elections and everyone is talking about what they are doing. The situation is dangerous. . . . The youth, unfortunately, are being pushed from the outside."[124] Later that same year, in what was to be the last stand of al-Gama'a al-Islamiyya within the Student Union, Ahmed 'Umar ran a spirited campaign in the election for president of the Cairo University Student Union. His opponent was handpicked by the regime. 'Umar had already served as the vice president of the Medical College Student Union and had considerable support from across the student population. However, when the votes were tallied, the election resulted in a tie, with 113 votes apiece. According to 'Umar, the election was decided by the drawing of lots, leading to the victory of the government candidate.[125]

Though it may have ended by chance, all indications pointed to the loss of the Islamic movement's status within the official avenues that had been afforded it for the better part of the decade. According to Badr's account, interference by state security agents ensured 'Umar's defeat and solidified the exclusion of al-Gama'a al-Islamiyya from any further participation in the Student Union.[126] In fact, the transition of the Islamic movement occurred as a result of both external as well as internal factors. On the one hand, the regime's determination to reverse the gains made by the Islamic youth movement forced student leaders to seek alternative modes of activism, often by disengaging from their long-standing interaction with state figures and institutions. On the other hand, the movement had already forged extensive links with the Muslim Brotherhood and had begun to merge many of its activities with those of the elder opposition group.

While these two developments appeared to go hand in hand, they were also furthered by the appearance of divisions within the ranks of al-Gama'a al-Islamiyya. In what could be described as a geographic fault line, groups within the universities of upper Egypt, especially those in Assiut and al-Minya, exhibited a more conservative outlook, one that expressed misgivings about the Islamic modernist mission of the Muslim Brotherhood, and sought to chart a more independent path. Leaders of these groups, including Karam Zuhdi in al-Minya and Nagih Ibrahim in Assiut, were successful in retaining sole use of the name "al-Gama'a al-Islamiyya" in the early 1980s, and distinguished it from its previous incarnation by taking it underground and infusing its activist program with a militant component, a phenomenon that has been examined elsewhere.[127]

Ultimately, however, the student movement of the 1970s was successful in cultivating an outlook that would prove critical for the continuation of Islamic activism in a new era. Its leaders fashioned a distinct ideological orientation that was shaped by a combination of a preexisting program delivered by classical texts and the teachings of an elder class of scholars, as well as their own cultural, socioeconomic, and political upbringing and experiences. The *tarbiya* phase of the youth movement had proved immensely successful, impacting the lives of tens of thousands of Egyptian youth, and providing them with a religious grounding that would anchor a common frame of reference for years.

While the movement's endeavors into political activism may not have yielded tangible results from a policy perspective, they nonetheless conditioned an entire generation in working through existing institutions, making precise claims, and doing so while framing them in an Islamic tone. Za'farani's statement that the Student Union experience taught the Islamic movement "how the country works" is of immense significance as one examines the youth movement's graduation from the university level and entry into the professional world. Madi claimed that Sadat's decision to combat the Islamic movement within the universities had the unintended consequence of transforming a student-led movement into a popular movement that quickly spread throughout society.[128] However, the argument could just as easily be made that, upon reaching maturity, and with most of its leaders having entered a new phase in their lives, the student movement had no other logical direction to take but to evolve beyond the realm of the university. Building upon its past successes, it would seek out other institutions, whether professional syndicates or the People's Assembly, with which to engage. It would also look to combine its efforts with those of another force, whose spirit had long hovered over the education and activism of al-Gama'a al-Islamiyya—a force whose name had been at one point in time synonymous with the Islamic movement.

5

The Young and the Old

IN AUGUST 1979, 'Umar al-Tilmisani, the general guide of the Muslim Brotherhood, was called into the office of Mansour Hasan, the minister of culture and information. Hasan beseeched Tilmisani to attend an upcoming event hosted by Anwar al-Sadat in the port town of Ismailia in commemoration of the establishment of the National Democratic Party. Upon Hasan's insistence, Tilmisani agreed to attend, though the Muslim Brotherhood and the Sadat regime had been at odds over recent state policies and Sadat's increasingly authoritarian behavior. The rift had deepened earlier that year with the conclusion of Egypt's peace treaty with Israel, a move strongly condemned by the Muslim Brotherhood and opposed by the majority of Egyptians.

Tilmisani arrived at the meeting hall, where he promptly took a seat in the back row. However, event organizers ushered him to a seat in the front row, directly opposite the podium where Sadat would be delivering his remarks. Tilmisani thanked the officials for that honor, and became optimistic that the gesture augured well for a new understanding between the Muslim Brotherhood and the regime.[1] The event, which would be televised nationally and featured an audience of prominent political and business leaders, provided an ideal backdrop for a clean slate in the strained relations between Sadat and the most vocal opposition movement in Egypt.

Instead, it was soon revealed that the entire scene was orchestrated as a full frontal propaganda assault on the Muslim Brotherhood. During his impassioned speech, Sadat recited a litany of charges against the Muslim Brotherhood generally and Tilmisani in particular. They were accused of sabotaging government policies, collaborating with Egypt's enemies, inciting Egyptian youth, and enflaming sectarian tensions. The elderly

Tilmisani was seated front and center, to be scolded like a schoolboy before the headmaster while the entire nation watched. "These words require a response," Tilmisani solemnly told the president. "When I finish what I have to say, respond as you wish," Sadat retorted, before re-launching into his tirade without missing a beat. He concluded each point emphatically, rhetorically asking, "Isn't that right, 'Umar?" addressing Tilmisani without any regard for his age or standing.

When the president finally concluded his remarks, Tilmisani rose to his feet. Perhaps thinking he was about to offer his sincere apologies to Sadat, the organizers rushed a microphone into his hands. To their surprise, Tilmisani took the opportunity to show the world "that there is one among those in Egypt who would tell the tyrant, 'you have committed outrages and transgressed.'"[2] Tilmisani took his time in responding to the accusations leveled against the Muslim Brotherhood, concluding with the following words:

> If anyone but you had made these accusations, I would have lodged my complaint to you. But when it is you, Muhammad Anwar al-Sadat, who is behind them, then I lodge my complaint with the wisest and fairest of judges. You have injured me so greatly.[3]

Sadat was stunned by this response by Tilmisani. He appeared particularly disturbed by the challenge to his personal piety. As his lips trembled, Sadat backtracked, "I did not intend to offend al-Ustadh 'Umar or the Muslim Brotherhood. Now withdraw your complaint!" Tilmisani responded, matter-of-factly, that "it has gone to the hands of one from whom I cannot retrieve it." With those words, the meeting was adjourned and Sadat once again came away from a carefully staged attempt to rehabilitate his image, only having done further damage to it.[4]

Indeed, as early as 1977, tensions between Sadat and the Islamic movement had become increasingly heightened. As his policy agenda became more apparent, from the economic liberalization measures to the pursuit of a separate peace with Israel, Sadat engendered a strong force of popular opposition. His handling of three major incidents that year only more deeply entrenched national sentiments against him. Sadat dismissed the Bread Riots—the large-scale protests against his economic policies—as the "uprising of the thieves." The fierce response by the state security apparatus to the wave of attacks and kidnappings by al-Takfir wal-Higra was deemed excessive and disproportionate by the mainstream Islamic movement, even as its leaders denounced the actions of the outlaw group. Finally, Sadat's trip to Jerusalem later that year broke a decades-long taboo by implicitly recognizing Zionist claims to the holy land. As he had not adequately prepared Egyptians for this dramatic break from long-standing policy, the move earned near universal condemnation, especially from the Muslim Brotherhood.

By the middle of 1979, when the widely publicized confrontation between Sadat and Tilmisani occurred, several other developments had contributed to the growing mistrust between the regime and the Muslim Brotherhood. In addition to the peace treaty with Israel, the response to the Iranian Revolution generated deep-seated hostility. The Muslim Brotherhood's perceived endorsement of the developments in Iran was viewed by Sadat as an ominous message that his own power would be threatened by a similar revolutionary force driven by religious fervor. Meanwhile, as Sadat invited Mohammad Reza Shah to take refuge in Egypt, the unilateral decision was considered an affront to the nation and was denounced in popular protests. Furthermore, the spread of civil unrest, motivated by sectarian divisions, in Cairo and upper Egypt, was also a source of consternation for Sadat, who accused the Islamic movement of deliberately attempting to destabilize his regime.

These events stood at the foreground of developments in Egypt during the late 1970s, resulting in a more deeply entrenched authoritarian regime and a more vocal and obstinate opposition movement. On a more fundamental level, though, it was a societal transformation, at work since the early part of the decade, which yielded the political stalemate that marked the abrupt end to the Sadat era in late 1981. Specifically, the successful reconstitution of the Muslim Brotherhood, a process that could not have been achieved without the active incorporation of the Islamic student movement, would come to define a new era of popular religious activism in Egypt.

This chapter charts the convergence of two major social forces: the Muslim Brotherhood, the traditional head of the Islamic movement, recently reestablished by the surviving group elders and brought under the leadership of Tilmisani; and the vibrant youth movement whose leadership comprised the religious contingent of students representing al-Gama‘a al-Islamiyya within Egypt's colleges and universities. As they coalesced into a unified force for Islamic activism, these groups successfully preserved the legacy of the Muslim Brotherhood while also charting a course for the movement's future role in Egyptian society. Given the immediate and long-term implications of this development, the examination of its multiple components is essential to any understanding of the evolution of the Islamic movement.

Just as in the early 1970s, the return of the Muslim Brotherhood was far from assured, by the middle of the decade, al-Gama'a al-Islamiyya's decision to bring its activist mission within the fold of a mother movement was by no means inevitable. It evolved out of a convergence of ideological visions, organizational mechanisms, and interactions with the state and society at large. The first of these factors was the most significant, in that it involved an intricate process of intellectual growth and discovery many years in the making. Early in their studies, youth leaders deferred their religious education to a class of elder scholars who guided the Islamic student movement toward the Muslim Brotherhood's ideological outlook. In fact, the student leaders who later refused to merge their groups with the Muslim Brotherhood were generally those most resistant to these intellectual influences during the initial years of the movement.

In the same vein, as the organizational structure of al-Gama'a al-Islamiyya expanded and took on a more complex shape, it gradually came to resemble the rigid hierarchical model for which the Muslim Brotherhood's organization was known. This uniformity laid the necessary groundwork, so that once the student leadership (and indeed, the decision was made at the highest levels of the student movement) became committed to the notion of joining the Muslim Brotherhood, the transition was as seamless as possible. From the point of view of key figures within the Muslim Brotherhood, the presence of a well-defined and centralized leadership within the student movement facilitated the recruitment of members and the appropriation of their programs.

The third element in the establishment of a unified Islamic movement under the Muslim Brotherhood banner encompassed the confluence of an activist program that appealed to a common base: the wider Egyptian society. As the mission of al-Gama'a al-Islamiyya looked to expand beyond the university setting and focused more on political issues, it became ripe for the contribution of the Muslim Brotherhood, which was considering means through which to reintroduce its program to society after a decades-long absence. This mutually beneficial arrangement saw to it that the activism of al-Gama'a al-Islamiyya did not necessarily have to end with the graduation of its leaders from the university, while the Muslim Brotherhood found a solution for the deficiency of active members by shoring up a bright and energetic new base.

Moreover, as Sadat's policies became more polarizing, both groups gradually became identified as the most formidable political opposition to the regime. By the late 1970s, there was no longer any discussion of whether the Islamic youth movement was operating on behalf of the Sadat regime, or whether the regime had any control over it. Instead, its fiercely independent and confrontational tone was reminiscent of the Muslim Brotherhood of past eras. For its part, as the Muslim Brotherhood was coming into its own, it discovered a venue through which to express its frustrations with the regime, in the form of student camps and conferences, while student leaders made particularly effective use of *al-Da'wa* magazine, the Muslim Brotherhood's own medium for the promotion of its mission.

In contrast to prior eras in the history of the Islamic movement, the 1970s were marked by fluidity in thought and action. As a result, the beginning of the next decade witnessed the consolidation of the respective gains made by the student movement and the reconstituted Muslim Brotherhood at the expense of a regime that had sought to cultivate these seemingly disparate forces for its own purposes. Therefore, it was no surprise when, during what would be his final speech before parliament in September 1981, as Sadat announced a wave of mass incarcerations, he lamented that "the Muslim Brotherhood is al-Gama'a al-Islamiyya and al-Gama'a al-Islamiyya is the Muslim Brotherhood."[5] To the dismay of the regime, it appeared that through the combined efforts of an elder generation of Islamic figures and a new generation of student activists, the Muslim Brotherhood was set to resume its place as the leading opposition movement in Egypt.

From One Movement to Many

Judging by the intellectual production of the Islamic movement, the 1970s were not a particularly fruitful period. The two decades of political repression that preceded it ensured that the scholarly class of Islamic activists had experienced severe restrictions on their activity, while a new generation of Egyptian youth possessed no adequate frame of reference, given their upbringing in the culture of Nasserism. Additionally, one of Nasser's main legacies was the transformation of Egypt's educational system, channeling the best and brightest of the nation's youth into the fields of medicine, engineering, and the natural sciences at the expense of law, the social sciences, the humanities, and Islamic studies.

Nevertheless, against this backdrop emerged a buoyant climate of spiritual discovery and the pursuit of Islamic knowledge for which this period became known, defying all expectations. The Sadat regime got more than it bargained for when it cultivated an air of free expression that allowed for the growth of an Islamic trend within the universities. And for their part, the Muslim Brotherhood elders were astonished to discover that the spirit of Islamic activism was alive and well, in spite of the group's absence from the scene. 'Abd al-Mon'eim Abul Futuh, one of the original founders of al-Gama'a al-Islamiyya at the Cairo University College of Medicine, recalled that "when we began Islamic activism in the university, we were a group united only by the drive and genuine desire to work toward the advancement of Islam, without any common intellectual or legal authority uniting us."[6]

Indeed, while it may not have produced a new class of scholars and thinkers, this era is distinguished by the fluidity with which the student movement interacted with a variety of distinct trends. This produced a moment of reassessment of the broad intellectual currents within the Islamic movement, and the cultivation of a new culture of activism suited to the needs of the Islamic *da'wa* in a new era of Egyptian history. As it engaged with a wide array of personalities, texts, and groups representing various trends within the Islamic movement, al-Gama'a al-Islamiyya, which by 1973 had become the face of Islamic activism in Egypt, secured for itself a central role in the construction of a new discourse.

In the early years of al-Gama'a al-Islamiyya's existence, student leaders took pride in their organizational as well as intellectual independence. They guarded that autonomy vigilantly. Students within the organization were free to pursue their Islamic education as they pleased. They studied classical texts and explored commentaries from a variety of viewpoints. Abul Futuh discovered an advantage for the youth in the absence of a dominant organization capable of bringing them under its control. Simple missionary groups and charity associations, such as al-Gam'iyya al-Shar'iyya and Ansar al-Sunna al-Muhammadiyya, lacked a defined structure and a stringent membership policy, limiting their ability to impact the student movement, while still allowing the new generation to gain an added perspective and to learn from the experiences of these groups.[7] Similarly, the Muslim Brotherhood's absence created a free and open environment that did not impose an organizational structure, but still afforded students access to its intellectual school, albeit through indirect channels.

The lack of a preexisting force to guide the student movement resulted in an organic intellectual environment in which choices were made naturally and the youth were free to adopt several approaches in the shaping of their Islamic outlook. Among the most popular trends were the Salafi, Jihadi, and naturally, the Muslim Brotherhood's intellectual tradition, better known as Ikhwani. Smaller trends, though influential nonetheless, included the Tablighi, Tahriri, Sufi, and those of the aforementioned charitable associations. During the formative period, it was not uncommon for a student to wade into the intellectual waters of a variety of competing trends, however contradictory it would later seem. In fact, most students would have been hard pressed to describe themselves as ultimately falling into one camp, having been inspired by different elements from some or all of the intellectual schools.

The Salafi trend of the 1970s did not have strong historical roots within Egyptian society. Its rise was owed in large part to Muhammad Hamid al-Faqi of Ansar al-Sunna. An Azhari sheikh who had lived and worked in Saudi Arabia during the early twentieth century, he published a number of influential Islamic texts that shaped the outlook of the youth on religious practices. Abul Futuh contended that Wahhabi thought emanating from the Saudi Salafi tradition "forced its way" into Egypt by the aggressive posturing of a newly enriched regional power. Hundreds of crates full of Wahhabi literature arrived free of charge to the offices of al-Gama'a al-Islamiyya throughout Egypt.[8] These books were widely distributed without much examination of their content. They impacted a considerable number of students, despite at times being too out of step with mainstream Islamic thought in Egypt, as in their prohibition of the celebration of religious milestones such as the Prophet's birthday.

The popular 'Umrah trips to the holy cities were another source of indoctrination for many young Egyptians. So enamored with the thought of learning about Islam from its source, some elected to stay behind and pursue a course of study with prominent Saudi scholars. They often returned to their universities in Egypt months later, eager to spread their newly acquired knowledge and correct the errors of their peers. They focused on issues of outward appearances, such as the growing of beards for men, which they argued was a requirement, and proper dress for both men and women. Salafi students also placed a heavier emphasis on segregation of the sexes, calling on officials to institute the practice throughout the country, at all levels of education.

Similarly, the early 1970s witnessed the rise of an Islamic trend that placed armed struggle at the forefront of its program. Inspired by the works of Sayyid Qutb, Mawlana Mawdudi, and their followers, a significant contingent of youth activists were filled with "a revolutionary and rebellious spirit" that propelled them toward seeking radical changes to the system.[9] For some, just seeing the photograph of Qutb as he clutched the bars of his prison cell prior to his execution brought on feelings of anger, frustration, and a desire to act.[10] In the culture of mass protest that was cultivated after the 1967 defeat, the youth did not expressly reject the use of violence to accomplish its aims. Once again, the boundless and amorphous nature of the student movement lent itself to what may otherwise have appeared to be a contradiction in terms. The movement's program could at once contain elements of self-contained spiritual development, popular social activism, and support for some form of violent contention against the state.

The *jihadi* trend, as it came to be termed, influenced a growing percentage of students who expressed solidarity with the spirit of Organization 1965's mission, without being properly informed of the ensuing debate within the ranks of the Islamic movement on the permissibility of rising up against the state. "Violence, for us, was religiously justified. The only disagreement was over the timing," recalled Abul Futuh.[11] While some students believed that rising up against the system was a long-term objective that required careful planning and preparation, others argued that it was an imperative and a top priority to be pursued immediately. This opinion grew out of a highly simplistic view of the world. All existing institutions were corrupted and needed to be removed and replaced with Islamic ones, on the basis of the all-encompassing system of the Shari'a. The restoration of the lost caliphate was central to this view, albeit in the abstract.

By their own admission, the youth lacked any sense of history or understanding of the modern world. "As a Gama'a Islamiyya that emerged without inheriting a tradition or a political model, we were shortsighted on the question of the state, its logic, and its philosophy," said Abul Futuh. This line of thought provided the rationale for the incident at the Technical Military Academy in 1974. Although the leadership of al-Gama'a al-Islamiyya played no role in the coup attempt, the conspirators had relied heavily on student recruits, including some who had also participated in Islamic programs at Cairo University. Movement leaders at the Medical College were stunned to discover that two of their colleagues, Mustafa

Yusri and 'Usama Khalifa, were among those charged by the government for participating in the attack on the Technical Military Academy. As head of the Student Union, Abul Futuh was compelled to defend them and even provided legal representation for their trial.[12]

However, this event caused the leadership of the Islamic student movement to reevaluate its approach to a number of questions on which it had never needed to take a definitive stance. Despite all subsequent attempts to delineate clear boundaries for the activist mission, the *jihadi* strain remained a consistent presence within the broader Islamic movement, especially outside major urban centers of the country, like in Assiut, where Karam Zuhdi and Nagih Ibrahim had established an autonomous chapter of al-Gama'a al-Islamiyya by the early 1980s. In addition, other activists were impacted by the practice of *takfir* and sought isolation from a corrupted society, creating a fundamental divide between them and the mainstream Islamic movement on the core functions of *da'wa*.[13]

The intellectual trend that captivated the hearts and minds of the student movement and came to dominate al-Gama'a al-Islamiyya was that of the Muslim Brotherhood. The Ikhwani tradition had a number of advantages over the other trends. First, it proposed a comprehensive vision for the Islamic movement, and did not simply focus on a narrow set of issues, as with several of the competing approaches. Second, it had a long-standing tradition within society, one whose presence had seeped into a new generation despite all efforts by the previous regime to erase it from the Egyptian collective memory. Finally, the Muslim Brotherhood had always placed youth at the center of its message, a quality that was to prove critical during the merger of two distinct generations in the 1970s. From the days of Banna, the organization had valued the recruitment and participation of Egypt's young Muslims and had relied on them as the engine that drove the mission toward its goals. As a result, much of the Ikhwani curriculum was composed in the language of youth and was fashioned in their image.

In spite of these apparent advantages, the Muslim Brotherhood faced several obstacles in advancing its program among the new generation. The long imprisonment of its leaders meant that there was a glaring absence of its key figures within society. For an organization that prided itself on charismatic leadership and recruitment through top-down interactions at the micro level, this placed it at a severe disadvantage. Even once the Muslim Brotherhood's leaders were freed, they lacked the communications networks and organizational infrastructure, essential tools for resuming their mission. They also had to overcome a sustained propaganda campaign against the Muslim Brotherhood by the state press. All of these factors had the effect of taking an intellectual project that once stood above all others and bringing it down to the level of an increasingly crowded marketplace of ideologies.

In their periodization of the Islamic student movement, youth leaders stressed that, in the years dating until roughly 1976, "it was all one movement," and that there had yet to be any true distinction between those who associated with one trend or another.[14] This may have been true in the organizational sense, as students continued to work together under the common umbrella of al-Gama'a al-Islamiyya, whose dynamism provided the opportunity for a multiplicity of viewpoints, even within the same activity. It was not uncommon therefore, to have a student conference that represented the viewpoints of scholars ranging from Ibrahim 'Ezzat of Jama'at al-Tabligh, Muhammad Nasiruddin al-Albani, a Salafi scholar, and Muhammad al-Ghazali, whose body of work had come to represent the Ikhwani modernist school. Even official state scholars representing al-Azhar, the preeminent center of Islamic learning in the Arab world, such as 'Abd al-Halim Mahmoud, would be invited to occasional campus events.

However, just as this "period of maturity" was celebrated for its diversity, it was also notable for the growing distinction between contending intellectual viewpoints.[15] The divisions appeared on the ideological plane, as al-Gama'a al-Islamiyya's leaders found themselves on the defensive, having to take positions on a number of issues that for years had been left to individual members to determine for themselves. In the aftermath of the events at the Technical Military Academy, for instance, student leaders were forced to contend with the prospect of armed insurrection against the state developing from within their ranks, and risking the destabilization—or worse, total dismantlement—of their movement. As a result, an article by Yousuf al-Qaradawi on "al-Ghulu fil Takfir" (The Excesses of Takfir) became requisite reading for members and was widely discussed within the movement.

Though he was no longer a member of the organization, Qaradawi represented the Muslim Brotherhood school of thought, and along with Ghazali, he played a pivotal role in disseminating its worldview among the youth. While a large proportion of youth leaders were captivated by the Ikhwani outlook, some were more hesitant, moving steadily toward their Salafi or *jihadi* inclinations. Coinciding with the deepening rifts within the Islamic movement, the return of Muslim Brotherhood figures onto the activist scene and their interactions with a number of important youth leaders provided the intellectual markers with which to distinguish the factions from one another.

Early Encounters

The first meeting between the new generation of Islamic activists and the elder cadre from the Muslim Brotherhood occurred in an unceremonious manner. As part of their professional training, the students at Cairo University's College of Medicine were permitted to see patients in a wing of Qasr al-'Aini Hospital that housed prisoners seeking medical treatment. Traditionally, this dispensation was granted to political prisoners representing all ideological trends except the Muslim Brotherhood, many of whom died in Nasser's prisons due to lack of adequate medical care. But as part of his bid to reintegrate the Muslim Brotherhood leaders into society, Sadat lifted this restriction upon his accession to power. As a result, for the first time, medical personnel (including young doctors in training) found themselves in close quarters with members of the banned organization, about whom much had been said publicly, all of it derogatory. For Abul Futuh and his peers, the experience was a dramatic eye-opener, dispelling "all the myths of terror and fear" that had been constructed by the Nasser regime, and instead confirming the narrative put forward by his local imam of a group "who fought and sacrificed their lives for the sake of their *da'wa*, and refused to compromise on it, even if it meant prison, torture, and even death."[16]

The students took advantage of these chance encounters, quietly discussing their activism with elders from the organization, including Fathi Rifa'i and Tilmisani, who spent some weeks in the medical wing prior to their release. Rifa'i, in particular, used the opportunity to introduce his young physicians to the curriculum of the Muslim Brotherhood. During one of their meetings, he managed to smuggle a handwritten copy of "Wajibat al-Akh al-Muslim" (The Duties of the Muslim Brother), one of Hasan al-Banna's famous letters. The version the students received was notable in that its content was edited for a new audience. It focused wholly on the message of the Muslim Brotherhood, removing any references to its organizational structure and objectives. As students proceeded to copy and distribute the letter, Abul Futuh recalled that, for many of them, this was their first real exposure to the writings of Banna.[17]

Similarly, in Alexandria, some student leaders met lower level Muslim Brotherhood members who had managed to avoid imprisonment during the Nasser years and who had become encouraged, following the shift in Sadat's policy, to engage with young activists in their communities.[18] Muhammad Hussein 'Isa was particularly influential among the youth in Alexandria.[19] In this way, the fear barrier was broken on both sides. Though its leaders proceeded with extreme caution given the state's legacy of repression, the Muslim Brotherhood discerned a real opening in the political environment, which could allow its reintegration into society and engagement with the youth. From the perspective of student activists, these brief encounters were enough to dispel the myth depicting the Muslim Brotherhood as a dangerous band of outlaws.

Instead, eager young minds became awed by personal stories of struggle and hardship, pain and sacrifice. A new narrative was taking shape, one that placed the Muslim Brotherhood at the heart of the Islamic movement. Though it had been absent from the scene for a generation and had yet to resume its mission in any meaningful way, its legacy was strong enough to propel it to a position of prominence in the minds of many student activists.[20] Seizing upon this opportunity, Muslim Brotherhood leaders continued to reconstruct the group's image and to shore up credibility by recounting the early years of its mission and the successes enjoyed under Banna's leadership. They countered the prevailing narrative of their associations with the Free Officers and the deterioration of the Muslim Brotherhood's relationship with Nasser. The stories of heroism and sacrifice and the gross injustices to which the Muslim Brotherhood had been subjected left a deep mark on impressionable young minds.

Following the release of Tilmisani and other group elders from prison, contacts remained intermittent and quite often indirect. As internal discussions on the future of the organization had yet to yield a final decision, Muslim Brotherhood officials hesitated to resume their public advocacy. The lack of an organizational foundation, coupled with the basic needs of salvaging their personal lives, and continuing fears of renewed state repression should the elders be suspected of infiltrating the student movement, kept most of them at arm's length from the youth. In the course of al-Gama'a al-Islamiyya's many public demonstrations, Abul Futuh recalled seeing a Muslim Brotherhood figure, Muhammad 'Abd al-Mu'ti al-Gazzar, standing at some distance from the protests and marveling at the religiously themed banners hoisted by student leaders. During that period, he never once approached the students or attempted to contact them, but later told Abul Futuh that "he was amazed at what he witnessed because he and his imprisoned colleagues imagined that once they were released, they would not discover any religiosity or Islam, or the youth to be this passionate."[21]

Our Daʿwa

Indeed, just as the youth experienced these fleeting interactions with former principal figures of the Islamic movement, they were also keenly aware that their actions were being monitored from afar. This development stimulated an open discussion within the upper echelons of leadership of the student movement on the future of their mission. By 1974, as the Muslim Brotherhood was slowly reconstituted under the leadership of Tilmisani, Abul Futuh and his peers discussed the possibility of merging their movement with that of a more established group. They explored three possibilities: the student movement would place itself at the hands of the Muslim Brotherhood; the Muslim Brotherhood would fall into the ranks of the broader Islamic movement led by the cadre of youth who founded al-Gamaʿa al-Islamiyya; or the two would remain completely separate from one another.[22] Elsewhere, the options were phrased slightly differently: in addition to their work within the university, would al-Gamaʿa al-Islamiyya contribute to the establishment of a new group with a wider mandate within Egyptian society, or would it join one of the many existing groups that had created a crowded field within the Islamic movement?[23]

In the course of these discussions, it appeared that there existed within the leadership of al-Gamaʿa al-Islamiyya, especially in Cairo and Alexandria, a critical mass who believed in combining their mission with that of the Muslim Brotherhood in some fashion. At this early juncture, the discussion revolved primarily around building a common intellectual project, with little discussion of organizational coordination. The appearance of ideological divisions within the ranks of the students, combined with the growth of frustrations by the impetuous youth, necessitated a process of learning from those more experienced than they were. The Muslim Brotherhood possessed a holistic view of their activist mission, while the students bickered over small, inconsequential matters of religious interpretation. Recognizing their "youthful, zealous, and impatient" nature, the student leaders resolved to forsake their desire for immediate change in exchange for "the cautious, slow approach favored by the Muslim Brotherhood toward the realization of an Islamic state."[24]

The process that followed featured the steady and methodical indoctrination of large segments of the student population in the curriculum of the Muslim Brotherhood. Although other external influences continued to play an active role, the *da'wa* that had come to be defined by Banna and carried forward by Hudaybi and Tilmisani took center stage in the discussions and events of the students. Ever cautious, the student leaders, often on the advice of their contacts within the Muslim Brotherhood, ensured that no direct mention of the organization was ever actually made. Any self-references to the Muslim Brotherhood within Ikhwani literature were removed, so that Banna's letters and speeches read like general advice for an Islamic activist of any era, and not a member of an organization with a particular structure and mission. This development ushered in a steady process of the refinement of views. Overly simplistic plans for the implementation of Islamic law were replaced by a complex vision for the Islamization of society. Contradictions inherent in the support for a variety of competing trends were slowly exposed and were reconciled with a more nuanced outlook that privileged peaceful interactions over violent confrontation and defined *jihad* in the context of *da'wa*.

Concerns over personal religious observances were given less importance in a new prioritization that favored one's commitment to the larger struggle at hand than to the length of one's beard or the shortness of one's pants. To be sure, the process was by no means a smooth one. Students occasionally expressed their frustrations with some of the practices of elder Muslim Brotherhood figures. Some whispered about the lack of strict observance of Salafi prayer traditions.[25] Others confronted them about their outward appearance. At times, some Muslim Brotherhood elders tried to calmly relate their perspective to the students. But in other instances, they avoided confrontation altogether. Abul Futuh recalled, "When they learned that the matter of beards and outward piety would alleviate our concerns, they grew their beards. Few of them actually opposed us on these peripheral issues."[26]

This symbiotic process allowed each side to discover the other and to adapt to its needs and expectations accordingly, though one side certainly had the upper hand. The knowledge, experience, and seniority of the Muslim Brotherhood ensured that they would remain the teachers and the students would stay true to their role. Often accused of being short-sighted, many student leaders were convinced of the long view put forward by the elders and began to see their mission as part of a broader project that would expand far beyond the university, even while that provided the base of its support and a safe haven for its activities. It was in this spirit that the first high-level meeting between a founder of the Islamic student movement and a key figure within the Muslim Brotherhood took place.

In 1974, following his release from prison, Kamal al-Sananiri requested a meeting with 'Abd al-Mon'eim Abul Futuh. As a high-ranking member of the Muslim Brotherhood, having learned at the hands of Hasan al-Banna and having been a key figure in the Secret Apparatus, Sananiri's legend had traveled far within the student movement. The youth had also heard the tale of how Amina Qutb, the sister of Sayyid Qutb, pledged to marry Sananiri after his own wife sought a divorce when she could not bear the many years of being apart during his imprisonment. At fifty-five years old, he had survived some of the darkest days of the Muslim Brotherhood, but had never wavered in his commitment to its mission. And now, so soon after he had won his freedom, Sananiri was already seeking to pick up where he left off, spreading the *da'wa* among the youth.

Abul Futuh was therefore flattered when he received the message to meet Sananiri at a shoe store on Qasr al-'Aini Street in Cairo. Owing to his extreme caution, Sananiri wanted to hold the meeting away from both of their homes and to maintain some level of secrecy around it. Sananiri was convinced that his movements were being tracked by state security agents and was not one to take chances. The shop was owned by a Muslim Brotherhood member who proceeded to bring his two special patrons pairs of shoes to try on as they discussed the future of the Islamic movement. Abul Futuh later stated that it was a highly sentimental meeting that he would never forget. "His words, his spirit, and everything about him were so new to me. . . . He would erupt with emotion as he described his ideas and insisted on continuing and completing what the group had started."[27]

From the perspective of a Muslim Brotherhood elder, the objective of the meeting was to send a feeler to the head of the Islamic student movement on the possibility of coordinating their efforts. The organization had just resolved the internal questions about the nature of its reconstitution, and had placed authority in the hands of Tilmisani. The new general guide oversaw the reestablishment of the long defunct Guidance Bureau and allowed a certain degree of autonomy to figures who believed in the importance of reorganizing the group around the young generation of activists. As a result, Sananiri, along with Mustafa Mashhur, another elder who had emerged from the disbanded Secret Apparatus, took the lead in the recruitment of the youth, a process that became known as *tawrith al-da'wa* (bequeathing the call).[28]

For his part, Abul Futuh believed that this meeting was a testament to the early successes enjoyed by al-Gamaʻa al-Islamiyya, especially as its mission had obtained a quasi-official status by virtue of its participation in the Student Union and its cordial relations with some regime officials. A second meeting was held, this time at Sananiri's home. This was followed by more frequent encounters and the inclusion of additional Muslim Brotherhood figures, including Mashhur, Ahmed Hasanain, Ahmed al-Malt, and ʻAbbas al-Sisi, whom Abul Futuh and local student leaders met in Alexandria.[29]

During these meetings, Sananiri, Mashhur, and the others hoped to gain a commitment by student leaders to orient themselves with the Muslim Brotherhood curriculum and to incorporate it more fully into their programs, even at the expense of the other intellectual trends. As one youth leader observed, with increasing divisions within the student movement, many leaders began to rely more heavily on the Muslim Brotherhood's ideological positions to issue responses and suppress competing visions. The *'usul*, or foundations of their arguments, were generally rooted in the works of Banna and the speeches and articles of Tilmisani.[30]

The curriculum, which gradually trickled down from the leaders to the rank-and-file members of al-Gamaʻa al-Islamiyya, consisted of the essential writings of Banna, as can be seen in the 1977 publication of three of his most famous letters under the title of *Daʻwatuna (Our Daʻwa)*.[31] As a schoolteacher by training, Banna had always oriented his message to young Egyptians. The fact that his writings were aimed at a youth audience made them easily accessible to a new generation of student activists nearly half a century later. Stemming from these inspirational works, Mashhur attempted a more systematic process of inculcating the Muslim Brotherhood mission to the youth. Known for his strong and at times overbearing personality, Mashhur made a deep impression on student leaders. He preached to them in close quarters, spending long hours on lessons from his own experiences and observations about student activism in a new era. He was never short of motivational words:

> Those who travel along the path must trust in that path and rest assured that it is the means to reach their goal, so that they are not misled and lost, and so that they are not overcome with doubt and mistrust as they proceed. . . . The path of *daʻwa* is worthy of that trust, for it is the foremost path that bonds the Muslim to all aspects of his life and bestows him all that he owns, from life, wealth, effort, thought, and time. His fate and future depend on it.[32]

Not only did Mashhur instill his eager listeners with the spiritual strength to succeed in an increasingly adversarial environment, he also offered practical advice to spread the *da'wa* in as coherent and efficient a way as possible.[33] His lessons were soon serialized in a segment in *al-Da'wa* magazine entitled "Min Fiqh al-Da'wa" (Understanding the Call). Mashhur demonstrated particular effectiveness at charting a historical course for the transmission of the Muslim Brotherhood program through the ages, ultimately becoming "a trust" in the hands of the new generation. In laying out Banna's legacy, Mashhur wrote on the importance of maintaining purity in missionary activities going forward:

> [al-Banna] stressed the importance of maintaining the educational program and the readiness of the individual Muslim to assume the doctrine, and the avoidance of the discourse of political parties; to focus on action and avoid argumentation and discussions that waste time and energy and stir up anger and frustration. He always concentrated on brotherhood and strengthening the bonds of love for the sake of God.[34]

With these lessons, young leaders gained a sense of belonging within the Muslim Brotherhood's intellectual school. As one student recalled, from this point forward, the foundations of the *da'wa* that his peers depended on were those of the Muslim Brotherhood, as found in Banna's writings and the lessons of Tilmisani and Mashhur.[35] Acknowledging that ideological conflicts could persist between the two generations, Abul Futuh stated, "as for the differences between us on tangential issues of legal interpretation, we gradually became convinced that the rift of disagreement would become narrower over time."[36]

Becoming a Brother

By 1975, a substantial portion of the leadership of the student movement had committed to pursuing an activist program within the framework put forward by Muslim Brotherhood thinkers and organizers. With only minor misgivings, a new generation had accepted the leadership of the elders and had initiated the process of bringing its movement under their command. When one of the young men announced his impending marriage to his colleagues, Mashhur reminded him, "Tell your wife that you have another wife. . . . it is the *da'wa*."37 Nothing short of total devotion to the mission would be acceptable.

In order to gain the dedication of the student movement, the educational period in which the *da'wa* was "bequeathed" proved critical. Badr recalled that the youth "were reared in the intellectual side of the Muslim Brotherhood before the organizational structure came."38 By the students' own account, the progression from converging toward a common ideological outlook to uniting under a defined organizational hierarchy occurred rather naturally. As they moved forward in their curriculum and entered into advanced internal discussions on collectively joining the reconstituted Muslim Brotherhood, it was no longer a question of "if" they would become official members, but "how" the process would be carried out.39

For all involved, the situation was unique. Never before had the Muslim Brotherhood attempted to absorb an entire preexisting movement within its ranks. Student leaders believed that a major strength of their movement was that it was self-contained. Throughout its existence, al-Gama'a al-Islamiyya had a limited mandate, but one that provided it with a degree of freedom that few other groups could claim. It was restricted to operating within the university community, but it enjoyed a wide array of privileges within it.40 By 1975, however, many of the foundational figures of the student movement either had already completed their studies or were nearing graduation. There emerged a widespread realization that they would soon be leaving their campuses, and accordingly, they sought a new organizational model to sustain their movement. The challenges awaiting them on the outside were perceived to be far greater than anything they had experienced within the safe confines of the scholastic world. Only an organization with a rich history of activism, deep roots within Egyptian society, and the demonstrated courage to face the strenuous obstacles along the way would suffice.

Through its celebrated legacy and the inroads it had made with the student movement in the mid-1970s, the Muslim Brotherhood became the ideal home for many students who looked to devote their lives to promoting the Islamization of their society. In the course of internalizing the Muslim Brotherhood's curriculum, student leaders also developed deep emotional bonds with the figures they encountered.41 The students were especially struck by the humility demonstrated by leading Muslim Brotherhood figures, especially in contrast to other guests who were less cordial and more demanding. Mashhur in particular was known to have spent long hours with the students. "He ate what we ate. He slept where we slept," recalled one student leader.[42] In his capacity as the head of the Youth and Universities Committee within the Guidance Bureau, Mashhur bore the responsibility of connecting with the student movement and ensuring that they found common ground with the Muslim Brotherhood leadership, in spite of the vast differences in age and experience. Abul Futuh recalled that during the summer camps, Muslim Brotherhood leaders would insist on staying overnight with the students and even joined them in the dawn exercises, despite their advanced age.[43]

Moreover, the bond that developed became one of trust and dependability, as the youth could often count on the elders for help and advice with their professional careers and the challenges of daily life, such as balancing their studies and activism. Even Tilmisani was no stranger to the students, making himself available to them at all hours of the day, whether for public lectures or for private consultations with youth leaders. They lauded him for his honest and plain-spoken style, gentle nature, and ability to deal with those who disagreed with him. Though he was in a vaunted position as head of the most prominent Islamic organization in Egyptian society, students did not hesitate to confront him on matters of religious belief and practice. Nor did he back down from the challenge. During a debate on the permissibility of music in Islamic law, Tilmisani stunned a crowded auditorium when he maintained that not only was there no objection to music in Islam, as the Salafis had ruled, but that he had taken up playing the 'oud (Arabic lute) in his younger days.[44]

During the course of internal deliberations among the leaders of al-Gama'a al-Islamiyya, the costs and benefits of formalizing their group's relationship with the Muslim Brotherhood were weighed and discussed. The concerns included the loss of the student movement's independence in thought and action, having to defer to the leadership of the elder generation, as well as the Muslim Brotherhood's official positions on the issues. But the movement also stood to gain from the legacy and experience of an organization that had stood the test of time for over a half century. While potentially stifling some of the intellectual diversity that existed among the students, the uniformity in thought was also an asset that would allow the student movement to evolve into an organized, coherent force in society. Moreover, the Muslim Brotherhood could offer the structural capacity to handle a movement that was reaching the limits of its infrastructural development with chapters at the college and university levels, and councils at the university and national levels. In spite of the success enjoyed by al-Gama'a al-Islamiyya within Egyptian universities, the rest of society, with its multiplicity of institutions, industries, and modes of life, remained largely untapped. While necessitating an internal reorganization, joining the Muslim Brotherhood would provide an instant avenue to propagate the call within the broader society.

Upon weighing the intellectual, emotional, and organizational factors that had come to shape the psyche of the student leadership over the course of the previous year, it was ultimately decided by leaders across the various universities that the time had come to enlist in the cause of the Muslim Brotherhood's *da'wa*. Abul Futuh had maintained contact with Sananiri, who by this point had become the officially designated recruiter of the Muslim Brotherhood.[45] Abul Futuh informed Sananiri of the students' decision. The Muslim Brotherhood was pleased to accept its first class of new members in many years, but placed certain restrictions on the process.

First, Sananiri stressed secrecy as a virtue. Given the highly sensitive nature of this development, which would be viewed with suspicion by the state as well as dissident students not in favor of joining, student leaders were instructed not to disclose their membership to their colleagues within the universities. The Muslim Brotherhood did not want to jeopardize the success that al-Gama'a al-Islamiyya enjoyed by either provoking a clampdown by the regime or a schism in the ranks of the student movement.

Second, the student leadership was told it could not join as a bloc. The Muslim Brotherhood had never absorbed an entire organized group, and was weary of such a possibility due to the risk of diluting its own organization. At a time when its organizational structure was in tatters and its membership numbers paled in comparison to those it was about to take on, the Muslim Brotherhood was especially vulnerable to a Trojan horse, essentially allowing a foreign entity to reshape the organization from the inside as it saw fit. Consequently, when 'Esam al-'Erian met with six close friends at his home, they unanimously decided to join the Muslim Brotherhood, but were surprised at the response they received. Sananiri told them, "We do not accept groups. This is a door that only one can enter at a time."[46]

Once again, the Muslim Brotherhood's leaders chose caution over immediate gains. Sananiri wanted to ensure that every new member had come to the choice of his own volition, not as a result of peer pressure or out of allegiance to one of the student leaders. Any hesitation or divided loyalties would lead to factionalism and the rise of blocs within the new cadre of Muslim Brotherhood members, something the elder leaders desperately wanted to avoid, especially given that the organization derived much of its strength from its strict hierarchical structure. Abul Futuh encountered a similar reaction, as he and his close friend and associate Sanaa' Abu Zayd were not allowed to join together.[47] This practice was widespread, although al-'Erian discovered that conditions in Alexandria were slightly more relaxed. Those who wanted to join could do so without added restrictions, but would face a probationary period before their membership would be made official. Ibrahim al-Za'farani and other Alexandria leaders benefited from this policy, and some students from Cairo even reportedly traveled to Alexandria, where joining the Muslim Brotherhood required less stringent conditions.[48]

The third major requirement involved the time-honored tradition of administering the bay'a, or oath of allegiance, to the general guide of the movement. Banna established the practice soon after the Muslim Brotherhood's establishment, as a nod to the oath that presaged the rise of a new caliph to power throughout the ages of Islamic history. With the abolition of the caliphate in the early twentieth century, Banna ensured that Muslims would not be completely without the focal point of moral, social, and spiritual authority that had sustained Islamic civilizations for thirteen centuries. All Muslim Brotherhood members had gone through this rite of passage, with some of the elders having given their bay'a to Banna himself. Following the settlement of the succession question within the Muslim Brotherhood, student leaders were among the first to offer their bay'a to Tilmisani.

While it could be interpreted as a symbolic display, the bay'a in effect formalized the entry of an individual into the Muslim Brotherhood and, in the case of the student leaders, instantly transformed the relationship dynamics between them and the elders. The reciprocal exchange of ideas was replaced with a top-down command structure in which no one dared question their superiors, let alone the general guide. The concept of sam' wa ta'a that al-Gama'a al-Islamiyya had instituted within its own ranks was adopted by the newest members of the Muslim Brotherhood, to great effect—except now it was the young amirs who would listen and obey.

Part and parcel of this pronouncement of faithfulness to the Muslim Brotherhood's leader was an acknowledgment of the group's authority to reorganize new recruits as it saw fit. Staying true to the traditional structure of the organization, students were placed into 'usar (sing., 'usra), or families, the basic unit of the Muslim Brotherhood, providing all members with a point of contact with group elders for instructional purposes. Once again, however, due to the circumstances surrounding the Muslim Brotherhood's reconstitution and recruitment of a large movement, this required a complex process of fusing the organizational visions of the young and the old. Abul Futuh recalled:

> The truth is that when we gave our *bay'a* to the Ikhwan, we did not give *bay'a* to an organization that existed in reality. Rather, we gave *bay'a* to an idea, a project, a legacy, for there was nothing that could be called an Ikhwani "organization" in the true sense of the word. There was only a group of individuals and historic leaders that took the reins of the true organization that existed, and that was al-Gama'a al-Islamiyya.[49]

In other words, the Muslim Brotherhood was "an empty house that was populated by the youth of al-Gama'a al-Islamiyya."[50] Using the traditional mode of establishing networks and forging linkages between leaders and members, the Muslim Brotherhood reoriented its new recruits to submit to the command of a regional official, usually from a student's hometown, village, or governorate. While helping to bring al-Gama'a al-Islamiyya under the hierarchy of the Muslim Brotherhood, this policy also addressed the problem of what to do with university graduates who were no longer active in the student movement. By 1976, graduates who had joined the Muslim Brotherhood were instructed to contact an elder in the organization in their hometown and to coordinate their activities through that leader.[51] A graduate returning home to Alexandria, for instance, would make contact with 'Abbas al-Sisi, who in turn would place him in a "family" populated with other members from a particular district or neighborhood.[52]

In the case of Abul Futuh and Abu Zayd, they were placed in a family along with a university professor, 'Abd al-Mu'ti al-Gazzar. Mubarak 'Abd al-'Azim, a science teacher who was part of an intermediary generation of Muslim Brotherhood members who had joined during the Nasser era, was appointed as the head of the family.[53] The group met in regular study circles for about a year, until Abul Futuh and Abu Zayd were relocated to another family, made up of more senior Muslim Brotherhood figures, including Mahmoud Abu Rayya, who had served as Hasan al-Banna's secretary and was placed in charge of the Muslim Brotherhood in Cairo. Given his lofty status within the student movement, it was natural that Abul Futuh would climb the ladder more quickly than many of his peers, and would become close to the center of decision making within the Muslim Brotherhood.

Just as the shape of student activism was altered by the adoption of the Muslim Brotherhood's school of thought and organizational discipline, the Muslim Brotherhood also had to adapt to a changing social and political environment. As part of his effort to create greater outreach efforts, Tilmisani arranged for the establishment of al-Maktab al-Siyassi (Political Bureau) within the Guidance Bureau. The decision aimed at counterbalancing the influence of the conservative faction of former Secret Apparatus members like Sananiri and Mashhur. While they focused more on internal matters of teaching new members the program of the Muslim Brotherhood and administering its central command structure, the Political Bureau appealed to the widespread sentiments among many youth that their mission should take on a public face, engaging with the state and society at large. Tilmisani appointed to the bureau several figures who represented the public activist wing of the Muslim Brotherhood, including Salah Shadi, Farid 'Abd al-Khaliq, 'Abd al-Mu'iz 'Abd al-Sattar, Ahmed Ra'if, and 'Abdullah Rashwan.[54]

Meanwhile, Salih al-'Ashmawi, a former member of the Muslim Brotherhood whom Hudaybi had expelled in the early 1950s, reconnected with Tilmisani, offering to bring his magazine, al-Da'wa, under the control of the Muslim Brotherhood once again. The publication became a focal point of the organization's activities, beginning with the first issue of the new edition in June 1976. In fact, the offices of al-Da'wa on Tawfiqiyya Street in downtown Cairo served as a makeshift headquarters for the Muslim Brotherhood's Guidance Bureau. Edited by Tilmisani, the magazine also served as a bridge between generations, as it featured reports and commentaries by important figures like Mashhur and Gaber Rizq, as well as student leaders like Badr Muhammad Badr and Muhammad 'Abd al-Quddus.

Facing the Fallout

By the late 1970s, the Muslim Brotherhood had successfully absorbed the great majority of the leadership of the student movement. In its brief time on the scene, al-Gama'a al-Islamiyya established itself as one of the most effective student activist organizations in Egypt's modern history,

but the strategic decision was made that the future of the Islamic movement depended on its ability to transcend the student movement. While
the two appeared synonymous for a brief historical moment, in reality
one was gradually overtaking the other. As a result, student leaders like
Abul Futuh, al-'Erian, and Za'farani pledged themselves to the mission of
the Muslim Brotherhood and conducted their affairs within the student
movement in accordance with the agenda of the mother organization.
Moreover, the program offerings to the general student body increasingly
represented the Muslim Brotherhood perspective, with many of its leading figures featuring prominently at camps and conferences, in the hopes
of widening the recruitment pool beyond the upper echelons of the student movement, to include the Islamic activist base.

The transformation was largely successful. Student leaders maintained that "the Muslim Brotherhood rescued al-Gama'a al-Islamiyya
from many problems, intellectual and organizational."[55] The rigidity of
Salafi thought, influential among the students, was narrowing the scope
of acceptable positions on a number of doctrinal issues. Meanwhile, the
jihadi tendency was also pervasive among some segments of youth who
were frustrated and disenchanted with the growing engagement with the
political system. For those who chose to adopt it, the Muslim Brotherhood's program addressed all of these competing trends and offered a
more promising and comprehensive outlook for the future. Badr characterized the difference in the student movement after many of its leaders
joined the Muslim Brotherhood as one of accountability. Leaders could
no longer simply take any position they wanted, a considerable development since the passions of youth were often ignited over hot button issues
like the tensions between Muslims and Copts. The requirement to adhere
to an official position developed by the senior leadership of the Muslim
Brotherhood often restrained a radical response that would otherwise
have emerged from al-Gama'a al-Islamiyya.[56]

However, the fact that the organizational structure and independence
of al-Gama'a al-Islamiyya remained fully intact, even after a number of
its leaders joined the Muslim Brotherhood, meant that internal conflicts
were inevitable. Abul Futuh and most of his peers had resolved to maintain an air of total secrecy about their membership in the Muslim Brotherhood. Those who did not join were largely unassuming, considering
only that their colleagues were sympathetic to the Ikhwani trend, while
they themselves were promoting an alternative outlook. Toward the end
of the decade, as al-Gama'a al-Islamiyya served to funnel increasingly

large numbers of students into the Muslim Brotherhood, one group was steadily expanding and rising in prominence, while the other remained stagnant, at least in terms of its leadership on the national stage of political activism.

This development was not lost on the dissenting minority within the leadership of the student movement. By 1979, quarrels and confrontations became a frequent occurrence across many universities. In Alexandria, for instance, during a meeting of al-Gama'a al-Islamiyya's leadership, Za'farani inadvertently let it slip that several leaders had taken the oath of membership in the Muslim Brotherhood. Usama 'Abd al-'Azim, a student leader associated with the Salafi trend, was stunned by the revelation, and proceeded to publicize it widely.[57] Accusations followed, with many outsiders charging that the secret Muslim Brotherhood members had staged a coup to take over the student movement from within. "The best defense," the student leaders decided, "was to go on the offensive."[58] Unapologetically, they acknowledged their affiliation with the Muslim Brotherhood and claimed that it was their right to join any group or organization as they saw fit.

Other factions had similarly started to become more organized, with blocs of Salafi students rallying around 'Abd al-'Azim, Muhammad Isma'il, and Ahmed Farid in Cairo and Alexandria. Elsewhere, the *jihadi* tendency was gaining momentum, especially in upper Egypt, under the leadership of Karam Zuhdi, Usama Hafiz, Nagih Ibrahim, 'Asim 'Abd al-Majid, and 'Esam Darbala. As these groups consolidated their movements with like-minded colleagues, their opposition to the mainstream leadership became more focused and provocative. The Salafi students accused the Ikhwani student leaders of taking liberties with Islamic practices and deviating from core doctrinal issues. The *jihadi* groups, meanwhile, asserted that the student movement had abandoned the call for struggle against a corrupt and unjust regime by focusing on tangential matters and reaching accommodation with the state.[59]

In this fashion, the fissures that had existed within the ranks of the student movement during much of the late 1970s erupted into deep chasms by the close of the decade. In some cases, as with the Salafi movement, the Muslim Brotherhood continued to pursue dialogue, though it was frequently unsuccessful and resulted only in heightening tensions. In other instances, as with the *jihadi* groups, communications broke down, and many of those who favored a militant path disappeared from the scene entirely, emerging only during the waves of violence that swept Egypt periodically. The Muslim Brotherhood maintained a key advantage in that its main recruits made up the uppermost level of leadership of the student movement, a prized asset for an organization that was looking to begin its mission anew by building on an existing movement. Meanwhile, most of the opposition figures from within the student movement made up the secondary tier of leadership: some were involved in the local councils at various chapters of al-Gama'a al-Islamiyya, but none of them was an amir. In a rare instance, that of the Assiut University chapter, did an opposition movement prove capable of taking the reins of leadership. A group led by *jihadi* figures was successful in ousting an Ikhwan-affiliated amir, Usama Sayyid Ahmed, and replacing him with one of their own.[60]

As the dividing lines became completely apparent, the Muslim Brotherhood student leaders no longer had reason to suppress their affiliation. By 1980, the dynamic within al-Gama'a al-Islamiyya had changed considerably. The Muslim Brotherhood leader was no longer introduced at official student events as "al-da'iya al-ustadh 'Umar al-Tilmisani" (the caller and teacher). Instead, he was introduced as "ustadhana, murshidana, sheikhana" (our teacher, our guide, our sheikh).[61] Official releases and publications issued by al-Gama'a al-Islamiyya included the Muslim Brotherhood's name on their letterheads and titles.[62] University campuses became a primary hub for the distribution of *al-Da'wa*. The public prayer services organized by student leaders that attracted tens of thousands of Egyptians during Islamic holidays featured Muslim Brotherhood banners and slogans. In short, the process of consolidation was complete. The Muslim Brotherhood had successfully assimilated the Islamic student movement intellectually, organizationally, and even on the level of day-to-day activities. Though there were two competing groups still claiming authority over the name al-Gama'a al-Islamiyya, by 1983, the group affiliated with the Muslim Brotherhood abandoned the name altogether, to dissociate itself from the militant actions of the group based in upper Egypt.

A Familiar Face

By the close of the decade, the Muslim Brotherhood had reclaimed the mantle of leadership over mainstream Islamic activism in Egypt. Battling tremendous odds, a movement that was once considered defunct, with its key figures executed, imprisoned, or exiled, suddenly experienced an unlikely resurgence. Within a few short years, the Muslim Brotherhood had settled the question of its return, had resolved its crisis of leadership, had forged links with the vibrant student movement, and had recruited its leaders into its ranks. By combining its traditional structural hierarchy with its knack for channeling the desires and aspirations of the new generation, the Muslim Brotherhood successfully cultivated a fresh organizational culture that promoted continuity when it could, but proved able to change when necessary.

For the student movement, the developments of this period led to mixed results. On the one hand, the early years of the movement were marked by the spontaneous and organic nature of youth activism, genuine intellectual curiosity that lent itself to the exploration of a multiplicity of viewpoints, and a fiery spirit that sustained a mass movement of political opposition. However, even the youth figures who lived this period acknowledged that the student movement faced greater challenges, ideological and structural, by not coming from an intellectual home within the elder generation, or building upon a proven organizational model. The reappearance of the Muslim Brotherhood gradually came to fill this void, a welcome advance in the minds of many, and an unauthorized intrusion for some. To some extent, the Muslim Brotherhood divided an otherwise unified movement that had found strength and harmony in its diversity. However, it could also be argued that the elder leaders simply exposed deep-seated conflicts within a young and inexperienced movement that would have eventually come to the fore in dangerous ways.

What the student leaders gave up in independence and spontaneity was made up for by the stability and coherence found in the Muslim Brotherhood curriculum and structure. Though it could not abate it entirely, the Muslim Brotherhood's aggressive response to the rise of militancy among some youth drastically minimized the spread of a potentially destructive force that undermined the essence of the group's mission to spread its message gradually within society. The Muslim Brotherhood had spent the better part of the previous decade articulating its response to the rise of a strain within Islamic thought that painted all of society with the brush of disbelief, and legitimated the use of force to oppose it. While the student movement of the 1970s was not privy to the debate between Hudaybi and the Qutbists as it unfolded during the latter prison years, they benefited greatly from the resolution of this question and the Muslim Brotherhood's ability to define its mission in relation to the external challenges that it faced.

The Muslim Brotherhood's successful consolidation of the Islamic movement was also not lost on the regime. In the span of ten years, Sadat had gone from releasing the Muslim Brotherhood members from Nasser's prisons to ordering their arrests on politically motivated charges. In between, the regime's policy toward the Islamic movement was never clearly laid out, and appeared to waver between co-optation and containment. As the organization formalized its reentry into society and began making significant inroads among the student movement, Sadat took the opportunity during a meeting with Tilmisani in al-Qanatir to offer the Muslim Brotherhood a path to legalization. The group would merely have to agree to register as a social association with the Ministry of Social Affairs. Then it would be granted full legal status to operate within the bounds provided for social and charitable groups. Tilmisani promptly rejected the offer. As a trained attorney, he understood the legal ramifications of Sadat's proposal. "I opposed it," he explained, "because under the law of social associations, the Ministry of Social Affairs has the right to dissolve any association at any time, as well as to appoint its officials and subject it to managerial and budgetary scrutiny."[63]

Not cowed by this initial rejection, Sadat continued to apply pressure on the Muslim Brotherhood to bring its mission in line with the agenda of his regime. By 1979, it became increasingly apparent to the regime that the organization had gained considerable ground, as an aide to Sadat noted that "[the Muslim Brotherhood] renewed its focus on teaching the young Muslim and instilling the doctrine. They did not count on clashing with any powerful political forces. They went in search of groups in civil society and universities until they controlled most of them."[64]

In light of these gains, Sadat once again arranged to meet with the general guide privately. This time, he offered to appoint Tilmisani to the Shura Council, the upper chamber in the Egyptian parliament.[65] Once again, Tilmisani refused the president's offer, explaining later that "when I am appointed and not elected, I am accountable to whoever has appointed me."[66] After the meeting, Tilmisani sent a message to Sadat stating that were he to be appointed against his will, he would resign the post immediately, so it would be better for the president to back down and avoid the embarrassing scene this would create.[67]

Even after the heated confrontation that occurred in August of that year, Sadat hoped to rely on the Muslim Brotherhood for assistance in diffusing an international crisis. Though the two sides had taken diametrically opposed positions on the Islamic revolution in Iran, the hostage crisis that developed there provided an opportunity for them to work hand in hand on a humanitarian issue. After early attempts to free all of the American hostages failed, US officials reportedly appealed to Sadat to enlist Tilmisani in the effort.[68] He was asked to meet directly with Ayatollah Khomeini and plead for the release of the hostages from a humanitarian and religious perspective. Sadat agreed to the mission, and an official from the US embassy met with Mashhur at the *al-Da'wa* offices to iron out the details. Sadat issued diplomatic passports for Tilmisani and his personal secretary, Ibrahim Sharaf, and requested that Sadat's trusted advisor, Mahmoud Gami', accompany them on the trip. Sadat also personally called Tilmisani and pressed him to do his utmost to free the hostages.

At the eleventh hour, Sadat called off the mission. He had heard a speech by Khomeini in which the Iranian leader expressed his admiration for the Muslim Brotherhood and claimed that he considered himself a student of Hasan al-Banna. In his increasingly paranoid state, Sadat came to fear that a conspiracy was at work to topple his regime with an Iranian-style Islamic revolution led by the Muslim Brotherhood. He simply could not afford to allow any contact or coordination between the Muslim Brotherhood and the Iranian revolutionaries, even if it meant backing out of a commitment to aid the United States.

Hoping to place further limits on the Muslim Brotherhood, Sadat recognized that its power to mobilize derived from its effective communications strategy. Before it compelled students to rise up in protest against the perceived political and social inequities of the time, the *da'wa* was first and foremost a simple educational mission, informing listeners about the world around them and the Islamic vision for self-empowerment and the betterment of society. To stem the growing tide of opposition to his policies, Sadat introduced Qanun al-'Ayb (Law of Shame) in April 1980. It established a court system to try individuals for "antisocial behavior" that included "inciting opposition to the state's economic, political, and social system, and disseminating false or extremist statements that damage national unity or social peace."[69]

This attempt by Sadat to silence all dissent aimed at his regime stemmed from his heightened sensitivity to sharp critiques that appeared within the independent press, especially in Islamic publications. Perhaps symbolizing the consolidation of its command over the entire Islamic movement, the Muslim Brotherhood maintained the publication most notorious for its verbal assault on Sadat's policies. In what would be his final address to parliament prior to his assassination, Sadat devoted the bulk of his lengthy speech to dissecting the content of the August 1981 issue of *al-Da'wa*. Like a prosecutor laying out his case, Sadat meticulously recited long passages from the magazine's pages and offered a point by point refutation of its arguments, though at times he was content simply to condemn the tone and language of the articles.

Unsurprisingly, that would be the last issue of *al-Da'wa* that the Muslim Brotherhood would ever produce in Egypt. Perhaps more ominously, Sadat used the opportunity to inform a stunned nation that earlier that morning, the Interior Ministry had conducted security raids across the country. Agents had arrested hundreds of opposition figures from across the political spectrum, but had placed the bulk of their energies on capturing the senior leadership of the Muslim Brotherhood and their counterparts from al-Gama'a al-Islamiyya. The members of these two groups, who had come together over a common ideological vision and a unified organization, were now reduced to a shared jail cell.

6

Constructing the Call

THROUGHOUT THE COURSE of the 1970s, there was no stronger sign of the re-emergence of the Muslim Brotherhood as a leading social movement organization than the publication of its periodical, *al-Da'wa*. Beginning with its inaugural issue in May 1976, not only did the monthly magazine present the new face of the organization, it offered the leadership an alternative base of operations, as the traditional Guidance Bureau had been defunct since the early years of the Nasser period.

It will be recalled that following their release from Nasser's prisons, veteran leaders were split on the future of the Muslim Brotherhood. Three camps advocated competing visions of the organization's future structure, ranging from a publishing house loosely affiliated with the Muslim Brotherhood of old to a group directly descended from its most hierarchically rigid unit, the Secret Apparatus.[1] Though the middle position represented by 'Umar al-Tilmisani eventually prevailed, both ends of the spectrum achieved valuable gains during this process. For the group advancing the former view, chief among these was the publication of a magazine that became the Muslim Brotherhood's most direct line to Egyptian society. In fact, *al-Da'wa* would develop into the main activism arm of the Muslim Brotherhood in the public sphere.[2] In addition to his position as general guide, Tilmisani would also take on the titles of president and managing editor of *al-Da'wa*. A more telling indication of the magazine's centrality to the reconstituted Muslim Brotherhood is the fact that the group's leaders did not maintain an official headquarters for the organization, but instead congregated at *al-Da'wa*'s offices.

Though the revival of the Muslim Brotherhood in the late 1970s could be examined in several ways, the study of *al-Da'wa* provides the most illuminating view into the group's reconstitution, as an organization and a holder of ideas. The magazine reflects the Muslim Brotherhood's meticulous efforts to develop a more coherent, broad-based message better than occasional speeches, brochures, posters, or slogans could. Even books authored by leaders within the organization, referenced throughout this study, provide only a glimpse of the internal debates that congealed on the pages of the magazine. While *al-Da'wa* was by no means the only publication broadcasting the views of the Muslim Brotherhood during this period, it was the most important, featuring regular contributions by the top brass of the organization and amassing a readership that reached 100,000.[3] Few independent publications could claim such a following in Sadat's Egypt.

This chapter builds upon the preceding discussion by demonstrating how, as the Muslim Brotherhood consolidated its gains in the organizational sphere, it also engaged in the active construction of its image in popular culture.[4] The "framing" process is marked by a fluidity in which "movement leaders and members continuously revise and modify frames, attempting to find new ways to connect with potential supporters and to reach new audiences."[5] In the case of the Muslim Brotherhood, the frames developed in the latter half of the 1970s took on a character markedly different from those of the early period of the movement.

The behavior of *al-Da'wa*'s editors is best understood as a function of the desire to rebuild the group's legitimacy and mobilize the maximum level of popular support. In its bid to accomplish this goal, the Muslim Brotherhood utilized preexisting reference points recognized by the majority of the nation's citizens. In the Egyptian context, this entailed a shared cultural heritage, common historical memory, and most of all, religious identity.

A thorough examination of the Muslim Brotherhood's chief publication reveals the conscious decisions undertaken by the leadership to present its message to a mass audience. Contrary to assertions made frequently by commentators on Islamic social movements, the content of mass-circulated media was not simply a reflection of group dogma or long-held religious doctrine. Rather, as the following discussion of the magazine's content demonstrates, decisions were made to fashion a specific discourse in light of contemporary social and political considerations. In this way, the Muslim Brotherhood was no exception to the general rule of social movements, recognizing the need to appeal to as broad an audience as possible while evading threats to its existence in the form of state repression.

The Written Word

Publication as the means by which to develop ideas and disseminate messages was a constant feature during this turbulent period in the history of the Islamic movement. Its importance as the primary method of communication was a relatively recent phenomenon in Islamic history, the product of a number of factors stemming from the Muslim world's interaction with modernity.[6] The decentralization of Islamic learning and knowledge allowed for the emergence of competing modes of thought, often outside traditional institutions. The role of the *'ulama*, the traditional religious class, became greatly diminished, allowing for a surge in lay Islamic activism with the emergence of groups such as the Muslim Brotherhood.

Technological innovations allowing for mass communication, increased movement of peoples, and efficient methods of printing information for distribution figured significantly, not only in the Islamic movement's means of spreading its message, but even in its conception of itself and the world around it. The global body of Muslims, or Ummah, took on a new meaning in the mid-twentieth century, as Muslim populations were at once divided into separate nation-states and united through their ability to communicate their shared experience and common outlook for the future. In a culture that had become dominated by print media, the regular publication of books, pamphlets, newspapers, and periodicals became the most effective tool of dispensing the organization's platform to the widest audience possible. Some scholars have even argued that the development of entirely new communities was spawned through print culture.[7]

The period of the 1970s in particular has been singled out as a point of departure from traditional means of disseminating information to the adoption of new technologies, a development that coincided with the Islamic resurgence.[8] This transformation resulted from a convergence of two primary factors. On the one hand, cultural changes necessitated that Islamic groups find new methods to reach ordinary citizens, while on the other hand, the state's aggressive economic opening altered the nature of the publication industry:

> In a shift that began in the Sadat era to a more market-driven production of books and pamphlets, the most significant growth has been in "Islamic books"—inexpensive, attractively printed texts written in a style accessible to readers who lack the literary skills of

the educated cadres of an earlier time. Often disregarding the vocabulary and grammar of formal Arabic in favor of colloquial diction, these books are available to a mass-educated public. They command press runs in the hundreds of thousands, while a book by Egypt's Nobel laureate is considered successful if it sells 5000–10,000 copies annually.[9]

So significant was this shift that even well-established "secularist and leftist" writers who preceded the Islamic resurgence adapted to the new trend, attempting to reach these segments of the Egyptian population.[10]

For its part, the Muslim Brotherhood had always relied on the publication of materials as a primary method of spreading its message. In addition to reviving Rashid Rida's *al-Manar* publication in the name of his organization, Hasan al-Banna's many speeches were repeatedly printed in collections for audiences that never saw him speak. In the years following the Free Officers Revolution, Hasan al-Hudaybi relied on secretly distributed pamphlets to counteract the state's onslaught against the Muslim Brotherhood in the realm of popular opinion.[11] One Western scholar made note of the use of medieval texts by Islamic jurists and thinkers, such as Ibn Taymiyya, resurrected in the late twentieth century by the Muslim Brotherhood. The reprinted editions came complete with new introductions by Muslim Brotherhood leaders relating old ideas to modern times.[12]

By the mid-1970s, the Muslim Brotherhood was faced with the prospect of reintroducing its message within a more competitive field that featured a variety of intellectual trends. In addition to *al-Da'wa*, two other Islamic periodicals made their mark during this period. The first was *al-I'tisam*, a magazine published by al-Gam'iyya al-Shar'iyya, the religious association established by Sheikh Mahmoud Khattab al-Sobki during Egypt's nationalist struggle following World War I. Founded by 'Ashur, Ahmed 'Isa in the late 1930s, the magazine expressed the group's Salafi orientation, often finding common cause with Banna and the Muslim Brotherhood.[13] In 1977, Hasan 'Ashur continued his father's legacy, developing *al-I'tisam* into a monthly publication that focused primarily on religious life, though it paid some attention to current political events, in particular its opposition to the Camp David Accords, which helped it amass a large following.

In 1979, Hussein 'Ashur, Hasan's younger brother, founded *al-Mukhtar al-Islami*, a journal characterized by its long scholarly pieces, an Islamic

Reader's Digest, as one study suggested.[14] This magazine took its inspiration from the Islamic Revolution in Iran, which distinguished it from the other Islamic monthlies, whose views on the events in Iran were more complex. Appealing to a narrower segment of the educated public, *al-Mukhtar al-Islami* often set the agenda of important political issues covered by the other periodicals, though its editors also credited the larger magazines with paving the way for its readership to expand.[15]

Because they covered similar subject matter and often expressed solidarity with *al-Da'wa*'s stances on the issues of the day, *al-I'tisam* and *al-Mukhtar al-Islami* have all been mistakenly identified as Muslim Brotherhood publications in various places.[16] In reality, only *al-Da'wa* represented the official Muslim Brotherhood position, though others may have shared its view on some matters, going so far as to republish *al-Da'wa* pieces on occasion.

Although these three magazines have been closely linked together in what Kepel referred to as the "Islamicist trinity," they were by no means the only religious publications circulating in Egypt during the latter half of the 1970s.[17] In addition to the well-established Azharite publications such as *Minbar al-Islami* and *al-Azhar*, magazines such as *al-Muslim al-Mu'asir* and *al-Tasawwuf al-Islami* also generated substantial followings within the Islamic movement. Sadat himself ordered the reprinting of the renowned Islamic modernist publication, Afghani and Abduh's *al-'Urwa al-Wuthqa*.[18] By September 1981, when the state banned all independent press, there were over a dozen regularly appearing Islamic publications throughout Egypt, an industry that had not even existed only a decade earlier.

Originating the Call

Leaders of the Muslim Brotherhood found no better way to announce the group's return than with the launch of *al-Da'wa* as its official mouthpiece in 1976. Though its editors claimed that the publication was simply the continuation of a previous run of a periodical of the same name, the latter edition of *al-Da'wa* was hardly the same as the original. The conditions experienced by the organization in the previous era were not conducive to the printing of a regular communiqué to be mass-produced and sold publicly on the market. Previous iterations of the magazine were much shorter in length, printed in small quantities, and did not appear regularly, especially at the height of Nasser's repression.

The first head of the Secret Apparatus and the former deputy of the Muslim Brotherhood, Salih al-'Ashmawi, founded *al-Da'wa* following Banna's death, as an attempt to strengthen an organization reeling from the sudden loss of its founder and charismatic leader. The magazine played an important part in presenting the Muslim Brotherhood's viewpoint at a time when its very existence was under threat of a government ban and a number of court cases against its members. It also fulfilled a secondary role, that of opposition to the leadership of Banna's successor, Hudaybi.[19] 'Ashmawi led a faction of prominent Muslim Brotherhood members who desired a change in the group's position on a host of issues, most significantly its relationship with the country's new political leaders, the Revolutionary Command Council. But in the end it was Hudaybi who emerged victorious from the threat to his leadership, ousting 'Ashmawi, along with other important figures such as Sayyid Sabiq and Muhammad al-Ghazali, in December 1953.

'Ashmawi continued to publish *al-Da'wa*, even after losing his affiliation with the Muslim Brotherhood. It covered general Islamic themes and avoided the confrontational path with the state to which Hudaybi's organization appeared to be heading. In fact, 'Ashmawi's exile from the group spared him entry into Nasser's prisons once the regime outlawed the Muslim Brotherhood and cast a wide net to apprehend most of its leaders and high-ranking members.

As staffers in the latter version of *al-Da'wa* would recount, 'Ashmawi published his magazine, even as Nasser dismantled any semblance of an independent press in Egypt. The magazine was not distributed, however. Because obtaining an official publishing license was a difficult ordeal, 'Ashmawi's sole objective at the height of Nasser's repression was to maintain the license to publish, the minimum requirement of which was the printing of five copies of any monthly publication.[20] By 1956, 'Ashmawi had ceased to produce new issues of *al-Da'wa*, and this process consisted entirely of reprinting five copies of past issues every month. Remarkably, this practice continued for two decades, throughout the Nasser period, and into the Sadat years.[21]

With his precious publishing license in hand, and the appearance of a fresh start for the Islamic movement, 'Ashmawi approached Tilmisani following the latter's emergence as de facto leader of the reconstituted Muslim Brotherhood. Putting his decades-old differences with Hudaybi behind him, 'Ashmawi placed his magazine at the service of the Muslim Brotherhood, which Tilmisani happily accepted. In June 1976, the first issue of the revived *al-Da'wa* was published, with nearly 60,000 copies distributed across Egypt.[22] The event was deemed so monumental that the BBC's news service announced the re-emergence of the Muslim Brotherhood on the basis of the printing of its magazine.[23]

Muslim Brotherhood leaders were quick to stress that neither 'Ashmawi nor Tilmisani, who had been appointed president of the magazine, sought permission from the Sadat government to publish the magazine. Instead, they relied on the preexisting license as the legal basis for publishing *al-Da'wa*.[24] Though it may have been true that Muslim Brotherhood leaders did not request official permission, the group's mouthpiece could never have appeared without at least tacit approval by Sadat. The events of 1981—only five years after the appearance of *al-Da'wa*'s first issue—would serve as a painful reminder that the state always maintained final control over the public activities of the Islamic movement.[25]

While 'Ashmawi and Tilmisani oversaw the general direction of the magazine, it was 'Abd al-Mon'eim Salim Jabbara, and later Gaber Rizq, who supervised the daily functions of *al-Da'wa*, from updating the layout and choosing the topics to be covered, to enforcing deadlines and soliciting advertisements. The magazine's offices were initially based in a small apartment in the Sayyida Zainab neighborhood of Cairo, and in 1978 moved to a more prominent location in Souq al-Tawfiqiyya, which later served as the Muslim Brotherhood's headquarters. According to Badr Muhammad Badr, a young staff writer for *al-Da'wa*, there were barely half a dozen reporters at the magazine, in addition to the editors. At a weekly meeting of the senior editors, the important topics of the day were discussed, usually yielding assignments for the staff reporters to pursue.[26] This was the formula generally followed in the latter years of the magazine's run, when current events took on more of a central focus than they had in earlier editions. Staff reporters were not restricted to covering particular issue areas, though any strengths they had were taken into account when issuing assignments. For instance, as one of the youngest members of the staff, Badr was placed in charge of the regular "Youth and University News" section of the magazine, in addition to a number of other topics on which he wrote.

The magazine's distribution quickly rose from the 60,000 copies of its first issue to 78,000 only seven months later. That figure appeared in the January 1977 issue's accounting statement.[27] Badr added that some later issues even reached 100,000 copies, with several selling out completely. The bulk of the distribution took place in Egypt, where *al-Da'wa* cost 12 piasters (written as 120 mallims in earlier issues). The rest of the

Arab world did have access to *al-Da'wa*, however, with more than 10,000 issues distributed outside Egypt, according to the January 1977 audit.

In addition to revenue generated by the magazine's sale, *al-Da'wa* also relied on advertising from both the public and private sector to sustain its publication. As one study of *al-Da'wa*'s advertising strategy showed, the editors relied heavily on former Muslim Brotherhood members who had become financially successful in Saudi Arabia and other Gulf countries. In fact, "three single advertisers represented half of all advertisements by private companies—al-Sharif plastics, al-Massara real estate company, and a foreign car dealer specializing in Japanese imports."[28] Perhaps representing the state's acknowledgment of *al-Da'wa* as an important publication, the National Bank of Egypt even took out full-page advertisements, highlighting its Shari'a-friendly financial services.[29]

As a consequence of its easier access to advertising revenue, *al-Da'wa* had a more attractive look and feel than any other Islamic publication in its time. The revived *al-Da'wa*, which began in June 1976, continued with almost perfect regularity, until it was closed down by government decree in September 1981.[30] Each issue ran roughly seventy pages and contained a variety of articles addressing current events, domestic and international politics, social and economic affairs, and religious thought and practice. To be sure, the Muslim Brotherhood had never before had an avenue to reach as wide an audience as its *al-Da'wa* readership would allow. As such, the organization's leaders would take great care to construct its message in as lucid and accessible a way as possible.

According to the magazine's young staffers, the Muslim Brotherhood's goal with *al-Da'wa* was to correct its image among Egyptians, in light of the "pressures" to which they had been subjected in years past. Put simply, it announced, "who they were, their ideas, their *da'wa*."[31] In its opening issue, an editors' note laid out the magazine's mission as "renewing *al-Da'wa*'s pact to remain the organ of an idea appealing for truth, believing in power, and calling for justice and freedom."[32]

Years later, in his memoir of the Sadat era, Tilmisani extolled the virtues of a professional, independent outlet capable of providing genuine information to its readers, a not-so-thinly veiled critique of the state-run media, which had been highly derisive of the Muslim Brotherhood's publication.[33] At one point, the mainstream press accused Tilmisani of exploiting "his *Da'wa* magazine" to inflame imams of mosques across the country in order to threaten national unity. While Tilmisani responded sarcastically that he was grateful for being credited with awakening the

nation's religious establishment, he resented the description of *al-Da'wa*
as his personal mouthpiece, depicting it as a collective effort by a movement that took its cues from the needs and attitudes of society. If Tilmasini
needed any more proof of *al-Da'wa*'s effectiveness, he would have it in
the years following Sadat's assassination, when virtually all independent
press outlets were allowed to resume publication with the notable exception of *al-Da'wa*. In fact, in 1984, the Egyptian government would pass a
law stating that a publishing license expired with the death of its owner
and could not be passed down to family members or associates. The law
was quite clearly aimed at permanently ending *al-Da'wa*'s run, whose
owner, Salih al-'Ashmawi, passed away in late 1983.[34]

Deconstructing the Call

Traditional studies of the Muslim Brotherhood have generally treated
the publication of *al-Da'wa* in markedly similar fashion. It was often portrayed as the rallying point for the Muslim Brotherhood in the 1970s.
During a critical time of reassessment within the Islamic movement, a
prominent periodical was the ideal vehicle to refine the organization's
message and rebuild its intellectual base. Furthermore, because of the
limited rights enjoyed by social movements under Sadat, the Muslim
Brotherhood seized the opportunity to publish a widely circulated magazine with a relatively high degree of freedom in an effort to reclaim its
once large following.

Nonetheless, when discussing *al-Da'wa*, scholars have tended to take
a narrow approach, analyzing it through the lens of traditional Western
thinking about fundamentalist movements. In a number of studies, the
only mention of *al-Da'wa*'s content were references to its heavy-handed
rhetoric against Israel and the United States, especially during the period
of the Camp David negotiations. As a result of this limited focus, many observers were left with the impression that *al-Da'wa*'s sole subject area (or
at best, primary subject area) was rehashing traditional Islamic perspectives on foreign relations, particularly with respect to Jews.[35] A number
of these analyses ascribed a particular form of radicalism to the Muslim
Brotherhood's writings on the issue, labeling their positions anti-Semitic
diatribes capable of radicalizing the Muslim masses through strong emotional rhetoric.[36]

Kepel's study of *al-Da'wa* was replete with such examples. The chapter's structure centered on the Muslim Brotherhood's identification of

"the enemies of Islam" in the course of the publication of its periodical. Likening them to the Evangelical Christian concept of the "Four Horseman of the Apocalypse," Kepel listed a quartet of foes named in the magazine over the course of its run. Though they appeared in many forms, he narrowed them down to: Jews, the Crusaders, communism, and secularism. As in many contemporary critiques of Islamic movements, these terms were not placed within their historical context. Nor was there a time frame within which the use of particular terminology occurred more frequently as part of a broader discourse. The impression one was left with upon reading such a one-dimensional analysis was that the central preoccupation of the Muslim Brotherhood was with the external enemies of Islam, existing from time immemorial, bent on the destruction of the faithful, and for which only a strong response would suffice. Kepel wrote:

> By making Jewry, the Crusade, secularism, and communism the four horsemen of the apocalypse, *al-Da'wa* demonstrates that, in the eyes of its readers, the lands of Islam now face an apocalyptic situation. Although all tendencies of the Islamicist movement fully agree on this observation, they differ when it comes to identifying the four horsemen. It is significant that the neo-Muslim Brethren have settled on four archetypes that are generally foreign to Egyptian society. This relieves them of the task of analyzing the internal causes of the difficulties of Islam, particularly as regards the relations between the state and civil society.[37]

Absent from this discussion was any possibility that in writing on such matters, *al-Da'wa* journalists and editors were engaged in a rational process of articulating their positions on a variety of issues of concern to their audience. There was an underlying assumption of uniformity in the course of five years of commentary on Egypt's foreign relations. A closer look at these articles would reveal developments over time and discernible differences among the various commentators expressing their outlook on these issues. In the final analysis, these articles did not exist in a vacuum. They were part of a larger context of the Muslim Brotherhood's framing mechanism, which tackled all of the pertinent issue areas affecting Egyptians. In fact, when compared to those articles dealing with domestic policy and social concerns, the commentaries on foreign policy were given far less attention and space by the editors of *al-Da'wa*.[38] The quasi-monthly series entitled "Israel: The Present and the Future," emphasized heavily in Kepel's analysis, appeared in the final pages of *al-Da'wa*'s issues, not nearly as prominent a position as articles covering other topics of more pressing concern.

In the few instances in which the scholarly community did not focus solely on the anti-Western rhetoric of *al-Da'wa*, it generally directed its attention toward single-issue concerns, such as the magazine's outlook on women as discussed in a regular section entitled "Toward a Muslim Home." Once again, the bulk of these discussions tended to adhere to the typical critique of modern Islamic movements, exhibiting little concern for the context of the particular problem. In the eyes of Western critics, the magazine's outlook on women was no more than a reflection of "Islam's treatment of women" throughout history. Though at least one author noted the role played by Zainab al-Ghazali, a long-standing figure in the Islamic movement and editor of "Toward a Muslim Home" in *al-Da'wa*, the conclusion drawn was that the Muslim Brotherhood's position on women remained largely underdeveloped and redundant.[39] Other studies very briefly engaged *al-Da'wa*'s position on other issues, such as its position on the Egyptian economy, which Ajami called "escapist polemics," or Telhami's aforementioned examination of the magazine's advertisements, which she described as "the most reliable indicator of organized Islamist economic power."[40]

To date, no study of the Muslim Brotherhood during this period adequately addressed the issues of *al-Da'wa* in a comprehensive fashion. Rather than approach single issues from a narrow perspective, the following section breaks down the framing processes within the magazine by contextualizing all the major issues covered by the editors. The underlying intellectual structure of *al-Da'wa*, along with pragmatic considerations of political limitations, audience, and opposition, often influenced its scope and content. All of the major issue areas covered by the periodical occurred within the framework of *da'wa*, a traditional Islamic concept that was refined and updated within the pages of its namesake.

Constructing the Call

Egypt's turbulent political climate during the mid-1970s had a visible impact on the direction of the mainstream Muslim Brotherhood and its reformist agenda. Seeking to develop its activist program within a rapidly changing society, the organization attempted to set forth its ideological beliefs in a flexible and easily accessible manner. All of its successive activities flowed from the articulation of the group's positions, which took place primarily in the pages of *al-Da'wa*. As was previously discussed, a feature of late twentieth-century Islamic activism was the shift in focus of the callers to the faith, the *du'a*, away from non-Muslims to non-practicing Muslims, thought to be in danger of leaving the faith and contributing to the general decline of religious life in society.

The *da'wa* work for this period revolved around what it meant to practice Islam in the modern age. In this regard, the initiatives undertaken by al-Azhar and other grand institutions across the Muslim world, intended to maintain Islamic life in society, were perceived by many Islamic movements as insufficient. Following the reconstitution of the Muslim Brotherhood in Egypt, *da'wa* took on an innovative approach, one that was to guide its entire program in the coming years. At the outset of its revival, it was clear that *al-Da'wa* aimed to offer readers a new interpretation of an old concept.

The initial step in this process involved defining the Muslim Brotherhood's *da'wa* in opposition to the alternative paths offered by the militant fringe of the Islamic movement and the state-supported religious establishment. In echoes of Hudaybi, the very first article directed toward the future *du'a* declared, "the principles of *da'wa* are united in the Qur'anic language of peace: 'and when the ignorant address them, they say: Peace.'"[41] The author's deliberate use of the verse citing "the ignorant," or *al-jahilun*, was a reference to the Qutbist discourse that dominated some segments of Egyptian society during the 1970s. While acknowledging the term's popular usage, the article offered a conciliatory approach to addressing the prevalent ignorance of Islam, using Hudaybi's call for "preachers, not judges," as a guide. Continuing along the same lines, in his inaugural editorial Tilmisani alluded to the Prophetic *da'wa* as the means by which the pagan tribes of Mecca ultimately accepted Islam—a feat they never would have thought possible at the outset of his mission.[42]

Another writer in the pages of *al-Da'wa*, Ahmed Gad, offered a scathing critique of the traditional conception of the term as practiced by religious elites functioning under the state. By placing the blame for Islam's continued subordination in society squarely on the shoulders of the state's religious establishment, the Muslim Brotherhood sought to position its own platform as a viable alternative to the norm. Gad wrote that "Islam's ordeal in this era arises from its *du'a* and their adherents more than those standing against its progress. By 'du'a,' I mean those employed in the

name of religious knowledge and given formal appointments of the official *da'wa*, and they are very many."[43]

In Gad's view, the state of *da'wa* in contemporary Egypt was at a historical low, consisting of preachers so ineffective that even ostensibly religious individuals were unaffected by their sermonizing. The traditional
vehicles for *da'wa* maintained a narrow focus on the ritualistic aspects of
the faith, leaving the needs of modern Egyptian society unfulfilled:

> They discuss the steps of ablution, or they describe how to conduct
> the Hajj, or even the rearing of a Muslim child, but on usury, po-
> litical oppression, and other violations of the limits of God, they
> are silent; it is as though these problems disappeared from their
> society or that Islam had made a pact of peaceful coexistence with
> them.[44]

Clearly, the aim of the Muslim Brotherhood's leaders was the construction of a new form of *da'wa*, one that offered a more comprehensive vision
of an Islamic society and transcended the limits set by the state. As stated
in other articles, the organization firmly held that its activities should
remain within the bounds of peaceful dialogue, preaching only to those
who would listen. In essence, change would only come if people desired
it and pursued it willingly. There was no room in the Muslim Brotherhood's *da'wa* for compulsion, coercion, or the use of force to achieve their
ends. This was an obvious allusion to the rising tide of extremism within
the Islamic movement, especially among the younger generation of zealous activists who aspired for immediate change. To them, Mustafa Mashhur urged prudence. The only way toward successfully accomplishing the
goals of the Islamic movement was to maintain a wider perspective. In
his sobering account of the arduous nature of this long-term strategy, he
contended:

> The path of *da'wa* is not furnished with flowers. It is long and ardu-
> ous, not simple and short. It is a struggle between truth and false-
> hood. It requires patience, perseverance, effort, dedication, and
> sacrifice. There should be no illusions about speedy results and one
> should not despair, for what is required simply is action. It is God
> who chooses the time and place for results. You may not even see
> them in your lifetime, but no matter, for we are judged according to
> our actions, not results.[45]

As a means of offsetting the obstacles with which the organization's mission was continuously confronted, Mashhur introduced an element of time to the discourse. He identified this time period as being a critical historical moment in the legacy of *da'wa* activity. Upon listing a number of parallels with the formative period of Islam, he wrote, "This phase is important and fundamental because it is the first step on the path and any mistake or deviation in understanding or knowledge will lead to negative results that will lead the *da'wa* off its path."[46] He emphasized the importance of a pure understanding of the Islamic sources, as well as the examples of the Prophet's companions and the latter-day Muslim leader in the figure of the Muslim Brotherhood's fallen founder. "This is what our Imam, the martyr Hassan al-Banna, stressed."

In the second stage of developing the *da'wa* concept, Mashhur authored a regularly appearing series entitled "The Path of *Da'wa*." After it was determined what *da'wa* was not, Mashhur set out to explain what it was. In laying the foundation for the revived concept, it was clear that he made a conscious effort to integrate his new conception of *da'wa* into the legacy of Islamic history:

> The path of *da'wa* is one. It was marched by the Prophet of God and his Companions before and it has been marched by the *du'a* since, through faith, action, love, and brotherhood. Their call is to faith and action followed by a unity of the hearts through love and fraternity. The strength of conviction was met with the strength of unity and their group became the standard bearers, whose message and call will undoubtedly spread and emerge victorious throughout the land.[47]

The importance of maintaining historical continuity lies in the desire for legitimacy that is often at the root of framing a social movement's discourse. By tracing the legacy of *da'wa* activity to the formative period of Islam, Mashhur effectively made the claim that the Muslim Brotherhood offered the most authentic form of Islamic activism. Nonetheless, he also cleared the path for innovation by highlighting the significant changes over time. The concept of *da'wa* was linked to the issue of civilizational decline. By reinstating religious consciousness and reasserting Islamic identity throughout society, Mashhur argued that Islam could once again emerge as a strong civilization at the forefront of human leadership.[48]

The tension between continuity and change continued as Mashhur outlined the steps of *da'wa*. According to him, "the general means of *da'wa* do not change. They have not been replaced and do not exceed these three basic principles: Deep faith; Precise orientation; Continuous action."[49] Despite the timeless nature of these principles, Mashhur explained in no uncertain terms the reformist goals of his platform. "Through these means," he wrote, "progress is made. Each step leads to a higher measure of success: there will be the Muslim individual, the Muslim home, the Muslim society, so that the extensive Islamic groundwork is set for the establishment of an Islamic government, which combines with others like it to form an Islamic caliphate across the Muslim world."[50] This brief description encapsulated the grand ambitions of the Muslim Brotherhood's *da'wa* project.

At first glance, it may appear as though Mashhur harkened back to the golden age of the Islamic empire. A more thorough look at this proposal, however, reveals that it was far from an anachronistic appeal to the romantic sentiments of some modern-day Muslims. Rather, this was a particularly significant statement because it signaled the first time in modern Islamic history that grassroots *da'wa* activity was utilized as part of a strategy for eventual political reform. The history of Islamic societies featured a pronounced gap between political authority and social movements—a gap that the Muslim Brotherhood sought to bridge through its reformulation of the *da'wa* concept.

As the series of articles on *da'wa* continued into the magazine's later issues, the discourse became more technical and was often responsive to the needs of the community of callers to the faith. This rigorous process of codifying the Muslim Brotherhood's *da'wa* project coincided with Mashhur's desire to rebuild a strong institutional structure on the order of the historic Secret Apparatus. In a three-part series of articles, Mashhur outlined what he identified as the primary phases of *da'wa*: proclamation, formation, and implementation.[51] He also gave considerable attention to what he labeled the "manners of *da'wa*," that is, the individual characteristics that make an effective *da'i*. Many articles addressed the legion of callers directly, describing in detail the ideal candidate for the crucial task of spreading the message. Among other things, he wrote that the individual must be:

> a positive role model for the type of Islam that he preaches for in his daily life; to have sincerity of faith in his chosen struggle so that

his message may reach the hearts of others; to think, speak, and act in accordance with the message of *da'wa*. To be versatile, dynamic, aware of all the different traditional schools of thought and current intellectual trends, to have a wide perspective.[52]

Beyond painting a portrait of the ideal type needed to carry out the mission, Mashhur also attempted to defuse the problems that arose during the course of the movement's development and expansion. An important aim of these articles was to ease the mounting frustrations of the youth regarding the popular perception within Sadat's Egypt of the widening contradiction between Islam's ideal vision of society and the corrupt reality surrounding Egyptians. Indirectly responding to incidents of violence, Mashhur wrote that these frustrations may lead to errors in judgment, but that the mission of *da'wa* nonetheless maintained that people had to be helped and that their intentions should not be questioned. He then offered counsel to those struggling in their daily lives while attempting to fulfill their charge. "Have patience, demonstrate resolve, and continue to inform people," he wrote. "Do not retaliate against the aggressors," Mashhur cautioned, even pointing to the example of early Islamic history, where passive assertion of faith was the only mode of resistance recommended by Muhammad. *Jihad*, Mashhur reminded his readers, exists in many forms, not only giving up one's life in battle.[53]

Picking up where Mashhur left off, famed Islamic scholar and former Muslim Brotherhood member Yousuf al-Qaradawi articulated the third stage of *da'wa* development. Whereas Mashhur emphasized strength and discipline in the ranks of the callers, Qaradawi worked toward the refinement of their sensibilities. In an early article, he commented on the similarities between *da'wa* and *jihad*, calling on young followers to go beyond *jihad*'s most commonly understood meaning of liberation by force, instead urging them to liberate their minds through a better understanding of their faith.[54] Qaradawi later initiated a regular series entitled "The Culture of the *Da'iya*," in which he described the intricacies involved in the promotion of an Islamic way of life. Knowledge alone was not sufficient, he argued, but a successful caller needed to know *how* to synthesize knowledge and implement it in everyday situations. In fact, beyond simply relying on religious knowledge, Qaradawi stressed to his readers the importance of learning across vast areas, including history, language, literature, and the sciences.[55] Through these articles, Qaradawi attempted to cultivate a *da'wa* culture steeped in traditional religious knowledge but also conversant with the contemporary language of Egyptian society.

The concept of *da'wa*, as it developed within the pages of the magazine, set the tone for the Muslim Brotherhood's activist program for the coming generation. Beyond the direct impact it had on the organizational structure, providing younger members with a sense of identity and mission, *da'wa* also informed the quality of issues addressed by the group. Even a cursory reading of *al-Da'wa*'s run reveals that its editors sought a comprehensive approach to the organization's platform, covering a vast array of issue areas through a unitary lens of *da'wa* as the starting point. In order to better analyze the framing mechanisms at work in the Muslim Brotherhood's chief publication, the plethora of issues can be organized into four broad categories.

The first includes the relatively large number of historical pieces offering an official perspective of the Muslim Brotherhood's formative years and subsequent suppression. For a monthly periodical, *al-Da'wa* devoted a considerable amount of space to dated materials, reflecting a strong desire to set the historical record straight and to frame the organization's contemporary activities in light of its rich experience.[56] These pieces quite often entailed a commemoration of the suffering witnessed by the Muslim Brotherhood's earlier generations at the hands of the state and in other instances, recounting tales of heroism displayed by the movement in the face of external enemies. In both cases, the goal was to establish an abiding legitimacy among Egyptians.

A second important point of interest reflected in the magazine was the organization's newfound engagement with the political process, albeit within certain limitations. For example, the question of Islamizing the Egyptian constitution at the time of its revision under Sadat was of vital concern to Tilmisani and others. In addition to the constitutional concerns, writers in *al-Da'wa* routinely addressed the policy issues of the day, such as the influx of Western cultural products that resulted from Sadat's *infitah*, or the revisions to Egypt's Personal Status Law, known as "Jehan's Law." In publicizing its positions on matters of governance, the Muslim Brotherhood cemented its position as the foremost opposition to the state.

The third focus of *al-Da'wa* includes all issues outside the domestic arena. Through its developed critique of the West, the Muslim Brotherhood provided commentary on the plight of Muslim nations at the hands of imperialism, colonialism, and internal strife. A central feature of these articles, however, was the continuing state of war between Israel and the

Arab states. Though Egypt had led the struggle against Zionism, Sadat's peace initiative saw the nation's standing plummet among neighboring countries and earned the ire of the Islamic movement. Using Islamic principles, Tilmisani sought credibility among the Egyptian masses in his strident attacks on the state's entry into the peace process.

The final category of issues is the broad category of religious life and culture. Though this covered everything from basic religious practices to more technical questions of applying principles of the Shari'a within public institutions, the significance of these pieces lay in their emphasis on the prominent role that Islam should play in society. As the critics of traditional *da'wa* noted, the discourse on Islam was decidedly individualistic in tone, ignoring the prevalent social problems for which religion offered an effective remedy. The majority of these types of articles addressed Islam's beneficial qualities in various aspects of public life. Together, these issues make up the four broad categories in which nearly all of the articles in *al-Da'wa* can be placed.

Commemoration of Suffering

Perhaps the most atypical aspect of the Muslim Brotherhood's publication was its strong devotion to historically oriented pieces. Unlike most periodicals, which tend to focus on current events, *al-Da'wa* gave considerable space to articles detailing the organization's history, documenting past experiences and reprinting the words of its fallen leaders. This is partially explained by political circumstances. Following a total suppression of the organization that lasted almost two decades, the Muslim Brotherhood was eager to pounce on the first opportunity to explain its own account of the events leading up to Nasser's crackdown. The official version of the state had dominated the public discourse so that a generation of Egyptians was raised knowing no other narrative.

In the very first issue of *al-Da'wa*, an article entitled "Abdel Nasser and the Massacre of the Ikhwan" established the tone for the ensuing historical revisionism. While introducing a recently published book entitled *The Silent Speak Out*, the editors laid the foundation for their historical frame:

> During the past twenty-two years, the people of Egypt have not heard or read about the Muslim Brothers except from a single, solitary source, in one tone of voice, filling their ears with the crimes of this group, its thirst for blood, desire for power, and collusion

with the British. The propaganda apparatus, with its vast resources that turned the 1967 defeat into victory, succeeded in deceiving this hapless population into dancing to these tunes and inflaming it with anger.[57]

From the outset, it was apparent that the Muslim Brotherhood believed that correcting the popular perception of the past was one of its most important missions in reaching out to contemporary Egyptian society. The article revealed the organization's relationship with Nasser, even asserting that he joined the Islamic movement during his days in the military, just prior to the coup. Following the first clash between the two, Nasser released the Brothers from prison and personally visited their leaders and welcomed them back into society. This action, overlooked by historians according to the author, confirmed that all of the early accusations of subversion and plotting were politically motivated fabrications.

Later articles pieced together the entire history of the Islamic movement, often focusing on particular time periods or highlighting important incidents. The group's early relationship with the monarch, touted by some of its opponents as a sign of the Muslim Brotherhood's elitism, was explained as a necessary tactic toward fulfilling the larger mission of the organization. The government's long-standing allegation of a 1954 coup attempt by the Secret Apparatus was addressed in detail. One article offered "the full truth," in its headline, before outlining the chain of events that led to the ban of the Muslim Brotherhood by Nasser.[58] At the time, much was made of the weapons cache discovered by authorities, which the group easily dismissed as a manipulation of the facts by Nasser's enforcers. In fact, they maintained, it was the Egyptian president who personally provided the Muslim Brothers with weapons in their struggle against the British in the Suez Canal Zone. There was never any plot (nor was one ever shown to have existed by the authorities) to turn those weapons against the state.

As for the infamous assassination attempt against Nasser in Alexandria by a member of the Muslim Brotherhood, the writers in al-Da'wa presented a meticulous point-by-point refutation of the government's accusation. In some instances, they offered physical evidence contradicting the official account of the incident, namely that the bullets pulled from the podium did not match the gun supposedly seized from the young would-be assassin.[59] Other arguments were framed from a strategic perspective—that the Muslim Brotherhood, as a strong supporter of the coup that brought the Free Officers to power, stood to gain nothing by under-mining the presidency in its early years. Resistance against foreign occu-pation, be it the Zionist project or British colonialism, did not translate as the strategy of choice in its tense relationship with the new government.

So important was this mission of setting the record straight for *al-Da'wa*'s editors that a new regular section addressing the particulars of the past relationship between the Muslim Brotherhood and the state began to appear prominently. In many ways, "The Muslim Brothers From the Pages of Yesterday," as it was called, sought to embarrass and expose the Egyptian regime by revealing the extent of the interaction at all levels of power. For the first time, Egyptians were given a firsthand account of the development of the Islamic movement in relation to the state. Criti-cal anti-state pamphlets and private letters from Hudaybi to Nasser were published in full. These typically addressed specific events or points of disagreement between the two, but at times also served as a platform for a general critique of the regime and a restatement of the Muslim Brother-hood's program.

This documentation of the organization's history served a number of purposes. It allowed the group an opportunity to meticulously outline its grievances against the regime, defining the diagnostic frame through historical experience and documented facts. The Muslim Brotherhood's remedy for the perceived ills of Egyptian society, or the prognostic frame, was shown to have been effective at times in the country's recent past. Hindsight, as it were, demonstrated the magnitude of the Muslim Broth-erhood's message through the directives of its founder and the experi-ences of his early followers. And finally, the publication of poignant accounts of the abuses suffered by members of the Muslim Brotherhood in the past served to motivate a new generation to act on the basis of the severe injustices of the regime and the historic sacrifices of the organiza-tion in particular.

Commemorating the suffering of Muslim Brotherhood members was an essential part of the magazine's mission. Throughout *al-Da'wa*'s run, anecdotes of numerous incidents documented the campaign of repres-sion against the organization's members. Headlines such as "Tales of Tortures" appeared regularly in *al-Da'wa*, promising "minute-by-minute" accounts of the traumatic abuses "from the tongues of the victims."[60] Ordinarily, these were anonymously written articles recalling the events leading up to arrests, interrogations, torture, and at times execution of Muslim Brotherhood activists. The editors of *al-Da'wa* engaged in an active construction of the martyrology of the organization. In some cases, friends, associates, and family members recalled the memory of the fallen victims, frequently surrounding them with an aura of purity, validity, and sacrifice.

In the story of one victim, Gamal Fawzi was described as being innocent of any wrongdoing. His only crime, according to his supporters, was his conviction in the precepts of the Islamic movement as it struggled peacefully against the regime. In a rare instance in which the victim's own words were printed, Fawzi described in his prison writings, prior to his execution, the suffering he had endured at the hands of the security services. Beginning with the raid of his home, Fawzi gave a vivid description of the soldiers entering "as though they had crossed the border and just defeated the Israelis." With guns pointed at him, his wife, and his children, they ransacked the house and took him to the intelligence agency's headquarters to be tortured. He recalled walking past rooms with pools of blood in them, before reaching the cell where his own blood would be spilled. He described in great detail the cruelty of the Egyptian interrogators as they sought information they were fully aware he did not possess, only to continue punishing him for crimes he did not commit.[61]

Similar stories appeared throughout the magazine's run. The formula was relatively consistent: sing the praises of the individual, noting his many virtuous qualities and accomplishments; chronicle the suffering endured at the hands of the security services, leading him to the path of martyrdom; and finally, castigate the regime for its violent abuses against the organization's members, while calling for accountability of those involved at the highest levels of power. In one typical commemorative article, this one chronicling the life of Yousuf Tal'at, the headlines running across the two-page spread captured his turbulent life and tragic death:

> Farouk tried to assassinate him; the British placed a bounty on his head; He fought in Palestine and the Canal; On the gallows, he said, "now I meet my Lord, while He is accepting of me; Oh Lord, please forgive me and forgive he who has oppressed me; Oh Lord, guide my people, for they do not know."[62]

That the Muslim Brotherhood constructed its martyrology with a specific purpose in mind is evident through its own explanation of this literature. Guarding against the potential accusations of inflaming popular sentiments or seeking the organization's own fame, the editors declared that their motivations were far more pure. "For if *al-Daʿwa* fills a few of its pages with the story of one of the victims of this tyranny, this is not to elicit people's emotions, harden their hearts against any particular person, or to declare that the Muslim Brothers have single-handedly carried the load of sacrifices."[63] However, the motivational framing of the Muslim Brotherhood relies precisely on those two results of its commemoration of suffering. By emphasizing the personal sacrifices of the Muslim Brotherhood in particular, the group hoped to swell its ranks with recruits, especially as it competed with the emerging fringe of the Islamic movement. Furthermore, by singling out the regime as being solely responsible for the state of terror and insecurity engulfing Egyptian society, it hoped to direct popular frustrations toward the state.

Throughout its chronicle of the Muslim Brotherhood's historical experience, *al-Daʿwa* aimed to deflect criticisms against the organization that arose from the fiery rhetoric of younger generations of Egypt's Islamic activists. It chose to highlight particular events in its history, such as the group's armed struggle against the Zionist project in Palestine and the continued British occupation of the Suez Canal Zone, in order to demonstrate the Muslim Brotherhood's commitment to justice in the face of oppression. In this sense, the Muslim Brotherhood represented all Egyptians by leading the national struggle. This notion was developed further as the group's leaders portrayed the government's assault on its members as an attack against all Egyptians. They wrote, "all people feel the lashes of the whip the day that the group of believers were lashed by the whip."[64]

Furthermore, the Muslim Brotherhood attempted to curtail the split within its ranks by commemorating the legacy of Sayyid Qutb as the quintessential victim of the government's anti-Islamist onslaught. In the many instances in which he appeared, including one feature article on the trials of his life, *al-Daʿwa*'s writers cemented Qutb's place in the history of the Muslim Brotherhood. Chronicling his life and the abuses he suffered, the editors established him as the single most prominent victim of the Nasser era. Qutb suffered not for his actions, they wrote, but for his words. He was innocent of any wrongdoing, the victim of a terrible crime and target of a vicious campaign that sought to stifle the voice of Islam in Egyptian society. In the most obvious sign that the Muslim Brotherhood had not abandoned Qutb nor his contribution to the larger movement, the editors of *al-Daʿwa* supplemented their claims that Qutb was killed only because of his writings by regularly reprinting excerpts from his books, especially his exegesis of Islamic scripture, *In the Shade of the*

Qur'an. This particular decision was the definitive signal that the "new look" Muslim Brotherhood continued to claim Qutb, a fallen martyr, as one of its own. In the face of rising opposition from hard-line elements within the Islamic movement, such a strong demonstration of resistance and sacrifice aimed to maintain the Muslim Brotherhood's credibility and to solidify its reputation as the foremost opposition movement to the oppressive Egyptian regime.

A second type of commemoration literature addressed the possibility of seeking justice for the martyrs in the current political climate. Though the Muslim Brotherhood rarely saw the benefit of pursuing legal action through the Egyptian courts, *al-Da'wa* published a number of articles advocating the prosecution of regime officials involved in the torture of Muslim Brotherhood members during the Nasser era. The appearance of official confirmation of the Muslim Brotherhood's claims lent more legitimacy to the group's commemorative efforts and ultimate struggle against the government. In most instances, these articles simply reiterated the facts made public by investigators, including the use of widespread administrative detentions, instances of torture, and sham trials. Lawyers conducting inquiries on behalf of the Muslim Brotherhood released their findings, which chronicled these systematic abuses, as in the Shams al-Shinnawi civil rights case.[65] In these articles, as much attention was given to the alleged perpetrators as their victims. In one case in which a lawsuit was filed for the death of three individuals, the editors seamlessly honored their memory and castigated those responsible for their deaths:

> The court considered the case of the martyr Muhammad Ali Abdullah, the martyr Isma'il al-Fayyumi, and the martyr Muhammad Awad, victims fallen to the various forms of torture while in the military prison. . . . [Men] with hardened hearts offering up blood to their false idols. Following these severe injustices, a compelling case was presented, with calls for the execution of those responsible for torturing and killing the victims. [66]

Though it is not clear from these articles whether any of these cases ended in legal victories for the victims (other sources seem to suggest they did not), the moral victory attained from the exposure of past abuses and the embarrassment suffered by many former and current regime officials were powerful enough to cement the Muslim Brotherhood's legacy and grant it the political and social capital it needed to proceed with its agenda.

For his part, Sadat allowed the publication to divulge its allegations against the authorities, even as it named individuals and singled out particular officials for prosecution. In the view of the Egyptian president, revealing the dark history of Nasser's era indirectly paved the way for his own cultivation of a democratic persona. Tilmisani clarified this point further, writing, "when the Muslim Brotherhood critiques the previous regime, it is not intended simply to embarrass and condemn certain individuals, but to learn the lessons of the past so as not to repeat them in the future."[67] Thus, the commemoration of suffering experienced by the previous generation of Islamic activists served as an important cornerstone of the Muslim Brotherhood's frame in the 1970s. It was an essential tool of self-definition, both within the organization and in relation to the rising tide of opposition.

Constitutional Calls

If the articles commemorating the Muslim Brotherhood's legacy were directed toward the younger generation affected by the growth of new movements, then the editorials and exposés devoted to the constitution and government policy represented the organization's tenuous relationship with the state. In the atmosphere of openness and pluralism that Sadat promoted upon his assumption of the presidency, and especially ratcheted up following the October War, the Muslim Brotherhood found an opportunity to demand its legitimate place in the political order. In the midst of this campaign, Tilmisani took the president at his word, even when the state's policies contradicted the freedom called for by Sadat. "The president declares his desire for reform," Tilmisani wrote, "while the great majority of the heads of governing institutions work to deliberately undermine his call."[68] Across the pages of *al-Da'wa*, the Muslim Brotherhood's leadership frequently called for institutional reform beginning with the constitution, at a time when it was undergoing a considerable facelift at the hands of Sadat.

Having been severely restricted in previous periods, the Muslim Brotherhood's engagement with the state occurred on a number of levels in the 1970s. Primarily, it focused on efforts to implement structural changes to governing institutions. In cases where the group was not actively pursuing these reforms by heeding Sadat's calls for democracy, Tilmisani and other leaders issued a sharp critique of the president's actual governing style. Various writers occasionally focused on particular issues concerning the functioning of governing institutions, including the parliament, the ministries, and the president's office. These policy grievances consisted of an identification of a particular problem, placing blame on a single official or group of officials, and proposing counter-measures.

The earliest issues of the magazine proceeded to place the Muslim Brotherhood's calls for Islamic governance within the broader context of Sadat's claims to democracy and the rule of law. Rather than reiterate the standard position on the role of Islamic law in governance, al-Daʿwa framed the discussion in relation to the government's discourse of reform. This allowed the Muslim Brotherhood's message to resonate with its audience, becoming a current feature of the public debate on the future of Egypt. In one of the earliest articles on the matter, a writer declared, "to realize true democratic rule, the constitution must be reformed."[69] This editorial responded to recent restructuring moves in the parliament by Sadat, which were not codified into law, and therefore were subject to reversal at any moment. The author made no mention of the Muslim Brotherhood's goal to maintain a religious character to the reforms, but sought only to reflect the interests of all Egyptians in codifying their rights.

In later issues, however, the Muslim Brotherhood expressed in no uncertain terms its frustrations with the failure of the government to meet its stated goals. As Sadat's democratization efforts reached a standstill in the late 1970s, al-Daʿwa published reports of the ever-widening gap between the state's lofty rhetoric and the unfortunate realities of Egyptian society. "[The government] issues many laws from time to time intended to organize society and provide peace and serenity. In spite of this fact, the people live under severe harassment, preventing them from basic security."[70] Editorials such as this claimed to expose the abuses committed by the state in defiance of its own calls for order and the rule of law. The writer posed the ultimate question: "If the officials in charge do not perform their duty in upholding the laws, then how can they request the people to help them in observing the law and calling for reform when they do not even follow their own laws?"[71]

By focusing on the perceived ills of Sadat's agenda for reform, the Muslim Brotherhood effectively juxtaposed the state's failures with its own alternative platform, claiming to hold the remedy for the diseases untreated by the establishment:

> If those officials believed in awakening the popular consciousness
> by upholding their laws before they ask others to do so, every citizen

would feel as though they had some responsibility to themselves and their society rather than simply out of fear of punishment. This religion is what causes the Muslim to be in private who he is in public. This religion is what teaches the Muslim to hold himself accountable before holding others accountable, and how to avoid in private what he would decry in public. This is all derived from one thing, the conscience of the believer, the certainty in his heart that God alone is all-knowing, holding all to account, with the power to do what no other ruler can do.[72]

Subsequent writings laid out the Muslim Brotherhood's position on the structure and substance of the Egyptian constitution, whose role was deemed central to the development of an Islamic society. The Egyptian constitution underwent numerous revisions in the modern period, especially during moments of political transition and turmoil. All of these versions, the Muslim Brotherhood leaders maintained, were short-sighted documents aimed at political expediency, in effect laying the groundwork for whoever happened to be aspiring toward power at the moment. What was actually needed, they argued, was a broader framework, one that recognized a source of universal values upon which to govern a Muslim society. "Therefore, the inspiration for our constitution must come from one who knows human nature and the condition of humanity, what harms it, and what benefits it. That is, the one God, the creator and facilitator."[73] As the religion of the majority of Egyptians, it was only logical, according to this line of argument, that Islam should inspire the system governing the nation.

In this way, the editors of *al-Da'wa*, led by Tilmisani in his opening editorials, made impassioned pleas to the state's lawmakers for a central place for Islam in the Egyptian constitution. To be sure, the Muslim Brotherhood frequently lauded statements by Sadat and other officials pledging to designate the Shari'a as the primary source of legislation in Egypt. Such remarks were frequently displayed on the pages of *al-Da'wa* as proof that the Muslim Brotherhood was gaining ground in Egypt and fulfilling its mission of infusing an Islamic ethos into the country's legal system. Nonetheless, the demands of effectively implementing the Shari'a went far beyond the symbolic gestures that Sadat was willing to make. The ensuing conflict between the Muslim Brotherhood and the regime usually centered on the exact role that the Shari'a should play in public life.

By late 1979, *al-Da'wa* was reflecting the mood among Islamic activists who felt betrayed by Sadat's revision of the constitution, which defined

Egypt in democratic socialist terms. His infamous comment that "there is no politics in religion or religion in politics" was viewed as an affront to the increased Islamization of Egyptian society meticulously documented in the magazine, as well as a departure from Sadat's previous comments. In the September 1979 issue, both Tilmisani and 'Ashmawi addressed the crisis over the constitution. The latter's commentary denounced the government's dismissive attitude toward the notion of an "Islamic constitution" and called for the formation of a committee to amend the constitution following the failures of Sadat's reforms.[74] Tilmisani gave a more sobering assessment, one that seemed resigned to the endless string of revisions:

> The secret behind the revisions and reforms of the constitutions from time to time has one root cause, though it may appear to have several. The Egyptian constitution relied on foreign sources for its content; they have their own manners, traditions, and principles, completely conflicting with our manners, traditions, and principles. The text of the constitution has demonstrated that it has inadequately protected freedoms, rights, and individual and collective security in Egypt. Had it been established on God's path, the religion of this Ummah . . . it would never have needed to be revised or amended from its establishment through today.[75]

The Muslim Brotherhood's leaders framed the discussion about the implementation of Islamic law through the prism of public interest. As chief competitor to the state's program, the Muslim Brotherhood put forward an alternative system to the one Egyptians had suffered through under the current government. In an edition of his semi-regular column excoriating state officials for their "conspiracy against the Shari'a," 'Ashmawi proclaimed, "In Egypt's constitution, Islam is stated as the official state religion and the Shari'a as its chief source of legislation. . . . Yet we hear constantly of women abducted and assaulted, passengers on trains and buses attacked and robbed by armed gangs."[76] Clearly, the issues of public safety and the rule of law were linked directly to the implementation of the Shari'a, which, according to its advocates, provided the necessary remedy to such issues of concern.

By the middle of 1980, 'Ashmawi wondered aloud why the discussion about legislating Islamic statutes had ceased completely to be a part of the public discourse. He contrasted that dilemma with the claim that most

Egyptians had expressed their desire for just such a change, especially in light of the social problems affecting their daily life. Instead of fulfilling these wishes, lawmakers failed to act on their earlier commitments, relegating Islamic law to a symbolic place in Egyptian society. The situation did not improve in successive months. In one of the most confrontational pieces to appear in *al-Da'wa*, Tilmisani authored an editorial calling on the entire government, from the president to the ministers and members of parliament, to resign their positions as a result of their failure to uphold the tenets of the constitution. The Muslim Brotherhood's leader began by declaring:

> In all the constitutional countries of the world, parties compete by various means available to them in order to accomplish the goal of implementing an agenda believed to be in the best interest of the nation. . . . It is of no importance who governs, but how they govern, in accordance with the one and only source. In that regard, what they all have in common is a respect for the constitution and the preservation of its principles.[77]

Tilmisani continued by arguing passionately that Egypt's government, led by its president, had abandoned its claim to legitimacy by repeatedly violating the constitution it had reformed. To be sure, the Muslim Brotherhood acknowledged that its provocative call was sure to increase tensions with the state. At a time when hostilities between the regime and the Islamic movement's fringe elements were already reaching a boiling point, the Muslim Brotherhood took special care to distinguish its sharp rebuke of the government from that of other groups. Its criticism was well intentioned, according to Tilmisani, and done in the spirit of brotherhood, from one Muslim to another:

> Do not look at what we have suggested in anger, for there is nothing between us and you except for the compassion of Muslims who desire for their country's leaders to be under the protection of God's law. . . . You are ministers of a state whose president has professed to be a Muslim and to govern an Islamic nation. What have you fulfilled from that mission?[78]

This statement represented a clear attempt by the Muslim Brotherhood's leader to balance his organization's need to express its position in strong terms, with recognition of the weight that such remarks might have in Egypt's tense political environment. As if to acknowledge the potential backlash that may arise from calling on government officials to step down, Tilmisani assured them that "we do not possess more than the word." That is, this plea was part of the larger discourse on the importance of Shari'a to society and not a public call to action.

As with its commemoration of suffering, the Muslim Brotherhood's framing of its constitutional concerns positioned the organization as the rightful defender of Egypt against the designs of those who would deny the will of the people to live as devout Muslims, free from foreign or domestic domination. Following the same model also meant that the writers of *al-Da'wa* would frame the discussion to allow for the maximum degree of popular support for their position and minimal government backlash. Regarding its relationship with the state's reforms, the Muslim Brotherhood would contend that the majority of Egyptians sided with the effort to Islamize the constitution. Such claims were difficult to prove, however, as there was no adequate measure of support because of a noticeable lack of any call to action on the part of the Muslim Brotherhood. In addition to its calls for constitutional reforms, another indicator of the Muslim Brotherhood's relationship to the state was its perspective on the Muslim world at large, especially through the lens of Egyptian foreign policy. As the following section demonstrates, this discourse also helped connect the organization to a far broader audience, that of the global community of Muslims.

War, Peace, and the Ummah

In the early part of the 1970s, as Sadat was solidifying his authority and the Muslim Brotherhood began a phase of reorganization, the foreign policy orientations of the two political forces were largely in line with one another. From the president's standpoint, the ideology of Arab nationalism that directed Egypt's foreign policy during the previous two decades was in need of complete dismantlement due to its failure to meet its primary objectives. From the perspective of the Islamic movement, the collapse of secular nationalism as the driving force behind the Arab world's international relations gave a boost to its assertion that a foreign policy rooted in the collective interest of the Muslim Ummah should guide the nation's leaders. Moreover, both parties were in agreement that the Israeli occupation of Arab lands since the devastating defeat in the Six Day War was the most pressing foreign policy issue facing Egypt.

Within only three years of his assumption of power, Sadat had already withdrawn from the orbit of the Soviet Union, redefined Egypt's role in the Arab world, and mounted a military campaign to force Israel's withdrawal from occupied lands. Contrary to the desires of many Egyptians, however, all of these actions held various deleterious consequences. The patronage of the Soviet Union was replaced by Sadat's courtship of US leaders. A realignment of regional power saw Egypt embrace former rivals at the expense of its allies, diminishing its influence across the Arab world. Finally, the 1973 war demonstrated the collective will of Arab forces, but failed to produce a military solution to Israeli occupation.

As the Muslim Brotherhood's leaders witnessed these events, a new message developed in accordance with the rapidly changing geopolitical climate around them. Though the essence of the group's long-standing mission—the need for an Islamic foreign policy—remained intact, the framing mechanisms experienced significant changes from earlier periods. Colonialism, for decades a major focus of the Muslim Brotherhood's critiques, was of less importance in an independent Egypt. Concerns over British rule gave way to scathing attacks on Soviet and American hegemony. Calls for unity under the banner of Islam outlasted the allure of Arab nationalism, which met its fate in the defeat of 1967. In urging the confrontation with Israel, the Muslim Brotherhood frequently recalled the sacrifices made by past generations and stressed the universal principles that would lead not only Arabs, but the entire Muslim world, to victory. The failure to produce a decisive victory in 1973 signaled the beginning of major tensions between Sadat and the Muslim Brotherhood. The president used the political capital gained from Egypt's strong showing to consolidate his authority and pursue a diplomatic solution to the occupation, while the Muslim Brotherhood cemented its position as the government's chief opposition movement in demanding continued hostilities with Israel.

As the Muslim Brotherhood's chief media outlet, *al-Da'wa* factored heavily in promoting the organization's views of Egyptian foreign policy, the Arab-Israeli conflict, and the state of the Muslim world. This outlook was reflected in a number of regular sections, feature news articles, and editorials. Every issue included a segment entitled "Our Islamic Nation," which compiled reports of developments in various corners of the Muslim world. Articles on Egyptian foreign relations usually focused on current events, such as the rounds of diplomacy with the United States and the changing status of Egypt in the Arab world. As the source of the continuous conflict in the region, Israel maintained a special place in the magazine. Guest contributors specializing in the field presented a history of the Zionist movement and the Jewish state in a number of articles. In addition, a regular feature by ʿAbd al-Monʿeim Salim entitled "Israel: The Present and the Future" provided a full analysis of the contemporary geopolitical situation and the domestic scene in Israel, prognosticating an imminent demise for the Zionist project. Finally, Tilmisani personally devoted a large amount of his opening commentaries to the Arab and Muslim world's conduct in relation to Israeli occupation, superpower hegemony, and regional politics. Together, these contributions represented the Muslim Brotherhood's worldview, presented to the group's audience in an accessible fashion.

The emergence of a bipolar global order in the latter half of the twentieth century presented a central problem for the Islamic movement. In the midst of Soviet and US competition for influence in all corners of the globe, the Muslim Brotherhood faced increasing challenges to carve a role for Islam in a region dominated by external forces. The aim of the new discourse was to empower Egyptians with a sense of their Islamic identity, while diminishing the seemingly omnipresent stature of the superpowers. A Muslim Brotherhood leader wrote in 1979 that the preceding decade signaled a shift away from the two orbits in much of the world.[79] The US withdrawal from Vietnam shattered the myth of its military invincibility, and the Soviet Union's image as a benevolent power proved spurious following its actions in Angola and Mozambique. The control over large masses of land and peoples was shrinking, and the time was ripe for Islam to assert itself as the path for nations to follow. The Iranian Revolution, though Shiʿite in character, proved that it could be done.

Nonetheless, a debate in the pages of al-Daʿwa contemplated the Iranian model and the unification of the Islamic movement worldwide as possible courses to follow.[80] In spite of the symbolic support given to such a project, the conclusion seemed to endorse a non-revolutionary, exclusively Egyptian track. Monthly pieces in "Our Islamic Nation" informed readers of the plight of Muslims from Morocco to Indonesia and beyond, but fell short of calling Egyptians—or their leaders—to action. The news and analysis provided in these articles served to keep readers informed of the larger Islamic world while properly contextualizing their place within it. The image of Muslims across the globe suffering under oppressive political and socioeconomic conditions was articulated in a deliberate way to give Egyptians a sense that they were part of a larger struggle for justice, to which all Muslims aspired. All that was required of the Muslim Brotherhood's following, at least in the immediate term, was the fulfillment of their duty toward their nation through the liberation of their land from foreign occupation and imperialism. By embracing the conflict against Israel as central to the broader struggle of Muslims against colonialism, imperialism, and Zionism, the people of Egypt could commit to making the necessary sacrifices to achieve victory.

The language of sacrifice was particularly important in the Muslim Brotherhood's discourse. In his pursuit of a separate peace with Israel, Sadat rationalized his independent track—widely perceived as abandonment of the Arab cause—by claiming that Egyptians had long shouldered the costs of war. A US-sponsored accord would lift the burden from the long-suffering Egyptian nation and restore its lost territory. Though this rhetoric was effective in generating significant Egyptian support for the negotiations at Camp David, the Muslim Brotherhood fought back in the form of numerous editorials decrying the desertion of the greater cause of the Ummah.

Moreover, according to a number of *al-Da'wa* articles, the defeat in 1967 signaled the end of the "fraudulent rhetoric of the past" in the program pursued by Nasser, and ushered in "a revelation of truth that the only path to victory is attachment to Allah as God, Islam as religion, and Muhammad as prophet and messenger."[81] The early 1970s brought "a new dawn" in which Egyptians, young and old alike, were affected by the heavenly message and worked toward a more complete victory. In the estimation of the Muslim Brotherhood, the war in October 1973 was a near-fulfillment of God's promise of victory, thwarted only by American interference, with its military and technological sophistication, which it provided to Israel.

In crafting their analysis of the events leading to the present negotiations, the editors of *al-Da'wa* were careful to avoid the scathing personal critiques against Sadat that were common at the time by other Islamic groups and Arab nationalists. One regular contributor, Salah Shadi, wrote:

> We will not say what others have said, that Sadat's visit to Jerusalem is in itself a horrendous crime or political ingenuity, for this distracts from discussion of the issue at hand and leads to arguments over pictures and symbols. And we do not say that Sadat is the one who accepted the offer for peace, for Nasser beat him to it after the defeat of 1967.[82]

This is a clear example of the great lengths that the moderate mainstream of the Islamic movement went to in order to avoid a direct confrontation with the regime. Such prudent remarks also served to distinguish the Muslim Brotherhood's critique of the ongoing peace process from that of the emerging extremist fringe, whose rhetoric began to focus solely on the figure of Sadat, especially following his 1977 trip to Jerusalem. As the stakes became higher, with the rise in anti-state violence (ultimately culminating in Sadat's assassination), the Muslim Brotherhood took great pains to avoid undermining the legitimacy of the regime, especially on matters of foreign policy. Rather, Tilmisani preached national unity and advocated the empowerment of the Arabs in the face of a common threat. In what was a fresh, Islamically oriented take on Nasser's pan-Arabism, the general guide of the Muslim Brotherhood envisioned victory through strong leadership and spiritual unity:

> There is a wide gulf between the Arab Muslim countries. The solution to Israel's occupation is with you, not America or Russia. There is no victory except from God and from the people and no worth to these people until they return to their religion and make their peace with God. They cannot do that while you are leaving them in a state of stagnation, weakness, and collapse. . . . You are able to achieve victory, if you wanted, and no one could stand in your way. Nothing stands between you and the implementation of God's law in your lands.[83]

This impassioned plea by Tilmisani reflected the organization's stance with regard to issues of international relations, up to and including the continuous state of war with Israel. Such challenges are viewed as moments of self-definition for the global community of Muslims. In the eyes of the Muslim Brotherhood, the emphasis on colonial power, Zionism, and later, the twin evils of communism and free market capitalism, played important roles in determining Muslim identity in the modern world. Only by addressing these threats head on through embodying traditional religious values, could the Ummah ever hope to secure its own existence and determine its own destiny.

The introspective nature of the discussion of foreign affairs was a common thread throughout the run of the magazine, especially in its final issues, when the future of the Egyptian state was to be forever altered by the course Sadat had taken. For every article on the illegality of Israel's occupation and the immoral enterprise of Zionism, there was a critical commentary on the state of the Arab and Muslim world in the face of these challenges. Indeed, as with every other topic area covered in *al-Da'wa*, the aim was to develop readers into conscientious, productive citizens by reawakening their absent sense of Islamic identity, revitalizing their weakened spiritual life, and prompting them to action. Because the level of international conflict was beyond their basic abilities as individuals, however, the quest for justice for Muslims across the region was a long-term goal that would only be achieved following the Islamization of society at home. This is why, contrary to a number of analyses of the magazine, the causes of Muslims worldwide, including the liberation of Egyptian land, took a backseat to issues of domestic concern in the course of *al-Da'wa*'s run.

Islam and Society

As the Muslim Brotherhood's work in the previous areas helped to define it as an opposition movement at odds with the state's program, those critical of the organization's efforts saw fit to paint it with the brush of extremism. The course of *al-Da'wa*'s run clearly demonstrates, however, that the emphasis on the engagement of society and the development of religious life sharply distinguished the Muslim Brotherhood from other trends of the Islamic movement. In fact, the overwhelming bulk of topics covered by the group's chief publication fell under the category of "Islam and society." This content also derived its importance from the fact that it represented the Muslim Brotherhood's relationship to Egyptian society at large, as opposed to its followers or the state.

In hoping to build a popular, grassroots movement that instituted Islamic culture and values in the everyday lives of Egyptians, Tilmisani set his group apart from those, such as al-Takfir wal-Higra, who chose to follow a divergent path toward isolation and militancy. Moreover, focusing on the needs of society allowed the Muslim Brotherhood more freedom to operate, as such a mission did not directly threaten the political establishment. In fact, while some of the articles did contain implications for social policy, most of the content related to Islam in society presented no opposition to the government. On one level, Sadat tolerated the effort to Islamize Egyptian society as an effective means to achieve his goal of de-Nasserization. These articles covered everything from Islamic practice, cultural interactions, and family life, to urban development, education, professional careers, and rural life—in other words, all the features of

Egyptian society. The Muslim Brotherhood writers infused an Islamic ethos in their discussion of all of these topics in an attempt to spread the organization's mission and to lay the groundwork for the ideal Islamic society to which they aspired.

Some of these articles were topical in nature, coinciding with the arrival of a particular occasion, such as the holy month of Ramadan or the Hajj season. These features served as reminders of the significance of religious rituals and to encourage a collective awareness of the faith's many tenets. One such piece, for instance, commemorated the anniversary of Muhammad's Night Journey and discussed the lessons for contemporary Egyptians from an event in the early history of Islam.[84]

Another category of articles reflected the Muslim Brotherhood's attempts to become deeply involved in the daily affairs of its audience. These included occasional feature segments, such as "With the Farmer," and regular installments of "Youth and Universities News" and "Toward a Muslim Home," among others. These pieces allowed the authors to tailor their message to distinctive audiences on the basis of their social standing.

Most of these articles followed the same general layout. They outlined a central theme or issue of concern for that particular month and addressed it in general terms from the body of thought developed by the movement over the course of its existence, and more directly from more current sources that tackled previously unforeseen questions. An article on the problems with university textbooks, for instance, included a page-long excerpt from a speech by Banna to students in which he espoused the virtues of *iman* (faith), *ikhlas* (sincerity), *hamasa* (zeal), and *'amal* (action) in pursuing higher education. By embarking on their mission in this spirit, Banna argued that the students would serve not only themselves, but their entire nation.[85] Coupled with this page from the Muslim Brotherhood's past, the editors of *al-Da'wa* also included an unsigned statement decrying the Ministry of Education's policy on university textbooks and calling for the government to meet the needs of students by developing a more up-to-date curriculum.

In this manner, the Muslim Brotherhood managed to appeal to a broad audience, offering a message that encompassed the goals of the Islamic movement intertwined with practical advice and support to the various elements of its constituency. Rural Egyptians and farmers were told that they provided a vital service to the rest of their countrymen and were entitled to more rights and benefits than what was provided by the government. In an article entitled, "How Will You Sell Your Cotton This Year?"

the Muslim Brotherhood's writer offered the cotton farmers three options: exporting to foreign markets, storing and selling wholesale to local companies, or joining the local cooperative to sell the produce in small quantities.[86] The article weighed the costs and benefits of each option, allowing the readers to decide for themselves what plan best suited them. Other pieces announced new technologies to ease the strains on farm workers, such as the development of a new industrial refrigerator to store potatoes.[87] If those efforts did not make clear that the Muslim Brotherhood appreciated the plight of the Egyptian farmer, more provocative entries demonstrated the group's understanding of the history of worker exploitation and a commitment to fight for their rights:

> After it was proven that the majority of farmers were the victims of the deviation into cooperatives, from one side, and the corruption of the supervising agency, from another side . . . for nearly fifty years, spent by the millions of farmers, toiling in the mills and grinders of "cooperative" corruption, whether under the era of feudal estates and parties or the era of the "socialist revolution" which filled the world with slogans of a war against corruption . . . when all that remained was the never-ending tragedy lived by millions of toiling farmers.[88]

Articles such as these concluded with fiery words addressed to the authorities responsible for the fate of farm laborers. During a crisis over a shortage of fertilizer, for instance, *al-Da'wa* confronted the minister of agriculture directly, questioning his handling of the situation and offering simple suggestions to ease the difficulties faced by many farmers.[89]

Reflecting a long-standing feature of modern Egyptian society, the Muslim Brotherhood regarded medical doctors as the highest trained professionals and the cornerstones of an advanced society. The articles addressing those in the field stressed the importance of developing an Islamic medical ethos.[90] The measure of progress could be seen in *al-Da'wa*'s later content, which no longer discussed a theoretical approach to Islamic medicine, but rather displayed the fruits of several years of activism within the Egyptian medical community. An October 1978 piece listed the many accomplishments of the Islamic Medical Union, an organization led by Muslim Brotherhood members. In addition to advancing an Islamic perspective on medical practice, the union offered numerous services to medical students and doctors alike, including: helping medical students with preparations for exams; building a library of medical reference materials, courtesy of a contribution from the *awqaf* minister of Kuwait; offering access to educational equipment and supplies; facilitating free medical services for impoverished communities; and initiating the building stage of an Islamic hospital.[91]

Another area of deep concern for the Muslim Brotherhood was the changes in the structure of Egyptian families brought about by modernity. The monthly section entitled "Toward a Muslim Home" addressed this issue directly, paying particular attention to the status of women in an Islamic society. Though the first few installments in this series were compiled by the editors, the section was eventually adopted by Zainab al-Ghazali, the only prominent female contributor to *al-Da'wa*. As a veteran of the Islamic movement in Egypt and leader of the Muslim Sisterhood, Ghazali was well positioned to articulate the magazine's discourse on gender.

Though the topic varied from issue to issue, the basic format remained similar to the previously discussed sections. Ghazali chose a topic of concern to Muslim families, addressed it through her knowledge of Egyptian society, including cultural and religious norms, as well as modern innovations. The second part of the piece usually featured an Islamic lesson relating to gender and the importance of the family. Based on traditional sources, such as the model of the early Islamic community, these lectures generally aimed to strike a chord with readers who failed to connect between the experiences of the past and the challenges of the present.

One of Ghazali's contributions captured the essence of the magazine's social mission. An article entitled "The Muslim Family in the Face of Challenges" defined the problem as perceived by the Muslim Brotherhood's school of thought. Ghazali used the image of a hurricane engulfing Egyptians, bringing "the winds of modernity" to a society with deep cultural and religious roots.[92] Identifying a pervasive campaign to undermine the Islamic character of society, she cautioned citizens against joining in that effort, however unwittingly. As with the general theme of much of the Muslim Brotherhood literature, this piece drew a picture of Islam under attack from near and afar. Social forces combined to form a rejectionist attitude that depicted Islam as regressive, misogynist, extremist, and anachronistic. Instead, these elements chose to promote excessive individualism and materialism, allowing for the spread of promiscuity, while modesty was equated with submission and the Muslim woman's headscarf was deemed an impediment to progress. Children were made to disobey their parents in the name of freedom and independence. The very basis of the family faced the danger of complete dismantlement, she wrote.

According to Ghazali's analysis, these developments were not in any doubt. The attack on Islamic values resonated with Egyptians and new trends took hold, all in the name of modernity. One of the consequences of this cultural transformation was the Personal Status Law promoted by Jehan al-Sadat, which provided women with, among other things, the right to unconditional divorce. Its proponents argued that the law "would provide happiness for the family," but Ghazali countered that it only led to more threats to the family unit's very being. The editors and contributors of *al-Da'wa* opposed this law as a dangerous plot targeting the family. The mainstream Egyptian media were depicted as prime culprits in executing this plot by smoothing the way for the transition to the new society. With seemingly no other opposition, the Muslim Brotherhood presented itself as the country's last line of defense against these developments. Ghazali and others stood in defense of the family, "the basic building block of society . . . the only frame of reference for the children."[93]

Upon identifying the essence of the problem as defined by the Muslim Brotherhood for decades, Ghazali concluded with the promise to monitor the issue closely and explore it in more depth in future issues. The second half of her two-page spread, though seemingly unrelated to the previous section, focused on the solution. This article profiled the historical figure of Khadija, the first wife of Muhammad, as an exemplar of courage, devotion, and good moral character for modern Muslim women. Following the traditional Qur'anic representation of the Prophet as a role model for all people, Ghazali prescribed a model specifically for women to follow. The life of Khadija contained many examples, she argued, that can be applied in the modern world. The focus was not on the differences in time and place, but on universal values that were to be observed in the lives of early Muslims such as the Prophet's wives, and applied in a contemporary setting.

The virtues of faith, patience, steadfastness, and compassion were described in vivid detail. The struggle facing Muslims was not limited to the early period, Ghazali wrote, but existed in the form of new challenges in the modern world. In this way, the author was able to seamlessly combine elements of the first part of her contribution, a critique of modernity, with the second piece on modern lessons from the example of a prominent woman in the early history of Islam.

In other articles, Ghazali was even more explicit about her position on gender roles. She viewed the notion of a woman working outside the home as a "disgraceful betrayal of the trust for which she was created."[94] Perhaps in an allusion to her own position as a prominent writer and activist, Ghazali does allow for the employment of women in certain circumstances, provided it does not adversely affect their domestic responsibilities. The Muslim Brotherhood's discourse on gender was indicative of the organization's larger aim in framing its social agenda, in this case attempting to stem the tide of foreign-inspired innovations and restore traditional values.

As the area on which Tilmisani focused the bulk of his group's efforts, social advocacy consisted in large part of defining roles that every social segment was meant to play in the nation's development. In addressing various professions separately, the writers in al-Da'wa sought to create a sense of individual responsibility. Doctors, lawyers, engineers, and farmers were approached in a personal manner in an attempt to appeal to each segment on its own terms. As detailed in prior chapters, students were given special attention because of the potential they held. If reached at a young age, they were expected to carry the mission of the Muslim Brotherhood and work toward its fulfillment wherever they went. The gender roles delineated by Ghazali were a central part of this overarching agenda.

The Islamic movement founded by Hasan al-Banna aimed to establish a social base capable of carrying out the group's mission. According to this vision, the Islamization of Egyptian society began by arming individuals with the knowledge and tools they needed to pursue an Islamic way of life in the course of their daily affairs. Perhaps more so than in any previous period, the content in al-Da'wa in the late 1970s addressed Egyptians in a clear and concise manner, motivating them to transform their way of life in accordance with the teachings of their religion, as interpreted and packaged by the leaders of the Muslim Brotherhood.

The articles in the magazine focusing on Islam and social life were the essence of Tilmisani's Muslim Brotherhood. They acted as the driving force behind the movement and were chief among all the topics covered in the pages of al-Da'wa. The remaining subject areas were ancillary to the overarching goal of embedding Islamic ideals in the social sphere. The Egyptian audience of al-Da'wa could not be expected to carry out the task of advocating for an Islamic form of governance if it had not internalized the teachings of their religion in its daily life. Nor could the legacy of the Muslim Brotherhood's historical experience have had the desired impact upon the new generation without their appreciation for the norms and values upon which previous generations based their actions.

Conclusion

LOOKING BACK ON the achievements of the Islamic movement in the 1970s, it is easy to lose sight of the disorderly and indeterminate nature of the movement, instead constructing a narrative that views the decade as the staging ground for the Muslim Brotherhood's triumphant return from the dustbin of history to the fore of Egyptian society and politics. But the reconstituted Muslim Brotherhood was shaped in large part by external factors that led to the emergence of a transformed and reconfigured organization. It reflected the established realities within Egyptian society, whether the state of political discourse or the dynamics of popular contention, as much as it demonstrated the fulfillment of the vision of its senior leaders. These figures, however, made it their central mission to preserve the legacy of the traditional organization that defined their lifelong experience with Islamic activism.

Therefore, the principal conflict of this era was one between the forces of continuity, fighting for the preservation of an existing order within the Islamic movement, and the forces of change, both internal and external, that sought to redesign the political, social, and cultural landscape upon which this Islamic activist mission was pursued. Examined through a conceptual framework, the dividing lines in this struggle become readily apparent.

The Muslim Brotherhood's senior leadership advanced an organizational model replicating the group's historical experience. Given the rise of many new groups contending for the leadership of the Islamic movement, 'Umar al-Tilmisani asserted the authority of the Muslim Brotherhood over all contenders. Its mobilizing power was one that had to be safeguarded, beginning with the organization's name. Responding to critics who suggested that the Muslim Brotherhood should not resume its mission until it has abandoned its name, Tilmisani put forward a list of ten reasons that such a proposal should be rejected in the strongest of terms.¹ He began by stating that "the Muslim Brotherhood has become a school. All of the callers learn through its institutions." Continuing, Tilmisani stressed the name's positive influence on the youth and commemorated the sacrifices on its behalf by countless activists over the years, including its founder: "What would we say to our martyr imam, Hasan al-Banna, who sacrificed his life in the cause of God, holding firm to this noble principle?" He concluded forcefully, posing the rhetorical question of who would lead the way, should the Muslim Brotherhood fold its tent:

> Who do we have as an inspirational guide, as a master to the generations, after the martyr imam and his successor, al-Hudaybi, to establish, raise, teach, lead, formulate, and implement? What guide can set the foundations, deliver the message, show the path, and gather the people around the book and the tradition with the same persistence, commitment, and loyalty?²

Beyond the name, senior figures argued for the continuation of the Muslim Brotherhood's historic organizational makeup. From the point of view of Kamal al-Sananiri and Mustafa Mashhur, the group's most effective mobilizing structure was its traditional hierarchy. Beginning at the top with the general guide and the Guidance Bureau, the organization had a power to mobilize its members down to the lowest rank-and-file follower. This was a feature of the Muslim Brotherhood that these figures were not eager to forfeit. In fact, they took important measures to strengthen the organizational structure. Learning from the failures of Hasan al-Hudaybi to exert the same level of authority over the organization as his charismatic predecessor, Mashhur emphasized strict discipline and obedience to the leader immediately above one's station in the chain of command. The result was an organizational structure that depended less on the charisma or leadership qualities of the general guide, and more on the ability of regional and local heads to enforce subservience.

From an intellectual standpoint, throughout the 1970s, the Muslim Brotherhood continued to frame its program as one of continuity with the positions established during the early days of the organization. For instance, 'Abd al-Mon'eim Abul Futuh recalled that Tilmisani publicly endorsed the organization's traditional view against the concept of political parties, while privately, his view had shifted to one of support for them in certain instances.³ Indeed, the cultural framing challenge for the Muslim Brotherhood was one of maintaining the vision articulated by its founder while also responding to the challenges of the day and demonstrating enough of an ability to adapt to shifting priorities within the intellectual currents of the Islamic movement. The disparity in content within the pages of *al-Da'wa*, from the republished pre-revolution tracts by Banna and Hudaybi's letters to Gamal Abdel Nasser, to articles on Anwar al-Sadat's peace initiative and the state of education in Egypt, are an indication that, try as it might, the Muslim Brotherhood could not afford to rely simply on its past to dictate its future.

External challenges set certain limits on the Muslim Brotherhood's reconstitution efforts. Though it never formulated a clear policy vis-à-vis the Islamic movement, the Sadat regime influenced its direction during every phase of its development. In fact, it is precisely the ad hoc nature of state policy toward Islamic activism that reverberated in the form of divisions within the movement. Sadat at once attempted to claim a stake for the regime in the Islamization of society, while also setting strict limitations on the application of this goal. He declared Islam as the source of all legislation in Egypt's revised constitution, but categorically rejected the call to implement traditional Islamic legal statutes. He removed the barriers to university activism, thus allowing the Islamic student movement to flourish, while refusing to lift the ban on the Muslim Brotherhood to operate freely within society and to advocate for Islamic government from within the halls of power.

Furthermore, the regime signaled an abrupt reversal from the religious rhetoric that defined the early part of the decade. A state that was to be built on the pillars of "science and faith" gave way to the proclamation that "there is no religion in politics and there is no politics in religion." Whereas Sadat framed the October War in religious language, the Camp David Accords were sold as a matter of national interest.⁴ The man once known as "the believer president" was garnering comparisons to Pharaoh by the end of his life.

Within this turbulent political atmosphere, the Muslim Brotherhood was forced to contend with the state's claims to religious authority. In a break from its past, when it did not have to challenge religious claims on the part of the ruling power, the organization expended tremendous energies refuting the state's assertions and pointing out its glaring inconsistencies. But by engaging the Sadat regime on this question so vigorously, the Muslim Brotherhood implicitly recognized it as a significant actor within the field of Islamic politics, thereby expanding the field for yet another competitor.

Not that this development was purely negative from the standpoint of the Muslim Brotherhood—by paving the way for the regime's entry into the discourse on Islam and politics, the Muslim Brotherhood created an avenue by which it could, in turn, directly engage the state on a number of policy areas that previous iterations of the Muslim Brotherhood, whether under the liberal/colonial regime or in the early revolutionary era, could not.[5] Debates ranging from the sources of legislation in the constitution to specific policy proposals dealing with war and peace, public morality, health, and education were all discussed in the fiery and contentious atmosphere of the mid-1970s. On occasion, the conflict left the realm of public discourse and emerged in the form of popular protest, as in the 1977 Bread Riots.

In measuring the political opportunities in place during various parts of the Sadat era, the Muslim Brotherhood at times struggled to strike the balance between maintaining its traditional outlook and adapting to a fluid political and social environment. At least twice, Tilmisani was offered the opportunity to join the government in some capacity, and both times he flatly refused, for fear of diluting the essence of his organization. Yet in other instances, the Muslim Brotherhood supported the engagement of its youth members with the regime by participating in Student Union elections. In fact, the organization built on this experience by expanding the scope its participation so widely that, by the early 1980s, the Muslim Brotherhood had come to control a number of professional syndicates and even forged political alliances with established parties and contested parliamentary elections.

It is this development, the engagement with the student movement, which most directly impacted the evolution of the Muslim Brotherhood's mission during the 1970s. The organizational dynamism and intellectual fluidity for which the Islamic student movement became known forced a recalculation on the part of elder leaders of the Muslim Brotherhood. In the course of their recruitment of the youth, they adopted many elements of their discourse, even as they attempted to challenge some aspects of the youth's beliefs and practices that they considered misguided. Even after the ideological questions were resolved, largely in favor of the Muslim Brotherhood's traditional program, Tilmisani and other leaders had to contend with the desire on the part of student leaders to maintain the outward focus of their activist mission. Upon the entry of the bulk of al-Gama'a al-Islamiyya's leaders into the Muslim Brotherhood in the mid-1970s, group elders struck a delicate balance between inculcating the students with the principles of an enclosed, self-contained organization and the demands of public activism.

This was a long-running debate within the upper ranks of the Muslim Brotherhood, some of whom wanted to abandon the notion of an internal organizational hierarchy unrelated to the group's public mission. Other figures, however, discerned a real need for such a structure, akin to the controversial Secret Apparatus, and it was those figures, including Mashhur and Sananiri, who gradually instituted this policy within the structure of the group. Whereas traditionally, the Secret Apparatus existed as a separate, self-contained entity from the rest of the Muslim Brotherhood's organization, these leaders gradually infused their philosophy across all levels of the group's ranks, so that by the mid-1980s, the Muslim Brotherhood's organizational structure was virtually inseparable from the strict internal hierarchy unrelated to its public mission.

Once again, the insular nature of this strategy stemmed from the concern over the loss of the Muslim Brotherhood's traditional vision in the face of increasing contestation, not only from the Sadat regime, but also from within some corners of the Islamic movement as well. While the Muslim Brotherhood successfully incorporated a large contingent of student activists into its ranks, not only did it have to address the intellectual and organizational dilemmas they posed, but it also had to contend with the vocal minority of Islamic activists who rejected the *da'wa* of the Muslim Brotherhood and put forward an alternative mission of their own.

Ultimately, this period proved to be as much about charting a new course for the organization by way of cultivating a fresh base of support as it was about preserving the legacy of the traditional Muslim Brotherhood of eras past. In due course, the youth members of the organization, who had successfully held the banner of popular activism during their college years, would take the reins of leadership and determine the Muslim Brotherhood's program for the coming decades. As Abul Futuh later observed, the ensuing period:

> was decisive in the construction of the Society of the Muslim Brotherhood and the development of its intellectual program and strategy for activism, the cultivation of its public image and its guiding principles as well. This period also saw the resolution of a number of issues that previously lacked clarity, such as the position

on violence and underground activity. It also established the foundations of the Muslim Brotherhood's organizational structure, the
rules governing its internal management, and the educational curriculum. . . . It is what allowed the Society to press forward strongly,
filling the void of popular activism in Egypt.[6]

Tilmisani's notion of *tawrith al-da'wa* was indicative of only one-half of
the equation. Not only was the call bequeathed to the next generation of
Islamic activists, it was also reimagined for a new era.

Epilogue

IN HER 2008 novel *Farag* (*Release*), Radwa 'Ashour tells the story of a generation disillusioned by the broken promises of an unfulfilled revolution. Even after experiencing the estrangement and dislocation caused by her father's political activism and subsequent imprisonment by the Nasser regime, the novel's narrator, Nada, finds herself drawn to the student movement of the early 1970s. The amorphous and non-ideological activism of this generation's youth contrasts with that of the previous one, and appears to cast their struggle as much against the failures of their parents as it did the early excesses of Sadat's rule. Before long, Nada too finds herself imprisoned, along with hundreds of her university comrades.

Unable to cope with the monumental struggle facing them upon their release from prison, many of Nada's colleagues give in to despair, abandoning a cause that they characterize as a "historical call" for the transformation of society toward "brotherhood, equality, justice, and happiness."[1] Instead, the characters engage in a prolonged period of self-criticism, internalizing the defeat of their "aborted dream" and experiencing such alienation through the subsequent years that one character dubs her generation "the stillborn." The novel's events are based in large part on actual events, including the rise to prominence and abrupt fall of Arwa Saleh and Siham Sabri, leaders of the student movement who may have spent only a short time in Sadat's jails, but exhibited a perpetual yearning for true liberation, finding it only upon taking their own lives, in 1997 and 2003, respectively.

To disentangle the complex social and political realities that would cause two bright and accomplished women to commit such an act in a cultural context in which suicide is seldom visible and rarely discussed, 'Ashour invokes Michel Foucault's concept of the disciplinary society. The structures and instruments of power, as they existed in the authoritarian environment of post-Nasserist Egypt, meant that not only would the state exercise complete control over the physical bodies of those it segregated from the rest of society through its political use of incarceration, but it ensured that even upon their return to society, dissidents faced a parallel set of constraints. Foucault likens these to the Panopticon, a disciplinary mechanism that employs a subtle coercive technique, primarily surveillance, "that assures the automatic functioning of power."[2]

By the time Sadat ordered the roundup of all political dissidents in September 1981, the process of subverting popular activism to the whims of the state had become complete. Only two forces proved capable of challenging this arrangement: the militant underground groups who relied on secrecy and violence in their contention against the regime; and the Muslim Brotherhood, with a disciplined and rigid internal hierarchical structure that permitted it to pursue a far-reaching social activist mission. Thirty years later, however, only the latter demonstrated durability in the face of continuing state repression.

When popular protests erupted across Egypt on January 25, 2011, the Muslim Brotherhood was poised to place its decades of experience in the service of a national movement to overthrow the regime of Sadat's successor, Hosni Mubarak. The movement that occupied Tahrir Square and other major public spaces in urban centers around the country for eighteen days was led by students and young professionals and was devoid of any particular ideological orientation. Like the movement that dominated Egyptian campuses in the late 1960s and early 1970s, these youth demonstrated strength through unity of purpose, determination, and courage, espousing universal convictions such as freedom, social justice, human dignity, and equality of opportunity for all. In short, they demanded a brighter future than the one their parents faced a generation earlier. Unlike the prior era, however, this period exhibited several critical features that would help determine the outcome of the popular revolt. From the technological advancements that facilitated wider mobilization, to the shifts in domestic and international political and economic conditions, and the evolution of modes of contention, the January 25 movement held an advantage over prior protests.

One can also add to these factors the decades of experience brought to the movement by an entire generation of activists who grew up with the regime and internalized its repressive tactics. Ultimately, as much as the toppling of Mubarak symbolized the coming of age of a cosmopolitan, tech-savvy generation, it also saw the fruition of a seemingly static dream long held by an older cadre of Egyptians.

For when the regime began grooming Gamal Mubarak to succeed his aging father over a decade earlier, the country's political order betrayed a more deeply entrenched authoritarianism. As the younger Mubarak, an investment banker by trade, began to assume control of a greater share of Egypt's political and economic institutions, along with a rising oligarch class, a panic set in among the country's activists, resulting in the establishment of the Kifaya (Enough) movement to oppose the regime's plans for hereditary rule. The unspoken tenor of the emerging national struggle suggested a visceral rejection of the notion that an octogenarian president would hand over the country to a son and his friends in their early forties—effectively bypassing an entire generation.

The passionate response with which this project was met served as a testament to the notion that a society could scarcely withstand an assault on the natural order of things, that is, barring a wide swath of the population from public service and the right to contribute to the growth and development of their nation. It is within this context, then, that the political developments in the months following the January 25 uprising should be understood. Barely a year after Mubarak's overthrow, five of the leading candidates to succeed him in Egypt's first democratic presidential elections in history came out of the 1970s generation of student leaders and activists.[3] Their rise to the fore of Egypt's post-revolutionary political scene was no mere accident. Rather, it was the product of a process that had been at work for several decades after the rise of the student movement and the concurrent reappearance of the Muslim Brotherhood as an organized force in Egyptian society. It is worthwhile to examine the major social and political developments over the course of the thirty-year period since Mubarak's ascent, placing particular emphasis on the figures who would later assume a dominant role in the short-lived post-revolutionary political transition.

When militants assassinated Sadat on October 6, 1981, the bulk of the community of activists, including virtually the entire Muslim Brotherhood leadership, had already been imprisoned weeks earlier as part of the regime's crackdown against dissent. Rather than a watershed moment that threatened to undo the social mission of Egypt's Islamic activism of the previous decade, this event only served to delineate the varying types of opposition faced by Egypt's ruling elites. Having solidified their control of al-Gamaʻa al-Islamiyya, militants based mostly in upper Egypt took their struggle underground, beginning a drawn-out war of attrition against the regime. By contrast, the student leaders who had joined the Muslim Brotherhood were released from prison within months and were allowed to resume their activities with only a few added restrictions, and under the watchful eyes of the state security apparatus.[4]

The following period witnessed a number of developments critical to the future of the mainstream Islamic movement. Two such transformations, occurring both in tension and in parallel with one another, have played a decisive role in the Muslim Brotherhood's progression in the aftermath of Mubarak's fall. The first involves the process of intensive focus on internal organizational development, or *tanzim*, that began in the late 1970s and continued through the subsequent era of institutional crystallization. The second reflects the growing desire, especially on the part of the newly admitted youth members of the Muslim Brotherhood, to continue their external outreach into Egyptian society and to establish a presence within civil society as well as state institutions. This process, which commenced with their entry into the Student Unions, continued with active participation in professional syndicates and culminated with the decision to field candidates in parliamentary elections beginning in 1984.

Both of these transformations were critical to the survival of the Muslim Brotherhood in the face of the continued factionalization of the broader Islamic movement and the external pressures from an authoritarian regime more determined to intervene in civil society than it had been under Sadat. Over the course of the ensuing decade, however, the rise of two distinct camps within the organization would prove detrimental to its internal cohesion and prospects for long-term survival.

Though it may have had its origins among the elder figures tasked with reconstituting the organization, the struggle between these two distinct impulses found its voice among the emerging leadership that came out of the 1970s student movement. In his role as a consensus figure, General Guide 'Umar al-Tilmisani encouraged both trends. On the one hand, he fulfilled the promise of *tawrith al-da'wa*, or bequeathing the mission to the next generation through strict hierarchical discipline within the group's ranks, while on the other hand, he sanctioned the call of recent college graduates to continue their public activism by joining the syndicates of their respective professions, and pursuing leadership positions within them to advance the broader Islamizing mission of the Muslim Brotherhood. Then, at a 1983 Cairo meeting of group representatives from across Egypt, Tilmisani announced that the organization would begin participating in the developing political process, including the upcoming parliamentary elections.[5]

In the mind of the group's leader, the Muslim Brotherhood's political objectives could be pursued without compromising the organization's structural integrity or risking the wrath of renewed state repression on the order of that witnessed under Nasser. This decision emboldened younger leaders, such as 'Abd al-Mon'eim Abul Futuh and 'Esam al-'Erian, former heads of the student movement, both of whom pursued entry into the Egyptian Doctors Syndicate and, in the case of al-'Erian, the parliament as well. He became the youngest person to serve in the body following the 1987 elections.

As Hesham al-Awadi demonstrated, the Muslim Brotherhood's wholesale entry into the public square coincided with the early Mubarak regime's quest for political legitimacy. By allowing greater participation by civil society in certain sectors of government and state institutions, Mubarak believed he would receive tacit recognition of his ruling authority by all opposition movements, including the Muslim Brotherhood.

For its part, the organization saw civic engagement as the path toward its own rehabilitation and acceptance by the state, something it had never fully achieved under Sadat. Once Mubarak overturned the stringent laws governing the state's professional syndicates, Tilmisani was free to usher in an era of continued participation by young members.[6] While by no means granting its members full political rights, this "honeymoon" between the Muslim Brotherhood and Mubarak, as al-Awadi has termed it, led the organization to achieve greater popular legitimacy than it had enjoyed previously, eventually forcing a recalibration on the part of the regime.[7]

Mubarak's reforms in anticipation of the 1990 elections and the resulting restrictions on the participation of the Muslim Brotherhood contributed to an internal shift within the organization that saw the ascendancy of the conservative elements at the expense of the accommodationists, whose years of political work had become frustrated by an increasingly autocratic regime. While the ability of Egypt's security apparatus to exploit the internal cleavages within the Muslim Brotherhood's leadership became a recurring theme in the 1990s and beyond, such external factors were only part of the story. Internally, the Muslim Brotherhood began to display important distinctions between two increasingly disparate factions.

To be sure, their conflict was not ideological in nature. The Muslim Brotherhood continued to exhibit the multiplicity of religious outlooks that was a feature of the 1970s Islamic movement. Rather, the institutional and political challenges that arose with the full-time resumption of the organization's mission necessitated the development of a pragmatic approach on the part of all of the figures involved. On the one hand, the group concerned primarily with the preservation of the Muslim Brotherhood's internal structure opposed public activism only insofar as it would dilute, or worse, destroy the central leadership's influence over its members. Future General Guide Mahdi 'Akef, long considered a leading member of the Guidance Bureau's conservative wing, had been vocal in his opposition to Tilmisani's efforts to pursue a more public political role for the Muslim Brotherhood.[8]

'Akef, along with Mustafa Mashhur and other senior figures of the conservative wing, began to rely more heavily on younger members who had not risen to positions of leadership within the student movement and could presumably be expected to fall in line with the more restrictive directives of the post-Tilmisani Guidance Bureau. Mohamed Morsi, who had not been particularly active within the student movement during his time at Cairo University through the late 1970s, was illustrative of this trend. Upon his return from the United States, where he pursued his doctorate, Morsi climbed steadily through the ranks of the Muslim Brotherhood's internal leadership structure. Similarly, Khairat al-Shater, who had attended Alexandria University but was not especially visible within the Islamic movement there, emerged as a key figure within the Muslim Brotherhood's central leadership in the late 1980s.

By the early 1990s, this group, which may be termed the conservative-pragmatists, had consolidated its control over the Guidance Bureau and had ensured the internal cohesiveness of the organization's structural hierarchy in the face of the Mubarak regime's repressive policies. On the other side, the accommodationist-reformers like Abul Futuh, who had devoted their activism to the Muslim Brotherhood's greater participation in the broader society and state institutions, were becoming increasingly marginalized and discredited due to the government's crackdown on their activities during this period. The 1990 elections boycott was followed by the failure of any out of 170 candidates fielded by the Muslim Brotherhood to be elected to the parliament in 1995, presumably due to fraud on the part of the regime.

In fact, the developments during that year proved to be critical to the recent history of the Muslim Brotherhood. The regime's decision to diminish the Islamic movement's presence in the public sphere extended beyond their exclusion from parliament. That year, the state security apparatus led a widespread crackdown on the organization, arresting and imprisoning hundreds of its members, seizing their assets, and subjecting its leaders to high-profile military tribunals. As one of the leading defendants in the trial, al-Shater was charged with a series of crimes, including, "creating an organizational structure throughout the governorates of the Republic and conducting secret meetings in which they professed principles contrary to the constitution," as well as "admitting a new generation of members after indoctrinating them in these principles . . . and creating the organizational hierarchy, including what is called the 'Organizational Consultative Assembly,' tasked with issuing orders and providing the financial means to accomplish the group's goals."[9]

For his role in being a chief organizer and financial officer within the Muslim Brotherhood, al-Shater was convicted and imprisoned by the military court, along with dozens of other group leaders. The case sent shock waves throughout the organization, not only because it effectively paralyzed its activities, at least in the short term, but because it also revealed the extent to which the state security apparatus had successfully infiltrated the Muslim Brotherhood and exposed its inner workings. From the perspective of rank-and-file members and lower level leaders like Sayyid 'Abd al-Sattar al-Meligi, who was himself named as a defendant in the case, the trial divulged organizational tactics and a decision-making process that was unknown to the members themselves, bringing to light years of doubts and frustrations about the Muslim Brotherhood's broader strategy.[10]

This internal fissure undoubtedly played a role in another major development during the same year, the establishment of Hizb al-Wasat, the Centrist Party. In late 1995, Abul 'Ela Madi entered discussions with other Muslim Brotherhood members about the possibility of leaving the organization to found a political party to compete in the Egyptian political process. Several weeks later, the group declared the formation of the party as a centrist Islamic alternative that was open to all Egyptians. In response, the general guide at that time, Ma'mun al-Hudaybi, requested the resignations of all members who chose to join the new party. A total of forty-six members did so. Although it did not include large numbers from the group's ranks, this signaled the most high-profile exodus from the Muslim Brotherhood in nearly four decades. The significance of this event also lay in the fact that it reflected an explicit rejection of the Muslim Brotherhood's organizational structure and operation, as opposed to its ideology. For all its emphasis on its moderate Islamist mission, al-Wasat Party did not depart much from the Muslim Brotherhood's intellectual school, relying on luminary figures such as Sheikhs Muhammad al-Ghazali and Yousuf al-Qaradawi as the basis for the party's Islamic reference.

The formation of al-Wasat Party brought back to the surface internal debates that had been at the heart of the Muslim Brotherhood's reconstitution over two decades earlier.[11] It was also a sign of things to come, as these same issues were to be revisited in the months before and immediately after Egypt's 2011 uprising. To be sure, although the emergence of two distinct camps within the Muslim Brotherhood was the primary development during the two decades preceding Mubarak's overthrow, the high degree of overlap across their approaches to activism prevented that fissure from resulting in an outright split. The conservatives approached the questions of engagement in society and confrontation with the regime far more cautiously than the accommodationists, but in the event that their political calculations indicated a high probability of success, not only could the conservatives be counted on to support a particular initiative, they could be expected to dominate it. This proved to be the pattern in a number of cases, whether it was the leadership of the professional syndicates or the parliamentary elections.

Though the conservative elements within the Muslim Brotherhood's leadership had expressed early misgivings about competing for the leadership of the professional syndicates, as it became apparent that the group could be expected to make considerable gains, they placed their active support behind the union elections, and the Guidance Bureau even handpicked the candidates for a number of key positions. Similarly, 'Akef's notable opposition to participation in parliament did not stand the test of time, as the Muslim Brotherhood made its strongest ever showing in national elections during his term as general guide. The historic elections of 2005 not only resulted in the Muslim Brotherhood taking hold of one-fifth of Egypt's lower house of parliament, or 88 seats, but it also solidified the hold of the conservatives over the organization's political strategy. As the Muslim Brotherhood's political activism was more tightly integrated into the central leadership's structural hierarchy, Morsi was selected to head the Parliamentary Committee within the

Guidance Bureau, overseeing the electoral strategy as well as the overall political agenda of the bloc once it was elected to parliament. Other conservative leaders from the Guidance Bureau, including Mahmoud 'Ezzat, Mahmoud Ghozlan, and Muhammad Badie', 'Akef's eventual successor as general guide, also began to play a greater role in the Muslim Brotherhood's political engagement.

Meanwhile, in what was considered a nod to the accommodationists by the Guidance Bureau, 'Esam al-'Erian took on a more prominent role in the organization's political activities, in some ways becoming the public face of its campaign to win the votes of the Egyptian people. Aside from emerging out of the leadership of the student movement of the 1970s, al-'Erian also found credibility in his distance from the core members of the Guidance Bureau, having been elected to the Muslim Brotherhood's general Shura Council but never serving within its executive office. On the other hand, noted student leader and Muslim Brotherhood reformer Abul Futuh had served in the Guidance Bureau since 1987. But while his presence provided the appearance that a multiplicity of viewpoints would be represented within the organization's highest body, Abul Futuh was largely ineffective at swaying the leadership on critical matters. Along with only a few other figures, Abul Futuh was consistently in the minority in the formulation of the group's broad strategy, even on matters of continued public engagement and political participation.

While the Muslim Brotherhood's 2005 electoral success was initially credited to the elements within the organization who pushed for greater civic engagement, internal state security documents released after the overthrow of Mubarak suggested that it was in fact the conservative leadership who struck a back-room deal with the regime that ensured the group's strong showing.[12] Once again, the regime's desire to temper the demands of the Islamic movement coincided with the pragmatic outlook favored by the Guidance Bureau.[13] Before long, however, Mubarak's security forces launched another crackdown against the group's top leaders in 2007, disrupting the internal organization and leading to the structural reshuffling two years later that consolidated the control of the conservative faction.

By late 2010, the Muslim Brotherhood's political gains had been entirely turned back, as parliamentary elections saw nearly all independent candidates defeated in the first round of voting, reportedly due to voter intimidation and fraud.[14] Rather than being upstaged by the Mubarak regime's electoral sweep, the Guidance Bureau made the determination to boycott the second round of the elections, effectively ending its recent run of successful political engagement, while also evading any direct confrontation with the regime. This decision was highly unpopular among the reformist wing of the Muslim Brotherhood, and the emerging fault line was exposed with the launch of the January 25, 2011, uprising.

Seemingly overnight, the internal conflicts brewing within the Muslim Brotherhood's organizational hierarchy for nearly three decades surfaced in the shadow of Egypt's largest ever mass protest movement. Led by a number of youth groups and civic organizations, the January 25 protests were the culmination of years of popular activism against the Mubarak regime's worst excesses, from economic exploitation and political corruption to police abuse, indefinite detentions, and torture. Throughout this burgeoning era of protest, the Muslim Brotherhood engaged the broad-based movement at only a peripheral level, through prominent figures such as Abul Futuh as well as the younger cadre of members.

Therefore, it came as no surprise when the Guidance Bureau refused to endorse the January 25 protests in a private meeting four days earlier.[15] Though this decision was reportedly based in part on the fear of retribution from state security officials, it was also in line with previous precedents set by the conservative leadership.[16] Nevertheless, the General Guide did not bar members from participating on an individual basis. This decision not only allowed a large contingent of Muslim Brotherhood youth to join their peers from other movements in Tahrir Square, it also paved the way for Abul Futuh, one of only a small number of high-profile Muslim Brotherhood figures who participated in the protest during its initial stages, to set himself apart from the organization.

It was only two days later, on January 27, in a move that reflected its pragmatic character, that the Guidance Bureau reversed course and put its full weight behind the popular protest that quickly expended in strength and scope the following day, dubbed the Day of Rage by the youth organizers. When the "Battle of Camel" occurred on February 2, the Muslim Brotherhood was poised to withstand the violent assaults on protesters by state security forces and armed thugs due to its organizational capacity and strict discipline across its ranks.

That institutional unity would not survive the final days of the uprising, however. The Guidance Bureau faced considerable backlash from younger members for its decision to engage in discussions with 'Umar Suleiman, Mubarak's intelligence chief and hastily appointed vice president. In the final week of his rule, Mubarak aimed to reach an agreement with the leading opposition figures with the hopes of remaining in power, while the Muslim Brotherhood's leadership appeared to be hedging its bets in the event that the protest movement failed to remove Mubarak. In a sign of things to come, the Muslim Brotherhood was, on the one hand, preserving its limited political gains within the closed system of Egypt's authoritarian regime, while also seeking to overthrow that very same dictatorship. It was only the determination of the Muslim Brotherhood youth in Tahrir Square, backed by the influential voice of Abul Futuh, that forced the organization's leadership to back down from a tentative deal with Suleiman that would have seen the Muslim Brotherhood withdraw from the protests in exchange for official recognition by the regime.

Less than two weeks after Mubarak's fall, the Muslim Brotherhood announced the launch of its political arm, Hizb al-Hurriyya wa al-'Adala, the Freedom and Justice Party (FJP). That the new party was an extension of the Guidance Bureau, and its conservative leadership was clear from the start. Morsi was named its president, while Sa'ad al-Katatni, previously the head of the Muslim Brotherhood's parliamentary bloc, was selected to be the party's secretary-general. Along with 'Esam al-'Erian, who had only recently joined the Guidance Bureau but was now committed to establishing its political arm, all three had to step down formally from their posts within the Muslim Brotherhood's governing body. But the distinction between the mother organization and the FJP remained nebulous. From his position as deputy general guide, al-Shater exerted tremendous influence over the political party in its initial stages. All Muslim Brotherhood members were instructed to join the FJP and to support its official position in ballot initiatives and its candidates during the parliamentary elections.

The successful bid by the conservative camp to dominate the Muslim Brotherhood's foray into electoral politics was a process three decades in the making. However, the radically altered conditions of Egypt's post-authoritarian political landscape ensured that long-standing internal divisions would finally boil to the surface. In defiance of the senior leadership's attempts to control their political preferences, a contingent of youth activists, led by Islam Lotfi, 'Abd al-Rahman Khalil, and Muhammad 'Abbas, announced the establishment of their own party. In sharp contrast to the FJP, al-Tayar al-Masri (the Egyptian Current) was open to all Egyptians, declared itself in favor of all of the tenets of the revolution, and did not style itself as Islamic in orientation. For their blatant disregard of the organization's directives, the Egyptian Current's founding members were expelled from the Muslim Brotherhood.

This was not to be the only exodus from the organization. Over the ensuing months, the Muslim Brotherhood's long-standing internal divisions resulted in the departure or expulsion of a number of high-profile figures, most of them former representatives of the 1970s student movement. Less than three months after Mubarak's overthrow, Abul Futuh announced his candidacy for Egypt's first free presidential election. As the FJP had previously declared that it would not challenge for the presidency, Abul Futuh intended to run as an independent and sought to appeal to a wide swath of the Egyptian public, not only those with sympathies toward the Muslim Brotherhood. For its part, not only did the Guidance Bureau disavow Abul Futuh's candidacy, it reportedly barred Muslim Brotherhood members from participating in his campaign.[17] Having already been dismissed from the organization's leadership following the 2009 internal elections, Abul Futuh's split from the Muslim Brotherhood became a mere formality in the aftermath of the 2011 uprising, but his expulsion came as a direct order from the general guide himself, Muhammad Badie'.[18]

In an obvious reference to Abul Futuh's candidacy, former General Guide 'Akef told the Egyptian press, "whoever wants to nominate himself can do so, but we are not endorsing anyone. We have our election lists and our internal principles to guide us and whoever does not abide by them will not remain one of us."[19] For his part, Abul Futuh continued to identify himself with the guiding mission of the Muslim Brotherhood, and reserved his disagreements to operational and policy matters.

In an April 2011 resignation letter addressed to the general guide, Ibrahim al-Za'farani affirmed that he saw no choice but to chart a separate course from the organization to which he had committed more than four decades of his life. Having served within the Consultative Assembly in Alexandria since the end of his student days, Za'farani had emerged as a reformist figure within the Muslim Brotherhood and was vocal in his condemnation of the 2009 electoral process that saw a major shift in the Guidance Bureau's makeup, followed by the election of Badie' as general guide just months later. In his view, the pressure brought to bear on high-ranking members during the elections ensured the total consolidation of power within the Guidance Bureau in the hands of the conservatives. At a time when most youth members and reformist leaders desired greater engagement with society and the broader opposition movement, Za'farani believed this core group of leaders was focused on narrow political gains at the expense of the organization's guiding mission, something that would become more costly in the post-Mubarak environment. He wrote, "after the 25 January revolution, I did not see any real change and there were signs that in my view showed the inability to keep the party separate from the work of *da'wa*, instruction, and social activism. When the Guidance Bureau appointed its members to the leadership of the party, in the process filling it with members of the *tanzim* of the Muslim Brotherhood."[20]

Furthermore, in his resignation letter Za'farani complained that the leadership's decision to prevent members from participating in any political party except the FJP "denies members of the Brotherhood the ability to assimilate into society."[21] In the days that followed, Za'farani announced the launch of Hizb al-Nahda (the Renaissance Party), an independent political party focused on a program of economic and social development for Egypt. The new party was quick to criticize what its leader perceived as the lack of vision in the FJP's political program.[22] Along with at least ten other junior leaders, joining Za'farani was another high-profile departure from the ranks of the Muslim Brotherhood's leadership, former Deputy General Guide Muhammad Habib. Having lost his seat in the Guidance Bureau in the recent internal elections, Habib also raised questions regarding the subsequent rise of Badie' to the position of general guide, charging that the Muslim Brotherhood's new leader was "selected and not elected."[23]

Other significant departures from the Muslim Brotherhood during the political organization phase of post-uprising included Haitham Abu Khalil and Khaled Dawud, founders of Hizb al-Riyada (the Pioneer Party), Mustafa al-Naggar, founder of Hizb al-'Adl (the Justice Party), and Hamid al-Difrawi, a reformist Muslim Brotherhood leader who left to establish Hizb al-Islah wal-Tanmiya (the Reform and Development Party). All told, in advance of the 2011 parliamentary elections, the Muslim Brotherhood's FJP had to contend with at least half a dozen parties established by former members, not including the rising number of Islamically oriented parties representing other trends such as the Salafis and the reformed jihadist groups.

From the standpoint of the Muslim Brotherhood, the subsequent months would prove what its most conservative elements had argued all along: namely, that strong organization and a disciplined structural hierarchy play a more decisive role than an open, all-inclusive approach that may have more broad appeal within society. The gains by Muslim Brotherhood offshoot parties—including the long established al-Wasat Party— were negligible when compared to the dominance demonstrated by the

FJP during all four stages of voting. The Muslim Brotherhood's coalition, the Democratic Alliance for Egypt, won 37.5 percent of the votes cast for the People's Assembly in late 2011, yielding a commanding 45 percent, or 226 seats in the lower house of parliament, of which all but 10 were representatives of the FJP.

Demonstrating its newfound political capital, built on years of developing strong social networks across Egypt, the Salafist coalition received 27.5 percent of votes and one-quarter of the available seats in parliament. Led by Hizb al-Nour (Party of the Light), the Salafi movement proved almost as adept at mobilizing its supporters to participate in the elections as had the Muslim Brotherhood. In fact, the movements shared common roots, having emerged out of the 1970s student movement that yielded, along with a reconstituted Muslim Brotherhood, the movement based out of Alexandria known as al-Da'wa al-Salafiyya (the Salafi Call). 'Emad 'Abd al-Ghaffour, the first head of al-Nour Party, was a veteran of the debates on Islam and society that permeated Egypt's university campuses into the early 1980s.

A junior partner in the Salafi coalition, Hizb al-Bina' wa-al-Tanmiya (the Building and Development Party), was a direct offshoot of al-Gama'a al-Islamiyya, the group that maintained the name that defined the 1970s student movement long after the bulk of its members had formally left to join the Muslim Brotherhood. The remaining members had distinguished themselves from their peers through their rejection of the Muslim Brotherhood's *da'wa* mission and political engagement in favor of direct confrontation with the regime, leading to the pursuit and imprisonment of its leadership. One such leader, 'Abbud al-Zumur, who was convicted of plotting the Sadat assassination, emerged as one of the heads of the Building and Development Party following his release from prison in March 2011, renunciation of militant action, and embrace of democratic politics.

A year after the dictator's overthrow, the emerging post-Mubarak political order appeared to signal a convergence of the mode of activism chosen by a broad swath of the Islamic movement for the first time in modern Egyptian history. The Muslim Brotherhood, its reformist offshoot groups, the Salafis, and the so-called reformed jihadists had all adopted party politics and democratic competition as the basis of their activism. The fiery debates that raged among student leaders in the late 1970s concerning the viability of broad social outreach and engagement with state institutions had resulted in a consensus on political participation as the primary vehicle for the fulfillment of the Islamic mission.

Not surprisingly, the parties representing the groups with the strongest internal structure and mechanisms for mobilization were by far the most successful during the elections. In contrast, the smaller parties made little to no gains in terms of actual representation. With the exception of the lone seat won by al-Naggar not on behalf of his Justice Party, but as an individual contested seat in a Cairo district, none of the new Muslim Brotherhood offshoots received any representation in the new Egyptian parliament. Even al-Wasat Party, with its decade and a half of experience in political organization, could only muster nine seats. Similarly, the Building and Development Party gained thirteen seats only through the strong showing by its main coalition partner, al-Nour Party.

These trends would carry forward into the next major political development in Egypt following the uprising, one that also was dominated by the 1970s student generation. Egypt's first free presidential election held tremendous symbolism for the sheer fact that it was to replace six decades of authoritarian rule with a popularly elected and democratically accountable president. Moreover, indications that the Supreme Constitutional Court intended to dissolve the elected parliament on technical grounds placed even greater weight on the outcome of the presidential elections.[24] In fact, it is in part under this pretext that the Muslim Brotherhood reversed its long-standing decision not to field a candidate for the presidential election when it announced in March 2012 that it planned to contest the race for Egypt's highest office.

As the qualification process threatened to exclude a number of high-profile candidates, from popular Islamist Hazem Salah Abu Isma'il to Mubarak-era intelligence chief Omar Suleiman, the Muslim Brotherhood's Guidance Bureau put forward not one but two candidates of its own. Its choice of the increasingly visible al-Shater and FJP party head Morsi as his backup reflected the group's preference for candidates with strong internal links to the organizational hierarchy. For a national election that demanded a strong candidate who exhibited wide appeal across the breadth of Egyptian society, this was a bold choice and a calculated risk on the part of the Muslim Brotherhood.

After Egyptians voted overwhelmingly with the Islamists in the national referendum and parliamentary elections, the election of a presidential candidate who represented that ideological trend appeared highly likely. Following the disqualification of Abu Isma'il and al-Shater by the Presidential Election Commission, the path to the presidency lay open before two candidates who symbolized the internal struggle within the

Muslim Brotherhood during the last three decades. Moving quickly to shed the "spare tire" image that beset him upon becoming his organization's second-choice candidate, Morsi set about to demonstrate that he was not merely the tool of the general guide or even al-Shater, the alleged orchestrator of the Muslim Brotherhood's mobilization strategy.

On the other side, as Abul Futuh's campaign was in full swing following the declaration of his candidacy over a year earlier, the pieces were beginning to fall into place. Not only had he earned the endorsement of virtually all Islamist groups who were disillusioned with the dominance of the Muslim Brotherhood, including the Salafis, the reformed jihadists, al-Wasat Party, and the other Muslim Brotherhood offshoots, he also gained support from liberal, leftist, and revolutionary youth groups. Billing himself as the "consensus candidate," Abul Futuh believed that not only would he appeal widely to all elements of Egyptian society, but that even the Muslim Brotherhood's rank and file members would support his candidacy.[25]

In addition to developing an electoral platform premised on rebuilding Egypt's economic capabilities, securing the hard-won freedoms of its citizens, and ensuring the country's regional and international independence, Abul Futuh also spent considerable time elucidating his legacy as a student leader and his decades as a Muslim Brotherhood activist. His famous 1977 televised confrontation with Anwar al-Sadat found new life on YouTube, as Abul Futuh's fiery protestations to an authoritarian ruler resonated with a younger generation of Egyptians.

Indeed, the legacy of this era took center stage during one of the most high-profile events of the campaign, a televised debate between two presidential front runners, Abul Futuh and former Mubarak foreign minister and Arab League secretary Amr Moussa. During the course of their heated exchange, Moussa took Abul Futuh to task for everything from his decades of service on the Muslim Brotherhood's Guidance Bureau to his student leadership days with al-Gama'a al-Islamiyya. On the latter point, Moussa conflated the earlier period of al-Gama'a al-Islamiyya's activism as a student group with the incidents of violence associated with the organization's branches in upper Egypt following its split from the mainstream movement and long after Abul Futuh had left it to join the Muslim Brotherhood. Moussa even went so far as to read a selected quotation from Abul Futuh's memoir in which he purportedly endorsed violence as a tactic during his youth. In his response, Abul Futuh appeared to equivocate on the question, claiming the line was taken out of context and misattributed. In the text itself, Abul Futuh repeatedly espoused the virtues of the 1970s era, marked by its lack of rigid ideological divisions and free-flowing discussions about approaches to Islamic activism. But the demands of a contemporary political campaign left no room for a nuanced outlook on the spirited and spontaneous nature of the student movement of a bygone era.

Similarly, Moussa played upon traditional tropes and growing fears of the Muslim Brotherhood when he asked Abul Futuh about the oath of allegiance that all group members must give to the general guide. Such a commitment, Moussa suggested, would mean that Egypt was in danger of electing a president whose loyalties were to a particular group, not the nation as a whole. Perhaps more alarmingly, such a president would take his marching orders from an unelected figure who was unaccountable to the Egyptian people. Abul Futuh seemed to acknowledge these concerns, but dissociated himself from them by affirming his resignation from the Muslim Brotherhood over one year earlier, and emphasizing the support he received from all corners of Egyptian society.

What was unstated but implicit in Abul Futuh's handling of the questions surrounding his historical and present relationship with the Muslim Brotherhood throughout the campaign was the decades-long conflict that had been simmering beneath the surface. Careful not to alienate potential supporters from within the organization, especially its youthful base that had supported him for years, Abul Futuh frequently lauded the achievements and sacrifices of the Muslim Brotherhood and the contributions it had made to Egyptian society. His decision to leave the organization in order to run for president as an independent candidate was a personal choice, he emphasized, and not reflective of any deep disagreements with the organization that shaped his intellectual outlook. Even his critique was measured. "The Muslim Brotherhood is a school that every Islamic activist should go through," he stated. "But eventually, one graduates from school."[26] This statement actively captures the essence of the division within the Muslim Brotherhood, defined not by ideological differences but organizational ones.

In fact, the ensuing drama surrounding the presidential elections best embodies the deepening divisions within the Muslim Brotherhood. After declaring that it would not run a candidate, and even publicly condemning Abul Futuh and eventually casting him out of the organization for his decision to compete for the presidency in spring 2011, the Guidance Bureau reversed course a year later. Rather than getting behind Abul

Futuh's campaign, which had gained significant momentum by that time, the group leadership fielded its own internal candidate, known for his deep loyalty and ability to follow orders. Moreover, the FJP focused its voter mobilization and media strategy on marginalizing Abul Futuh.

This strategy, coupled with the internal weaknesses of the Abul Futuh campaign, resulted in a smashing success for the Muslim Brotherhood and a resounding defeat for the independent candidate. When the votes were tallied following the May 25, 2012 election, the Morsi campaign, which had only come into being a couple of months earlier, led in the voting with 5.7 million votes and just under one-quarter of all ballots cast, even exceeding the support to Ahmed Shafiq, the remnant of the former regime who effectively mobilized the state apparatus in his favor. Abul Futuh, on the other hand, came in fourth in the voting, with just over four million votes and 17.5 percent of total ballots after dark horse Nasserist candidate Hamdeen Sabahi made a late surge to finish third, capturing over 20 percent of votes.

The Muslim Brotherhood's strong showing in the first round and Morsi's eventual victory over Shafiq in the runoff, coupled with Abul Futuh's disappointing result, served to clarify a primary point of contention that marked the Muslim Brotherhood's recent history. The inward focus on building a strong structural hierarchy and enforcing strict discipline throughout the ranks paid tremendous dividends for the organization, as seen in its extraordinary ability to mobilize supporters consistently for the two years after the uprising. The reformist approach pursued by Abul Futuh and others may have appealed to a wider swath of Egyptians, but it failed to materialize the support necessary for success within the limits set by Egypt's emerging political order.

In the short term, the remarkable achievements by the Muslim Brotherhood appeared to support the arguments long made by its increasingly conservative leadership. No organization without a strong internal structure could have survived the authoritarianism of the Mubarak era and hope to contend for political power in its wake. In the long term, however, the results of this approach are far from certain. If the short-lived Morsi presidency was any indication, the Muslim Brotherhood's supposed strengths during the authoritarian era emerged as the cause of its undoing at the dawn of Egypt's democratic moment. Having consolidated the Muslim Brotherhood's electoral gains by winning Egypt's highest office, Morsi faced the monumental task of fulfilling the demands of the revolution against the increasingly resilient remnants of the former regime. Not only did Morsi prove unequal to the task, but the Muslim Brotherhood's exclusivity, a hallmark of its conservative leadership, was now on display for the entire nation. Within months of taking office, Morsi had alienated all elements of the revolutionary factions and political opposition within Egypt.

Preferring to maintain its narrow political gains, the Muslim Brotherhood's leadership aimed to avert an all-out conflict with a regime that remained very much in control of many of the state's most powerful institutions, including the state security apparatus that had tormented the movement for over half a century. On the other end, the fragmented and disorganized political factions rallied around their opposition to Morsi's mishandling of the revolutionary demands and his increasingly autocratic behavior, embodied in a November 2012 presidential decree that included a provision granting him legislative and executive powers that were not subject to judicial oversight. Coupled with the dire economic situation, continuing lack of security in parts of the country, and a mounting media campaign aimed at delegitimizing the Morsi government, the picture looked increasingly bleak for the Muslim Brotherhood barely a year into its experiment with governance.

When the military, led by Minister of Defense 'Abd al-Fattah al-Sisi, stepped in to remove Morsi from office on July 3, 2013, it did so to the cheers of many Egyptians who preferred a return to military rule over a democratic transition led by an exclusivist social movement organization. By then, there was little that the Muslim Brotherhood and its supporters could do but lodge their protests at this assault on the legitimacy of the elected president. By mid-August, as security forces stepped in to break up the sit-ins at Rab'aa al-'Adawiyya and al-Nahda squares, over a thousand civilians were killed in the most violent show of force by the Egyptian state in modern history. Along with Morsi, virtually the entire leadership of the Muslim Brotherhood and the FJP were arrested and charged with a litany of crimes that included murder, treason, and incitement. In the months that followed, the Muslim Brotherhood's supporters were subjected to continued violent crackdowns and detentions. The group's assets were seized, its media shut down, and its activities curtailed. Even its charitable associations and social service institutions, long left untouched by Mubarak, were closed. In a move that recalled the total repression of the 1950s, by January 2014, the interim government that took power after the military coup had declared the Muslim Brotherhood an outlawed group.

It took over two decades for the group to recover from the repression of the Nasser era. This time, however, the Muslim Brotherhood has the added benefit of that experience. With its leadership reeling from the total war policy pursued by Sisi, the Muslim Brotherhood faces the long-term challenge of reconciling the competing approaches to Islamic activism that have characterized its development over the course of the preceding three decades. The post-uprising exodus of a number of key reformers, along with the alarming rate at which it became isolated from society even after repeated electoral victories, are indicative of the fact that the organization must adapt to the new challenges confronting its activist mission. In the face of nearly unprecedented external pressures stemming from the new political reality, internal self-reflection is a difficult but necessary task. As much as the leadership viewed structural continuity and internal stability as markers for the group's ability to survive periodic bouts with repression, the rapid unraveling of the Morsi presidency revealed an even greater need to engage with broader segments of society and to pursue a more fluid and open model of Islamic activism. As its leaders find themselves in the all-too-familiar position of outlawed opposition, the longstanding struggle between elements grasping onto the group's structural integrity and those urging for change in the Muslim Brotherhood's outlook toward Egyptian society will continue to define the pursuit of its historic mission therein.

Notes

FOREWORD

1. Richard P. Mitchell, *The Society of the Muslim Brothers*, reprint edition (New York: Oxford University Press, 1993), xiii–xiv.
2. Saad Eddin Ibrahim, "Anatomy of Egypt's Militant Islamic Groups: Methodological Note and Preliminary Findings," *International Journal of Middle East Studies* 12, No. 4, December 1980, 448.
3. Anna Jerome, "What Underlies Resurgence of Egypt's Militant Islamic Groups," *Christian Science Monitor*, April 10, 1980, p. 7.
4. Saad Eddin Ibrahim, "Egypt's Islamic Militants," *MERIP Reports*, No. 103, February 1982, 10.
5. Carrie Rosefsky Wickham, *The Muslim Brotherhood: Evolution of an Islamist Movement* (Princeton: Princeton University Press, 2013), 44.
6. Barbara H. E. Zollner, *The Muslim Brotherhood: Hasan al-Hudaybi and Ideology* (London: Routledge, 2009), 3.
7. Gilles Kepel, *Muslim Extremism in Egypt: The Prophet and Pharaoh* (Berkeley: University of California Press, 1986), 128.
8. Zulkifly Abdul Malek, "From Cairo to Kuala Lumpur: The Influence of the Muslim Brotherhood on the Muslim Youth Movement of Malaysia (ABIM)," (master's thesis, Georgetown University, 2011), 38–39.
9. John L. Esposito and John O. Voll, *Makers of Contemporary Islam* (New York: Oxford University Press, 2001), 109.

INTRODUCTION

1. 'Umar al-Tilmisani, *Ayyam Ma'a al-Sadat* (Cairo: Dar al-I'tisam, 1984), p. 102.
2. Interview with Muhammad 'Abd al-Quddus.
3. Tilmisani, p. 102.

4. Some prominent examples include: Kurshid Ahmad, Islamic Resurgence: Challenges, Directions and Future Perspectives: A Roundtable with Kurshid Ahmad (Tampa: WISE, 1994); Hillal Dessouki, ed., Islamic Resurgence in the Arab World (New York: Praeger, 1982); John Esposito, Voices of Resurgent Islam (New York: Oxford University Press, 1983); John Voll, Islam: Continuity and Change in the Modern World (Syracuse: Syracuse University Press, 1994); Emmanuel Sivan, in James P. Jankowski and Israel Gershoni, ed., Rethinking Nationalism in the Arab Middle East (New York: Columbia University Press, 1997); Bassam Tibi, The Challenge of Fundamentalism: Political Islam and the New World Disorder (Berkeley: University of California Press, 2002).

5. An example of this is the classical study by Daniel Lerner, *The Passing of Traditional Society: Modernizing the Middle East* (Illinois: Free Press, 1958).

6. Particularly emblematic of this trend was the 1990 article by Bernard Lewis in the *Atlantic*, entitled "The Roots of Muslim Rage."

7. Examples of this literature include: Gilles Kepel, *Jihad: The Trail of Political Islam* (Cambridge, MA: Harvard University Press, 2002); Bassam Tibi, *The Challenge of Fundamentalism: Political Islam and the New World Disorder* (Berkeley: University of California Press, 1998); John L. Esposito and John O. Voll, *Islam and Democracy* (New York: Oxford University Press, 1996).

8. Examples include: Olivier Roy, *The Failure of Political Islam* (Cambridge, MA: Harvard University Press, 1994.

9. Examples of this trend include the works by Bernard Lewis, *What Went Wrong: Western Impact and Middle Eastern Response* (New York: Oxford University Press, 2002); and *The Crisis of Islam: Holy War and Unholy Terror* (New York: Modern Library, 2003).

10. This includes Quintan Wiktorowicz, ed., *Islamic Activism: A Social Movement Theory Approach.* (Bloomington: Indiana University Press, 2004); Carrie Rosefsky Wickham, *Mobilizing Islam: Religion, Activism, and Political Change in Egypt* (New York: Columbia University Press, 2002);
    Janine A. Clark, *Islam, Charity, and Activism: Middle-class Networks and Social Welfare in Egypt, Jordan, and Yemen* (Bloomington: Indiana University Press, 2004); and Ziad Munson, "Islamic Mobilization: Social Movement Theory and the Egyptian Muslim Brotherhood," *Sociological Quarterly* 42, No. 4, 2001, pp. 487–510.

11. Doug McAdam, John D. McCarthy, and Mayer N. Zald, eds., *Comparative Perspectives on Social Movements: Political Opportunities, Mobilizing Structures, and Cultural Framings* (New York: Cambridge University Press, 1996), p. 3.

12. Within the realm of the state, political opportunities are created in a number of ways, including the following: (1) opening access to participation for new actors; (2) political realignment within the polity; (3) the appearance of influential allies; (4) emerging splits within the elites; and (5) decline in the state's capacity or will to repress dissent. In Sidney Tarrow, *Power in Movement: Social*

Movements and Contentious Politics (New York: Cambridge University Press, 1998), p. 76.

13. McAdam et al. p. 3.

14. Charles Tilly. And Sidney Tarrow, *Contentious Politics* (Boulder: Paradigm Publishers, 2007), p. 8.

15. Wiktorowicz, pp. 10–12.

16. Ibid., pp. 12–13.

17. McAdam et al., p. 6.

18. David A. Snow. And Robert D. Benford, "Ideology, Frame Resonance, and Participant Mobilization," in Bert Klandermans, ed., *From Structure to Action: Comparing Movement Participation across Cultures, International Social Movement, International Social Movement Research*, Vol. 1, 1988.

19. The literature on framing is not free from criticism. Wiktorowicz stated that the frame is an important interpretive device, though its explanatory function is limited. Wickham concluded her study of the contemporary Muslim Brotherhood by challenging the rationalist assumptions of the theory, given its problematic nature in the case of religious frame creation in Egypt. "The promotion of a new ethic of civic obligation differs profoundly from a more narrow appeal to the 'rational' self-interests of potential recruits. In fact, Islamists called on graduates to struggle against the natural human inclination to seek pleasure, wealth, and power." Wickham, p. 147 Wiktorowicz, p. 19.

20. Harris contended that the movement failed because it did not appeal to Western-educated Egyptians with its traditional rhetoric. Christina Phelps Harris, *Nationalism and Revolution in Egypt: The Role of the Muslim Brotherhood* (The Hague: Mouton, 1964).

21. L. Carl Brown, *The Society of the Muslim Brothers* by Richard P. Mitchell, Reviewed in *Journal of Interdisciplinary History*, Vol. 2, No. 3. Winter 1972, p. 344.

22. Ibid. p. 345.

23. For instance: John Esposito, *The Islamic Threat: Myth of Reality?* (New York: Oxford University Press, 1999).

24. Emmanuel Sivan, *Radical Islam: Medieval Theology and Modern Politics* (New Haven: Yale University Press, 1985).

25. Shepard included both the militant organizations and the mainstream moderates under the category of "radical Islamism." Though their methods may differ, he contended that they ultimately aspire toward the same goal: "More than others, the radical Islamists emphasize the urgency of putting the *Shari'a* into practice. It is not only an ideal to be known and revered, but a law to be put into effect and obeyed." Shepard articulated a typology of intellectual currents in Egypt that include secularism, Islamic modernism, radical Islamism, traditionalism, and neo-traditionalism. In William E. Shepard, "Islam and Ideology: Toward a Typology," *International Journal of Middle East Studies*, Vol. 19, 1987, pp. 307–315.

26. Ibrahim cites the figure of 3,000 to 5,000 arrested by Sadat's sweeps of radical groups. Saad Eddin Ibrahim, "Anatomy of Egypt's Militant Islamic Groups: Methodological Note and Preliminary Findings," *International Journal of Middle East Studies*, Vol. 12, No. 4, December1980, p. 425.

27. A number of studies endorse the view of a "different" Muslim Brotherhood through their use of other names to refer to the organization under Tilmisani's leadership. Kepel labels it the "neo-Muslim Brethren." Hinnebusch refers to it as the "*Da'wa* Group," while Abed-Kotob uses the term "Accommodationists."

28. Gilles Kepel, *Muslim Extremism in Egypt: The Prophet and Pharaoh* (Berkeley: University of California Press, 1993).

29. Ibid., p. 128.

30. Davis offered this analysis of the methodology employed in the works referenced above: "Efforts to gain a deeper understanding of Islamic political movements require a more systematic historical methodology and a more sophisticated understanding of social structure and ideology. The concept of revival or resurgence of Islam, and its attendant notions of fundamentalism and Islamic society, work against such an understanding due to their transhistorical nature. Likewise, mechanistic attempts to link ideology and social class in a one-to-one relationship fail to comprehend many of the subtleties involved in the social mobilization of supporters of Islamic movements and the manner in which the construction of ideologies can serve to promote either hegemony or conflict in society." Eric Davis, in Barbara Stowasser, ed., *The Islamic Impulse* (Washington, DC: Center for Contemporary Arab Studies, 1987), p. 56.

31. John O. Voll, in Yvonne Haddad, John Voll, and John Esposito, eds., *The Contemporary Islamic Revival: A Critical Survey and Bibliography* (New York: Greenwood Press, 1991), p. 26.

32. Richard P. Mitchell, in Stowasser, p. 77.

33. John O. Voll, in Martin E. Marty and R. Scott Appleby, eds., *Fundamentalisms Comprehended* (Chicago: University of Chicago Press, 1995), p. 373.

34. Ibid. p. 380.

35. Examples of these studies include: William E. Shepard, *Sayyid Qutb and Islamic Activism: A Translation and Critical Analysis of Social Justice in Islam* (Leiden, New York: E. J. Brill, 1996); Brynjar Lia, *The Society of the Muslim Brothers in Egypt (1928–1942)* (Reading, England: Ithaca Press, 1998); Barbara H. E. Zollner, *The Muslim Brotherhood: Hasan al-Hudaybi and Ideology* (New York: Routledge, 2009); John Calvert, *Sayyid Qutb and the Origins of Radical Islam* (New York: Columbia University Press, 2010); Carrie Rosefsky Wickham, *The Muslim Brotherhood: Evolution of an Islamist Movement* (Princeton: Princeton University Press, 2013).

36. Clark's study of Islamic medical clinics in Egypt provided one such example. Utilizing the growing literature on political opportunity structures, she

described the success of Islamic medical clinics as a result of the state's failures to provide for its citizens. Clark, p. 75. In her social movement history of the Muslim Brotherhood through the 1980s, Wickham maintained that the rise of Islamic activism was not a spontaneous occurrence, but rather a result of resource mobilization on the part of this elite sector and its ability to frame its grievances effectively. She developed the concept of *lumpen intelligentsia*, a class of ambitious, educated, urbanized, Egyptians who would come to make up the base of support for the Muslim Brotherhood. In Wickham, p. 37.

37. Charles Tilly, *Social Movements, 1768–2004* (Boulder: Paradigm Publishers, 2004), p. 3.

38. Using Tarrow's definition, social movements are "collective challenges, based on common purposes and social solidarities, in sustained interaction with elites, opponents, and authorities." Tarrow, p. 4.

CHAPTER I

1. Sayyid 'Abd al-Sattar al-Meligi, *The History of the Islamic Movement in the Field of Education (1933–1993)* (Cairo: Maktabat Wahba, 1993).

2. Raymond William Baker, *Egypt's Uncertain Revolution under Nasser and Sadat.* (Cambridge, MA: Harvard University Press, 1978), pp. 119–122.

3. Baker, p. 26.

4. Richard P. Mitchell, *The Society of the Muslim Brothers* (New York: Oxford University Press, 1969), p. 96.

5. Ibid., p. 97.

6. Ibid.

7. Anwar El-Sadat, *Revolt on the Nile* (New York: The John Day Company, 1957), p. 29.

8. Ibid., p. 30.

9. Ibid., p. 92.

10. Ibid., p. 111

11. Ibid.

12. Mitchell, p. 100.

13. Ibid., pp. 101–104.

14. See Mitchell. See also Joel Gordon, *Nasser's Blessed Movement: Egypt's Free Officers and the July Revolution* (New York: Oxford University Press, 1992); and Barbara H. E. Zollner, *The Muslim Brotherhood: Hasan al-Hudaybi and Ideology* (New York: Routledge, 2009).

15. Mitchell, p. 111.

16. Ibid., p. 133.

17. Barbara H. E. Zollner, *The Muslim Brotherhood: Hasan al-Hudaybi and Ideology* (New York: Routledge, 2009), p. 41.

18. Ibid., p. 42

19. Qutb was personally associated with many of the Free Officers and was one of the only civilians to attend their meetings during the planning stages. Olivier Carre, *Mysticism and Politics: A Critical Reading of Fi Zilal al-Qur'an by Sayyid Qutb (1906–1966)* (Boston: Brill, 2003), p. 7.

20. Sayyid Qutb, "In the Shade of the Qur'an," in Albert J. Bergesen, ed., *The Sayyid Qutb Reader: Selected Writings on Politics, Religion, and Society* (New York: Routledge, 2008), p. 47.

21. Gilles Kepel, *Muslim Extremism in Egypt: The Prophet and the Pharaoh* (Berkeley: University of California Press, 1993), p. 43.

22. Ibid., p. 46.

23. Ibid., pp. 27–28.

24. Zollner, p. 52.

25. Specifically, the concepts of *hakimiyya* and *jahiliyya* as used in a contemporary context in Mawdudi's work, informed by his experience in the Indian subcontinent, were adapted by Qutb in his later works. Zollner, p. 53.

26. Sayyid Qutb, *Milestones* (American Trust Publications: Indianapolis, 1990), p. 15

27. Haddad, pp. 95–96.

28. Qutb, p. 120.

29. Ibid., p. 134.

30. This practice became known as *takfir* and was the trademark of a small Islamic movement organization in the 1970s.

31. Sayed Khatab, *The Political Thought of Sayyid Qutb: The Theory of Jahiliyyah* (New York: Routledge, 2006), p. 54.

32. Emmanuel Sivan, in Martin E. Marty and R. Scott Appleby, eds., *Fundamentalisms Comprehended* (Chicago: University of Chicago Press, 1995), p. 55.

33. Though not officially published until 1977, the book was completed and first appeared in 1969. Hasan al-Hudaybi, *Du'ah la qudah: Abhath fi al-'aqidah al-Islamiyah wa-manhaj al-da'wah ilá Allah* (Cairo: Dar al-Tiba'ah was-al-Nashr al-Islamiyah, 1977).

34. Among the names that are mentioned as contributors are: Ma'mum al-Hudaybi, Mustafa Mashhur, 'Umar al-Tilmisani (all future general guides), and Shaykh Hasan Ma'mun, Shaykh Ahmad Muhammad 'Abd al-'Al Haridi, and Shaykh Mahmoud 'Abd al-Majid (all senior scholars at al-Azhar). Zollner, pp. 66–69.

35. Ibid., pp. 40–42.

36. Hassan al-Hudaybi, *Du'ah la qudah: Abhath fi al-'aqidah al-Islamiyah wa-manhaj al-da'wah ilá Allah* (Cairo: Dar al-Tiba'ah was-al-Nashr al-Islamiyah, 1977), pp. 8–10.

37. According to Voll, "For Hudaybi and the other old-guard Brotherhood leaders, the problem was that Egyptians needed to be educated and called to the faith, not that Egyptians had ceased to be Muslims. Hudaybi rejected the practice

of *takfir*, thereby rejecting the rationale for active revolution." John O. Voll, in Marty and Appleby, p. 373.

38. Joseph S. Szyliowicz, *Education and Modernization in the Middle East* (Ithaca, NY: Cornell University Press, 1973), p. 122.

39. Ibid., pp. 122–123.

40. Ibid., p. 182.

41. Ahmed Abdalla, *The Student Movement and National Politics in Egypt (1923–1973)* (Cairo: American University of Cairo Press, 2008), p. 24.

42. Szyliowicz, p. 189.

43. Abdalla, p. 40.

44. Ibid., p. 42.

45. Ibid., p. 65.

46. Ibid., pp. 75–77.

47. Ibid., p. 48.

48. Ibid., p. 47. From FO 141, 1077 (1946).

49. Ibid., p. 48.

50. Szyliowicz, p. 196.

51. Ibid., pp. 260–261.

52. Abdalla, p. 101.

53. Ibid., p. 120.

54. Ibid., p. 124.

55. Ibid., pp. 130–131.

56. Ibid., p. 137.

57. Szyliowicz, p. 296. Quoted in Abdalla, p. 140.

58. Wa'il 'Uthman, *Asrar al-Harakah al-Tullabiyyah: Handasat al-Qahira, 1968–1975*, 2nd ed. (2006), Cairo: n.p., p. 25.

59. Ibid., p. 26.

60. Abdalla, pp. 150–151.

61. 'Uthman, pp. 29–31.

62. Abdalla, p. 158.

63. Ibid., p. 159.

64. Ibid., p. 174.

65. A prominent example is Fouad Ajami, *The Arab Predicament: Arab Political Thought and Practice since 1967* (New York: Cambridge University Press, 1992).

66. Abdalla, pp. 174–175. 'Uthman, pp. 32–33.

CHAPTER 2

1. Abdalla, p. 129.

2. Interview with 'Adli Mustafa. And Interview with Wa'il 'Uthman.

3. 'Uthman, p. 41.

4. Interview with 'Uthman.

5. Ibid. And Interview with Mustafa.

6. 'Uthman, pp. 37–38.

7. Ibid., p. 56.

8. Ibid., p. 41.

9. 'Abd al-Mon'eim Abul Futuh acknowledged this characterization of al-Gam'iyya al-Diniyya's early wall magazines. In Hosam Tammam, ed., 'Abd al-Mon'eim Abul Futuh (Cairo: al-Shorouk, 2010), p. 29.

10. 'Uthman. p. 43.

11. In the wake of the 1969 fire at al-Aqsa mosque in Jerusalem, an attempt by student leaders to organize a student militia was swiftly and quietly squelched by the government.

12. Kirk J. Beattie, Egypt during the Sadat Years (New York: Palgrave, 2000), p. 99.

13. 'Uthman, p. 63.

14. Ibid.

15. Whether this happened before or after the leftist students rejected the agreement is a matter of some dispute. Another factor was the involvement of Student Union representatives, who met separately with officials and probably played an important part in nixing the agreement. 'Uthman, p. 63. Abdalla, pp. 180–183. Beattie, p. 100.

16. Abdalla, p. 183.

17. Abdalla, p. 199; and 'Uthman, pp. 89–90.

18. Abdalla, p. 198.

19. Beattie, p. 81.

20. Abdalla, p. 179.

21. Arab Report and Record, August 16–31, 1971. Cited in Beattie, p, 81.

22. 'Uthman, p. 115.

23. Ibid. And Interview with Mustafa.

24. 'Uthman, p. 112.

25. Ibid., p. 114.

26. Shabab al-Islam Press Release No. 3 November, 1972.

27. Shabab al-Islam Press Release No. 4 November, 1972.

28. 'Uthman, p. 116.

29. Interview with 'Uthman.

30. Both Mustafa and 'Uthman stated that they gave no consideration to the regime's offer. Subsequent events seem to corroborate that account.

31. 'Uthman, pp. 117–118.

32. Ibid., p. 119.

33. In addition to the Shabab al-Islam leadership, this incident is also referred to by Sadat confidant Mahmoud Gami'. In Mahmoud Gami', 'Arift al-Sadat (Cairo: Maktabat al-Masri al-Jadid, 1998), p. 157.

34. 'Uthman, p. 90.

35. Mustafa recalled that the fifth individual was likely to have been al-Simari, but could also have been Muhammad Khalil. Interview with 'Adli Mustafa.
36. Ibid.
37. Interview with Wa'il 'Uthman.
38. Ibid. And Interview with 'Adli Mustafa.
39. 'Abdalla, p. 200. And 'Uthman, pp. 89–90.
40. 'Abdalla, p. 200.
41. Ibid. p. 201.
42. 'Uthman, p. 94.
43. Interview with Wa'il 'Uthman.
44. Interview with 'Adli Mustafa.
45. Al-Sayyid 'Azzazi, "A Call for the Unification of the Islamic Movement in the University," *Wa Islamah*, No. 2, April 1975, p. 14.
46. Interview with 'Adli Mustafa.
47. Ibid.
48. Ibid. And Interview with Wa'il 'Uthman. Additionally, 'Abd al-Mon'eim Abul Futuh confirms the notion of blind allegiance to the leader by the members of al-Gam'iyya al-Diniyya. In Tammam, p. 47.
49. Interview with 'Adli Mustafa.
50. Badr Muhammad Badr, *Al-Gama'a al-Islamiyya fi Gami'at Masr* (n.p., 1989), pp. 14–15. And 'Esam al-'Erian. *al-Ahrar*, September 26, 1973.
51. Salwa Muhammad al-'Awwa. *al-Gama'a al-Islamiyya al-Musallaha fi Masr (1974–2004)* (Cairo: Maktabat al-Shuruq al-Duwaliyya, 2006), pp. 73–74.
52. Interview with 'Adli Mustafa.
53. Interview with Wa'il 'Uthman.
54. Interview with 'Adli Mustafa.
55. Interview with Wa'il 'Uthman.
56. These political opportunities include a range of possible variables, including "the level of formal informal access to political institutions and decision-making, the degree of political system receptivity to challenger groups, the prevalence of allies and opponents, the stability of the ruling elite coalition, the nature of state repression, and state institutional capacity." Quintan Wiktorowicz, ed., *Islamic Activism: A Social Movement Theory Approach* (Bloomington: Indiana University Press, 2004), p. 14.
57. Alexis de Tocqueville, *The Old Regime and the French Revolution*, translated by Stuart Gilbert (New York: Doubleday Anchor, 1955), pp. 176–177. Quoted in Sidney Tarrow, *Power in Movement: Social Movements and Contentious Politics* (New York: Cambridge University Press, 1998), p. 74.
58. Interview with 'Adli Mustafa.
59. Ibid.
60. Ibid.
61. Interview with 'Uthman.

CHAPTER 3

1. 'Adel Hammoudah, "The Quick Divorce Between Sadat and the Muslim Brotherhood," *Sabah al-Kheir*, No. 1651, August 27, 1987, p. 21.
2. Gilles Kepel. *Muslim Extremism in Egypt: The Prophet and Pharaoh* (Berkeley: University of California Press, 1993), pp. 62–63. See also: Saad Eddin Ibrahim, *Egypt Islam and Democracy: Critical Essays* (Cairo: American University of Cairo Press, 1996), p. 36.
3. Emmanuel Sivan, *Radical Islam: Medieval Theology and Modern Politics* (New York: Yale University Press, 1990), p. x.
4. Ibid.
5. Ibid., pp. 21, 27.
6. Ibid., p. ix.
7. 'Abd al-Hamid Kishk. Quoted in Kepel, p. 189.
8. Charles Hirschkind, *The Ethical Soundscape: Cassette Sermons and Islamic Counterpublics* (New York: Columbia University Press, 2006), pp. 58–59.
9. Interview with 'Esam al-'Arian. Interview with Abul 'Ala Madi.
10. Ahmed Ra'if. *al-Bawwaba al-Sawda'*, (Cairo: al-Zahra', 1986), p. 247.
11. www.burhaniya.info.
12. Sayed Khatab, *The Political Thought of Sayyid Qutb: The Theory of Jahiliyyah* (New York: Routledge, 2006), p. 54.
13. Barbara H. E. Zollner, *The Muslim Brotherhood: Hasan al-Hudaybi and Ideology* (New York: Routledge, 2009), pp. 45–46.
14. Ibid., pp. 46–47.
15. Zollner, pp. 46–47. And Kepel, p. 75.
16. Kepel, pp. 75–76.
17. An amendment to the Egyptian constitution passed in 1980, at the height of heated critiques of Sadat's policies, further affirmed this desire to represent Islamic norms in the state, establishing Shari'a as "the principle source of legislation."
18. Anwar al-Sadat. "Message to the Conference of the YMCA in Egypt and America," March 25, 1976. Anwar Sadat Archives, University of Maryland.
19. Ibid.
20. John L. Esposito, *Islam and Politics* (New York: Syracuse University Press, 1984), p. 236.
21. Ibid. p. 237.
22. Saad Eddin Ibrahim, *Egypt Islam and Democracy: Critical Essays* (Cairo: American University of Cairo Press, 1996), p. 3.
23. Kepel, p. 94.
24. After 1967, Nasser released a thousand "least threatening" Muslim Brotherhood members. In Bruce K. Rutherford, *Egypt after Mubarak: Liberalism, Islam, and Democracy in the Arab World* (Princeton: Princeton University Press, 2008), p. 82.

25. Kirk J. Beattie, *Egypt during the Sadat Years* (New York: Palgrave, 2000), p. 81.
26. Ra'if, p. 561.
27. Ibid.
28. Interview with 'Esam al-'Erian.
29. Examples of this literature include: Ahmed 'Abd al-Majid, *al-Ikhwan wa 'Abd al-Nasir* (Cairo: al-Zahra', 1991). See also: Salah Shadi, *Safahat min al-Tarikh* (Cairo: Dar al-Tawzi' wal-Nashr al-Islami, 2006). 'Ali Siddiq, *Al-Ikhwan al-Muslimun: Bayna Irhab Faruq wa 'Abd al-Nasir* (Cairo: Dar al-'Itisam, 1987). Jabir Rizq, *Madhabih al-Ikhwan fi Sujun 'Abd al-Nasir* (Cairo: Dar al-'Itisam, 1977). *Al-Da'wa* magazine (1976–1981) also contained a regular section detailing the experiences of this period.
30. Kepel, p. 28.
31. Ibrahim, p. 6.
32. Interview with al-'Erian.
33. Ra'if, pp. 590–591.
34. Interview with 'Abd al-Mon'eim Abul Futuh.
35. Beattie, pp. 81–82.
36. Ibid., p. 82.
37. Mahmoud Gami', *'Arift al-Sadat* (Cairo: Maktabat al-Masri al-Jadid, 1998), p. 189.
38. Anwar El-Sadat, *Revolt on the Nile* (New York: The John Day Company, 1957), p. 111.
39. Kepel, p. 105.
40. Interview with al-'Erian.
41. Interview with Sayyid 'Abd al-Sattar al-Meligi.
42. Mahmoud 'Abd al-Halim, in Hosam Tammam, *Tahawulat al-Ikhwan al-Muslimin* (Cairo: Maktabat Madbouli, 2006).
43. Mahmoud 'Abd al-Halim, *Al-Ikhwan al-Muslimun Ahdath Sana'at al-Tarikh: Ru'yah min al-Dakhil* (Alexandria: Dar al-Da'wah, 1979), Vols. 1–3.
44. Sayyid 'Abd al-Sattar al-Meligi, *al-Ikhwan wal-Tanzim al-Sirri* (Cairo: Maktabat Wahba, 2009), p. 51.
45. Ibid.
46. Interview with al-Meligi.
47. In Tammam.
48. 'Abd al-Mon'eim Abul Futuh, in Hosam Tammam, ed., *'Abd al-Mon'eim Abul Futuh* (Cairo: al-Shorouk, 2010), p. 87.
49. According to Ahmed al-Malt. Abul Futuh in Tammam, p. 88.
50. Abul Futuh in Tammam, p. 88.

CHAPTER 4

1. Hosam Tammam, ed., *'Abd al-Mon'eim Abul Futuh* (Cairo: al-Shorouk, 2010), p. 60.
2. Ibid., p. 61.

3. Omayma Abdel-Latif, "Abdel-Moneim Abul-Futuh: A Different Kind of Syndicalism," *al-Ahram Weekly*, No. 743, May 19–25, 2005.

4. Haggai Erlich, *Students and University in 20th Century Egyptian Politics* (London: Frank Cass, 1989), p. 203.

5. Ibid., p. 202.

6. Ibid., p. 204.

7. Ibid., p. 202.

8. Abul Futuh recalls the culture shock that he and his friends experienced on entering Cairo University. In contrast to many of the students already there who represented the middle and upper classes, he and his friends came from far more modest backgrounds and could seldom afford to acquire books. In some instances, they would have to combine their meager allowances in order to obtain reading materials. In Tammam, p. 29.

9. Erlich. p. 203.

10. Raymond A. Hinnebusch, Jr., *Egyptian Politics under Sadat* (Boulder: Lynne Rienner Publishers, 1988), p. 199.

11. Ibid.

12. Interview with 'Abd al-Mon'eim Abul Futuh.

13. Ibid.

14. Interview with Ibrahim al-Za'farani.

15. Ibid. In contrast, Abul Futuh stated that his family benefited from Nasser's land reforms, with his father and uncles receiving plots of land from the state "when they previously did not own anything." In Tammam, p. 21.

16. Hamied Ansari, *Egypt: The Stalled Society* (Albany: State University of New York Press, 1986), pp. 184, 195.

17. Interview with Abul Futuh. Interview with Za'farani. Interview with Gamal 'Abd al-Salam. Abul Futuh also recalled that in the early stages of the student movement, "none of us had a particular outlook or a distinct religious vision. Most of us were religious as a result of our birth and upbringing in a broadly religious society." In Tammam, p. 33.

18. Tammam, p. 23.

19. Ibid. pp. 22–23.

20. Ibid.

21. Other notable scholars included Yousuf al-Qaradawi, 'Abd al-Hamid Kishk, 'Abd al-Sabur Shahin, Muhammad Mitwalli al-Sha'rawi, and Ahmad al-Mahallawi.

22. Tammam, p. 25.

23. Ibid.

24. Ibid.

25. Michael Slackman. "A Poet Whose Political Incorrectness Is a Crime," *New York Times*, May 13, 2006.

26. "Ahmed Fu'ad Negm: The '67 Defeat Made Me into a Poet," *al-Mu'tamar*, June 1, 2007.

27. Ibid.
28. Ibid.
29. Interview with 'Esam al-'Erian.
30. Tammam, p. 28.
31. Sayyid 'Abd al-Sattar al-Meligi, *Tarikh al-Harakah al-Islamiyyah fi Sahat al-Ta'lim (1933–1993)* (Cairo: Maktabat Wahba, 1993), p. 40.
32. Interview with Za'farani.
33. Tammam, p. 30. Badr described this meeting as the first official summer camp of the Islamic student movement, though given the simplicity and disorganized nature of the meeting, in contrast to later camps, this was probably an overstatement. In Badr Muhammad Badr, *Al-Gama'a al-Islamiyya fi Gami'at Misr: Haqaiq wa Wathaiq* (n.p., 1989), p. 11.
34. Tammam. p.29.
35. Ibid.
36. Ibid. pp. 36–38.
37. Ibid. p. 36.
38. Ibid. p. 33.
39. Badr, p. 23.
40. At 'Ain Shams University, Sayyid 'Abd al-Sattar al-Meligi recalled that the Student Union budget for religious activities was limited to 75 Egyptian pounds annually. As amir of al-Gama'a al-Islamiyya at 'Ain Shams, Meligi would later participate in union elections, motivated in part by the desire to expand his group's access to union funds. In Meligi, p. 42. And Interview with Sayyid 'Abd al-Sattar al-Meligi.
41. Tammam, p. 40.
42. According to Abul Futuh, Hasan 'Abid Rabbo had no knowledge of the arts, and had never left his small village before coming to Cairo University. This reflected a widespread view among the youth in the Islamic movement that the arts had been a tool for spreading immorality and the denigration of the faith. In Tammam, p. 41.
43. Ibid. p. 48.
44. Ibid. p. 47.
45. Ibid. p. 50.
46. Meligi, p. 44.
47. Tammam, p. 47.
48. Although there was a slight variation in names, the movement at Alexandria University followed a parallel trajectory. According to Za'farani, the first religious organization was titled "Gam'iyat al-Dirasat al-Diniyya" (Association of Religious Studies), then it was changed to "al-Gam'iyya al-Diniyya" before settling upon "al-Gama'a al-Islamiyya" after the decision was made at Cairo University. Interview with Za'farani.
49. This development occurred during the same time period of the October War, which was painted in Islamic terms by the political establishment and the

state media. The youth leaders were deeply affected by the cultural swelling of an Islamically oriented battle for liberation. Interview with al-'Erian. Interview with Mamduh al-Ridi.

50. Meligi recalled that within months, the name was in use at every university, and that there had been no objections to its adoption. On the contrary, he wrote, "It was as though we had been awaiting it." In Meligi, p. 44.

51. Tammam, p. 49. And Interview with al-'Erian.

52. Badr, p. 24.

53. Interview with Abul Futuh.

54. Tammam, p. 49.

55. Ibid.

56. Ibid., p. 48.

57. Interview with 'Abd al-Salam. Incidentally, 'Awda was the son of 'Abd al-Qadir 'Awda, a prominent Islamic intellectual and Muslim Brotherhood deputy guide until his arrest, trial, and execution by the Nasser regime in 1954.

58. Interview with Za'farani.

59. Ibid.

60. Interview with Abul 'Ela Madi.

61. Ibid.

62. Meligi asserted that the regime attempted to overturn the gains of al-Gama'a al-Islamiyya as early as 1977, intimidating its candidates and promoting ones more favorable to the regime, such as Mahmoud Tal'at Jalal, who became president of the National Student Union, though he was also sympathetic to the aims of al-Gama'a al-Islamiyya. Regime intrusion obstructed the activities of the union, until it was nullified outright in 1979. In Meligi, pp. 53–56.

63. Ibid. p. 52.

64. Tammam, p. 52.

65. Badr, p. 13.

66. In Badr, pp. 14–15. In Tammam, p. 55. And 'Esam al-'Erian, Untitled article in *al-Ahrar*, September 26, 1983.

67. Tammam, p. 55.

68. Badr, pp. 14–15.

69. Ibid., p. 15.

70. Some even leave open the possibility that Shabab al-Islam was the complete brainchild of Muhammad 'Uthman Isma'il. Abul Futuh, in particular, believes this active creation of a new group occurred only after it became clear that al-Gama'a al-Islamiyya would not be co-opted by the regime, due to the principled stance of its leaders and its adversarial political positions vis-à-vis the Sadat regime. Tammam, pp. 55–56. And Badr, p. 14. Abul Futuh acknowledged that Isma'il also attempted to coordinate regime efforts with leaders of al-Gama'a al-Islamiyya, but they declined. Interview with Abul Futuh.

71. Tammam, p. 53.
72. Interview with 'Abd al-Salam. And Tammam, p. 55.
73. Meligi said as much in his recollection that Abu Talib, Ahmed Kemal Abul Magd, and Rif'at al-Mahjoub "reached out secretly to the religious minority of students." In Meligi, p. 41.
74. Tammam, p. 56.
75. Ibid., pp. 56–58.
76. Ibid., p. 56.
77. Hinnebusch, p. 70.
78. Badr, p. 19.
79. This period has also been referred to as *marhalat al-tarshid*, or the guidance phase. In Meligi, pp. 43–44.
80. Badr, p. 31.
81. Sayyid 'Abd al-Sattar al-Meligi wrote that these camps were the "trademark" of the *tarbiya* phase. In al-Meligi, p. 49. Abul Futuh stated that they were necessary "to cultivate the leadership of the Islamic student movement in a natural and spontaneous way." In Tammam, p. 46.
82. In fact, amirs sought and received official permission from university authorities before organizing the camps on university grounds. In Meligi, pp. 44–45.
83. Ibid. p. 49.
84. Tammam, p. 46.
85. Meligi, p. 50.
86. Badr, p. 34.
87. Interview with 'Abd al-Salam.
88. Interview with Abul Futuh. And Tammam, pp. 45–46.
89. Interview with Madi.
90. This figure (number of students) appears in a September 26, 1983, article by 'Esam al-'Erian in *al-Ahrar*, cited in Badr, p. 32. The figure (cost of trip) was relayed by Abul 'Ela Madi. Interview with Madi. Abul Futuh and 'Umar each recalled that it cost them 25 Egyptian pounds. In Tammam, p. 68. And Interview with 'Umar.
91. Interview with Madi.
92. Badr, p. 27.
93. Ibid.
94. Ibid. p. 33. Abul Futuh stated that when the tradition began in 1976, 40,000 Egyptians attended the service in Alexandria, led by Sheikh Mahmoud 'Eid, and 50,000 attended the service in Cairo, led by Sheikh Yousuf al-Qaradawi. In Tammam, p. 50.
95. Tammam, p. 29.
96. Ibid. p. 45.
97. Ibid.
98. Interview with Za'farani.

99. Interview with Ridi. Also, Interview with Badr.

100. Badr, p. 29.

101. Ibid., p. 34.

102. Ibid., p. 49.

103. Ibid., p. 53.

104. Ibid., pp. 55–57.

105. Interview with Badr.

106. Official efforts to repeal Law 44 of 1979 began with the parliament in 1980 and were completed by judicial decision in 1985. In Amira El-Azhary Sonbol, *The New Mamluks: Egyptian Society and Modern Feudalism* (Syracuse: Syracuse University Press, 2000), p. 185. And Dale F. Eickelman and James Piscatori, *Muslim Politics* (Princeton: Princeton University Press, 1996), p. 169.

107. Badr, p. 59.

108. Ibid., p. 65.

109. Ibid., pp. 66–67.

110. Ibid., pp. 75–76.

111. Ibid., pp. 76–77.

112. Ibid., p. 80.

113. Tammam, p. 106.

114. Ibid.

115. Ibid., p. 107.

116. Ibid., p. 110.

117. Ibid., p. 111. Additionally, Badr recalled that as early as 1978, students at other universities were intimidated into withdrawing from elections, usually through pressure placed on their parents. There were also reports of election fraud. In Badr, pp. 87–88.

118. Tammam, pp. 111–112. Interview with Badr.

119. Meligi, pp. 55–56.

120. Interview with Za'farani.

121. Interview with Abul Futuh. Interview with Madi. In Badr, p. 88.

122. A conference was also held at al-Azhar, which included the participation of over ten thousand students, in condemnation of the new law governing the Student Union. In Meligi, pp. 57–62.

123. Badr, p. 73.

124. Ibid., pp. 92–93.

125. Interview with Ahmed 'Umar.

126. Badr, pp. 87–88. Meligi provided a similar account of regime obstruction of the national union. In Meligi, pp. 54–56.

127. For example, see Gilles Kepel, *Muslim Extremism in Egypt: The Prophet and the Pharaoh* (Berkeley: University of California Press, 1993).

128. Interview with Madi.

CHAPTER 5

1. 'Umar al-Tilmisani, *Ayyam Ma'a al-Sadat* (Cairo: Dar al-I'tisam, 1984), p. 34.
2. Ibid.
3. Ibid. p. 35.
4. This story is also recounted by Mahmoud Gami', a Sadat confidant who sat in the second row of the event. He recalled that he was "shocked" by the "vicious attack" against Tilmisani. After the meeting, he reports that Sadat apologized to Tilmisani and embraced him. In Mahmoud Gami', *'Arift al-Sadat* (Cairo: Maktabat al-Masri al-Jadid, 1998), p. 274.
5. Sadat was contesting the claim made by Muslim Brotherhood leaders that they were not affiliated with some branches of al-Gama'a al-Islamiyya suspected of militant activities. But that distinction was not made during the speech, which depicted al-Gama'a al-Islamiyya as a monolithic group, though it had ceased to be at the time. Anwar al-Sadat. Speech before Egyptian parliament. September 5, 1981.
6. Hosam Tammam, ed., *'Abd al-Mon'eim Abul Futuh* (Cairo: al-Shorouk, 2010), p. 67.
7. Ibid., p. 63.
8. Ibid., p. 67.
9. Ibid.
10. Interview with Gamal 'Abd al-Salam.
11. Tammam, p. 69.
12. Ibid., p. 65.
13. Interview with 'Esam al-'Erian. And Interview with Hamid al-Difrawi.
14. Interview with Sayyid 'Abd al-Sattar al-Meligi. The same sentiment was expressed by Hamid al-Difrawi, Badr Muhammad Badr, and 'Abd al-Mon'eim Abul Futuh. Interview with al-Difrawi. Interview with Badr Muhammad Badr. Interview with Abul Futuh.
15. Interview with Difrawi.
16. Tammam, p. 39.
17. Ibid., p. 40.
18. Interview with Badr. Interview with Ibrahim al-Za'farani.
19. Abul Futuh claimed that 'Isa did not explicitly represent himself as a member of the Muslim Brotherhood, though he stood for their views. In Tammam, p. 74.
20. Meligi maintained that the early success enjoyed by the Muslim Brotherhood was due to the youth's "emotional attachment" to the experiences of the elders. Interview with Meligi.
21. Tammam, p. 74.
22. Ibid. p. 73.
23. Interview with Badr.

24. Interview with Kamal Habib.

25. Interview with Badr.

26. Tammam, p. 79.

27. Ibid. p. 75.

28. Sayyid 'Abd al-Sattar al-Meligi, *Tarikh al-Harakah al-Islamiyyah fi Sahat al-Ta'lim (1933–1993)* (Cairo: Maktabat Wahba, 1993), p. 36. And Interview with al-'Erian.

29. Tammam, p. 78.

30. Interview with Badr.

31. Hasan al-Banna, *al-Rasa'il al-Thalath: Da'watuna* (Cairo: Dar al-Tiba'ah wal-Nashr al-Islamiyyah), 1977.

32. Mustafa Mashhur, "al-Thiqa fil Da'wa," *al-Da'wa*, No. 21, March 1978, p. 6.

33. Mashhur, *Tariq al-Da 'wa* (Cairo: Dar al-Tiba'ah wal-Nashr al-Islamiyyah, 1979).

34. Mashhur, "Min Fiqh al-Da'wa," *al-Da'wa*, No. 22, March 1978, p. 6.

35. Interview with Badr.

36. Tammam, p. 82.

37. Ibid., p. 80.

38. Interview with Badr.

39. Ibid.

40. For example, Islamic conferences with independent religious scholars were only allowed within the university walls, and Islamic camps would never have been approved for religious associations outside of al-Gama'a al-Islamiyya. The public Eid prayers were only held under the auspices of the student movement.

41. Interview with al-'Erian.

42. Interview with Abul 'Ala Madi. Abul Futuh recalled that, in spite of Mashhur's age, he insisted on riding behind a student on his motorcycle rather than burden the students by having them hire him a cab. In Tammam, p. 80.

43. Tammam, p. 82.

44. Ibid., pp. 83.

45. Whereas Mashhur's role as head of the Youth and Universities Committee in the Guidance Bureau was more official, it revolved around education and raising awareness, while Sananiri worked through the logistics of organizational membership, such as administering the *bay'a* (oath) to new members, and placing them within their respective groups in the new hierarchy.

46. Interview with al-'Erian.

47. Interview with Abul Futuh.

48. Interview with al-'Erian. Interview with Za'farani.

49. Tammam, p. 91.

50. Ibid.

51. Interview with Abul Futuh. Interview with Meligi. And Interview with Badr.

52. The practice was widespread and covered urban centers as well as the country-side. Abul Futuh provided other examples. Ahmed al-Bas was the contact in al-Gharbiyyah governorate; Muhammad al-'Adwi in al-Mansurah; 'Ali Ruzza in Ismailiya; al-Dissouqi Buqnayna in al-Buhaira; 'Abd al-'Aziz al-'Azzazi in Suez; 'Abd al-'Aziz Hammoudeh in Port Said; in Tammam, pp. 91–92.
53. Ibid., p. 93.
54. Interview with Meligi. And in Tammam, p. 85.
55. Interview with Ahmed 'Umar.
56. Interview with Badr.
57. Interview with Abul Futuh. And in Tammam, pp. 89–90.
58. Ibid., p. 90.
59. This line of argument was given prominence later by al-Jihad leader 'Abd al-Salam Faraj in his book *al-Farida al-Gha'ibah* (*The Neglected Duty*). Faraj was executed in 1982 for his role in Sadat's assassination.
60. Tammam, p. 92.
61. Interview with Abul Futuh.
62. Tammam, p. 89. To distinguish themselves from the Muslim Brotherhood–affiliated student group in Cairo and elsewhere, the opposition student movement based in al-Gama'a al-Islamiyya at Assiut University used the religious slogan "la ilaha illa Allah" (There is no God but God) in their publications, contrasting with the other group's use of the Muslim Brotherhood slogan "Allah akbar wa lillahi al-Hamd" (God is greatest and to Him all praise is due); Additionally, the Assiut group devised its own logo, featuring one sword hovering above its slogan, to distinguish it from the Muslim Brotherhood's traditional logo of two swords crossed over a Qur'an. Interview with Abul Futuh. And Interview with Habib.
63. Karim Yahya. "Hiwar ma'a 'Umar al-Tilmisani," *al-Ahali*, September 29, 1982.
64. Gami', p. 157.
65. Admission to the Shura Council is accomplished through direct elections (for two-thirds of the seats) and presidential appointments (roughly one-third of the seats).
66. Yahya.
67. During the speech in which Sadat confronted Tilmisani, he alleged that he "considered" appointing Tilmisani to the Shura Council, implying that no offer had ever been made, a claim Tilmisani obviously disputed.
68. Gami', p. 273.
69. Denis Jospeh Sullivan and Sana Abed-Kotob, *Islam in Contemporary Egypt: Civil Society vs. the State* (Colorado: Lynne Rienner Publishers, 1999), p. 93.

CHAPTER 6

1. Interview with Sayyid 'Abd al-Sattar al-Meligi. The first view was represented by 'Abbas al-Sisi (early on), Mahmoud 'Abd al-Halim, and 'Abd al-Halim

Khafaga. The second view was represented by Mustafa Mashhur, Ahmed Hassanain, and Kamal al-Sananiri.

2. It should be noted that the second camp also benefited from the publication of *al-Da'wa*. Mashhur used it as a regular platform for the articulation of his ideological views.

3. John L. Esposito, *Islam and Politics* (Syracuse, NY: Syracuse University Press, 1984), p. 237. And in Wickham, p. 96. Other estimates of *Da'wa's* circulation range from 60,000 to 80,000. Interview with Badr Muhammad Badr. Interview with Muhammad Abd al-Quddus.

4. This chapter relies heavily on the social movement theory literature on cultural framing. Cultural framing is defined as the process by which a movement packages its agenda, articulating issues of concern, their remedies, and calls to action. Benford and Snow list three core framing tasks: the diagnostic frame, which identifies particular problems and issues of concern for a movement; the prognostic frame, which articulates the solution; and the motivational frame, which "provides the 'call to arms' or rationale for engaging in ameliorative collective action, including the construction of appropriate vocabularies of motive." Robert D. Benford and David A. Snow, "Framing Processes and Social Movements: An Overview and Assessment," *Annual Review of Sociology*. Vol. 26, 2000, p. 617.

5. Rory McVeigh, Daniel J. Myers, David Sikkink, "Corn, Klansmen, and Coolidge: Structure and Framing in Social Movements," *Social Forces*. Vol. 83, No. 2, December 2004, pp. 653–690.

6. Francis Robinson, "Technology and Religious Change: Islam and the Impact of Print," *Modern Asian Studies*, Vol. 27, No. 1, February 1993, p. 242.

7. Dale F. Eickelman and James Piscatori, *Muslim Politics* (Princeton: Princeton University Press, 1996), pp. 121–123.

8. Eickelman, Dale F. and Jon W. Anderson, "Print, Islam, and the Prospects for Civic Pluralism: New Religious Writings and Their Audiences," *Journal of Islamic Studies*. Vol. 8, No. 1, 1997, pp. 47.

9. Ibid., p. 48.

10. Ibid. For more information, see Yves Gonzalez-Qiujano, *Les Gens du livre: Champ inteUcctuel et edition dans l'Egypte republicaine (1952–1993)*, These de doctorat de l'Institut d'Etudes Politiques de Paris, Mention Sciences Politiques, 1994.

11. Mitchell, pp. 139–143.

12. Sivan, Emmanuel, *Radical Islam: Medieval Theology and Modern Politics* (New Haven: Yale University Press, 1985), p. x.

13. "Salafi" here refers to the original concept as put forward by the Islamic modernist thinkers, in whose footsteps Sobki and Banna established their organizations.

14. Kepel, p. 104.

15. "Fifty Years of al-I'tisam Magazine," *al-Mukhtar al-Islami,* February 1989, pp. 32, 35.
16. Rudi Matthee, in Juan R. I. Cole and Nikki R. Keddie, eds., *Shi'ism and Social Protest* (New Haven: Yale University Press, 1986), pp. 251–252. In Saad Eddin Ibrahim, *Egypt, Islam, and Democracy: Critical Essays* (Cairo: American University of Cairo Press, 1996), pp. 41–42. And in Asef Bayat, *Making Islam Democratic: Social Movements and the Post-Islamist Turn* (Stanford: Stanford University Press, 2007), p. 217.
17. Kepel, p. 104. Sivan also refers to *al-I'tisam* and *al-Mukhtar al-Islami* as *al-Da'wa*'s "sister monthlies," p. 134.
18. Hasan Hanafi. "The Relevance of the Islamic Alternative in Egypt," *Arab Studies Quarterly,* Vol. 4, No. 1–2, 1982, p. 57.
19. Zollner, pp. 32, 147–148.
20. Interview with 'Abd al-Quddus.
21. Ibid. And Interview with Badr.
22. Interview with 'Abd al-Quddus.
23. Interview with Badr.
24. Ibid. And Interview with 'Abd al-Quddus.
25. In September 1981, Sadat banned all independent publications. Though he did not withdraw their publishing licenses, he used a state of emergency to stop them from appearing and imprisoned many journalists and editors.
26. Interview with Badr.
27. *al-Da'wa,* No. 8, January 1977, p. 17.
28. Ghada Hashem Telhami, *The Mobilization of Muslim Women in Egypt* (Gainesville: University of Florida Press, 1996), p. 40.
29. Ibid., pp. 39–40.
30. There was an absence of one issue, May 1979, which failed to appear. The final issue appeared in September 1981, at which time Sadat banned the publication of Islamic literature.
31. Interview with 'Abd al-Quddus.
32. Editors, "Dear Reader," *al-Da'wa.* No. 1, June 1976, p. 1.
33. Tilmisani, pp. 66–67.
34. Interview with 'Abd al-Quddus.
35. Sivan, p. 48. Kepel, pp. 110–112. And Johannes J. G. Jansen, *The Dual Nature of Islamic Fundamentalism* (Ithaca, NY: Cornell University Press, 1997), pp. 125–126.
36. Jansen writes that a Western reader would be reminded of "certain examples of Nazi propaganda" when reading *Da'wa,* p. 126.
37. Kepel, p. 124.
38. Articles dealing with foreign policy constitute on average less than one-fifth of the articles in *Da'wa.* Of the regularly appearing series entailing international affairs, half deal with places other than the United States and Israel.

39. Valerie J. Hoffman, in Martin E. Marty and R. Scott Appleby, eds., *Fundamentalisms Comprehended* (Chicago: University of Chicago Press, 1995), pp. 215–216.

40. Fouad Ajami, *The Arab Predicament* (New York: Cambridge University Press, 1981), p. 225. And Telhami, p. 39.

41. 'Abd al-Athim al-Mut'ani, "The Manners of the Caller," *al-Da'wa*, No. 4, September 1976, p. 12. The verse quoted is from Qur'an 25:63.

42. 'Umar al-Tilmisani, "Al-Da'wa . . . on the Path," *al-Da'wa*, No. 1, June 1976, pp. 2–3.

43. Ahmed Gad. "On *da'wa* and *du'a*," *al-Da'wa*, No. 8, January 1977, p. 30.

44. Ibid.

45. Mashhur, p. 10.

46. Mashhur, "From the *fiqh* of *Da'wa*: The Path of *da'wa*," *al-Da'wa*, No. 8, January 1977, p. 33.

47. Mustafa Mashhur. "From the *fiqh* of *Da'wa*: The Path of *da'wa*," *al-Da'wa*, No. 7, December 1976, p. 10.

48. Ibid., p. 11.

49. Ibid.

50. Ibid.

51. This series begins with issue number 10 (March 1977) and continues through issue number 12 (May 1977).

52. Mustafa Mashhur "From the *fiqh* of *Da'wa*: The Path of *Da'wa*," *al-Da'wa*, No. 10, March 1977, p. 16.

53. Mustafa Mashhur. "From the *fiqh* of *Da'wa*: The Path of *Da'wa*," *al-Da'wa*, No. 15, August 1977, p. 6.

54. Yousuf al-Qaradawi. "Islam Is *Da'wa* and *Jihad*," *al-Da'wa*, No. 10, March 1977, pp. 4–6.

55. Yousuf al-Qaradawi. "The Culture of the *Da'iya*," *al-Da'wa*, No. 16, September 1977, pp. 14.

56. Although this is true of a number of Islamic periodicals, it was especially pronounced in *al-Da'wa* because of the inability to respond to continuous assaults on its reputation throughout the Nasser period and into the Sadat period.

57. "Abdel Nasser and the Massacre of the Ikhwan," *Da'wa*, No. 1, July 1976, p. 18.

58. Saleh Abu Rafiq. "The Full Truth: What They Say about the Muslim Brothers and Weapons . . . and the British," No. 2, August 1976, pp. 20.

59. "Abdel Nasser and the Massacre of the Ikhwan," *Da'wa*, No. 1, July 1976, p. 18.

60. "Tales of Torture: Minute-by-Minute, on the Tongues of the Victims," *Da'wa*, No. 2, August 1976, pp. 8–9.

61. Ibid.

62. "Muslims on the Path: The Martyr Yousuf Talat," *Da'wa*, No. 3, September 1976, pp. 4–5.

63. Ibid.

64. "Cases of Torture of the Muslim Brothers," No. 11, April 1977, p. 10.

65. Ibid., p. 13.

66. "Cases of Torture of the Muslim Brothers," No. 12, May 1977, pp. 4–5.

67. 'Umar al-Tilmisani, "The Muslim Brothers, the Previous Era and the Future Era," *Da'wa*, No. 17, October 1977, p. 3.

68. 'Umar al-Tilmisani. "Not the Last Turn," *al-Da'wa*, No. 11, April 1977, p. 2.

69. Rashad al-Shibr Engoumi. "To Realize Democratic Governance, the Constitution Must Be Reformed," *Da'wa*, No. 2, August 1976, pp. 16–17.

70. Editorial, "Those Charged with Enforcing the Laws Are the First to Break Them!" No. 20, January 1978, p. 15.

71. Ibid.

72. Ibid.

73. "On the Occasion of the Reform of the Constitution," *al-Da'wa*, No. 44, January 1980, p. 38.

74. Salih 'Ashmawi. "Is There an Islamic Constitution?" *al-Da'wa*, No. 40, September 1979, pp. 12–13.

75. 'Umar al-Tilmisani. "On the Reform of the Constitution, We Have an Opinion," *al-Da'wa*, No. 40, September 1979, pp. 4–5.

76. Salih Ashmawi. "Why Did the Discussion about Implementing the *Shari'a* Disappear?" *Da'wa*, No. 49, June 1980, p. 14.

77. 'Umar al-Tilmisani. "This Government Must Resign," *Da'wa*, No. 55, November 1980, p. 4.

78. Ibid., p. 6.

79. Abdel Munim Salim Jabbarah, "Until When Will We Remain in the Crusader or Communist Orbit?" *Da'wa*, No. 38, July 1979, pp. 8–9.

80. Jaber Rizq, "Does the Model of the Iranian Revolution Fit All Islamic Movements in the World?" *Da'wa*, No. 49, June 1980, pp. 34–36.

81. Salah Shadi, "The Jews, Peace, and the Arabs," *Da'wa*, No. 21, February 1978, p. 47.

82. Ibid.

83. 'Umar al-Tilmisani, "To the Muslim Rulers: Do You Not Fear God?" *Da'wa*, No. 20, January 1978, pp. 2–3.

84. "Remembrance of the Night Journey," *Da'wa*, No. 2, August 1976, pp. 32–33.

85. "The Youth and the Universities: The Martyr Hasan al-Banna Talks to Students," *Da'wa*, No. 5, November 1976, pp. 46–47.

86. "With the Farmer: How Will You Sell Your Cotton This Year?" *al-Da'wa*, No. 28, September 1977, p. 48.

87. "A New Refrigerator for Potatoes," *al-Da'wa*, No. 28, September 1977, p. 48.

88. Rashad al-Shubra Bikhoumi, "Fifty Years of Farmers Suffering in the Hell of Cooperatives," *al-Da'wa*, No. 5, October 1976, pp. 48–49.

89. "The Fertilizer Crisis: Causes, Consequences, and Solutions," *al-Da'wa*, No. 3, August 1976, pp. 54–55.

90. "Ali Mahmoud Diab, "In Medical Science, Toward an Islamic Conception," *al-Da'wa*, No. 4, September 1976, pp. 34–35.
91. "Questions about the Islamic Medical Union," *al-Da'wa*, No. 29, October 1978, pp. 42–43.
92. Zainab al-Ghazali, "Toward a Muslim Home: The Muslim Family in the Face of Challenges," *al-Da'wa*, No. 44, January 1980, pp. 33–34.
93. Ibid.
94. Zainab al-Ghazali, "The Woman and Work," *al-Da'wa*, No. 32, January 1979, p. 44.

CONCLUSION

1. 'Umar al-Tilmisani, *Ayyam Ma'a al-Sadat* (Cairo: Dar al-I'tisam, 1984), pp. 48–50.
2. Ibid., p. 50.
3. Hosam Tammam, ed., *'Abd al-Mon'eim Abul Futuh* (Cairo: al-Shorouk, 2010), p. 86.
4. The regime also attempted to justify the peace treaty with Israel in religious terms, even soliciting an Islamic legal ruling in support of it, but these explanations were secondary to overtly political considerations. Moreover, the rulings had little popular resonance as the treaty was widely viewed within the Islamic movement as an affront to God's will.
5. While Banna certainly proposed Islamic legislation to the government and Hudaybi explored the possibility of participating in the revolutionary regime, the intricate nature of Tilmisani's engagement of the policies of the Sadat regime make this period unique in the organization's history.
6. Tammam, p. 130.

EPILOGUE

1. Radwa 'Ashour, *Farag* (Cairo: Dar al-Shorouk, 2008), p. 91.
2. Michel Foucault, *Discipline and Punish: The Birth of the Prison* (New York: Vintage Books, 1977), p. 201.
3. They were: 'Abd al-Mon'eim Abul Futuh, Hamdeen Sabahi, Mohamed Morsi, Khairat al-Shater, and Hazem Salah Abu Isma'il. The latter two were disqualified by the Presidential Elections Commission prior to the first round of voting in May 2012.
4. For instance, the Muslim Brotherhood was not allowed an official publication. Thereafter, its official monthly, *al-Da'wa*, was published in Europe.
5. Badr Muhammad Badr, in Hesham al-Awadi, *In Pursuit of Legitimacy: The Muslim Brotherhood and Mubarak, 1982–2000* (London: I. B. Tauris, 2005), pp. 56–57. In fact, in another report, according to Abul 'Ela Madi, Tilmisani

approved the establishment of a party to fulfill the Muslim Brotherhood's political objectives. *Hizb al-Shura*, the Consultative Party, was to be led by retired judges and lawyers with no official connection to the Muslim Brotherhood. In Ahmed al-Fakhrani, "Those Who Split from the 'Obedience to the Brotherhood' from the Time of Banna to the Leadership of Badie'," *al-Masry al-Youm*, April 7, 2012.

6. Ibid. pp. 57–58.

7. Hesham al-Awadi. "Mubarak and the Islamists: Why Did the 'Honeymoon' End?" *Middle East Journal*, Vol. 59, No. 1, Winter 2005, pp. 62–80.

8. Al-Awadi, p. 39.

9. Muhammad Salim al-'Awwa, *Qadiyyat al-Ikhwan al-Muslimin 1995* (Cairo: Dar al-Shorouk, 2012), p. 27.

10. Interview with Sayyid 'Abd al-Sattar al-Meligi.

11. In fact, Madi explicitly stated that the idea for al-Wasat Party came out of an internal effort by the Muslim Brotherhood to establish a political arm in the late 1980s. Hizb al-Islah, or the Reform Party, was the product of a committee within the Consultative Assembly chosen to develop the party's structure and platform. Along with Madi, Abul Futuh and al-'Erian were tasked with carrying out the initiative, but it was soon abandoned to concerns over its supposedly "extremely secular" outlook, according to senior Muslim Brotherhood leaders. In al-Fakhrani.

12. Though they acknowledge having met with state security officials prior to the 2005 elections, Muslim Brotherhood leaders denied the presence of any formal agreement. However, former Deputy General Guide Muhammad Habib admitted that the General Guide Mahdi 'Akef entered into negotiations over the number of parliamentary seats the Muslim Brotherhood would gain from the elections. Shayma' 'Abd al-Hadi, "The Muslim Brotherhood Formally Admits Meeting State Security Officials during 2005 Elections," *al-Ahram*, June 13, 2012. Interview with Muhammad Habib, Al-Tahrir Network, June 6, 2012.

13. Official state security documents suggest that meetings with Morsi and al-Shater resulted in agreements by the Muslim Brotherhood's top officials to temper their performance in the elections through standing down from particular districts and limiting their campaigning in other districts. Ahmed 'Abd al-Fattah, "State Security Documents: Agreement with al-Shater and Morsi on Election Rolls during 2005 Elections," *al-Masri al-Youm*, March 6, 2011.

14. Robert F. Worth and Mona El-Naggar, "Fraud Charges Mar Egypt Vote," *New York Times*, November 28, 2010.

15. Interview with 'Usama Yasin, "Shahed 'Ala al-Thawra," Al-Jazeera Network, June 11, 2011.

16. In his interview with Al-Jazeera, 'Usama Yasin states that state security officials delivered explicit threats to Muslim Brotherhood leaders that their active

endorsement and participation in the January 25 protests would be met with a swift and brutal response by the regime.

17. Muhammad Gharib, "Abul Futuh Decides to Nominate Himself for Presidential Elections," *al-Masry al-Youm*, May 10, 2011.

18. Al-Fakhrani.

19. In the same article, another Muslim Brotherhood official explicitly calls for Abul Futuh to resign as a member of the Muslim Brotherhood. Sa'ad al-Din, Mahmoud, "Muslim Brotherhood Leaders: We Will Not Endorse Abul Futuh as a Candidate for President No Matter What the Circumstances," *al-Youm al-Sabi'*, May 12, 2011.

20. Al-Fakhrani.

21. Ibid.

22. Hani al-Waziri, "Al-Za'farani's Party Directs Strong Criticisms to the Program of the Freedom and Justice Party," *al-Masry al-Youm*, April 6, 2011.

23. Al-Fakhrani. Habib ultimately left al-Nahda Party in late 2012 to preside over the launch of a new civic organization, which its founders named Gam'iyyat al-Ihya' wal-Tajdid al-Da'wiyyah, focused on revival and renewal of the Islamic call.

24. The Supreme Constitutional Court considered the question of the legality of the parliamentary elections throughout spring 2012 and ultimately ruled to dissolve the entire People's Assembly on June 14, 2012, only two days before the presidential run-off between Mohamed Morsi and Ahmed Shafiq.

25. Amin Saleh and Rihab 'Abdullah, "Presidential Election Candidates Seminar Series: Abul Futuh," *al-Yawm al-Sabi'*, February 17, 2012.

26. Interview with 'Abdel Mon'eim Abul Futuh.

Bibliography

'Abd al-Fattah, Ahmed. "State Security Documents: Agreement with al-Shater and Morsi on Election Rolls during 2005 Elections," *al-Masry al-Youm*, March 6, 2011.

'Abd al-Hadi, Shayma'. "The Muslim Brotherhood Formally Admits Meeting State Security Officials during 2005 Elections," *al-Ahram*, June 13, 2012.

'Abd al-Halim, Mahmoud. *al-Ikhwan al-Muslimun Ahdath Sana'at al-Tarikh: Ru'yah min al-Dakhil*. Alexandria: Dar al-Da'wah, 1979. Vol. 1–3.

'Abd al-Khaliq, Farid. *al-Ikhwan al-Muslimun fi Mizan al-Haqq*. Cairo: Dar al-Sahwa, 1987.

Abdalla, Ahmed. *The Student Movement and National Politics in Egypt (1923–1973)*. Cairo: American University of Cairo Press, 2008.

'Abd al-Majid, Ahmad. *al-Ikhwan wa "Abd al-Nasir: al-Qissah al-Kamilah li-Tanzim 1965*. Cairo: al-Zahra', 1991.

Abdel-Latif, Omayma. "Abdel-Moneim Abul-Futuh: A Different Kind of Syndicalism," *al-Ahram Weekly*, No. 743, May 19–25, 2005.

Abdo, Geneive. *No God But God: Egypt and the Triumph of Islam*. New York: Oxford University Press, 2000.

Abed-Kotob, Sana. "The Accommodationists Speak: Goals and Strategies of the Muslim Brotherhood of Egypt," *International Journal of Middle East Studies*, Vol. 27, No. 3, August 1995, pp. 321–339.

Abou El Fadl, Khaled M. *The Great Theft: Wrestling Islam from the Extremists*. New York: HarperCollins Publishers, 2005.

Abul Futuh, 'Abd al-Mon'eim. *Mujaddidun la Mubaddidun*. Cairo: Tatwir lil Nashr, 2005.

Ahmad, Kurshid. *Islamic Resurgence: Challenges, Directions and Future Perspectives: A Roundtable with Kurshid Ahmad*. Tampa: WISE, 1994.

"Ahmed Fu'ad Negm: The '67 Defeat Made Me into a Poet," *al-Mu'tamar*, June 1, 2007.

Ahmed, Makram Muhammad. *Mu'amarah am Muraja'ah*. Cairo: Dar al-Shurouq, 2003.

Ajami, Fouad. *The Arab Predicament: Arab Political Thought and Practice since 1967*. New York: Cambridge University Press, 1992.

al-Ahram newspaper. Cairo, 1969–1984.

al-'Anani, Khalil. *Al-Ikhwan al-Muslimun Fi Misr: Shaikhukhah Tusari' al-Zaman?* n.p., 2007.

al-Ansari, Talal. *Mudhakkarat Talal al-Ansari*. n.p., n.d.

al-Awadi, Hesham. *In Pursuit of Legitimacy: The Muslim Brothers and Mubarak (1982–2000)*. London: Tauris Academic Studies, 2004.

Al-'Awwa, Muhammad Salim. *Qadiyyat al-Ikhwan al-Muslimin 1995*. Cairo: Dar al-Shorouk, 2012.

al-'Awwa, Salwa Muhammad. *al-Gama'a al-Islamiyya al-Musallaha fi Masr (1974–2004)*. Cairo: Maktabat al-Shuruq al-Duwaliyya, 2006.

al-Banna, Gamal. *al-Da'wat al-Islamiyya al-Mu'asira ma laha wama 'Alayha*.

———. *Risala ila al-Da 'wat al-Islamiyya*. Cairo: Dar al-Fikr al-Islami, 1991.

———. *Ma Ba'd al-Ikhwan al-Muslimin*. Cairo: Dar al-Fikr al-Islami, 1996.

al-Banna, Hasan. *al-Rasa'il al-Thalath: Da'watuna*. Cairo: Dar al-Tiba'ah wal-Nashr al-Islamiyyah, 1977.

———. *al-Salam fil-Islam wa-buhuth ukhrá: majmu'at kitabat Hasan al-Banna*. Dimyat: Mu'assasat Ghandur, 1985.

al-Baquri, Ahmed Hasan. *Baqaya Dhikrayat*. Cairo: Markaz al-Ahram, 1988.

al-Bishri, Tariq. *Al-Haraka al-Siyasiyya fi Misr: 1945–1952*. Cairo: Dar al-Tawzi' wa al-Nashr al-Islamiyyah, 1972.

al-Da'wa magazine. Cairo, 1976–1981.

al-Din, Ahmed Bahaa'. Cairo: *Muhawarat ma' al-Sadat*. Dar al-Hilal, n.d.

al-'Erian, 'Esam. *al-Ahrar*, September 26, 1973.

al-Fakhrani, Ahmed. "Those Who Split from the 'Obedience to the Brotherhood' from the Time of Banna to the Leadership of Badie," *al-Masry al-Youm*, April 7, 2012.

al-Ghazali, Muhammad. *Al-Tariq min Huna*. Cairo: Dar al-Shurouq, 2005.

al-Hudaybi. Hasan. *Du'ah la qudah: Abhath fi al-'aqidah al-Islamiyah wa-manhaj al-da'wah ilá Allah*. Cairo: Dar al-Tiba'ah was-al-Nashr al-Islamiyah, 1977.

———. *al-Islam wa-al-da'iyah: Maqalat, Bayanat, Nasharat, Rasa'il, Mudha'at Hasan al-Hudaybi*. Cairo: Dar al-Ansar, 1977.

———. *Dusturuna*. Cairo: Dar al-Ansar, 1978.

Alianak, Sonia. *Middle Eastern Leaders and Islam: A Precarious Equilibrium*. New York: Peter Lang, 2007.

al-'Itisam magazine. Cairo, 1977–1981.

al-Jamal, Hasan. *Jihad al-Ikhwan al-Muslimin fi al-Qanah wa-Filastin: riwayat shahid 'ayan*. Cairo: Dar al-Tawzi' wa-al-Nashr al-Islamiyah, 2000.

al-Kharbawi, Tharwat *Qalb al-Ikhwan*. Cairo: Dar al-Hilal, 2010.

'Allam, Fu'ad. *al-Ikhwan wa-Ana*. Cairo: al-Maktab al-Masri al-Hadith, 1996.

al-Meligi, Sayyid 'Abd al-Sattar. *Tarikh al-Haraka al-Islamiyyah fi Sahat al-Ta'lim (1933–1993)*. Cairo: Maktabat Wahba, 1993.

"al-Musawwar fi Liman al-Turra," *al-Musawwar*, No. 2991, February 5, 1982.

al-Qaradawi, Yousuf. *al-Ikhwan al-Muslimun*. Cairo: Maktabat Wahba, 1999.

———. *Ibn al-Qarya wa al-Kuttab: Malamih Sirah wa Masirah, (Vol. 3)*. Cairo: Dar al-Shurouq, 2006.

———. *al-Sheikh al-Ghazali kama 'Ariftahu: Rihla Nisf Qarn*. Cairo: Dar al-Shurouq, 2008.

al-Sadat, Anwar. *Revolt on the Nile*. New York: The John Day Company, 1957.

———. "Message to the Conference of the YMCA in Egypt and America," Anwar Sadat Archives, University of Maryland. March 25, 1976.

———. *In Search of Identity: An Autobiography*. New York: Harper & Row, 1978.

al-Shobaki, Amr, ed. *Azmat al-Ikhwan al-Muslimin*. Cairo: al-Ahram Center, 2009.

al-Sisi, 'Abbas. *Fi Qafilat al-Ikhwan al-Muslimin*. Alexandria: Dar al-Tiba'a wa al-Nashr, 1986.

———. *Hikayat 'an al-Ikhwan*. Cairo: Dar al-Tawzi' wa al-Nashr al-Islamiyyah, 1997. Vol. 1–2.

al-Tilmisani, 'Umar. "Risala ila al-Shabab," *al-Musawwar*, No. 2993, February 19, 1982.

———. *Ayyam Ma'a al-Sadat*. Cairo: Dar al-I'tisam, 1984.

———. *Dhikrayat . . . La Mudhakkarat*. Cairo: Dar al-Tima'a wa al-Nashr al-Islami, 1985.

———. *Risalati ila al-Shabab*. Alexandria: Dar al-Da'wa, 1986.

———. *La nakhafu al-salam wa-lakin!* Cairo: Dar al-Tawzi' wal-Nashr al-Islamiyyah, 1992.

Al-Waziri, Hani. "Al-Za'farani's Party Directs Strong Criticisms to the Program of the Freedom and Justice Party," *al-Masry al-Youm*, April 6, 2011.

Amin, 'Adel. *The Egyptian Student Uprising (1972–1973)*. Vols. I–II. Cairo: al-Maktab al-Fana, 2003.

Ansari, Hamied. "The Islamic Militants in Egyptian Politics," *International Journal of Middle East Studies*, Vol. 16, No. 1, March, 1984, pp. 123–144.

———. *Egypt: The Stalled Society*. Albany: State University of New York Press, 1986.

Appleby, R. Scott, Samuel C. Heilman, James Piscatori, Nancy T. Ammerman, Robert Eric Frykenberg, and Martin E. Marty, editors. *Accounting for Fundamentalisms: The Dynamic Character of Movements*. Chicago: University of Chicago Press, 1994.

Arquilla, John, and David Ronfeldt. *Networks and Netwars: The Future of Terror, Crime, and Militancy*. Santa Monica, CA: RAND, 2001.

Ashour, Omar. *The De-radicalization of Jihadists: Transforming Armed Islamic Movements*. New York: Routledge, 2009.

'Ashour, Radwa. *Farag*. Cairo: Dar al-Shorouk, 2008.

Aulas, Marie-Christine. "Egypt Confronts Peace," *MERIP Reports*, No. 72, November 1978.

Ayubi, Nazih N. M. "The Political Revival of Islam: The Case of Egypt," *International Journal of Middle East Studies*, Vol. 12, No. 4, December 1980, pp. 481–499.

Badr, Badr Muhammad. *Al-Gama'a al-Islamiyya fi Gami'at Misr: Haqaiq wa Wathaiq.* n.p., 1989.

Bainbridge, William Sims. *The Sociology of Religious Movements.* New York: Routledge, 1997.

Baker, Raymond William. *Egypt's Uncertain Revolution under Nasser and Sadat.* Cambridge, MA: Harvard University Press, 1978.

———. *Sadat and After.* Cambridge, MA: Harvard University Press, 1990.

———. *Islam Without Fear: Egypt and the New Islamists,* Cambridge, MA: Harvard University Press, 2003.

Bari, Zohurul. *Re-emergence of the Muslim Brothers in Egypt.* New Delhi: Lancer Books, 1995.

Bayat, Asef. *Making Islam Democratic: Social Movements and the Post-Islamist Turn.* Stanford: Stanford University Press, 2007.

Bayyumi, Zakariah Sulaiman. *Al-Ikhwan al-Muslimun bayna Abd al-Nasser wa al-Sadat, min al-Manshiyya ila al-Manassa, 1952–1981.* Cairo: Maktabat Wahba, 1987.

———. *Al-Ikhwan al-Muslimun wa al-Jama'at al-Islamiyyah fi al-Hayat al-Siyasiyyah al-Misriyyah, 1928–1948.* 2nd ed. Cairo: Maktabat al-Wahbah, 1991.

Beattie, Kirk J. *Egypt during the Sadat Years.* New York: Palgrave, 2000.

Benford, Robert D., E. Birke Rochford, Jr., Steven K. Worden, and David A. Snow. "Frame Alignment Processes, Micromobilization, and Movement Participation," *American Sociological Review,* Vol. 51, No. 4, August 1986, pp. 464–481.

Benford, Robert. D. and David A. Snow. "Framing Processes and Social Movements: An Overview and Assessment," *Annual Review of Sociology,* August 2000, Vol. 26, pp. 611–639.

Bergesen, Albert J., ed. *The Sayyid Qutb Reader: Selected Writings on Politics, Religion, and Society.* New York: Routledge, 2008.

Brynjar, Lia. *The Society of the Muslim Brothers in Egypt (1928–1942).* Reading, England: Ithaca Press, 1998.

Butterworth, Charles E. "Political Islam: The Origins," *Annals of the American Academy of Political and Social Science,* Vol. 524, Nov. 1992, pp. 26–37.

Calvert, John. *Sayyid Qutb and the Origins of Radical Islam.* New York: Columbia University Press, 2010.

Carre, Olivier. *Mysticism and Politics: A Critical Reading of Fi Zilal al-Qur'an by Sayyid Qutb (1906–1966).* Boston: Brill, 2003.

Chandler, Jennifer. "The Explanatory Value of Social Movement Theory," *Strategic Insights,* Vol. 6, Issue 5, May 2005.

Clark, Janine A. *Islam, Charity, and Activism: Middle-class Networks and Social Welfare in Egypt, Jordan, and Yemen.* Bloomington: Indiana University Press, 2004.

Cole, Juan R. I., and Nikki R. Keddie, eds. *Shi'ism and Social Protest.* New Haven: Yale University Press, 1986.

Dessouki, Hillal. "Arab Intellectuals and al-Nakba," *Middle Eastern Studies*, Vol. 9, No. 2, May 1973, pp, 187–195.

———. ed. *Islamic Resurgence in the Arab World*. New York: Praeger, 1982.

Dhahni, Siham. "Man al-Mas'oul 'an Bidayat al-Gama'at al-Islamiyyah?" *Sabah el Kheir*, No. 1350, November 19, 1981.

Diani, Mario, and Doug McAdam, eds. *Social Movements and Networks: Relational Approaches to Collective Action*. New York: Oxford University Press, 2003.

Eickelman, Dale F., and James Piscatori. *Muslim Politics*. Princeton: Princeton University Press, 1996.

Eickelman, Dale F., and Jon W. Anderson. "Print, Islam, and the Prospects for Civic Pluralism: New Religious Writings and Their Audiences," *Journal of Islamic Studies*. Vol. 8, No. 1, 1997, pp. 43–62.

El Guindi, Fadwa. "Veiling Infitah with Muslim Ethic: Egypt's Contemporary Islamic Movement," *Social Problems*, Vol. 28, No. 4, April 1981, pp. 465–485.

El-Sadat, Anwar. *Revolt on the Nile*. New York: The John Day Company, 1957.

El-Shazly, Saad. *The Crossing of the Suez*. San Francisco: American Mideast Research, 2003.

Erlich, Haggai. *Students and University in Twentieth Century Egyptian Politics*. London: Frank Cass & Co., 1989.

Esposito, John L. *Voices of Resurgent Islam*. New York: Oxford University Press, 1983.

———. *Islam and Politics*. Syracuse: Syracuse University Press, 1984.

———. *The Islamic Threat: Myth of Reality?* New York: Oxford University Press, 1999.

Esposito, John L., and John O. Voll. *Islam and Democracy*. New York: Oxford University Press, 1996.

Euben, Roxanne L. *Enemy in the Mirror: Islamic Fundamentalism and the Limits of Modern Rationalism*. Princeton: Princeton University Press, 1999.

Foucault, Michel. *Discipline and Punish: The Birth of the Prison*. New York: Vintage Books, 1977.

Gami', Mahmoud. *'Arift al-Sadat*. Cairo: Maktabat al-Masri al-Jadid, 1998.

Gerges, Fawaz A. "The End of the Islamist Insurgency in Egypt? Costs and Prospects," *The Middle East Journal*. Vol. 54, No. 4, Autumn 2000, pp. 592–612.

Ghanim. Ibrahim al-Bayyumi. *Al-Fikr al-Siyasi li al-Imam Hasan al-Banna*. Cairo: Dar al-Tawzi' wa-al-Nashr al-Islamiyyah, 1992.

Gharib, Muhammad. "Abul Futuh Decides to Nominate Himself for Presidential Elections," *al-Masry al-Youm*, May 10, 2011.

Gibb, H. A. R. *Modern Trends in Islam*. Chicago: University of Chicago Press, 1947.

Glock, Charles Y., and Rodney Stark. *Religion and Society in Tension*. Chicago: Rand McNally, 1965.

Goodwin, Jeff, and James M. Jasper, eds. *The Social Movements Reader: Cases and Concepts*. Malden, MA: Blackwell Pub, 2003.

Gorman, Anthony. *Historians, State and Politics in Twentieth Century Egypt: Contesting the Nation.* London: RoutledgeCurzon, 2003.

Habermas, Jurgen. *On the Pragmatics of Social Interaction: Preliminary Studies in the Theory of Communicative Action.* Cambridge, MA: MIT Press, 2001.

Habib, Muhammad. *Dhikrayat D. Muhammad Habib: 'An al-Hayat wa-al-Da'wa wa-al-Siyasa wa-al-Fikr.* Cairo: Dar al-Shorouk, 2012.

Haddad, Yvonne. *Contemporary Islam and the Challenge of History.* Albany: State University of New York, 1982.

Halliwell, John Clifford. *Sayyid Qutb and Literary Exegesis.* MA thesis, American University of Cairo, 2006.

Halpern, Manfred. *The Politics of Social Change in the Middle East and North Africa.* Princeton: Princeton University Press, 1963.

Hammoudeh, 'Adel. "Asra' Talaq bayn al-Sadat wal-Ikhwan al-Muslimin," *Sabah al-Kheir,* No. 1651, August 27, 1987.

Hanafi, Hasan. "The Relevance of the Islamic Alternative in Egypt," *Arab Studies Quarterly,* Vol. 4, No. 1–2, 1982, pp. 54–74.

Harris, Christina Phelps. *Nationalism and Revolution in Egypt: The Role of the Muslim Brotherhood.* The Hague: Mouton, 1964.

Hawwa, Saeed. *The Muslim Brotherhood: Objectives, Stages, Methods.* Translated by Abdul Karim Shaikh. Delhi: Hindustan Publications, 1983.

———. *Hadhihi Tajrubatana wa Hadhihi Shahadati.* Beirut: Dar 'Ammar, 1988.

Haykal, Muhammad Hasanayn. *Li-Misr La Li-'Abd al-Nasir.* Cairo: Dar al-Siyasah, 1980.

———. *'Inda Muftaraq al-Tariq.* Beirut: Sharikat al-Matbu'at lil-Tawzi' wal-Nashr, 1983.

Heyworth-Dunne, J.. *Religious and Political Trends in Modern Egypt.* Washington, DC: McGregor & Werner, Inc., 1950.

Hinnebusch, Raymond A., Jr. *Egyptian Politics under Sadat: The Post-Populist Development of an Authoritarian-Modernizing State.* Boulder: Lynne Rienner Publishers, 1988.

Hirschkind, Charles. *The Ethical Soundscape: Cassette Sermons and Islamic Counterpublics.* New York: Columbia University Press, 2006.

Husaini, Ishaq Musa. *The Muslim Brethren: The Greatest of Modern Islamic Movements.* Westport, CT: Hyperion Press, 1956.

Ibrahim, Abdullah Muhammad. "Abdullah Muhammad Ibrahim: Muslim Brotherhood Second-in-Command," *MERIP Reports,* No. 103, Feb. 1982.

Ibrahim, Saad Eddin. "Anatomy of Egypt's Militant Islamic Groups: Methodological Note and Preliminary Findings," *International Journal of Middle East Studies,* Vol. 12, No. 4, December 1980, pp. 423–453.

———. "Egypt's Islamic Militants," *MERIP Reports.* No. 103, Feb. 1982.

———. *Egypt Islam and Democracy: Critical Essays.* Cairo: American University of Cairo Press, 1996.

Imam, 'Abd Allah. *Inqilab 15 Mayu.* Cairo: Dar al-Mawqif al-Arabi, 1983.

Interview with 'Abd al-Mon'eim Abu al-Futtuh.

Interview with Abul 'Ela Madi.

Interview with 'Adli Mustafa.

Interview with Ahmed Kamal Abul Magd.

Interview with Ahmed 'Umar.

Interview with Badr Muhammad Badr.

Interview with 'Esam al-'Erian.

Interview with Gamal 'Abd al-Salam.

Interview with Gamal al-Banna.

Interview with Hamid al-Difarwi.

Interview with Ibrahim al-Za'farani.

Interview with Kamal Habib.

Interview with Mamduh al-Ridi.

Interview with Muhammad 'Abd al-Quddus.

"Interview with Muhammad Habib," Al-Tahrir Network, June 6, 2012.

Interview with Muhammad Moro.

Interview with Sayyid 'Abd al-Sattar al-Meligi.

"Interview with 'Umar al-Tilmisani," *al-Musawwar*, No. 2989, January 1982.

"Interview with 'Usama Yasin, Shahed 'Ala al-Thawra," Al-Jazeera Network, June 11, 2011.

Interview with Wa'il 'Uthman.

Isma'il, Salwa. "Confronting the Other: Identity, Culture, Politics, and Conservative Islamism in Egypt," *International Journal of Middle East Studies*, Vol. 30, No. 2, May 1998, pp. 199–225.

Jankowski, James P., and Israel Gershoni, eds. *Rethinking Nationalism in the Arab Middle East*. New York: Columbia University Press, 1997.

Jansen, Johannes J. G. *The Dual Nature of Islamic Fundamentalism*. Ithaca, NY: Cornell University Press, 1997.

Juergensmeyer, Mark. *The New Cold War? Religious Nationalism Confronts the Secular State*. Berkeley: University of California Press, 1993.

Kepel, Gilles. *Muslim Extremism in Egypt: The Prophet and the Pharaoh*. Berkeley: University of California Press, 1993.

———. *The Revenge of God: The Resurgence of Islam, Christianity, and Judaism in the Modern World*. Malden, MA: Polity Press, 1994.

———. *Jihad: The Trail of Political Islam*. Cambridge, MA: Harvard University Press, 2002.

Khatab, Sayed. *The Political Thought of Sayyid Qutb: The Theory of Jahiliyyah*. New York: Routledge, 2006.

Kirkpatrick, David D., and David E. Sanger, "After First Talks, Egypt Opposition Vows New Protest," *New York Times*, February 6, 2011.

Lerner, Daniel. *The Passing of Traditional Society: Modernizing the Middle East*. Chicago: Free Press, 1958.

Madi, Abul 'Ela. *Jama'at al-'Unf al-Misriyya wa Ta'wilatiha lil-Islam*. Cairo: Maktabat al-Shorouq al-Duwaliyya, 2006.

Mahmood, Saba. *Politics of Piety: The Islamic Revival and the Feminist Subject*. Princeton: Princeton University Press, 2011.

Marty, Martin E., and R. Scott Appleby, eds. *Fundamentalisms Comprehended*. Chicago: University of Chicago Press, 1995.

Mashhur, Mustafa. *Tariq al-Da'wa*. Cairo: Dar al-Tiba'ah wal-Nashr al-Islamiyyah, 1979.

McAdam, Doug, John D. McCarthy, and Mayer N. Zald, eds. *Comparative Perspectives on Social Movements: Political Opportunities, Mobilizing Structures, and Cultural Framings*. New York: Cambridge University Press, 1996.

McVeigh, Rory, Daniel J. Myers, and David Sikkink. "Corn, Klansmen, and Coolidge: Structure and Framing in Social Movements," *Social Forces*. Vol. 83, No. 2, December 2004, pp. 653–690.

Mitchell, Richard P. *The Society of the Muslim Brothers*. New York: Oxford University Press, 1969.

Moro, Muhammad. *Al-Islam al-Siyasi Shakhsiyyat*. Cairo: Maktabat Jazeerat al-Ward, 2011.

Munson, Ziad. "Islamic Mobilization: Social Movement Theory and the Egyptian Muslim Brotherhood," *Sociological Quarterly* Vol. 42, No. 4, 2001. pp. 487–510.

Mustafa, Hala. *al-Islam al-Siyasi fi Misr: Min Harakat al-Islah ila Jama'at al-'Unf*. Cairo: Mu'asassat al-Ahram, 1992.

Otterman, Sharon. "Muslim Brotherhood and Egypt's Parliamentary Elections," *Council on Foreign Relations*, December 1, 2005.

Pargeter, Alison. *The Muslim Brotherhood: The Burden of Tradition*. London: Saqi Books, 2010.

Qutb, Sayyid. *Ma'alim fi al-tariq*. Cairo: Dar al-Shuruq, 1970.

———. *Milestones*. Indianapolis: American Trust Publications, 1990.

———. *Social Justice in Islam*. New York: Islamic Publications International, 2000.

Ra'if, Ahmed. *al-Bawwabah al-Sawda'*. Cairo: al-Zahra' lil 'Ilam al-'Arabi, 1986.

Ramadan, Abd al-'Aziz. *Al-Ikhwan al-Muslimun wa al-Tanzim al-Sirri*. Cairo: Maktabat Madbuli, 1985.

Rizq, Jabir. *Madhabih al-Ikhwan fi Sujun 'Abd al-Nasir*. Cairo: Dar al-'Itisam, 1977.

Robinson, Francis. "Technology and Religious Change: Islam and the Impact of Print," *Modern Asian Studies*, Vol.27, No. 1, February 1993, pp. 229–251.

Roy, Olivier. *The Failure of Political Islam*. Cambridge, MA: Harvard University Press, 1994.

Rutherford, Bruce K. *Egypt after Mubarak: Liberalism, Islam, and Democracy in the Arab World*. Princeton: Princeton University Press, 2008.

Sa'ad al-Din, Mahmoud. "Muslim Brotherhood Leaders: We Will Not Endorse Abul Futuh as a Candidate for President No Matter What the Circumstances," *al-Youm al-Sabi'*, May 12, 2011.

"Sadat to Legalize Muslim Brotherhood?" *MERIP Reports*, No. 47, May 1976.

Saleh, Amin, and Rihab 'Abdullah. "Presidential Election Candidates Seminar Series: Abul Futuh," *al-Youm al-Sabi'*, February 17, 2012.

Sayyid-Marsot, Afaf Lutfi. *Egypt's Liberal Experiment (1922–1936)*. Berkeley: University of California Press, 1977.

———. *A History of Egypt: From the Arab Conquest to the Present*. New York: Cambridge University Press, 2007.

Shabab al-Islam Press Releases (Nos. 1–6), 1972.

Shadi, Salah. *Safahat min al-Tarikh: Hisad al-'Umr*. Cairo: Dar al-Tawzi' wa-al-Nashr al-Islamiyyah, 2006.

Sharaf, Sami. *'Abd al-Nasir: Hakadha Kana Yahkumu Masr*. Cairo: al-Madbouli al-Saqhir, 1996.

Shehata, Samer, and Joshua Stacher. "The Brotherhood Goes to Parliament," *Middle East Report*, Vol. 36, Fall 2006.

Shepard, William E. "Islam and Ideology: Toward a Typology," *International Journal of Middle East Studies*. Vol. 19, 1987, pp. 307–336.

———. *Sayyid Qutb and Islamic Activism: A Translation and Critical Analysis of Social Justice in Islam*. Lieden: Brill, 1996.

Shoukri, Ghali. *Egypt: Portrait of a President*. London: Zed Press, 1981.

Shurbagi, Ahmed Hasan. *Mahmoud Abd al-Halim: Sheikh Mu'arikhi al-Harakat al-Islamiyyah*. Alexandria: Dar al-Da'wah, 2002.

Siddiq, 'Ali. *Al-Ikhwan al-Muslimun: Bayna Irhab Faruq wa 'Abd al-Nasir*. Cairo: Dar al-'Itisam, 1987.

Sivan, Emmanuel. *Radical Islam: Medieval Theology and Modern Politics*. New Haven: Yale University Press, 1990.

Slackman, Michael. "A Poet Whose Political Incorrectness Is a Crime," *New York Times*, May 13, 2006.

Smith, Jackie, Charles Chatfield, and Ron Pagnucco. *Transnational Social Movements and Global Politics: Solidarity Beyond the State*. Syracuse: Syracuse University Press, 1997.

Snow, David A., and Robert D. Benford. "Ideology, Frame Resonance, and Participant Mobilization," in Bert Klandermans, ed., *International Social Movement Research*, Vol. 1. Greenwich, CT: JAI Press, 1988, pp. 197–217.

Snow, David A., and Susan E. Marshall. "Cultural Imperialism, Social Movements, and Islamic Revival," In Louis Kriesberg, ed. *Research In Social Movements, Conflicts, and Change*, Vol. 7. Bradford, UK: Emerald Group Publishing, 1984.

Sonbol, Amira El-Azhary. *The New Mamluks: Egyptian Society and Modern Feudalism*. Syracuse: Syracuse University Press, 2000.

Starrett, Gregory. *Putting Islam to Work: Education, Politics, and Religious Transformation in Egypt*. Berkeley: University of California Press, 1998.

Stowasser, Barbara, ed. *The Islamic Impulse*. Washington, DC: Center for Contemporary Arab Studies, 1987.

Sullivan, Denis Jospeh, and Sana Abed-Kotob. *Islam in Contemporary Egypt: Civil Society vs. the State.* Boulder: Lynne Rienner Publishers, 1999.

Szyliowicz, Joseph S. *Education and Modernization in the Middle East.* Ithaca: Cornell University Press, 1973.

Talhami, Ghada Hashem. *The Mobilization of Muslim Women in Egypt.* Gainesville: University of Florida Press, 1996.

Tammam, Hosam. *Tahawulat al-Ikhwan al-Muslimin.* Cairo: Maktabat Madbouli, 2006.

———. *Ma' al-Harakat al-Islamiyya fil 'Alam.* Cairo: Maktabat Madbouli, 2009.

———.ed. *'Abd al-Mon'eim Abul Futuh.* Cairo: al-Shorouk, 2010.

Tarrow, Sidney. *Power in Movement: Social Movements and Contentious Politics.* New York: Cambridge University Press, 1998.

———. *The New Transnational Activism.* New York: Cambridge University Press, 2005.

Tibi, Bassam. *The Challenge of Fundamentalism: Political Islam and the New World Disorder.* Berkeley: University of California Press, 1998.

Tilly, Charles. *From Mobilization to Revolution.* Reading, MA: Addison-Wesley Pub, 1978.

———. *Popular Contention in Great Britain, 1758–1834.* Cambridge, MA: Harvard University Press, 1995.

———. *Social Movements, 1768–2004.* Boulder: Paradigm Publishers, 2004.

———. *Regimes and Repertoires.* Chicago: University of Chicago Press, 2006.

Tilly, Charles, Doug McAdam, and Sidney Tarrow. *The Dynamics of Contentious Politics.* New York: Cambridge University Press, 2001.

Tilly, Charles. and Sidney Tarrow. *Contentious Politics.* Boulder: Paradigm Publishers, 2007.

Tucker, Judith. "While Sadat Shuffles: Economic Decay, Political Ferment in Egypt," *MERIP Reports*, No. 65, March 1978.

'Uthman, 'Uthman Ahmed. *Safahat min Tajribati.* Cairo: al-Maktab al-Masri al-Hadith, 1994.

'Uthman, Wa'il. *Hizb Ullah fi Muwajahat Hizb ul-Shaytan.* Cairo: n.p. 1975.

———. *Ightial al-Sahwa al-Islamiyya.* Cairo: n.p. 2005.

———. *Asrar al-Harakah al-Tullabiyyah: Handasat al-Qahira, 1968–1975.* Cairo: n.p. 2nd ed. 2006.

Voll, John O. "Fundamentalism in the Sunni Arab World," in Martin E. Marty and R. Scott Appleby, eds. *Fundamentalisms Observed.* Chicago: University of Chicago Press, 1991.

———. *Islam: Continuity and Change in the Modern World.* Syracuse: Syracuse University Press, 1994.

Wa Islamah. No. 2, 1972.

Wickham, Carrie Rosefsky. *Mobilizing Islam: Religion, Activism, and Political Change in Egypt.* New York: Columbia University Press, 2002.

Wiktorowicz, Quintan, ed. *Islamic Activism: A Social Movement Theory Approach.* Bloomington: Indiana University Press, 2004.

Worth, Robert F., and Mona El-Naggar. "Fraud Charges Mar Egypt Vote," *New York Times,* November 28, 2010.

Yahya, Karim. "Hiwar maʿa ʿUmar al-Tilmisani," *al-Ahali,* September 29, 1982.

Yousef, al-Sayyid. *Al-Ikhwan al-Muslimun wa al-Dawla al-Islamiyyah.* Cairo: Al-Arabi, 1997.

Zollner, Barbara H. E. "Prison Talk: The Muslim Brotherhood's Internal Struggle during Gamal Abdel Nasser's Persecution: 1954 to 1971." *International Journal of Middle East Studies,* Vol. 39, No. 3, 2007, pp. 411–433.

———. *The Muslim Brotherhood: Hasan al-Hudaybi and Ideology.* New York: Routledge, 2009.

Index

on global Islamic community, 192,
205–207
government's closure of, 183–184
historically oriented pieces in,
192–199
on Iranian Revolution, 206
on Islamization of Egyptian society,
209–210, 212–214
on Israel, 184–186, 192–193,
205–206, 208–209, 217
on Jehan's Law, 192
Kepel on, 184–186
martyrology of Muslim Brotherhood
members in, 195–198
mass audience and impact of, 17,
176–177, 180, 182–183, 187,
210–211, 214
on medical profession, 211–212
re-launch of, 76, 100, 107, 181–183
Sadat and, 17, 174–175, 182, 199–200,
202, 207, 217
Shari'a and, 183, 193, 201–202, 204
on Six Day War, 207
university distribution of, 171
on women and gender, 186, 212–214
al-Da'wa al-Salafiyya, 234
Da'watuna (al-Banna), 161
Dawud, Khaled, 233
democracy
Islam and, 5
Sadat's rhetoric on, 1, 64, 199–200
student movement's calls for, 63
Democratic Alliance for Egypt, 234
ad-Dhahabi, Muhammad Husayn, 84,
143
al-Difrawi, Hamid, 233
The Doctrine of the Muslim (al-Ghazali),
116
Du'a la Quda (Hudaybi), 76
"The Duties of the Muslim Brother"
(al-Banna), 156
Dylan, Bob, 114

Egyptian Constitution
al-Da'wa on, 199–204
Sadat and, 192, 201–202, 250n17
Egyptian Current (political party), 231
Egyptian educational system
British colonialism and, 35–36
Free Officers and, 40
Nasser and, 41, 45–46, 53, 80, 109,
150
Sadat and, 109–110
student movement and, 19, 35, 40–41
al-'Erian, 'Esam
on development of oppositional
culture, 113–114
Egyptian Doctors Syndicate and, 225
Egyptian parliament and, 225
Freedom and Justice Party (FJP) and,
231
al-Gama'a al-Islamiyya leadership
and, 121–122
al-Gam'iyya al-Diniyya leadership
and, 119
Guidance Bureau and, 229, 231
Hizb al-Islah (Reform Party) and,
265n11
Muslim Brotherhood membership of,
165–166, 169, 229, 231
on the Muslim Brotherhood's
released prisoners, 91
on Muslim Brotherhood's returning
exiles, 94–95
student movement and, 229
'Ezzat, Ibrahim, 81, 155. *See also* Jama'at
al-Tabligh
'Ezzat, Mahmoud, 229

Faith and Science (television program),
81
al-Fanniya al-'Askariya. *See* Technical
Military Academy
al-Faqi, Muhammad Hamid, 152
Faraj, 'Abd al-Salam, 78

Printed in the USA/Agawam, MA
October 23, 2015